Recent developments in cultural history and literary criticism have suggested new ways of addressing the interpretation of reading. How did people read in the past? Where, when and why did they read? How were the manner and purpose of reading envisaged and recorded by contemporaries – and why? Drawing on fields as diverse as medieval pedagogy, textual bibliography, the history of science, and social and literary history, this collection of fourteen essays highlights both the singularity of personal reading experiences and the cultural conventions involved in reading and its perception. An introductory essay offers an important critical assessment of the various contributions to the development of the subject in recent times. *The practice and representation of reading in England* constitutes a major addition to our understanding of the history of readers and reading.

THE PRACTICE AND REPRESENTATION OF READING IN ENGLAND

THE PRACTICE AND REPRESENTATION OF READING IN ENGLAND

EDITED BY
JAMES RAVEN, HELEN SMALL
AND NAOMI TADMOR

CAMBRIDGE
UNIVERSITY PRESS

CAMBRIDGE UNIVERSITY PRESS
Cambridge, New York, Melbourne, Madrid, Cape Town, Singapore, São Paulo

Cambridge University Press
The Edinburgh Building, Cambridge CB2 8RU, UK

Published in the United States of America by Cambridge University Press, New York

www.cambridge.org
Information on this title: www.cambridge.org/9780521480932

First published 1996
This digitally printed version 2007

A catalogue record for this publication is available from the British Library

Library of Congress Cataloguing in Publication data

The practice and representation of reading in England /
edited by James Raven, Helen Small and Naomi Tadmor.
p. cm.
Includes bibliographical references and index.
ISBN 0 521 48093 0 (hardback)
1 Books and reading – Great Britain – History.
I Raven, James, 1959– II Small, Helen III Tadmor, Naomi
Z1003.5.G7P73 1996
028′.9′0941 – dc20 95–13247 CIP

ISBN 978-0-521-48093-2 hardback
ISBN 978-0-521-02323-8 paperback

Contents

Illustrations

Tables

Contributors

JOHN BREWER is Professor of Cultural History at the European University Institute, Florence. His publications include *Party Ideology and Popular Politics at the Accession of George III* (1976), *The Common People and Politics 1750–1790s* (1986) and *Sinews of Power: War and the English State, 1688–1783* (1989). He is also the co-editor with Roy Porter of *Consumption and the World of Goods* (1993).

JAN FERGUS is Professor of English at Lehigh University, Bethlehem, Pennsylvania. She is the author of *Jane Austen and the Didactic Novel* (1983) and *Jane Austen: A Literary Life* (1991). She is currently completing a study of the bookselling records of the Clays of Warwickshire.

KATE FLINT is University Lecturer in Victorian and Modern English Literature at the University of Oxford. She is the author of *Dickens* (1986) and the editor of *The Victorian Novelist: Social Problems and Social Change* (1987). Her study of women and reading, *The Woman Reader 1837–1914*, was published by Oxford University Press in 1993.

ADAM FOX is Lecturer in the Department of Economic and Social History at the University of Edinburgh. He is currently working on a book, to be published by Oxford University Press, which examines the relationship between oral and literate culture in early modern England.

LISA JARDINE is Professor of English at Queen Mary and Westfield College, University of London. She is the author of *Francis Bacon: Discovery and the Art of Discourse* (1974), *Still Harping on Daughters: Women and Drama in the Age of Shakespeare* (1983) and, most recently, *Erasmus, Man of Letters* (1993). With Anthony Grafton, she is the co-author of *From Humanism to the Humanities: Education and the Liberal Arts in Fifteenth- and Sixteenth-Century Europe* (1986) and, with Julia Swindells,

What's Left? Women in Culture and the Labour Movement (1990). *Reading in the Renaissance*, co-authored with Anthony Grafton and William H. Sherman, is forthcoming.

ADRIAN JOHNS is Lecturer in the History of Science at the University of Kent. His publications include studies of the work of printers, writers and natural philosophers in Restoration England, and he is currently writing a book on natural philosophy and the publishing trade in Early Modern Europe, to be published by Chicago University Press.

JOHN KERRIGAN is Fellow of St John's College, Cambridge and University Lecturer in English. The author of numerous essays on English, Irish and American poetry, and of *Revenge Tragedy: Aeschylus to Armageddon* (1996), he has edited, among other works, Shakespeare's *Sonnets and A Lover's Complaint* (1986), and has published various studies of textual problems in Shakespeare and Renaissance drama.

JAMES RAVEN is University Lecturer in Modern History and Tutorial Fellow of Mansfield College, Oxford. He is the author of *British Fiction, 1750–1770: A Chronological Check-List of Prose Fiction Printed in Britain and Ireland* (1987) and *Judging New Wealth: Popular Publishing and Responses to Commerce in England 1750–1800* (1992). His *The Commercialization of the Book* is forthcoming from Cambridge University Press.

SUZANNE REYNOLDS is Lecturer in Medieval Literature in the School of English, University of Birmingham. She has recently completed a book entitled *Medieval Reading: Grammar, Rhetoric, and the Classical Text* to be published by Cambridge University Press in 1996.

WILLIAM H. SHERMAN is Assistant Professor of English at the University of Maryland at College Park. He is the author of *John Dee: The Politics of Reading and Writing in the English Renaissance* (1994). A collaborative study of reading in the Renaissance, co-authored with Anthony Grafton and Lisa Jardine, is forthcoming.

HELEN SMALL is Lecturer in English at the University of Bristol. She is the author of *Love's Madness: Medicine, the Novel, and Female Insanity, 1800–65* (Oxford, 1996), and is co-editing Charles Dickens, *Little Dorrit* (Penguin Books).

NAOMI TADMOR is Kitson Clark Lecturer and Fellow in History at New Hall, Cambridge. She has published on the history of the family and on relations between history and literature in the eighteenth century, and she is currently completing a book on concepts of the family in the eighteenth century, entitled *Family and Friends: Household, Kinship and Patronage in Eighteenth-Century England.*

ANDREW TAYLOR is Lecturer in the Department of Literature and Language at Northern Kentucky University. He is working on a study of reading in late-medieval England, provisionally entitled *To Drive the Night Away*.

Acknowledgements

Most of the essays in this volume were first delivered at a conference entitled 'The Practice and Representation of Reading in Britain from the Fourteenth to the Nineteenth Centuries', sponsored by the Cambridge Project for the Book, and held at Magdalene College, Cambridge, in March 1992. We are grateful to the British Academy, the French Cultural Delegation, Gonville and Caius College and Magdalene College for their funding assistance. Without the organizational skills of Elsa Meyland-Smith the conference could not have taken place. Our sincere thanks to her and to Trevor Eaton, Margaret Jones, Richard Luckett, David McKitterick and Marian Martin. The editors and contributors are also indebted to the following for substantial and stimulating contributions to the conference: Mark Amsler, Mark Bland, Eamon Duffy, Laurence Fontaine, Peter H. Pawlowicz, Gary Waller, Françoise Waquet and Helen Weinstein. We are particularly grateful to Roger Chartier who, with Lisa Jardine, set the conference on its course with an opening address, and provided a wealth of helpful criticism in discussion of individual papers. We also appreciate the invaluable part played by those who chaired the original sessions: Patrick Collinson, D. F. McKenzie, the late William A. Moffett, Margaret Spufford and Morag Shiach.

Several people have provided generous assistance to the editors in preparing this volume. We would particularly like to thank Richard Beadle, Stephen Bending, Neil Hitchin, Jane Hughes, Arnold Hunt, Elisabeth Leedham-Green, Keith Manley and Margaret M. Smith.

Plate 1 'Novel Reading in a Vault at Blackheath, 1802'

Plate 2 Illustration from an early fifteenth-century copy of Bartholomaeus Anglicus, *De proprietatibus rerum*. London, British Library, Royal 17E iii

CHAPTER I

Introduction: the practice and representation of reading in England

James Raven, Helen Small, Naomi Tadmor

Plate 1, reproduced opposite, shows an unsigned sketch after the manner of Rowlandson, issued by William Holland from his 'Caricature Warehouse' in 1802. Entitled 'Novel Reading in a Vault in Blackheath', it depicts a young gent and his lady friend absorbed by a copy of Matthew Lewis's sensational work of Gothic horror, *The Monk.* Lewis's best-known novel was published in 1796, and immediately attacked as salacious and blasphemous. Polite cuts were made to the fourth edition and its publisher took desperate measures to dispose of the remaining copies of earlier versions. In the none-too-salubrious surroundings of a London privy (the sketch plays on the more vulgar meaning of the burial 'vault' in Lewis's novel[1]), the pair read *The Monk tête à tête*, unaware that they are being watched by a pudgy Peeping-Tom. The gentleman, legs crossed, is reading aloud to his companion, but her fascination is such that she leans over to try to follow the text with her own eyes. From her indecorous posture – legs splayed, arms akimbo, skirt raised over one ankle – and from the evident titillation on the face of the voyeur, we are given a strong hint as to the nature of the passage that has claimed their attention.

The image in plate 2 depicts a very different scene of reading: a chaste one, clearly dedicated to higher motives than the surreptitious reading of *The Monk.* The illustration comes from a manuscript copy of *De proprietatibus rerum*, composed by Bartholomaeus Anglicus (Bartholomew de Glanville) in the mid-thirteenth century, and first translated into English in the late fourteenth century. An encyclopaedic work, with large sections on the functioning of the body, *De proprietatibus rerum* was extensively copied and then printed during the next two centuries.[2]

1 *Oxford English Dictionary*, 4c.

2 M. C. Seymour (gen. ed.), *On the Properties of Things: John Trevisa's Translation of 'Bartholomeus Anglicus De Proprietatibus Rerum': A Critical Text*, 3 vols. (Oxford, 1975–88), III, 3.

The richly illuminated volume in which this image appears was made at Bruges in the early fifteenth century, probably for presentation to Edward IV (it is listed in a catalogue of the royal collection drawn up for Henry VIII in 1535). The picture appears at the head of Book IV, a section devoted to 'the properties of man's body', the elements and humours believed to condition health and sickness. A master is seated on a chair in front of four students, who have taken their places on two benches arranged before him. It is clear that a lecture is being delivered in the orderly setting of a classroom. Two books can be seen. One is prominently displayed on a special stand attached to the master's chair. The text is open, and his hand points to a relevant passage. The other book seems to be a copy of the same text, and is placed on a low lectern before the students. Only one of them is obviously engaged with it. Of the others, one watches the master, another looks toward a shelf bearing two flasks and two glass vessels of samples (probably urine); but the student closest to the viewer gazes away from the scene, and while he may be ruminating on his teacher's words it seems equally possible that the lecture has failed to hold his attention. 'Reading' in this instance is a communal activity, in which authoritative interpretation and explication lie with the master, but a range of response is evident in the postures and expressions of those supposedly engaged in study together.

These two starkly contrasting depictions of the activity of reading are drawn from opposite ends of the period discussed in this volume and, unglossed, their juxtaposition might appear to reinforce a familiar distinction between a 'medieval' form of reading, understood as public, hierarchical and closely directed; and a 'modern' reading experience defined as private and anarchic. In fact, neither image can be simply described as 'public' or 'private' and both invite a more challenging set of questions about reading in the past. How and why do people read? In what circumstances do they take up the written or printed word? What do they make of the signs on the page? What do they and others think happens when they read, and what do they imagine might be the consequences of that reading? More particularly, how has the practice and representation of reading altered or been seen to alter over the centuries? How do we accommodate these changes in our understanding of literary creativity and reception?

The subject of reading has undergone radical revision in recent years. As Susan Suleiman pointed out fifteen years ago, the word *reader* 'once relegated to the status of the unproblematic and the obvious' has become the subject of intense debate. In 1980, she noted:

> one rarely picks up a literary journal on either side of the Atlantic without finding articles (and often a whole special issue) devoted to the performance of reading, the role of feeling, the variability of individual response, the confrontation, transaction, or interrogation between texts and readers, the nature and limits of interpretation – questions whose very formulation depends on a new awareness of the audience as an entity indissociable from the notion of artistic texts.[3]

Suleiman was introducing a collection of essays which included some of the most influential critics of the 1970s and early 1980s writing on very diverse aspects of reading. Her essay is an adept summary of the text-centred approach which characterized theoretical approaches to reading at that time and which found its most influential expression in Wayne Booth's formulation of 'the implied reader',[4] Gérard Genette and Gerald Prince's account of the narratee,[5] Wolfgang Iser's phenomenology of reading,[6] Stanley Fish's work on interpretive communities,[7] and, more recently, Brian Stock's concept of 'textual communities'.[8] Fifteen years later, one term seems strikingly absent from Suleiman's account of the field and from the collection itself. Few writers on the subject of reading today are likely to be so behindhand with the term 'history'. [9]

It would be easy to assume that the growing prominence of 'the history of reading' over the last ten years is just one reflection of a generally increased emphasis on history across literature and the social sciences; but it is also the result of other kinds of change within the academy. In England, where disciplinary boundaries retain perhaps more definition than in continental Europe or in North America, and

3 Susan R. Suleiman, 'Introduction', in Suleiman and Inge Crosman (eds.), *The Reader in the Text: Essays on Audience and Interpretation* (Princeton, NJ, 1980), pp. 3–4.

4 Wayne C. Booth, *The Rhetoric of Fiction* (Chicago, IL, 1961), esp. p. 138.

5 Gérard Genette, *Figures III* (Paris, 1972), pp. 265–7; Gerald Prince, 'Introduction à l'étude du narrataire,' *Poétique* 14 (1973): 178–96.

6 Most importantly, Wolfgang Iser, *The Implied Reader: Patterns of Communication in Prose Fiction from Bunyan to Beckett* (Baltimore, MD, 1974) and *The Act of Reading: A Theory of Aesthetic Response* (Baltimore, MD, 1978).

7 Stanley Fish, *Is there a Text in this Class? The Authority of Interpretive Communities* (Cambridge, MA, 1980) was published the same year as *The Reader in the Text.* See also his earlier *Surprised by Sin: The Reader in 'Paradise Lost'* (London, 1967).

8 Brian Stock, *Listening for the Text: On the Uses of the Past* (Baltimore, MD, 1990), pp. 140–58.

9 For an overview particularly relevant to this context, see David Simpson, 'Literary Criticism and the Return to "History" ', *Critical Inquiry* 14 (1988): 721–47.

where interdisciplinarity consequently has more force as a concept, the growth of interest in reading is closely allied to the questioning of traditional demarcations between academic fields that has characterized so much research in the humanities over the last ten to fifteen years. The history of reading is far from being a new subject,[10] but it is, unquestionably, changing its character.[11] Some of the kinds of work now contributing to the 'history of reading' would once have seemed so diverse in their methodologies and in their objects of enquiry as to have had little contact with each other. The great range of new contributions relating to an historical understanding of reading therefore makes it timely to review the various kinds of research which have shaped this volume, and to assess the ways in which a more interdisciplinary approach is changing our sense both of the nature of the field, and of its wider significance.

Most studies of reading in England have, until fairly recently, focused on the objects of reading – manuscript and print materials – and have derived their accounts of changing readerships primarily from developments in the production and distribution of texts. Early studies such as A. S. Collins's *Profession of Letters* (1929), H. S. Bennett's three-volume history of *English Books and Readers* in the Renaissance (1952–70), Richard Altick's *The English Common Reader* (1957), and Ian Watt's *The Rise of the Novel* (1957) remain classics.[12] Their work is, however, undergoing significant refinement and, in places, substantial revision in the light of new historical questions and new bibliographical sources and techniques. Major cataloguing projects and the specialist work of a new generation of historical bibliographers have meant that it is now possible to chart with far more accuracy the timing and character of the upturn in English domestic publication from the early modern period onward. Indeed, the current state of retrospective national bibliography in England is remarkably advanced by comparison with much of Europe.[13] Thanks to the progress of the early modern and the eight-

10 A select bibliography can be found at the end of this book.

11 On developments in the history of reading during recent years, see particularly Alain Bentolila (ed.), *Recherches actuelles sur l'enseignement de la lecture* (Paris, 1976); Robert Darnton, 'First Steps towards a History of Reading', *Australian Journal of French Studies* 23 (1986): 5–30; David D. Hall, 'The History of the Book: New Questions? New Answers?', *Journal of Library History* 21 (1986): 27–38; Jonathan Rose, 'Rereading the English Common Reader: A Preface to a History of Audiences', *Journal of the History of Ideas* 53 (1992): 47–70; Roger Chartier (ed.), *Histoires de la lecture: un bilan des recherches* (Paris, 1995).

12 Full references are given in the select bibliography.

13 See, for example, the remarks of Roberto Bruni, report, *Publishing History* 29 (1991): 78–81.

eenth-century short-title catalogues,[14] we can now state that by comparison with the 400 or so surviving books known to have been published in England in the first decade of the sixteenth century, about 6,000 were published during the 1630s, almost 21,000 during the 1710s, and more than 56,000 in the 1790s.[15] Work on the nineteenth-century short-title catalogue continues, but recent estimates (based on publishers' catalogues and circulars) suggest a figure of around 325,000 separate items published during the 1870s.[16]

Nevertheless, there are many difficulties in the way of deriving information about past readership sizes from bibliographical evidence alone. It is difficult to establish clear criteria that will enable scholars to perform systematic comparisons between different periods. Most obviously, fundamental differences in production and distribution make meaningful comparisons between manuscripts and printed materials highly problematic.[17] For example, we have no consolidated inventory of all the extant manuscript books that were produced in England up to the end of the fifteenth century. What fraction of the total output is represented by these survivors is a question that remains entirely open, beyond saying that it is likely to be a very small fraction indeed.[18] For the period after 1475, short-title catalogues have gradually transformed our

[14] See *The Incunabula Short-Title Catalogue*, ed. Lotte Hellinga (British Library on-line); *A Short-Title Catalogue of Books Printed in England, Scotland, and Ireland and of English Books Printed Abroad 1475–1640*, 2nd edn rev., ed. A. W. Pollard, G. R. Redgrave and Katharine F. Pantzer (London, 1976–91) (abbreviated hereafter as *STC*); *Short Title Catalogue of Books Printed in England, Scotland, Ireland, Wales, and British America and of English Books Printed in other Countries 1641–1700*, 2nd edn rev., ed. Donald Wing (New York, 1972–88); and *ESTC on CD-ROM* (the British Library, 1992).

[15] Maureen Bell and John Barnard, 'Provisional Count of *STC* Titles, 1475–1640', *Publishing History* 31 (1992): 48–64; and *ESTC* (database August 1992). Bell's work is based on vol. III of *STC* (1991): 'The next stage of the statistical survey will be to refine the raw title-counts still further, using the machine-readable version currently being prepared by the British Library', *Book Trade History Group Newsletter* 15 (1992), p. 5.

[16] Simon Eliot, *Some Patterns and Trends in British Publishing, 1800–1919, Occasional Papers of the Bibliographical Society* 8 (London, 1994), p. 12, fig. 4.

[17] See Lotte Hellinga, 'The Codex in the Fifteenth Century: Manuscript and Print', in Nicolas Barker (ed.), *A Potencie of Life: Books in Society* (London, 1993), pp. 63–88.

[18] Some impression of the number, type and distribution of manuscripts and early printed books in institutional hands may be derived from N. R. Ker, *Medieval Libraries of Great Britain: A List of Surviving Books*, 2nd edn (London, 1964), with *Supplement* by A. G. Watson (1987). The scantier evidence for the rise of lay readership is surveyed by Malcolm B. Parkes, 'The Literacy of the Laity', in David Daiches and Anthony K. Thorlby (eds.), *Literature and Western Civilization: The Mediaeval World* (London, 1973), pp. 555–79, repr. in Parkes, *Scribes, Scripts and Readers: Studies in the Communication, Presentation and Dissemination of Medieval Texts* (London, 1991), pp. 257–97; see also Jeremy Griffiths and Derek Pearsall (eds.), *Book Production and Publishing in Britain 1375–1475* (Cambridge, 1989). The lack of an enumerative study of medieval English manuscript books and their survival rate is discussed by Richard Beadle, 'Middle English Texts and their Transmission 1350–1500: Some Geographical Criteria', in M. Laing and K. Williamson (eds.),

ability to conduct such research, but the catalogues understandably differ (sometimes substantially) in their principles of selection and organization. Even confining ourselves to book-production, the gaps in the historical record are large: the exact size of most editions before the nineteenth century remains unknown. Publication numbers have to be projected from specialist studies of the few remaining printing ledgers and occasional printers' and booksellers' jottings, except in rare cases where the print runs of a particular publishing house have survived. The ledgers of the eighteenth-century printing house of William Bowyer are one such exception[19] – and an important one – but, while they tell us a great deal about the business of one major London printing house, they cannot inform us of the practices of other London booksellers and publishers. In addition, the proportion of books surviving to what was actually produced is almost impossible to calculate with accuracy.[20] In the cases of other types of printed matter, the processes of production are even more obscure. Painstaking and valuable research has been devoted to chapbooks, periodicals and newspaper production.[21] However, many details of their publication history are sketchy, despite important case studies, and the readerships that can be assumed for these materials remain elusive.

Moreover, estimates of publication output are only meaningful as a guide to contemporary readership sizes if the nature of the market is understood. Although new work on booksellers' records has greatly improved our knowledge of the sale and distribution of print,[22] three

Speaking in Our Tongues: Proceedings of a Colloquium on Medieval Dialectology and Related Disciplines (Cambridge, 1994), pp. 64–91, 107ff. See also Susan H. Cavanaugh, *A Study of Books Privately Owned in England 1300–1450*, 2 vols. (Ann Arbor, MI, 1980).

19 Keith Maslen and John Lancaster (eds.), *The Bowyer Ledgers: The Printing Ledgers of William Bowyer Father and Son* (London, 1991).

20 See David McKitterick, 'The Survival of Books', *The Book Collector* 43 (1994): 9–26.

21 On cheap book production and distribution, see Victor Neuburg, *Chapbooks: A Guide to Reference Material*, 2nd edn (London, 1972); Bernard Capp, *Astrology and the Popular Press: English Almanacks, 1500–1600* (London, 1979); Margaret Spufford, *Small Books and Pleasant Histories: Popular Fiction and its Readership in Seventeenth-Century England* (London, 1981); and Tessa Watt, *Cheap Print and Popular Piety, 1550–1640* (Cambridge, 1991). For serials and newspapers, see Roy McKeen Wiles, *Serial Publication in England before 1750* (Cambridge, 1957); Robert D. Mayo, *The English Novel in the Magazines, 1740–1815* (Evanston, IL, 1962); G. A. Cranfield, *The Development of the Provincial Newspaper, 1700–1760* (Oxford, 1962); Carolyn Nelson and Matthew Seccombe, *British Newspapers and Periodicals, 1641–1700: A Short Title Catalogue of Serials Printed in England, Scotland, Ireland and British America* (New York, 1987); and Michael Harris, *London Newspapers in the Age of Walpole: A Study of the Origins of the Modern English Press* (London, 1987).

22 Important work on English booksellers' trade records includes Elisabeth Leedham-Green *et al.* (eds.), *Garrett Godfrey's Accounts c. 1527–1533*, Cambridge Bibliographical Society Monograph no. 12 (Cambridge, 1992); John Barnard and Maureen Bell, 'The Inventory of Henry Bynneman (1583): A Preliminary Survey', *Publishing History* 29 (1991): 5–46; and John Barnard and

key issues need more attention. First, throughout the sixteenth and seventeenth centuries, commercial manuscript circulation continued side by side with the book industry.[23] The proportion of available manuscript texts compared to printed matter varied, as did the types of text produced by hand or print, but even in the eighteenth and nineteenth centuries the sovereignty of print was on occasion challenged by written communications.[24] Second, no tally of new publications, however carefully recovered, can take account of the diverse and extensive trade in second-hand books which, at least by the mid-seventeenth century was developing its own specialist markets and sales procedures. And third, until the early eighteenth century, England was a net importer of books, particularly scholarly texts, so that any understanding of print and book collecting in the early modern period must include an appreciation of the European trade.[25] Thus, even when taken together, figures derived from these different areas of study can only give us a rough minimum guide to the number of items that circulated at a given time. Gauging the size of 'the English readership' or even of specialist readerships from the manuscript and printed materials known to have existed will, in the majority of instances, continue to require cautious projections from the partial evidence that remains.

In those cases where the evidence for literature in circulation at a given time is particularly elusive, the problem facing historians of reading is only more apparent: how are we to make the move from statistics for manuscript or book production to a knowledge of the

Maureen Bell, *The Early Seventeenth-Century Book Trade and John Foster's Inventory of 1616* (Leeds, 1994). See also Jan Fergus and Ruth Portner, 'Provincial Bookselling in Eighteenth-Century England: The Case of John Clay Reconsidered', *Studies in Bibliography* 40 (1987): 147–63; Fergus, 'Eighteenth-Century Readers in Provincial England: The Customers of Samuel Clay's Circulating Library and Bookshop in Warwick, 1770–72', *Papers of the Bibliographical Society of America* 78 (1984): 155–213; Jan Fergus and Janice Farrar Thaddeus, 'Women, Publishers, and Money, 1790–1820', *Studies in Eighteenth-Century Culture* 17 (1987): 191–207.

23 See particularly Harold Love, *Scribal Publication in Seventeenth-Century England* (Oxford, 1993).

24 See Iain McCalman, *Radical Underworld: Prophets, Revolutionaries and Pornographers in London, 1795–1840* (Cambridge, 1988), and Albert Goodwin, *The Friends of Liberty: The English Democratic Movement in the Age of the French Revolution* (London, 1979).

25 On the importation of scholarly books in the early modern period see Lotte Hellinga, 'Importation of Books Printed on the Continent into England before *c.* 1520', in Sandra Hindman (ed.), *Printing the Written Word: The Social History of Books, circa 1450–1520* (Ithaca, NY, 1991), pp. 205–24; and Elizabeth Armstrong, 'English Purchases of Printed Books from the Continent 1465–1526', *English Historical Review* 94 (1979): 268–90. For later periods, see Giles Barber, 'Book Imports and Exports in the Eighteenth Century', in Robin Myers and Michael Harris (eds.), *Sale and Distribution of Books from 1700* (Oxford, 1982), pp. 77–105; and James Raven, 'Selling Books Across Europe, *c.*1450–1800: An Overview', *Publishing History* 34 (1993): 5–19.

kinds of people reading those texts, the forms their readings took, and the meanings they ascribed to them? In working from production and distribution data, we are necessarily recovering what has been described as 'dependency readerships': readerships that can be assumed from certain modes of access to literature and from specific distributive circuits and agencies.[26] Such readerships can be sub-divided according to the literary form or the subject matter in question, and identified as, for example, 'professional', 'scholarly', 'clerical' or (a neglected group) 'military' readers.[27] Further distinctions can be made on the basis of status, place of residence, gender, language or dialect, religious or sectional interest, social habits and, crucially, purchasing power.

An important consideration shaping the potential size of readership is the issue of who could afford to buy certain kinds of printed matter. Printed materials always varied enormously in price. In the late seventeenth century, for example, a broadsheet ballad could be bought for 1d, while twenty-four page chapbooks might cost up to 6d. Books were substantially more expensive. The price of a specific item depended upon its size and quality and upon the type of binding required, and might range from a few shillings to several guineas. As a result, the readership that can be assumed for broadsheets and ballads is obviously more extensive than that for expensive scholarly texts. Moreover, contrary to a common historical assumption, commercial advances in the eighteenth century did not produce a sudden change in the real price of many books. The production and distribution of printed materials clearly increased dramatically, but if the price of books is considered in relation to purchasing power, most types of new publication in fact became more, not less, costly. Part-issues, cheaper 'reprint' series and a flourishing second-hand market did assist many modest buyers, but the prices in sales catalogues and book auctions[28] at the end of the century reflect a widening price gap between the

[26] James Raven, 'Du qui au comment: A la recherche d'une histoire de la lecture en Angleterre', in Chartier (ed.), *Histoires de la lecture*, pp. 141–63.

[27] A thorough-going application of this approach is Miriam Usher Chrisman's description of 'reader-markets' in *Lay Culture, Learned Culture: Books and Social Change in Strasbourg, 1480–1599* (New Haven, CT, 1982), esp. pp. 59–75.

[28] See A. N. L. Munby and Lenore Coral, *British Book Sale Catalogues 1676–1800: A Union List* (London, 1977); Graham Pollard and Albert Ehrman, *The Distribution of Books by Catalogue, from the Invention of Printing to A.D. 1800* (Cambridge, 1965); Ian Maxted, '"4 Rotten Cornbags and Some Old Books": The Impact of the Printed Word in Devon', in Myers and Harris (eds.), *Sale and Distribution of Books*, pp. 37–76; and Michael Frearson, 'The Distribution and Readership of London Corantos in the 1620s', in Robin Myers and Michael Harris (eds.), *Serials and their Readers, 1620–1914* (Winchester, 1993), pp. 1–25.

materials sold by the newly established 'remainder' merchants and the relatively expensive wares of the antiquarian booksellers. Not until the nineteenth century, with fundamental changes in the technology of printing and distribution, did books genuinely become an affordable commodity for many.

Readerships and reading have of course been transformed across the centuries not just by technological changes in print production, but by such factors as the development of the carrying trade, provincial retailing, book auctions, and, from the early eighteenth century, by bookclubs and circulating libraries.[29] In most cases, however, those changes were gradual rather than sudden. Detailed case-studies have enriched our information about some of the means of book distribution, including publication by subscription which provides useful information about the number and the identity of people who supported the production of specific items and who can be presumed to have been among their first readers.[30] In most cases, however, the information available tells us frustratingly little about the motives which led people to buy or borrow specific texts and it tells us nothing at all about how those texts were read. Perhaps most basically, it tells us almost nothing about what counted as 'reading'. Reading, as Margaret Spufford has insisted in her study of late seventeenth-century spiritual autobiography, 'was a much more socially diffused skill than writing' and the two skills were not necessarily interdependent.[31] If we discard assumptions of a simple overlap between reading and writing, we have to rethink fundamentally the means by which we appraise the history of reading. It becomes necessary to take into account not only how many were able to read a text, even a particular text, but what

29 Among the many studies of books clubs and reading societies in England, see particularly: Paul Kaufman, 'The Community Library: A Chapter in English Social History', *Transactions of the American Philosophical Society* ns 57, pt 7 (1967); Kaufman, 'English Book Clubs and their Role in Social History', *Libri* 14 (1964): 1–31; Devendra P. Varma, *The Evergreen Tree of Diabolical Knowledge* (Washington, DC, 1972); Thomas Kelly, *Early Public Libraries: A History of Public Libraries in Great Britain before 1850* (London, 1966); and James Raven, 'The Noble Brothers and Popular Publishing, 1737–89', *The Library* 6th ser., 12 (1990): 293–345.

30 On subscription lists, see P. J. Wallis and F. J. G. Robinson, 'The Potential Uses of Book Subscription Lists', in A. Jeffreys (ed.), *The Art of the Librarian* (Newcastle upon Tyne, 1973), pp. 133–9; P. J. Wallis, 'Book Subscription Lists', *The Library* 5th ser., 29 (1974): 255–86; R. C. Alston, F. J. G. Robinson and C. Wadham (comps.), *A Check-List of Eighteenth-Century Books Containing Lists of Subscribers* (Newcastle upon Tyne, 1983).

31 Margaret Spufford, 'First Steps in Literacy: The Reading and Writing Experiences of the Humblest Seventeenth-Century Spiritual Autobiographers', *Social History* 4 (1979): 407–35. See also Eamon Duffy, 'The Godly and the Multitude in Stuart England', *The Seventeenth Century* 1 (1986): 31–55; and David Vincent, *Literacy and Popular Culture: England 1750–1914* (Cambridge, 1989).

that reading involved. It also becomes necessary to rethink the relationship between the written word and the surrounding oral culture.

Like the history of the book, the history of literacy is problematic. What counts as literacy? What range of skills? What level of ability? The study of literacy has a fundamental part to play in the history of reading, yet it is essential to recognize that there can be no clear-cut procedure for the historical measurement of functional literacy.[32] In the absence of other sources, historians of literacy have necessarily had to deduce reading skills from the existence of rudimentary writing skills. Yet a mark in a parish register – the only guide to the writing competency of most of the population until the twentieth century – does not necessarily signify illiteracy. David Cressy's warning that low literacy rates in a given period or place 'should not be taken as indicators of retardation or deprivation, awaiting rectification by progress' is still a necessary one.[33] Moreover, it is possible that some of those who did not or could not sign their names, possessed simple reading skills. Here again, the evidence can give us only a rough minimum from which to infer the size of the potential readership.

Research on reading has increasingly concentrated on the more precise though less extensive evidence surrounding the acquisition of reading skills in the past, particularly in the medieval and Renaissance periods. Research into the pedagogical conditions governing first experiences of reading has derived key information from such varied sources as the glosses and commentaries on medieval educational texts, the iconography of medieval portrayals of St Anne teaching her daughter, the Virgin Mary as a child, to read the Psalter, the rare marginalia in early modern schoolbooks, primers, bibles and prayer-books, and the occasional representations and illustrations of reading in

32 The literacy debate is too complex to be treated in the detail it deserves here. Key discussions of this issue are: R. S. Schofield, 'The Measurement of Literacy in Pre-Industrial England', in Jack Goody (ed.), *Literacy in Traditional Societies* (Cambridge, 1968), pp. 311–25; Linda Auwers, 'Reading the Marks of the Past: Exploring Female Literacy in Colonial Windsor, Connecticut', *Historical Methods* 13 (1980): 204–14; David Cressy, *Literacy and the Social Order: Reading and Writing in Tudor and Stuart England* (Cambridge, 1980); Rab Houston, 'The Literacy Myth? Illiteracy in Scotland 1630–1760', *Past and Present* 96 (1982): 81–102; and Julia Boffey, 'Women Authors and Women's Literacy in Fourteenth and Fifteenth-Century England', in Carol M. Meale (ed.), *Women and Literature in Britain, 1150–1500* (Cambridge, 1993), pp. 159–82. Wider implications are addressed in Jack Goody and Ian Watt, 'The Consequences of Literacy', in Goody (ed.), *Literacy*, pp. 27–68 and Brian V. Street, *Literacy in Theory and Practice* (Cambridge, 1984).

33 David Cressy, 'Literacy in Context: Meaning and Measurement in Early Modern England', in John Brewer and Roy Porter (eds.), *Consumption and the World of Goods* (London, 1993), pp. 305–19.

hornbooks and chapbooks. Much attention has been given to developments in education during the Reformation. Similarly, the methods of the charity schools and workers' institutes which played so crucial a part in the reading education and experience of working-class men, women and children in the eighteenth and nineteenth centuries have attracted increasing interest in recent years.[34]

Certain kinds of information about the ways in which people read can also be derived from contemporary accounts of the spaces, the furniture and the aids designed for reading. Reconstructing the way in which books were physically organized tells us much about the kinds of reading that were possible and that were held desirable.[35] In several cases, we have the benefit of extensive records concerning particular collections, including library inventories and catalogues (some assisted by the survival and identification of parts of the original collection),[36] probate records,[37] and marks of ownership and use.[38] The situations

34 On the history of teaching reading skills in England, see Mitford M. Mathews, *Teaching to Read: Historically Considered* (Chicago, IL, 1966); M. T. Clanchy, *From Memory to Written Record: England 1066–1307* augmented 2nd edn (Oxford, 1993); Tony Hunt, *Teaching and Learning Latin in Thirteenth-Century England*, 3 vols. (Cambridge, 1991); W. J. Frank Davies, *Teaching Reading in Early England* (London, 1973); Rosemary O'Day, *Education and Society 1500–1800: The Social Foundations of Education in Early Modern Britain* (London, 1982); R. A. Houston, *Literacy in Early Modern Europe: Culture and Education, 1500–1800* (London, 1988); R. K. Webb, *The British Working Class Reader, 1790–1848: Literacy and Social Tension* (London, 1955; repr. New York, 1971); and, relatedly, Patricia Cline Cohen, *A Calculating People: The Spread of Numeracy in Early America* (Chicago, IL, 1982); and Keith Thomas, 'Numeracy in Early Modern England', *Transactions of the Royal Historical Society* 5th ser., 37 (1987): 103–32.

35 See David McKitterick, 'Bibliography, Bibliophily, and the Organization of Knowledge', in David Vaisey and David McKitterick (eds.), *The Foundations of Scholarship: Libraries and Collecting, 1650–1750* (Los Angeles, CA, 1992), pp. 29–61; Jack A. Clarke, *Gabriel Naudé, 1600–1653* (Hamden, CT, 1970).

36 See Sears Jayne, *Library Catalogues of the English Renaissance* 2nd edn (Godalming, 1983); and Archer Taylor, *Book Catalogues: Their Varieties and Uses* 2nd edn, rev. by W. P. Barlow, Jr (Winchester, 1986). There is no full list of the many studies of private and institutional book collections appearing in recent years, but a valuable survey is given by David McKitterick, 'Book Catalogues: Their Varieties and Uses', in Peter Davison (ed.), *The Book Encompassed: Studies in Twentieth-Century Bibliography* (Cambridge, 1992), pp. 161–75.

37 See E. S. Leedham-Green, *Books in Cambridge Inventories: Book-Lists from Vice-Chancellor's Court Probate Inventories in the Tudor and Stuart Periods*, 2 vols. (Cambridge, 1986); R. J. Fehrenbach and E. S. Leedham-Green (eds.), *Private Libraries in Renaissance England: A Collection and Catalogue of Tudor and Early Stuart Book-Lists*, 2 vols. (Marlborough, 1992–3); and Christian Coppens, *Reading in Exile: The Libraries of John Ramridge (d. 1568), Thomas Harding (d. 1572) and Henry Joliffe (d. 1573), Recusants in Louvain* (Cambridge, 1993). See also Lorna Weatherill's analysis of book ownership in the late seventeenth century based on 3,000 wills and inventories drawn from eight parts of England – *Consumer Behaviour and Material Culture in Britain, 1660–1760* (London, 1988). Unfortunately, these sorts of probate inventories virtually disappear after a change in the law in the early eighteenth century.

38 See John Harrison, *The Library of Isaac Newton* (Cambridge, 1978); Jackson Campbell Boswell, *Milton's Library: A Catalogue of the Remains of John Milton's Library and an Annotated Reconstruction of Milton's Library and Ancillary Readings* (New York, 1975); and Brian North Lee, *Early Printed Book*

which would require the historian's attention for a comprehensive account rapidly escalate, however: the monastery cell and refectory, the pew and pulpit, the classroom, the private study, the private library, the institutional library and, later, different types of booksellers' shops and circulating libraries, debating societies, coffee houses, and – those favourite targets of satirists – the boudoir, the billiard room and the garden grotto, not forgetting the privy. The places in which reading happens, and the company the reader may keep undoubtedly change the nature of that reading. To read in solitude for a long uninterrupted stretch is a very different process from intermittently perusing the same text while the reader is in the hands of the hairdresser, or from dipping into it while browsing through a bookshop. Or again, a priest's reading from the Bible in church is different from a monastic reading of the same text during a meal, and different again from a soldier's encounter with that text on the eve of a battle.[39]

Clearly, other kinds of evidence are also needed in order to understand the modes of reading that obtained in the past, the ways in which it was practised and the meanings attached to it. In this respect, changes within the field of textual bibliography have been particularly important for historians of reading. Until twenty-five years ago, textual bibliography tended to be concerned with the means by which printed texts were produced from their manuscript originals. Broad changes in the field of literary criticism, and modifications in editorial practice argued for – most notably – by Jerome J. McGann, have disrupted this consensus. No longer believing in the possibility or the desirability of returning to a purely authorial text, the 'social approach to editing'[40] represented by McGann is relatively reader-oriented. It sees the meaning of literary works as being shaped by their emergence into the public domain: contingent, in other words, on the materiality of the text (its binding, paper, print type and composition) and on its contexts (the places in which it appears, the kinds of material which may appear in conjunction with it, the reputation of the publishing house and so forth). McGann's historicization of the act of reading is not as fully developed

Labels: A Catalogue of Dated Personal Labels and Gift Labels Printed in Britain to the Year 1760 (Pinner, 1976); Brian North Lee, *British Bookplates: A Pictorial History* (Newton Abbot, 1979); and Brian North Lee, *British Royal Bookplates and Ex-Libris of Related Families* (Aldershot, 1992).

39 See David Cressy, 'Books as Totems in Seventeenth-Century England and New England', *Journal of Library History* 21 (1986): 92–106, for a discussion of the contrasting symbolic uses of the book and its reading.

40 For discussion and critique, see T. H. Howard-Hill, 'Theory and Praxis in the Social Approach to Editing', *TEXT* 5 (1991): 31–46.

as his historical analysis of composition and publication,[41] but his mode of textual criticism potentially has much to tell us about the ways in which the reading practices which could be brought to bear on a text in the past were assisted by the text itself, both explicitly and implicitly. The evidence ranges from title page ascriptions and subscription lists to the less obtrusive signs which mark out a text for particular kinds of reader, down to the punctuation of the text – a practice largely overlooked until recently, but one which, as Malcolm Parkes and John Lennard have shown, profoundly affects the experience of reading.[42]

More immediate evidence of the ways in which certain kinds of text were read can sometimes be gleaned from visual representations of the reading of manuscript and print. Often these were offered within the texts themselves as elaborately decorated letters and factotums, or through simple woodcuts and engraved illustrations. Influential literary portrayals of the act of reading in England first appear during the late fourteenth century. For example, Chaucer's innovatory representations of himself as a reader, and of some of the figures who appear reading in his poems, were directly imitated by several of his fifteenth-century followers, and the resonances of such reading scenes have echoed in English writing ever since.[43] More broadly, pictorial representations range from paintings on the walls of churches to family miniatures. Implicitly, and often explicitly, readers were told by such visual and literary illustrations how to read and what to expect from their reading – but often the representation of reading was being mocked or castigated rather than idealized.[44] Throughout the period considered

41 For his current position see 'How to Read a Book', *The Library Chronicle of the University of Texas at Austin* 20 (1990): 13–37, repr. in Jerome J. McGann, *The Textual Condition* (Princeton, NJ, 1991), pp. 101–28.

42 See M. B. Parkes, *Pause and Effect: An Introduction to the History of Punctuation in the West* (Aldershot, 1992); Parkes, *Scribes, Scripts and Readers*; John Lennard, *But I Digress: The Exploitation of Parentheses in English Printed Verse* (Oxford, 1991); Tobin Nellhaus, 'Mementos of Things to Come: Orality, Literacy, and Typology in the *Biblia pauperum*', in Hindman (ed.), *Printing the Written Word*, pp. 292–321; and Mindele Treip, *Milton's Punctuation and Changing English Usage 1582–1676* (London, 1970).

43 See Paula Neuss, 'Images of Writing and the Book in Chaucer's Poetry', *Review of English Studies* ns 32 (1981): 385–97.

44 Studies of literary representations of reading are too numerous to cite here. Many of them are referred to in individual chapters of this volume. German research into the problematic issue of interpreting iconographic representations of reading is more advanced than in England and includes English examples. See Erich Schön, *Der Verlust der Sinnlichkeit oder die Verwandlungen des Lesers: Mentalitätswandel um 1800* (Stuttgart, 1987); Eva-Maria Hannebutt-Benz, *Die Kunst des Lesens: Lesemöbel und Leseverhalten vom Mittelalter bis zur Gegenwart* (Frankfurt am Main, 1985); Heinke Wunderlich, *'Buch' und 'Leser' in der Buchliteratur der 18. Jahrhunderts* (Heidelberg, 1980); and Carsten-Peter Warncke (ed.), *Ikonographie der Bibliotheken* (Wolfenbüttel, 1993).

by this volume, a sense of the potentially dangerous consequences of reading reverberates in the warnings of educationalists and moralists, from the campaign against Wycliffe Bibles to early nineteenth-century polemics against radical pamphleteering. Behind the lampoons and satires and stern rebukes that issued from so many guardians of public morality there can be seen a clear recognition that – once in the hand of the individual reader – the respectful reception of the written word was far from guaranteed.

For direct evidence of how books were received, however, we have the occasional testimony of readers themselves. Carlo Ginzburg's study of the sixteenth-century miller of Friuli, Domenico Scandella,[45] and Robert Darnton's work on the letters of the Protestant merchant of seventeenth-century La Rochelle, Jean Ranson,[46] remain key works in this respect, responsible for attracting greater interest in the historical value of the experience of the individual reader. In England, important information about the use of books has been derived from letters and autobiography, the earliest including the fifteenth-century correspondence of the Paston family of Norfolk and the sixteenth-century letters of the Lisle family.[47] More recently, a great deal of interest has also centred on the annotation practices of particular readers, with notable English examples including Gabriel Harvey and Charles Darwin.[48] Much of the significance of Ginzburg's and Darnton's examples, however, lies in their insistence on directing attention away from the illustrious intellectuals and the wealthy patrons of the literary arts to more humble men and women and their understanding of the printed word.

The fact that individual testimonies survived at all has to be attributed to singular experience, activity, luck or to a combination of those factors. The vast majority of readers left far fewer direct traces of the kinds of reading material they valued, and the way in which they

45 *The Cheese and the Worms: The Cosmos of a Sixteenth-Century Miller*, trans. Anne and John Tedeschi (London, 1980).

46 *The Great Cat Massacre and other Episodes in French Cultural History* (London, 1984), pp. 215–56. Comparably rich material has also been provided by recent editions of the memoirs of early modern literate artisans, most notably: Valentin Jamerey Duval, *Mémoires: enfance et éducation d'un paysan au XVIIIe siècle*, ed. Jean-Marie Goulemot (Paris, 1982); and Daniel Roche (ed.), *Journal de ma vie: Jacques-Louis Ménétra, vitrier an XVIIIe siècle* (Paris, 1982).

47 H. S. Bennett, *The Pastons and their England: Studies in an Age of Transition* (Cambridge, 1922), pp. 108–13, 261–2; Norman Davis (ed.), *The Paston Letters: A Selection in Modern Spelling*, 2 vols. (Oxford, 1983); and Muriel St Clare Byrne (ed.), *The Lisle Letters*, 6 vols. (Chicago, IL, 1981), references to books indexed VI, 329.

48 See Lisa Jardine and Anthony Grafton, ' "Studied for Action": How Gabriel Harvey Read his Livy', *Past and Present* 129 (1990): 30–78.

obtained, perused and disposed of it – if they left any at all. Yet, perhaps the greatest value of those testimonies which remain to us is that they oblige us to make the move from the general outline to the specificity of experience and then back again to reflect on the significance of individual readings for the general historical account. Familiarity with any one of the readers listed above prompts a recognition that reading can be highly individualistic – culturally conditioned, certainly, but not in any easy sense reducible to a cultural norm. Among the most important challenges facing historians of reading must be the question of how to integrate the broad narrative of the expansion of readerships over the centuries (complex enough in itself) with the actual experience of men and women.

How can we, in Roger Chartier's words, 'organize this indistinguishable plurality of individual acts according to shared regularities?'[49] As numerous historians have noted, we need a continued refinement of our thinking about 'collective experience',[50] but – as urgently – we need an approach to the history of reading that will be various enough in its methodologies and in its objects of study to establish and explore the often conflicting, contradictory ways in which general social changes and individual experience interact. Only then can we understand not just what materials people read in the past, but how they read them, why they read them and, wherever possible, what it meant to them. The essays included in *The Practice and Representation of Reading in England* seek to forward such a project by addressing subjects as diverse as medieval pedagogy, Renaissance letters, early modern physiology, eighteenth-century libraries and nineteenth-century public performance. In bringing these essays together, the intention has been not only to give a representative sample of the work now being done under the rubric of history of reading in England, but to demonstrate the value of such collaborative research.

The collection opens with an essay on the twelfth century which raises central questions about the kinds of activity which constituted

[49] Roger Chartier, 'Texts, Printing, Readings', in Lynn Hunt (ed.), *The New Cultural History* (Berkeley, CA, 1989), pp. 154–75 (p. 156).

[50] In this respect, see particularly Robert D. Hume's call to investigate 'historical reader-response groups' in 'a kind of historicization of Stanley Fish' – Hume, 'Texts within Contexts: Notes Toward a Historical Method,' *Philological Quarterly* 71 (1992): 69–100 (pp. 80 and 84). It is perhaps only fair to recall the stress laid by Stanley Fish in refinements to his thinking (and considered a dilution of his reader-response methodology by some of his critics) on the fact that no one can know whether he or she is a member of the same interpretive community; Fish, 'Interpreting the *Variorum*', *Critical Inquiry* 2 (1976): 465–85 (p. 485).

reading in the past. Suzanne Reynolds's 'Let him Read the *Satires* of Horace: Reading, Literacy and Grammar in the Twelfth Century' examines the reading of classical verse texts as part of the educational curriculum of young men in medieval England. She uses the evidence of medieval grammatical texts to develop a detailed account of the highly directed ways in which teachers of grammar taught their students to 'read' the classical authors. She describes a culture in which 'reading' possessed a very different meaning from those it acquired later. This is reading as a communal practice with carefully delineated educational criteria – occasionally disturbed by an anxiety that other, less desirable readings of the classics might be possible.

The situations considered by Suzanne Reynolds undoubtedly come under the heading of what we would consider 'public' reading. The nature of the public/private divide – its uses, and its legitimacy as a historical category – is an area of lively historical interest, and it is taken up in several of the chapters which follow. Andrew Taylor's essay 'Into his Secret Chamber: Reading and Privacy in Late Medieval England', is the first to examine the wide range of activities which fell within the rubric of 'private reading' in the past. Taylor looks at the reading practices of the aristocracy and gentry in the late fourteenth and early fifteenth centuries, focusing primarily on collaboration between the laity and the clergy in the production of devotional literature, with its quite specific guidelines for readers. As he shows in his analysis of this material, public and private forms of reading were not always easily distinguishable from each other, co-existing in a more complex way in fourteenth-century England than has often been assumed.

It has already been noted in this Introduction that the evidence for individual reading practices in the medieval period is frustratingly elusive, requiring careful and resourceful use of incomplete sources. By the sixteenth century, records of individual readers are still rare, but some very illuminating evidence does survive. The next chapter examines a rich source of information about one individual's reading practices in this period. William H. Sherman's account of 'The Place of Reading in the English Renaissance' concentrates on the creation of the largest library in Elizabethan England – John Dee's collection at Mortlake, near London. This account of Dee's own and other people's use and appreciation of his library building and the collection it housed shows the library as a centre of scholarly, political and, not least, social pursuits. In exploring the diverse functions of the library at Mortlake,

Sherman challenges some entrenched orthodoxies about the nature of the gentleman scholar's library and of the acts of reading it promoted and enshrined.

The valuation of certain kinds of reading within Renaissance humanism is also the subject of chapter five. Lisa Jardine's essay also brings the volume back to the subject of pedagogy through an account of the teaching and practice of letter-reading in sixteenth-century England. 'Reading and the Technology of Textual Affect' is concerned with the influence on England of one of the foremost intellectual figures in the European Renaissance: Desiderius Erasmus. Looking principally at the reception of Erasmus's familiar letters and his treatise on letter-writing, *De conscribendis epistolis*, she retrieves an understanding of the art of writing and reading letters intimately connected with contemporary ideas about moral and emotional authenticity. 'Reading and the Technology of Textual Affect' takes Erasmus's concept of the well-conceived and executed affective letter form to a reading of *King Lear*, revealing the extent to which the moral chaos imagined by Shakespeare's play involves the betrayal of ethical and emotional standards bound up with Erasmian expectations of the letter form.

John Kerrigan's chapter on textual bibliography and the editing of Renaissance texts pursues the issues raised above about the role of the reader in editorial theory and practice. After a brief survey of changing approaches to textual bibliography in the twentieth century, the example of editions of George Gascoigne is used to show how editing which exalts hypothetical authorial intentions over anticipated and actual reader responses produces flawed results. Yet the 'social approach to editing' associated with McGann, though freer of false assumptions, can be shown to have neglected the diversity of individual reading practices which Renaissance authors and printers admitted and, on many occasions, actively encouraged in their audiences. Analysing addresses 'To the Reader' in a range of early modern texts, Kerrigan provides the basis for a new model of editing and for a more fully informed 'historicist textual criticism' (in the words of McGann): one which stresses the importance of the reading process within the decision-making of editors as well as the historically shaped variety of reading practices in the literary audience.

In the next chapter, Adam Fox explores the interaction of orality and literacy in provincial England, investigating the nature of reading in popular culture before the Civil War. Evidence for popular reading in the early seventeenth century is slight, largely dependent on the survival of printed texts and contemporary descriptions of their reception. Fox overcomes this difficulty by exploring archives of legal material from the period. Formal records of the scandalous ballads and humorous verses presented in court to support charges of libel enable him to retrieve a genuinely popular literature: one not only produced for the people but produced by them. As he shows, 'reading' in these instances was a communal activity, and the texts were both unstable and dynamic. Familiarization with the verses was closely interlinked with other activities such as singing, reciting and, not least, listening, so that the written words were kept alive and repeatedly transformed by their audience.

In chapter eight, Adrian Johns pursues what is arguably the most elusive and the most basic aspect of the experience of reading: what readers believe happens when they pursue and interpret the signs on the page. 'The Physiology of Reading in the Restoration' explores the writing of seventeenth-century scientists, philosophers and moralists to provide for the first time an account of the different physiological operations – the functioning of eye, nerve and brain – that were seen to constitute the physical embodiment of the reading process. The picture that emerges is one of an intimate involvement of reader with text – a picture with far-reaching implications for this and later periods in its emphasis on the potential hazards of that involvement.

One of the most recurrent anxieties to surface in relation to the physiological effects of reading was its perceived impact on women. Warnings against the damaging influence of the novel on the female body and mind in particular were endemic in the eighteenth century and long afterward. Chapter nine addresses the conventional representation of eighteenth-century female readers as supine, passive ladies of leisure, idling away their time with the latest romance. '"In the even my wife read to me": Women, Reading and Household Life in the Eighteenth Century' looks in detail at the forms taken by that convention both in the period and in later historical reflections on it. Naomi Tadmor uses the evidence of two very different households to correct the stereotype. Samuel Richardson's personal correspondence speaks from a social world far removed from that of the Sussex shopkeeper and diarist, Thomas Turner, but both sources depict women combining novel-reading with a rigorous routine of work, religious discipline and social activity, belying contemporary and later assumptions about the pernicious effect of fiction on the female body and mind.

Women readers, and particularly their reading of novels, feature strongly in chapter ten of this volume, where James Raven returns to the subject of the library. His essay takes up questions introduced in earlier chapters about the reading practices reflected and promoted by the very different places in which readers encountered literature. This chapter highlights the difficulty in distinguishing between private and public libraries in the eighteenth century, and argues that the ambiguity between the two categories was itself a key contemporary concern. In a period of unprecedented library building, both commercial and private, Raven identifies a conflict between support for the growth of the print industry and moral and political alarm about the implications of an expanded readership. He finds evidence of such reaction expressed in the physical arrangement of libraries and in their contemporary representations, and argues that recognition of the resistance expressed toward the extension of reading should act as a corrective to any easy assumption that the growth of a 'mass' English readership was an unproblematic precursor of democratization and modernity.

How far access to the printed word was genuinely expanding in the period cannot be assessed until we have a clearer picture of the social breakdown of the consumption of print. Jan Fergus's research into the bookselling records of the Clays of Daventry, Rugby, Lutterworth and Warwick has already been referenced above.[51] In the next chapter she extends her work in a new direction, concentrating on what the Clay records can tell us about one of the primary targets of moralists' anxieties: the reading of servants in the period. Her analysis of the books borrowed and purchased by fifty provincial servants in the late eighteenth century adds significantly to our knowledge of a group of readers who left few individual traces of their involvement with literature. Fergus shows a range of men and women of different ranks and occupations, all employed as servants and actively engaged in reading for pleasure and for personal improvement.

Several of the essays in this volume have made close use of the records of individual readers: Dee, Erasmus, Boyle, Richardson and Turner. In chapter twelve, John Brewer uses a remarkably detailed personal testimony to reconstruct the reading of one late eighteenth-century reader – Anna Larpent, wife of John Larpent, Inspector of Plays in the Office of the Lord Chamberlain. Anna Larpent was closely

[51] See p. 7.

involved with her husband's work and, during the 1790s, she not only kept a diary-record of her extensive reading, but regularly described the situations in which she read, the motives for her reading, and her assessments of specific books. Her access to literature was uniquely privileged, but, as Brewer argues, the value of that uniqueness is partly the challenge it presents to general or statistical assessments of reading in this period and, by extension, in any other. Not least, it emphasizes the necessity of giving full credit to the diversity of ways in which any one individual may engage with the printed word.

Inaccurate though the image of the idle, frivolous female novel-reader was, the stereotype did not disappear with the close of the eighteenth century. The force of its durability and the degree to which novels themselves continued to feed this representation is explored in Kate Flint's account of William Makepeace Thackeray's celebrated satire on Victorian England, *Vanity Fair*. Kate Flint's chapter examines the representation of reading in *Vanity Fair*, drawing on Thackeray's many addresses to the reader, his comic allusions to the merits and demerits of various reading practices, his barbed depictions of contemporary tastes in literature and, above all, the distinctions he made between male and female readers. She goes on to show just how profoundly, for all his wit as a satirist, Thackeray continued to attribute exclusively to men the clarity of insight essential to his definition of good reading practice.

The final chapter of this volume re-examines a concept which has all but disappeared from recent work on the history of reading: that of the 'general reading public'. Like many of the previous chapters, 'A Pulse of 124' is concerned with conflicting reactions to the extension of reading. Helen Small looks at the role played by the concept of 'the reading public' within the particular context of late nineteenth-century concern about reform of the franchise and incorporation of the working classes. 'A Pulse of 124' argues that in Charles Dickens's highly successful public reading tours of the 1850s and 1860s there can be found a revealing cultural extension of contemporary political debates. The chapter assesses mid-Victorian celebrations of Dickens's Readings as a forum in which all classes were able to come together, united in their enjoyment of a common sensibility. It also looks at the recurrent undertones of anxiety about the security of that vision of a harmonious general public expressed through reading.

These essays are arranged chronologically, but it is intended that they should be read with the connections between them in view. As a collection, they repeatedly challenge popular assumptions about continuity and change in the history of reading. That history has often been understood as a linear development in which 'oral' modes are gradually replaced by 'literate', and in which primarily 'public' forms of reading give way to 'private' ones as individuals gain a growing autonomy from their environment. This volume shows very clearly that such narratives are misleading. Far subtler and more various narratives are necessary if we are to understand the relations between material and cultural dimensions of existence as they are expressed in the activity of reading.[52] The essays collected here pursue numerous historical traces to reconstruct the nature of reading in the past, ranging from quantitative evidence of the consumption of printed matter, to the testimony of individual readers. Different chapters treat the 'reader' as the consumer of manuscript and print, the visitor to a library or bookshop, the implied addressee of a particular text, and the guilty subject of many a stern moralist's warning. They also offer written and pictorial illustrations of readers engaging with their choice of literature in very different situations, postures and companies, with divergent ends in mind. A common view informs all these contributions: a conviction that the history of reading is also a history of the culture in which it takes place, requiring close attention to what it was possible to think, to perceive and, not least, to feel, in particular situations at particular moments in the past. At a time when it is far from clear in what form literature will survive the technological innovations of the late twentieth century, and in which the circumstances and purposes of reading are under constant review, a fuller sense of what is involved in the history of reading should sharpen our awareness of how extensive the repercussions of current changes may be.

52 The phrase 'material and cultural dimensions of existence' is taken from William J. Gilmore *Reading becomes a Necessity of Life: Material and Cultural Life in Rural New England, 1780–1835* (Knoxville, TN, 1989), p. 9.

CHAPTER 2

'Let him read the Satires *of Horace': reading, literacy and grammar in the twelfth century*

Suzanne Reynolds

In the learned culture of the Middle Ages, reading most often occurred in the context of specific and clearly defined educational disciplines. These ranged from the art of grammar (*grammatica*), the foundation of the educational system, to theology, its peak and consummation. Between these two poles, reading was of course fundamental to areas of learning as diverse as, say, rhetoric and arithmetic. But the differences between the art of grammar and the pursuit of theological wisdom lay not only in the texts that were read but, just as importantly, in the way of reading. Strategies for dealing with the sacred page of the Bible, where a hierarchical system of exegetical approaches operated, were not of course appropriate for dealing with treatises on syntactic theory. Even closely related disciplines like the trivium arts of grammar and rhetoric, read the same texts in different ways and for different purposes. The art of grammar is particularly interesting from this point of view, for its very aim was to teach the Latin language by teaching students how to read classical Latin texts. Here, 'reading' is explicitly and profoundly shaped by the overarching purpose of achieving literacy in Latin, the ability to understand spoken and written Latin texts.

This is the context for Alexander Nequam's remark that the young student (the *puer*) should read Horace, Virgil, Ovid, Statius and other classical Latin authors (*auctores*) as an essential part of his training in grammar.[1] Writing in the last years of the twelfth century, Nequam

I would like to thank Richard Beadle and the staff–postgraduate medieval studies seminar of the School of English, University of Birmingham for very helpful discussion of several points in this essay. I have recently completed a book on the reading practices I discuss briefly here.

1 Nequam prescribes these texts in his *Sacerdos ad altare accessurus*, preserved in a unique manuscript, Cambridge, Gonville and Caius College 385/605 (henceforth G), pp. 7–61; the text as a whole, with parts of the commentary, is now edited in Hunt, *Teaching and Learning*, I, 258–73 (pp. 269–70 for this list); for further information on this text see C. H. Haskins, *Studies in the History of Mediaeval Science* (Cambridge, MA, 1924), pp. 372–73 and for Nequam himself see R. W. Hunt, *The Schools and the Cloister: The Life and Writings of Alexander Nequam 1157–1217*, edited and revised by Margaret Gibson (Oxford, 1984).

implicitly allied his educational curriculum to a tradition with a very long history. However, we have tended to leave this postulated interaction of grammatical and literary discourses unquestioned, assuming that the implication of this text – that the basics of a foreign language be learnt by 'reading' complex texts in verse – is perfectly straightforward.[2] Of course, this is far from the case, and the use of literary texts in *grammatica* raises many important questions. When Nequam says that the *puer* should read (*legat*) these authors, when he has previously learnt only the most elementary of grammatical skills, what force can 'read' possibly have in these circumstances?[3] How far is the nature of that 'reading' shaped by the discipline of which it seems to form a part? And how does this reading practice in turn reflect on our notion of grammar as a discipline in the Middle Ages?

It is true to say that reading, in the broadest terms, is the practice which drew grammatical and literary concerns together – it lay at the heart of *grammatica*'s notoriously double-sided nature. For Quintilian, writing in first-century Rome, grammar's doubleness was aphoristically simple. It was the science of speaking correctly (*scientia recte loquendi*) and the explication of the poets (*enarratio poetarum*).[4] In practice, this entailed a notion of correctness based upon the usage of the classical authors, the poets. But this alliance of correctness and exposition grew increasingly complex as the language of students became further divorced from the language of the authoritative texts they were studying.[5] Quintilian's students were of course learning correct usage from texts written in their mother tongue. By the twelfth century however, students of grammar in the monastic and cathedral schools of England and Northern France,[6] were 'reading' texts of Latin classical authors as

2 See for example R. R. Bolgar, *The Classical Heritage and its Beneficiaries* (repr. Cambridge, 1973), p. 197.

3 Before tackling the authors, the young student will have read Donatus' *Ars minor*, the alphabet and other 'boyish rudiments'; see Hunt, *Teaching and Learning*, 1, 269; for the *Ars minor*, see Louis Holtz, *Donat et la tradition de l'enseignement grammaticale: étude sur l'Ars Donati et sa diffusion (IVe-IXe siècles) et édition critique* (Paris, 1981), pp. 585–602; for the learning of the alphabet and the 'boyish rudiments' in the later Middle Ages, see Danièle Alexandre-Bidon, 'La lettre volée: apprendre à lire à l'enfant au moyen age', *Annales: Economies, Sociétés, Civilisations* 44 (1989): 953–92.

4 *Institutio oratoria* (*IO*) 1, 4, 2, ed. M. Winterbottom, 2 vols. (Oxford, 1970), 1, 2.

5 Servius' fourth-century commentary on Virgil has been examined in the light of this tension; see Robert A. Kaster, *Guardians of Language: The Grammarian and Society in Late Antiquity* (London, 1988), pp. 176–97.

6 In the twelfth century, this region was fairly homogenous in cultural terms, and it is often impossible to tell which side of the Channel a manuscript comes from; see R. M. Thomson, 'England and the Twelfth-Century Renaissance', *Past and Present* 101 (1983): 3–21. On the schools see G. R. Evans, *Old Arts and New Theology: The Beginnings of Theology as an Academic Discipline* (Oxford, 1980), pp. 8–15.

works in a completely foreign language. For them, reading those texts was synonymous with learning the Latin language itself, and with learning to read; until the later Middle Ages, learning to read inevitably meant learning to read Latin. In this way, *grammatica*'s first aim, to generate skills in Latin (*ut sciamus componere litteras in sillabam, sillabas in dictiones, dictiones in oratione*, 'so that we might know how to combine letters into a syllable, syllables into words, words into a phrase') becomes the basic model for reading the authors.[7] This surely is what makes sense of Nequam's curriculum – very basic grammatical knowledge, followed by the reading of Horace and others, followed in turn by the more advanced and complex grammatical treatises of the authoritative Donatus and Priscian.[8]

How then are we to reconstruct the students' 'reading' of the texts signalled by Nequam when he wrote *sermones Oracii* ... *legat* ('let him read the *Satires* of Horace')? The most obvious use of classical texts in grammar takes the form of the examples used in grammatical treatises or florilegia. Along with examples from the Bible, or examples of the grammarian's own invention, classical literature was the storehouse of examples, and grammarians used them to illustrate, reinforce and refute grammatical points.[9] However, the exposition undertaken in these examples is only one rather limited mode of 'reading' the classical authors. Of far more importance for a study of reading practice within the art of grammar are the many grammatical glosses and commentaries on classical texts. Here we have a reversal of the structure and physical layout of the grammatical treatise which uses literary examples; the glosses occupy the marginal and interlinear spaces on the page, surrounding the text with explanations of its linguistic detail. This is the site in which the double demand of grammar, that it instil correct usage and explain the poets, is most urgently played out. The

7 See Franz H. Bäuml, 'Varieties and Consequences of Medieval Literacy and Illiteracy', *Speculum* 55 (1980): 238; Alexandre-Bidon, 'La lettre', p. 985. The example is taken from an anonymous twelfth-century commentary on Priscian, the *Circa hanc artem* (Cambridge, St John's College D. 12, fols. 51ra-79rb (fol. 51rb)).

8 Hunt, *Teaching and Learning*, I, 270. The grammatical texts referred to are: Book III of Donatus's *Ars maior*, the *Barbarismus* (on the figures and tropes) (edited in Holtz, *Donat*, pp. 603–74), dating from the fourth century AD; Priscian, *Institutiones grammaticae* (henceforth *IG*), written in sixth-century Constantinople, edited in H. Keil, *Grammatici latini* (henceforth *GL*), 7 vols. (repr. Hildesheim, 1961), II, 1–597 and III, 1–384; Priscian's *Partitiones*, a grammatical analysis of the first line of each of the twelve books of the *Aeneid* (*GL*, III, pp. 459–515).

9 G. Evans, 'The Use of Biblical Examples in Ralph of Beauvais' Commentary on Donatus', *Studi medievali* 24 (1983): 371–2; Irène Rosier, 'Le traitement spéculatif des constructions figurées au XIIIe siècle', in Rosier (ed.), *L'Héritage des grammairiens latins de l'Antiquité aux Lumières* (Paris, 1988), pp. 201–2.

medieval grammatical commentator is forced constantly to negotiate between the authority of the complex classical text, and the requirement to teach the basics of the Latin language itself.

In order to reconstruct the reading that these glosses point to, we have to look at them in terms of their function – how the gloss interacts with the text, what it is using the text for. Glosses on Priscian, Ovid, Arator and Prudentius have been studied from a functional point of view, but these studies have not attempted to integrate the glosses into the disciplinary context of *grammatica*.[10] In this essay, I shall present a typology of glossing, or reading strategies, according to the scheme of medieval grammar, although space permits me only to look at a limited range of glosses on the word and on the phrase. This approach enables us to evaluate how far and to what extent the reading embodied in the glosses is shaped by the more theoretical concerns in twelfth-century grammar. It also enables us to see that these readings of classical texts were the instruments in *grammatica*'s initial and most elementary aim of teaching Latin.

Before going any further, it is necessary to state quite clearly the nature of the evidence that these glosses provide. In later periods, and for other more advanced types of glossing and commentary, annotation seems to provide a fairly direct route to a particular reading, even to a particular reader.[11] (This is not to say that such readings are isolated from contextual pressures, political and cultural). The case here is quite different. We have, since the first publication of Michael Clanchy's *From Memory to Written Record* in 1979, been keenly aware of the very strict separation of the skills of reading and writing in this period.[12] Being able to read, even being able to read Latin, in no way implies the capacity to record anything in writing. The skills and office of the scribe were quite separate, and it is interesting in this respect to note that Nequam's grammatical curriculum does not include writing at all, and that he discusses it instead in the final two chapters of the *Sacerdos*,

10 See A. Schwarz, 'Glossen als Texte', *Beiträge zur Geschichte der deutschen Sprache und Literatur* 99 (1977): 25–36; R. J. Hexter, *Ovid and Medieval Schooling: Studies in the Medieval School Commentaries on Ovid's 'Ars amatoria', 'Epistulae ex ponto' and 'Epistulae Heroidum'*, *Münchener Beiträge zur Mediävistik- und Renaissance-Forschung* 38 (Munich, 1986); G. R. Wieland, *The Latin Glosses on Arator and Prudentius in Cambridge University Library, MS Gg. 5. 35*, *Studies and Texts* 61 (Toronto, 1983).

11 For example Grafton and Jardine, '"Studied for Action"' and the account of a later reader of Horace in Anthony Grafton, 'Teacher, Text and Pupil in the Renaissance Classroom: A Case Study from a Parisian College', *History of Universities* 1 (1981): 37–70.

12 Clanchy, *From Memory to Written Record*. See also D. H. Green, 'Orality and Reading: The State of Research in Medieval Studies', *Speculum* 65 (1990): 267–80.

which deal with the scribe and his craft.[13] Writing was a more or less professional, technical skill. What then are we to do with elementary readings that are recorded in written glosses? The kind of reader who would need the information they convey is by definition the kind of reader who cannot write; in terms of the twelfth-century hierarchy of literate skills, someone who could write would have no need of them. We are forced to the conclusion that the glosses are the traces of a reading undertaken by experts for the less expert, that is to say, by teachers for their pupils. Thus, the nature of the reading is determined by the needs of the pupils even though it is not actively undertaken by them. Put another way, the mode of reading is directly dependent on the level and literacy of the students even though they do not, in our sense of the word, read the text at all. It remains at all times and in all senses in the teacher's hands. The students memorize the text and its exposition. Only when they are considerably more advanced and are able to write do they make notes, using wax tablets or scraps of parchment.[14] This reading is therefore a communal activity, communicated orally, and the glosses are merely the written traces of a fuller reading practice. Indeed, we have in one and the same set of glosses a witness to what one scholar has termed the 'eye' reading of the *magister*, that is to say a reading of the written word on the page, and the 'ear' reading of the students, who hear the text being read.[15] This is why Nequam's curriculum employs the terms *audire* (to hear) and *legere* (to read) almost interchangeably to denote the use of texts in the classroom.[16]

This essay will concentrate on glosses on the *Satires* of Horace, a text that was particularly useful to the twelfth-century teacher of Latin for two principal reasons.[17] In the first place, its highly topical and demotic language provided an excellent opportunity for the learning of useful, everyday Latin, and the text was often glossed with lexical equivalents. Secondly, the *Satires* presented a common-sense morality at the literal level of the text, so that the teacher of basic Latin can at the same time communicate a basic morality. Thus, a literal (grammatical) reading is

[13] G, pp. 58a-61a; Hunt, *Teaching and Learning*, I, 272.

[14] On wax tablets and their uses in classroom settings see Elisabeth Lalou, 'Les tablettes de cire médiévales', *Bibliothèque de l'École des Chartes* 147 (1989): 130–1.

[15] Terms used in Susan Schibanoff, 'The New Reader and Female Textuality in Two Early Commentaries on Chaucer', *Studies in the Age of Chaucer* 10 (1988): 71–108 (p. 76).

[16] G, pp. 47–52; see Hunt, *Teaching and Learning*, I, 269–70.

[17] All references are to Horace, *Opera*, ed. D. R. Shackleton Bailey (Stuttgart, 1985); translations from Horace, *Satires, Epistles and Ars Poetica*, edited and translated by H. Ruston Fairclough (London, 1978).

possible and the pagan text does not need to be christianized through allegorical analysis, even though, as we shall see later, glosses do occasionally manifest Christian anxiety.[18]

We have already seen how grammar divides language into the constituent parts of the letter, the syllable, the word and the phrase. The first two elements are dealt with by learning the alphabet and the full range of syllabic combinations before the learner begins to tackle a text. The most elementary approach to texts, to what we can call 'reading', therefore takes the form of a word by word analysis. Glosses on words have two principal functions – to offer definitions, synonyms and so on, or to examine the grammatical form of the words in the text. They are either lexical or morphological in emphasis; the same dualistic approach is also fundamental to grammatical doctrine in this period. The *Satires* are glossed with a wealth of lexical equivalents, principally Latin synonyms, but with many translation glosses using Anglo-Norman, Old French and Medieval Occitan. In this respect, they represent the literary equivalent of the genre of heavily glossed, versified dictionaries of everyday life which abounded in the latter half of the twelfth century, such as Nequam's *De utensilium nominibus* ('On the names of useful things') and the *De utensilibus* ('On useful things') of Adam of Petit Pont.[19] The function of all vernacular, and some Latin lexical glosses, is to explain an unfamiliar word by suggesting a more familiar one. Other Latin lexical glosses aim to enlarge the Latin vocabulary of the students for whom they are intended. Some glosses perform both these functions, and more. For example, the early thirteenth-century glossator of an English twelfth-century Horace manuscript (Cambridge, Peterhouse 229, henceforth C), glosses the word 'cucu[l]lum' (cuckoo) as follows: 'that is a cuckoo, *hic cucullus*, a cloak, *hic cuculus*, a cuckoo'.[20] The gloss translates the text, differentiates the word in the text from a confusingly similar form (the choice is between one 'l' or two), and provides an indication of the gender of the word (masculine) by using the demonstrative adjective *hic* ('this') as a kind of article. This gloss is closely related in both form and function to the techniques of medieval mono- and bi-lingual wordlists, a very important strand of medieval lexicography. For example, in a

18 On the idea of allegory as ideological 'recuperation', see Morton W. Bloomfield, 'Allegory as Interpretation', *New Literary History* 3 (1972): 301–17.

19 Both texts now edited in Hunt, *Teaching and Learning*, I, 165–89.

20 *idest cuculum: hic cucullus, cufel, hic cuculus, cuku* : C, fol. 46^r, *Satires* I, 7, 31, p. 197, trans. p. 93. The vernacular glosses from this manuscript are published in Hunt, *Teaching and Learning*, I, 64.

mid-thirteenth century Latin-French glossary of Anglo-Norman provenance, we find the following two glosses: 'hec cucula, *cufle*' and 'hic cuculus, *cucu*'.[21]

The C glossator seems especially concerned with differentiating near synonyms and combating equivocation, in other words with ensuring 'correct' and precise understanding of the text. In one case, the word *inula* (an onion-like herb) is glossed with a vernacular equivalent *eschalunies* (which is found in other Horace manuscripts and in contemporary glossaries), and a phonetically similar Latin term: *hinnulus in silvis, hinule queruntur in ortis* ('a young deer (*hinnulus*) is found in the woods, herbs (*hinule*) in the garden').[22] The aim is both to augment vocabulary and to forestall any possible confusion between near homonyms. A gloss on Nequam's *De naturis rerum* (which may originate with the author), articulates the difference in much the same way: *hec hinula est scalonia: hic hinnulus est fetus cerve* ('the *hinnula* is a spring-onion, the *hinnulus* is a young deer').[23] A much closer, verbal parallel exists in a gloss on the *Distigium* of John of Garland: *hinnulus est fetus cerve ... dicit magister J. de Gallandia* (sic), *ubi dicit hinnulus in silvis, hinule queruntur in ortis, scilicet escalogne gallice* ('the *hinnulus* is a young deer, says Master John of Garland, where he says the hind is found in the woods, herbs in gardens, that is herbs which are *escalogne* in French').[24] A precise verbal parallel does exist in John of Garland's *Accentarium.*[25] It is impossible to establish precisely whether the C glossator knew the work of John of Garland directly (the thirteenth-century date of the hand makes this a distinct possibility), or whether both the glossator and John of Garland were drawing on a common source or a commonplace tradition. In either case, it is clear that we need to locate lexical glosses on literary works in the context of contemporary texts concerned with definition. Glosses, dictionaries and lexicographical treatises are united in their use of a common strategy to differentiate ambiguous forms.[26] Word by word reading of texts is identical to approaches to the word in medieval *grammatica.*

21 See A. Ewert, 'The Glasgow Latin-French Glossary', *Medium Aevum* 25 (1957): 154–63 (pp. 161 and 163).

22 C, fol. 49^{v}; *Satires* II, 2, 44, p. 212, trans. p. 141. See Tony Hunt, *The Plant Names of Medieval England* (Cambridge, 1989), p. 148.

23 Alexander Nequam, *De naturis rerum et De laudibus divinae sapientiae*, ed. T. Wright (London, 1863), p. 274.

24 See Tony Hunt, 'Vernacular Glosses in Medieval Manuscripts', *Cultura neo-latina* 39 (1979): 35.

25 *hinnulus in silvis, hinnule queruntur in ortis*: John of Garland, *Accentarium*, in manuscript G, pp. 68–140 (p. 78) with vernacular glosses *foun* and *scalon*: see Hunt, *Teaching and Learning*, I, 146.

26 The best survey of medieval lexicography with further bibliography is Cl. Buridant, 'Lexicographie et glossographie médiévale', *Lexique* 4 (1986): 9–46.

The use of *hic, hec, hoc* as 'articles' is of particular importance in this respect. These glosses take us into the realm of morphology, which in medieval *grammatica* was always analysed in terms of the eight parts of speech. Twelfth-century grammarians isolated three main criteria for establishing this classification, by looking at words first in terms of their abstract, non-referential *significatio* ('signification') (for example, 'nouns signify substance'), secondly through their function (*officium*), and last through their various secondary significations (*consignificationes*), which were manifested in their accidents.[27] Morphological glosses aim to examine these accidents, that is the inflections or 'endings' of the words of the text. The form of such glossing is fairly uniform and the following example from C is typical: *primores* (leaders) is annotated *primor, primoris* ('the leader, of the leader'), that is to say the oblique plural form in the text is glossed not by a lexical equivalent but by itself, in nominative and genitive singular forms.[28] These two forms are the key to the whole morphology of a noun, and their use in glosses undoubtedly stems from the declension paradigms in the *Ars minor* of Donatus (the sole grammatical text read by the *puer* in Nequam's curriculum before he started to study the *auctores*). There, nominative and genitive are the first two cases to be given for each declined noun, for once these are known the form of the remaining cases should be obvious.[29] In the declension of adjectives, the glossator's concern is less the form of the genitive than the nominative forms of the three genders. In C, *vafer* (cunning) for example is glossed *vafer, fra, frum*, giving masculine, feminine and neuter forms.[30] Such configurations are often followed by a synonym gloss so that both morphological and lexical information is offered. *Petum* (squinting) for example, is explained *petus, ta, tum, idest petulantem* ('lascivious').[31] However, the synonym is given in the accusative case like the lemma, while the adjectival forms convert it to the nominative. This clearly

27 See principally Karin Margareta Fredborg, 'The Dependence of Petrus Helias' *Summa super Priscianum* on William of Conches' *Glose super Priscianum*', *Cahiers de l'Institut du Moyen Age Grec et Latin* (*CIMAGL*) 11 (1973): 1–57; Irène Rosier, 'Les parties du discours au confin du XIIe siècle', *Langages* 92 (1988): 37–49.

28 C, fol. 49ʳ: *Satires* II, 1, 69; p. 209, trans. p. 133.

29 An interpolation from Priscian's *Institutio de nomine et pronomine et verbo* in one manuscript of the *Ars minor* argues for the genitive as the basis of the taxonomy of the five-declension system: 'As for the declensions of the nouns – which are discovered in the genitive singular case – how many are there? Five' (*Declinationes nominum quae in genitivo casu singulari requiruntur, quot sunt? V*): *Ars minor*, p. 587. See *GL* III, 443.

30 *Satires* I, 3, 130: C, fol. 41ᵛ, p. 180, trans. p. 43.

31 *Satires* I, 3, 45: C, fol. 41ʳ, p. 176, trans. p. 37.

demonstrates a division between semantic and formal approaches to the word within the same gloss.

Glosses on the noun and adjective can take an alternative form, where the grammatical information embodied in the ending is supplemented by the inclusion of the prepositional terms, *hic*, *hec* or *hoc*. In C, *guttus* (flask) is explained by *hic guttus, platel* and *hillis* (sausages) by the comment *hillis, hec hilla, le anduil.*[32] As well as providing a vernacular, Anglo-Norman equivalent, the gloss uses the nominative form of the word from the text along with the demonstrative adjective. This is intended to help inculcate the grammatical gender of individual words, a crucial factor in determining the declension to which they belonged. *Hic, hec* or *hoc* only occur with the nominative glosses and not the genitive forms that accompany them, precisely because the genitive *huius* is the same for all three genders, and so cannot serve to differentiate them. Moreover, their combination with vernacular equivalents confirms the elementary level at which such glosses operated. The same function for *hic, hec, hoc* is attested in other pedagogic contexts. For example, a glossator of Ovid's *Art of Love* sought to negate the homosexuality of the text by suggesting that for the ancients, *puer* referred to girls as well as boys: *hic et haec puer.*[33] Elsewhere, a Latin-Occitan word list employs these terms for nouns of the third declension only, where the gender is not clearly signalled by the ending.[34] And in C, adjectives of the third declension are subjected to similar treatment. *Limis* (askew) is glossed by *hic et hec limis et hoc lime* and *comis* (courteous) by *hic et hec comis.*[35]

Is this strategy the result of vernacular pressures? It is often assumed that the mother tongue of the students is the model for how they learned Latin, so that we might postulate that the Latin demonstrative is employed as an article in accordance with the grammatical structure of Old French. However, it is important not to look hastily to the vernacular when the grammatical tradition itself may have a more pressing claim to be considered the basis of glossing tactics. Even the humble 'article' has its own history. The article was important to Latin writers such as Quintilian and Priscian by virtue of its absence, an irritating divergence from the pattern of

[32] *Satires* I, 6, 118: C, fol. 45^{v}, p. 195, trans. p. 85; *Satires* II, 4, 60: C, fol. 54^{v}, p. 231, trans. p. 191.

[33] See R. J. Hexter, '*Latinitas* in the Middle Ages: Horizons and Perspectives', *Helios* 14 (1978): 73.

[34] See Ch. Samaran, 'Une *Summa grammaticalis* du XIIIe siècle, avec gloses provençales', *Bulletin du Cange* 31 (1961): 194–212.

[35] *Satires* II, 5, 53; C, fol. 55^{v}, p. 235, trans. p. 203; *Satires* II, 8, 76; C, fol. 59^{r}, p. 249, trans. p. 245.

Greek.[36] But Isidore of Seville, ever pragmatic, allowed for a certain degree of flexibility in this matter:

Articuli autem dicti, quod nominibus artantur, id est conligantur, cum dicimus 'hic orator'. Inter articulum autem et pronomen hoc interest, quod articulus tunc est, quum nomini coniungitur, ut 'hic sapiens'. Cum vero non coniungitur, demonstrativum pronomen est, ut hic et haec et hoc.[37] ('[The words] which are drawn to nouns, that is tied to them, are called articles, as when we say *hic orator*. There is this difference between the article and the pronoun, that it is the article when it is joined to the noun, for example, *hic sapiens*. But when it is not joined, then it is a demonstrative pronoun, like *hic* and *haec* and *hoc*').

Suddenly we are very close to glossatorial practice. Moreover, Priscian, whose *Institutiones grammaticae* was the bedrock of medieval grammatical thought, also allowed that in certain circumstances, *hic* and its cognates might be considered articles. To be more precise, this use is permissible in declensions, the very context in which the glosses operate.[38] This association of *hic, hec, hoc,* with grammatical declension is made absolutely explicit in Donatus's *Ars minor,* where each noun and adjective declension is accompanied with the appropriate demonstrative pronoun. Moreover, a tenth- or eleventh-century grammatical manuscript in Barcelona demonstrates that the use of *hic, hec* and *hoc* as articles for pedagogical purposes persisted long after Donatus and Priscian: *Iusticia est nomen prime declinacionis generis femini cum numero singulari nomen pronomen vel articulus preponitur 'haec'*[39] ('Justice is a feminine noun of the first declension which in the singular is prefaced by the noun or pronoun or article *haec*'.) Indeed, the two most important Priscian-commentators of the first half of the twelfth century both address the question of the article in some detail. William of Conches' 1140s version of his *Glose super Priscianum* confirms Priscian's statement that Latin does not have an article, but examines three possible contenders for this role, *idem, hic* and *qui.* His verdict on *hic* reinforces Priscian's distinction between correct usage and pedagogic function; *hic* can be used *extra orationem in doctrina puerorum dictionibus preponi in declinando ad discernendum genus, casum et numerum*[40] ('in

[36] See Quintilian, *IO* I, 4, 19, vol. I, p. 26; for Priscian see *IG* XVII, 27 (*GL* III, 124); *IG* II, 16 (*GL* II, 54); *IG* II, 17 (*GL* II, 55); *IG* XI, 1 (*GL* II, 548).

[37] Isidore, *Etymologiae*, ed. W. M. Lindsay, 2 vols. (Oxford, 1985), I: I, viii, 4.

[38] *IG* XVII, 27 (*GL* III, 124).

[39] See the *Declinationes nominum* in Barcelona, Archivo de la Corona de Aragon, Ripol. 59, fols. 1r-250r (fol. 49v). I am extremely grateful to Vivien Law for this reference.

[40] William of Conches, *Glose super Priscianum*, Paris, Bibliothèque Nationale, fonds latin 15130 (W), fol. 25va on Priscian *IG* II, 16 (*GL* II, 54).

the instruction of young students and outside speech, to be placed before words in declining, for distinguishing number, gender and case'). This function is therefore explicitly located in elementary pedagogic practice. In his commentary on the same passage, Peter Helias too allows for the use of *hic* only in metalinguistic contexts.[41] Both grammarians associate the use of *hic* in declensions with the practice of the *pueri*, the least expert students of Latin, and their position is adopted by several other grammarians writing later in the twelfth century.[42]

Neither William nor Peter use this opportunity to remark on the existence of an article in the European vernaculars, although both were in the habit of referring to them for purposes of comparison in other contexts.[43] Moreover, later grammarians such as Nequam, Robert Kilwardby and Roger Bacon do point out the existence of the article in French but never compare it to the use of *hic* in declensions. For all these writers, it marked an essential difference between their mother tongues and the Latin language.[44] When glossators use *hic* glosses, they are perpetuating a long-established pedagogic, grammatical method which is effective precisely because of its proximity to vernacular forms. This is not the same as saying that they are imposing vernacular forms onto the Latin text.

An exactly parallel situation – a negotiation between grammatical tradition and vernacular context – arises when we look at the syntax glosses which attempt to unravel the very complex, periodic style of the

41 Peter Helias, *Summa super Priscianum*, Paris, Bibliothèque de l'Arsénal 711, fol. 17rb: *Quoniam vero hic et hec preponuntur in declinatione ad discernenda genera et casus, sicut quidam articuli apud grecos, inde videntur esse articuli, sed non sunt* ('But since hic and hec are placed before (the noun) in a declension to distinguish the genders and cases, just as certain articles do according to the Greeks, therefore they are seen to be articles, but they are not').

42 See for example the *Promisimus* commentary on Priscian in Oxford, Bodleian Library, Laud lat. 67 (L), fols. 20^{r}-88^{v} (fol. 23ra), which likewise states that the aim of *hic* is 'to distinguish gender, case and number' (*discernere genus et casum et numerum*). See also R. W. Hunt, 'Studies on Priscian in the Eleventh and Twelfth Centuries II: The School of Ralph of Beauvais', in G. L. Bursill-Hall (ed.), *The History of Grammar in the Middle Ages: Collected Papers* (Amsterdam, 1980), p. 76, n. 5; Hugh of Saint Victor, *Opera propaedeutica*, ed. R. Baron (Notre Dame, IN, 1966), p. 90.

43 See Karin Margareta Fredborg, 'Universal Grammar according to some twelfth-century Grammarians', *Historiographia Linguistica* 7 (1980): 75–82.

44 See P. Wolff, 'Alexandre Neckham et l'article', in *Études de civilisation médiévale (IXe-XIIe siècles): Mélanges offerts à Edmond-Réné Labande* (Poitiers, 1975), pp. 763–6; Karin Margareta Fredborg *et al.*, 'The Commentary on the *Priscianus maior* ascribed to Robert Kilwardby', *CIMAGL* 15 (1975): 106–7; S. Lusignan, 'Le français et le latin aux XIIIe-XIVe siècles', *Annales* 42 (1987): 959–61; see also S. Heinimann, 'Die Lehrer vom Artikel in den romanischen Sprachen von der mittelalterlichen Grammatik zur modernen Sprachwissenschaft', *Vox romanica* 24 (1965): 27–30.

Horatian text.[45] We turn here to the phrase, the next step in *grammatica*'s work. I have examined elsewhere the structures that the glosses apply to the text – reuniting subject and postponed verb, relinking adjective and substantive nouns, imposing a clausal structure – but the nature and origin of these reading structures remains a matter of some debate.[46] Some scholars have seen them as the most accurate record available to us of the 'normal' word order of early European vernaculars; others assert that they correspond to a pan-European system of analysis.[47] I would argue however, that *grammatica* itself, which in the twelfth century shifts dramatically towards an interest in the study of syntax, provides a more likely context.[48]

In English and French Horace manuscripts of this period, the glosses tend to convert the text into a subject-verb-predicate word order, where a main clause is established and is then followed by further co-ordinating or subordinating clauses. In other words, the periodic style of the classical text, based on suspense and separation of related parts, is overturned. The opening lines of the seventh Satire are particularly susceptible to this kind of analysis. The following example is from Rome, Biblioteca Casanatense, 537, fol. 66^{r}:

Proscripti Regis Rupili pus atque venenum
g a
hybrida quo pacto sit Persius ultus, opinor
d e c f b
omnibus et lippis notum et tonsoribus esse.[49]

The glossed elements are brought together in the order subject-verb-predicate (*a-c*: 'I am sure it is well known') followed by further complements (*e-f*: 'by all blear-eyed men and barbers'); the relative

45 For the differing syntaxes of Classical and Medieval Latin see J. Martin, 'Classicism and Style in Latin Literature', in R. L. Benson and G. Constable (eds.), *Renaissance and Renewal in the Twelfth Century* (Oxford, 1982), pp. 537–68 and Aldo Scaglione, *The Classical Theory of Composition* (Chapel Hill, NC, 1970).

46 Suzanne Reynolds, '*Ad auctorum expositionem*: Syntactic Theory and Interpretative Practice in the Twelfth Century', *Histoire Épistémologie Langage* (*HEL*) 12 (1990): 31–51.

47 Articles representing these two approaches are respectively, Fred C. Robinson, 'Syntactical Glosses in Latin Manuscripts of Anglo-Saxon Provenance', *Speculum* 48 (1973): 443–75 and Michael Korhammer, 'Mittelalterliche Konstruktionshilfe und Altenglische Wortstellung', *Scriptorium* 34 (1980): 18–58.

48 The best surveys of twelfth-century syntactical thought are Karin Margareta Fredborg, 'Speculative Grammar', in Peter Dronke (ed.), *A History of Twelfth-Century Western Philosophy* (Cambridge, 1988), pp. 177–95; C. H. Kneepkens, 'Master Guido and his View on Government: On Twelfth-Century Linguistic Thought', *Vivarium* 16 (1978): 108–41; C. H. Kneepkens, 'On Mediaeval Syntactic Thought with Special Reference to the Notion of Construction', *HEL* 12 (1990): 139–76.

49 *Satires* 1, 7, 1–3, p. 195, trans. p. 91.

clause, marked by the gloss g above *quo* follows immediately ('how the mongrel Persius took revenge on the foul and venomous Rupilius Rex'). The distancing of the verb (*opinor*) from its dependent infinitive (*esse*) is overturned, and a main clause is created out of the text. A further example from the Peterhouse manuscript confirms this approach, this time using dots rather than letters of the alphabet to refashion the text (C, fol. 51r):

> ••
> ... tamen me
> ••
> cum magnis vixisse invita fatebitur usque
> ••
> Invidia ...

(yet Envy, in spite of herself, will ever admit that I have lived with the great).[50] Here the glossed terms are the object (*me*, of the accusative and infinitive dependent clause), the deponent main verb *fatebitur* (will admit) and the subject, *invidia* (Envy). The glossator targets this passage because it would have caused confusion; not only are the elements of the initial clause separated from each other, they are also inverted (object-verb-subject).

How far can these pedagogical manoeuvres be related to contemporary reflections on syntax in the more familiar form of commentaries on the *Priscianus minor* (Books xvii and xviii of Priscian's *Institutiones*)? It is clear that the glosses are founded in the notion of a normal word order to which the literary text should be referred and through which it may be clarified. In their unravelling of literary examples, grammatical texts too participate in this notion.[51] In the grammatical tradition, the *locus classicus* for the discussion of word order was Priscian's *Institutiones grammaticae* xvii, 105, which established that the noun should by nature (*naturaliter*) precede the verb, as action, signified by the verb, is an accident of substance, signified by the noun.[52] In his commentary on the *Institutiones*, William of Conches examined the concept of a word order that is 'natural', and affirmed that the nominative (the subject case) should be followed by the verb, in turn followed by the oblique cases, then adverbs. This *ordo naturalis* (natural word order), is directly related to the work of exposition or explanation (*necesse est in*

[50] *Satires* ii, 1, 75–6, p. 210, trans. p. 133.
[51] See Fredborg, 'Speculative Grammar', p. 187.
[52] *GL* iii, 164.

expositione, 'it is necessary for exposition'), that is to say the reading of texts.[53] William's remarks form part of a long tradition which, following Priscian, characterized the word order of literature (crafted rhetorical writing) as the more beautiful artificial order (*ordo artificialis*), and contrasted it with the order of grammatical exposition or *expositio*, the *ordo naturalis*. In other words, the mode of reading combats textual rhetoric. In this way, artificiality in word order became a defining characteristic of literariness: any composition employing natural word order had the status of a grammatical exercise, and throughout the Middle Ages, it was usually reserved for paraphrase and the rewriting of grammatical and logical examples.[54] This is what lies behind the rather compressed formulation in Geoffrey of Vinsauf's *Poetria nova*, that *quae sociat constructio, separat ordo* ('that which construing (*constructio*) brings together, (artificial) ordering separates').[55]

Geoffrey's use of the term *constructio* is of some importance. According to Peter Hispanus' commentary on the *Priscianus minor* (*c.* 1175), *constructio* is *actus construentis quem in lectione exercemus* ('the act of construing which we perform while reading').[56] A comment on the first line of Priscian's *Institutiones* in the gloss *Promisimus* shows this meaning of *constructio* as a form of reading at work: *Notandum vero quod iste prior versus difficilis est construendum, quare videndum est que sit eius summa, ut facilior sit constructio* ('but it should be noted that this first line is difficult to construe, which is why its general meaning is to be understood first, so that the construing (*constructio*) will be easier').[57] William of Conches explicitly associated *constructio* with the *ordo naturalis*: *necesse autem est in expositione ad suum naturalem ordinem dictiones reducere, quod sine sciencia construendi facile fieri non potest* ('for it is necessary to convert the words to

[53] W, fol. 86ra. Cited in C.H. Kneepkens, '*Ab omni homine habetur aliquod capud*: A Note on the Concept of Word-Order in 12th-Century Grammatical Thought', *Vivarium* 25 (1987): 147.

[54] It is recommended by grammarians as diverse as Peter Helias, *Summa super Priscianum constructionum*, James E. Tolson (ed.), *CIMAGL*, 27–8 (1978): 16; Hugh of Saint Victor, *Opera propaedeutica*, p. 106; Alexander Villa Dei, *Doctrinale*, ed. D. Reichling (repr. New York, 1974), pp. 88–9 and Ralph of Beauvais, *Glose super Donatum*, ed. C. H. Kneepkens (Nijmegen, 1982), p. 11. For studies of this idea, see U. Ricken, 'L'ordre naturel du français: naissance d'une théorie', in André Joly and Jean Stéfanini (eds.), *La grammaire générale des Modistes aux Idéologues* (Villeneuve d'Ascq., 1977), pp. 210–13; Irène Rosier, 'Transitivité et ordre des mots chez les grammairiens médiévaux', in *Matériaux pour une histoire des théories linguistiques*, ed. Sylvain Auroux *et al.* (Lille, 1984), p. 184.

[55] See E. Gallo, *The Poetria Nova and its Sources in Early Rhetorical Doctrine* (Paris, 1971), pp. 70–1.

[56] *Summa absoluta cuiuslibet*, ed. C. H. Kneepkens, *Het Iudicium Constructionis. Het Leerstuk van de Constructio in de 2de Helft van de 12de Eeuw*, 4 vols. (Nijmegen, 1987), IV, 1.

[57] L, fol. 20ra.

their natural order during their exposition, which cannot be done easily without a knowledge of construing').[58] Even Dante was to use the conjunction of construing and natural word order in his hierarchy of styles.[59]

Ordo naturalis reconstructs the text according to a model which reunites the parts of a phrase that are syntactically related. It is a way of reading that exactly mirrors the glosses on Horace. Of course, it is impossible to argue with absolute certainty that the expository *ordo naturalis* of the grammarians is the only model for the glossators' refashioning of the text. Glossing traditions themselves may have had an important part to play, for we find very similar 'construe marks' in Insular manuscripts from as early as the ninth century.[60] The precise nature of the interdependence of these two traditions, grammatical and glossatorial, is impossible to formulate. But we can say that both are founded in a model of proximity or contiguity – those parts which are related stand next to each other – and moreover, that contiguity was also becoming of increasing significance in the syntax of Romance vernaculars in the same period.[61] In all three contexts, those parts of speech which are related semantically – subjects and verbs, verbs and objects, adjectives and substantives – are usually contiguous in the phrase.

This is the context for some seemingly enigmatic glosses in another Horace manuscript. British Library, Harley 3534, produced in England or Northern France at the end of the twelfth century, is another workmanlike copy of Horace with plentiful contemporary glosses. At fourteen points in the exposition of the *Satires* the superscript graph *or* is found, followed a line or more later by a superscript *do*. A gloss *ordo* is thus created, spanning up to four lines of verse. In six of these cases, the glossed passage is notable for the suspension of the main verb (which is distanced from its subject and object), or from its negative. In other words, suspense or separation – the most characteristic feature of the periodic style – are once again the focus of attention. The following example from the sixth Satire contains a radical separation of subject (*ego*: I) and verb (*narro*: I narrate):

58 W, fol. 86ra.

59 See Aldo Scaglione, 'Dante and the Rhetorical Theory of Sentence Structure', in J. J. Murphy (ed.), *Medieval Eloquence* (London, 1978), pp. 254–8.

60 See the articles by Korhammer and Robinson (n. 47 above) for bibliography.

61 See the remarks in L. Foulet, *Petit syntaxe de l'ancien français* (Paris, 1923), p. 350 and Frede Jensen, *The Syntax of Medieval Occitan* (Tübingen, 1986), p. 385.

or
non ego me claro natum patre, non ego circum
me Satureiano vectari rura caballo,
do
sed quod eram narro.[62]

(My tale was not that I was a famous father's son, not that I rode about my estate on a Saturian steed: I told you what I was). A series of separate syntactic groups depend on the same verb *narro*, which is left unexpressed until the end of the period. The H glosses imply a relocation of this verb to relate it to the first expression of its subject: it will then be implicit through the whole passage. The aesthetic of suspense is again negated in the name of exposition; the artificial order of the text is, as it were, naturalized.

The injunction *ordo* was thus applied to difficult passages where conversion to a more natural or logical word order would help clarify the sense. The glosses were founded in the current didactic and expositional practice of *constructio*; the order they prescribed was the *ordo naturalis*. The glosses probably represent an activity undertaken by the glossator during his exposition; alternatively, these passages might have been set as challenging construing tests for the learners. The *ordo* glosses are found only on fols. 73^{r}-76^{v} (*Satires* I, 3, 124–I, 6, 97) and fols. 80^{v}-82^{v}, (*Satires* II, 1, 54–II, 3, 36), suggesting that they were to form the focus of perhaps one or two lessons in the first instance with random recapitulations later in the reading of the text.

This approach to secular, pagan poetry is in marked contrast to the reverence with which the word order of the sacred text was treated in contemporary vernacular translations of the Psalms. There the structures of Old French were abandoned in order to mirror the style of the Scriptures absolutely.[63] But the reading practice embodied in the Horatian glosses essentially 'un-writes' the text, attempting to make it comprehensible and useful by negating that which, in medieval terms, constituted its literariness. Moreover, this reading strategy is espoused and propounded by the art of grammar. As with the *hic, hec, hoc* glosses, the pedagogical efficiency of this strategy may reside in its undoubted closeness to developing vernacular forms, but the model itself is not directly dependent on vernacular structures. It may also be possible that *grammatica*'s championing of natural word order grew out of

62 *Satires* I, 6, 58–60, p. 192, trans. p. 81; H, fol. 76^{r}.
63 See H. Nordhal, '*Verborum ordo mysterium*: Petite étude sur l'antéposition absolue du verbe dans la traduction en ancien français du Livre des Psaumes', *Neophilologus* 62 (1978): 342–8.

expository glossing traditions, in other words, that what is put forward as a metalinguistic ideal is in fact based on traditional, pragmatic approaches to texts.

There are three remarkable features of this reading practice. First, it does not depend exclusively on the vernacular, but negotiates between vernacular and grammatical models. Second, it takes place at the most elementary levels of textual activity. The third feature, directly dependent on the second, is the complete lack of anxiety about using the pagan texts to teach grammar to young Christian students.[64] This is particularly striking given that from the eleventh to the thirteenth centuries, anxiety about the reading of pagan texts tends to surface in works which prescribe reading *curricula* for young students of the Latin language.[65] Even in Nequam's *Sacerdos,* where an impressive range of classical authors is recommended, there is undeniable hesitation at some moments, especially when it comes to Ovid: *Elegias Nasonis et Ovidium metamorfoseos audiat sed et precipue libellum de remedio amoris familiarem habeat. Placuit tamen viris autenticis carmina amatoria cum satiris subducenda esse a manibus adolescencium.* ('He may listen to the *Elegies* and *Metamorphoses* of Ovid, but he should be particularly familiar with the *Remedy for Love.* Certain trustworthy writers are of the opinion that the love poetry of Ovid should not be allowed to fall into the hands of adolescents.')[66]

This anxiety only rarely penetrates the glosses on Horace's *Satires.* One example occurs in a manuscript now in the Vatican (Biblioteca Apostolica Vaticana, Reg. lat. 1780 (V)), whose glosses represent the most advanced literal reading of Horace that I have encountered, analysing figures and tropes, rhetorical structure and mythological and antiquarian matters.[67] At the beginning of *Satires* 1, 8, the glossator asserts that Horace's intention is to reprehend sorceresses (*reprehendere veneficas*).[68] However, the gloss then goes a step further and, after having claimed that the aim of this Satire was to reprehend the *fidem romanorum* ('the belief of the Romans'), he writes: *Hic reprehendit Oratius veneficas ... introducens Priapum deum earum opera testificantem ... vel ut beatus Geronimus perhibet, ritus gentilium (et) idolatriam deridet inducens ipsum Priapum deum*

64 Cf. R. J. Hexter, '*Latinitas* in the Middle Ages', pp. 77–80.

65 For a survey of this issue and bibliography see Aldo Scaglione, 'The Classics in Medieval Education', in Aldo S. Bernardo and Saul Levin (eds.), *The Classics in the Middle Ages, Medieval and Renaissance Texts and Studies* 69 (Binghampton, NY, 1990), pp. 343–62.

66 Hunt, *Teaching and Learning,* 1, 269–70.

67 On this manuscript, see K. Friis-Jensen, '*Horatius liricus et ethicus*: Two Twelfth-Century School Texts on Horace's Poems', *CIMAGL* 57 (1988): 89 and 147.

68 v, fol. 72^r, p. 197, trans. p. 97.

ortorum. ('Here Horace reprehends sorceresses ... introducing the god Priapus testifying to their deeds ... and as St Jerome asserts, he derides the rite of the pagans and idolatry, (by) introducing Priapus, god of the gardens.')[69] This is far from a casual reference. The glossator is referring very closely to the passage in the Commentary on Isaiah where Jerome quotes the opening lines of this Satire in his condemnation of false images.[70] Just for a moment, Horace's text is read through Jerome, through an explicitly Christian filter. The conventional way to read such a situation is to see it as a manifestation of the perennial problem of using pagan texts in a Christian curriculum. But if we look at the gloss in its own context, it becomes clear that it is the result of an advance in literacy. The audience for whom these glosses were intended has moved beyond basic grammatical facts to argumentation and aesthetics. As their increasing skills render the text more accessible, the teacher intervenes to nullify its dangerous aspects. In this way, we can see that students' access to the text was limited either by ignorance, or, when that safeguard failed, by an interpretative intervention by the teacher.

The Horatian text was thus entirely in the hands of the teacher-glossator, and most medieval students simply did not understand without his help. But the glossing practice of treating the text as a series of verbs, nouns and figures woven together in a bizarre order must nevertheless be seen as the result of the needs of the learners for whom it was being glossed. Passive in some respects, the *pueri* nevertheless determined the kind of reading that took place. For many of them, the text was no more or no less than a linguistic resource, a field of grammatical practice. In fact, this was the inevitable result of perpetuating grammar's association with classical literary texts in an era when Latin was to all readers a foreign language. This context can serve to explain a puzzling remark in the *accessus* to Horace in v: *Quedam enim sciuntur ut sciantur sicut evangelia, quedam propter aliud ut auctores* ('for some things are known in order that they might be known, like the Gospels, other things (are known) for something else, like the authors').[71] That something else may be as prosaic as acquiring basic grammatical skills. The remark takes us to the heart of the reading I have delineated; it was a communal practice, shared by a learned expositor and an

69 v, fol. 72r.

70 Jerome, *Commentariorum in Esaiam*, XII, xliv, 104, ed. M. Adriaen, *Corpus christianorum series latina* 73A (Turnhout, 1963), p. 500, on Isaiah XLIV. 6–7.

71 Friis-Jensen, '*Horatius liricus et ethicus*', p. 147.

illiterate audience, who read or experienced the text in very different ways. The glosses are not the record of an individual reading undertaken in isolation – they are shaped by expository traditions, by the needs, level and vernacular of the students, and by a purpose, to learn Latin. They share this purpose with the art of grammar, and are profoundly indebted to it for their strategies and models.

CHAPTER 3

Into his secret chamber: reading and privacy in late medieval England

Andrew Taylor

In 1395, after waiting impatiently for some weeks for an audience, Froissart was finally ushered into King Richard II's outer chamber, where he presented the king with a collection of his poems:

Than the kynge desyred to se my booke that I had brought for hym. So he sawe it in his chambre, for I had layde it there redy on his bedde. Whanne the kynge opened it, it pleased hym well, for it was fayre enluymned and written, and couered with crymson veluet, with ten botons of syluer and gylte, and Roses of gold, in the myddes with two great clapses gylte, rychely wrought. Than the kyng demaunded me wherof it treated, and I shewed hym howe it treated of maters of loue; wherof the kynge was gladde and loked in it, and reed in many places, for he coulde speke and rede frenche very well. And he tooke it to a knyght of his chambre, namyed syr Rycharde Creadon, to beare it in to his secrete chambre [*chambre de retraite*].[1]

The presentation of a book was an important ritual moment, one depicted in highly conventional form in innumerable contemporary illuminations.[2] It marked a symbolic exchange of the poet's cultural and the prince's social prestige. Froissart's presentation of his book thus provides a convenient instance of the increased status of reading and of the court poet in Ricardian England. It is an indication of the bookishness that has been so often taken to mark the demise of

I would like to thank Joyce Coleman and my editors for valuable cautions against a cavalier use of the term 'private', A. I. Doyle, Leslie Korrick, Nicholas Watson and Siegfried Wenzel for their helpful suggestions, and A. I. Doyle for permission to cite from his work on Harley 1706 and Douce 322. This study was supported with a grant from the Social Sciences and Humanities Research Council of Canada.

1 *The Thirde and Fourthe Boke of Sir Johan Froyssart*, trans. John Bourchier, Lord Berners (London, 1525), repr. New York and Amsterdam, 1970, fol. 255^{v}–256^{r} and Kervyn de Lettenhove (ed.), *Oeuvres de Froissart*, 25 vols. (Brussels, 1871–7), xv, 167.

2 This particular moment is depicted in at least two manuscripts of Froissart's *Chroniques*, British Library, Harley 4380, fol. 23^{r}, and New York, Pierpont Morgan Library, M. 804, fol. 1^{r}. For a discussion of such images see Brigitte Buettner, 'Profane Illuminations, Secular Illusions: Manuscripts in Late Medieval Courtly Society', *The Art Bulletin* 74 (1992): 75–90.

professional minstrelsy and oral narration.[3] At the same time, Froissart's account complicates the simple categories oral/written by showing a single book functioning in a number of ways: as a luxury commodity and visual delight, as an occasion for public reading and discussion (since it appears that Richard read sections aloud), and as a personal chamber book, to be read alone or with select intimates. Richard's casual skimming, his interest in the topic rather than the treatment, in fragments rather than the whole, and in the cover and illustrations rather than the text, are all suggestive of the range of uses and kinds of appropriation imposed upon or elicited by a book as a material object.[4] Appropriately enough, the scene closes with the book disappearing from view into the inner sanctum of the King's private chamber. Because the royal chamber might aptly be called the black hole of record keeping, a place where the king's expenses '*pro secretis suis*' were sheltered from the scrutiny of the exchequer or wardrobe clerks and thus from the scrutiny of the modern historian, the episode epitomizes the methodological difficulties that we face when we endeavour to expose private reading.[5]

The chamber, a realm of private solace in which dreaming and reading intermingle, is both a symbol and a material condition of a certain kind of leisure reading we now take very much for granted. LeRoy Joseph Dresbeck notes that the threefold combination of fireplace, flue and chimney stack, a technological innovation necessary for the comfortable heating of small rooms, was in use by the early twelfth century and became increasingly common in the thirteenth and fourteenth.[6] In these

3 See Gervase Mathew, *The Court of Richard II* (London, 1968), pp. 3–11; M. B. Parkes, 'The Literacy of the Laity', in David Daiches and Anthony Thorlby (eds.), *The Mediaeval World* (London, 1973), p. 572; and Richard Firth Green, *Poets and Princepleasers: Literature and the English Court in the Late Middle Ages* (Toronto, 1980), p. 105. For a discussion of the continuity of minstrelsy, see Michael Chestnutt, 'Minstrel Reciters and the Enigma of the Middle English Romance', *Culture and History* 2 (1987): 48–67; and Andrew Taylor, 'Fragmentation, Corruption, and Minstrel Narration: The Question of the Middle English Romances', *The Yearbook of English Studies* 22 (1992): 38–62.

4 For examples of the range of appropriation of printed books, see de Certeau, 'Reading as Poaching', pp. 165–76; and Roger Chartier, *Les usages de l'imprimé* (Paris, 1987), p. 8 and 'Texts, Printing, Readings', in Lynn Hunt (ed.), *The New Cultural History* (Berkeley, CA, 1989), pp. 154–75.

5 See Thomas F. Tout, *Chapters in the Administrative History of Mediaeval England*, 6 vols. (Manchester, 1920–33), I, 53, II, 356, and Green, *Princepleasers*, p. 5.

6 See Dresbeck 'The Chimney and Fireplace: A Study in Technological Development Primarily in England during the Middle Ages', unpublished Ph.D. dissertation, University of California, Los Angeles (1971). On the creation of private space in the late Middle Ages, see Dominique Barthélemy and Philippe Contamine, 'The Use of Private Space', in Georges Duby (ed.), *A History of Private Life II, Revelations of the Medieval World*, trans. Arthur Goldhammer (Cambridge, MA, 1988), pp. 395–505.

warm and well-lit chambers one could read in bed, read and eat or drink, read oneself asleep, read and fantasize. Retreating from the public *praelectio* of the hall, one could read to oneself in peace and quiet; one could read silently. As Paul Saenger has shown, silent reading, which became common among clerics in the twelfth century and gradually spread to the laity, permitted a new intimacy in reading, linking it with devotional practice and the development of religious individualism and at the same time encouraging a rebirth of erotica.[7] Yet the chamber rarely offered perfect solitude. The king, for one, was never without a select group of courtiers in attendance. Chamber reading among the aristocrats and gentry might mean someone reading alone 'to drive the night away', but it could as readily involve a select and intimate group poring over the illuminations together or listening as one member read aloud. There was no clear separation between the public and private realms.

Of the various ways of reading, that which would seem most dependent on isolation is meditative devotional reading, a specialized mode of apprehension involving the ability to dwell in sustained reverie on a text. This is reading in slow time, reading as a form of prayer. It developed in the cloister, as a form of *lectio divina*, one which, in Jean Leclercq's memorable term, entailed the 'mastication' of the text.[8] It was a mode of reading both intense and private, reading suited to a monastic cell. By the late Middle Ages it appears that it was being practised widely by the laity.

Late medieval meditation took a number of forms. When undertaken most studiously it involved a series of mental exercises including protracted attempts to visualize and even feel the pains of Christ's Passion, often culminating in hysterical weeping or mystical visions.[9] Some, like Saint Colette of Corbie, apparently practised the art without recourse to external aids,[10] but many used books, icons or

7 Paul Saenger, 'Silent Reading: Its Impact on Late Medieval Script and Society', *Viator* 13 (1982): 367–414; Saenger, 'Books of Hours and the Reading Habits of the Later Middle Ages', *Scrittura e Civilità* 9 (1985): 239–69; and his 'Physiologie de la lecture et séparation des mots', *Annales: Economies, Sociétés, Civilisations* 44 (1989): 939–52.

8 Jean Leclercq, *The Love of Learning and the Desire for God*, trans. Catherine Misrahi (New York, 1961), pp. 18–22, 89–93.

9 For an overview of this development see, in particular, the introduction to James H. Marrow, *Passion Iconography in Northern European Art of the Late Middle Ages and Early Renaissance* (Kortrijk, 1979).

10 Her regular meditation on the Passion is described by Peter of Vaux in his account of her life, *Acta sanctorum ... editio novissima*, March, 1 (Paris, 1863), 560. Colette did, however, have special devotional pictures of the Passion and was deeply upset when they were broken (p. 562).

images in books to help them concentrate.[11] The early sixteenth-century devotional manual *The Pomander of Prayer* notes that 'if the persone be unlettered and moche encombred with wandryings cogitations of theyr herte than it is expedient for suche to have afore theyr eyes some devoute remembrance or object or some picture of the passion of Chryste or som saynt'. To prevent distraction, it recommends 'lyttel books in the whiche is conteyned pictures of the articles of the lyfe and passion of our Lorde Jesu'.[12] For many, meditation meant meditative reading. Even the illiterate Margery of Kempe's visions of Christ's body, 'mor ful of wowndys þan euyr was a duffehows (dove-house) of holys ... þe reuerys of blood flowyng out plentevowsly of euery membre', may reflect the devotional books read to her by a priest in Lynn.[13]

In some ways this form of meditation is not far removed from erotic reading, since both cultivate the habit of extensive fantasizing on short passages, and encourage readers to visualize the events in vivid and intimate terms even to the extent of inserting themselves in the picture.[14] Visualizing oneself standing at the foot of the cross while Christ was crucified or by the side of the Virgin and her child could also merge with what we would now consider erotic daydreaming as mystics imagined themselves in the embrace of Christ.[15]

One of the clearest examples of the deliberate effort to cultivate the

11 See Sixten Ringbom, 'Devotional Images and Imaginative Devotions: Notes on the Place of Art in Late Medieval Private Piety', *Gazette des Beaux-Arts*, 6th ser. 73 (1969): 159–70; and Vincent Gillespie, '*Lukynge in haly bukes*: *Lectio* in Some Late Medieval Spiritual Miscellanies', in James Hogg (ed.), *Spätmittelalterliche Geistliche Literatur in der Nationalsprache*, *Analecta Cartusiana* 106, 2 vols. (Salzburg, 1984), II, 1–27. Gillespie draws attention to the way in which familiar images become in effect a text, and meditation upon them a form of *lectio*.

12 Cited from a copy of R. Redman's edition of 1531 now in the John Rylands Library, Manchester, by Robert A. Horsfield, '*The Pomander of Prayer*: Aspects of Late Medieval English Carthusian Spirituality and Its Lay Audience', in Michael Sargent (ed.), *De Cella in seculum: Religious and Secular Life and Devotion in Late Medieval England* (Cambridge, 1989), p. 212. For examples of such illustrated manuscripts, see below, n. 53.

13 Sanford Brown Meech and Hope Emily Allen (eds.), *The Book of Margery Kempe*, EETS, os 212 (London, 1940), esp. p. 70. Margaret Aston suggests that the pattern of Margery's visions reflects, in particular, the *Revelations* of St Bridget, one of the works read to her by a priest of Lynn; see 'Devotional Literacy', in Aston, *Lollards and Reformers* (London, 1984), pp. 120–1. Margery's reference to Christ's wounded body closely echoes a passage in Rolle's *Meditation B*. See John C. Hirsh, 'Author and Scribe in *The Book of Margery Kempe*', *Medium Aevum* 44 (1975): 145–50.

14 See, for example, the complaints of Jean Gerson, Chancellor of the University of Paris, against the danger of an excessively corporeal meditation on images of the Crucifixion, cited in Ringbom, 'Devotional Images and Imaginative Devotions', pp. 169–70, n. 52.

15 See Caroline Walker Bynum, *Holy Feast and Holy Fast: The Religious Significance of Food to Medieval Women* (Berkeley, CA, 1987), esp. pp. 246–51.

habit of visualization by a broader public can be seen in a popular Italian handbook on prayer for young girls, the *Zardino de Oration*, which dates from 1454. Here we find detailed instructions for the preparation of a personal theatre of the mind:

> The better to impress the story of the Passion on your mind, and to memorise each action of it more easily, it is helpful and necessary to fix the places and people in your mind: a city, for example, which will be the city of Jerusalem – taking for this purpose a city that is well known to you. In this city find the principal places in which all the episodes of the Passion would have taken place ... And then too you must shape in your mind some people, people well known to you, to represent for you the people involved in the Passion ... When you have done all this, putting all your imagination into it, then go into your chamber. Alone and solitary, excluding every external thought from your mind, start thinking of the beginning of the Passion, starting with how Jesus entered Jerusalem on the ass. Moving slowly from episode to episode, meditate on each one, dwelling on each single stage and step of the story.[16]

The careful mental construction of physical settings in an attempt to give prayer visionary intensity culminates in the spiritual exercises of Loyola, and it is there that it is more generally known.[17] The technique, which draws on the mnemonics of classical rhetoric, also appears to have been in widespread use in England in the later Middle Ages, although it had yet to be so clearly defined.[18] English readers might find similar advice in *The Blessed Lyf of Jesu Christ*, a translation of the pseudo-Bonaventurean *Meditationes Vitae Christi* made by Nicholas Love shortly before he became Prior of the Carthusian monastery of Mount Grace in 1410.[19] The *Blessed Lyf* lays out a regular schedule of readings in which the reader is led towards extreme affective piety by vividly imagining scenes from the Nativity and Passion. The introduction specifically instructs the reader how this is to be done:

> Wherfore thou that coueytest to fele truly the fruyte of this book, thou moste with al thy thouȝt and al thyn entente in that manere make the in thy soule present to tho thynges that ben here writen, seide, or done of oure lord Jesu;

16 Cited in Michael Baxandall, *Painting and Experience in Fifteenth-Century Italy*, 2nd edn (Oxford, 1988), p. 46, Italian text, pp. 163–4.

17 See W. H. Longridge, *The Spiritual Exercises of Saint Ignatius Loyola with a Commentary and Translation of the Directorium in Exercitia* (London, 1930), pp. 85, 304–5; and Alexandre Brou, *Ignatian Methods of Prayer*, trans. W. Young (Milwaukee, WI, 1949), pp. 95–103.

18 The composition of place closely resembles what Mary Carruthers, *The Book of Memory: A Study of Memory in Medieval Culture* (Cambridge, 1990), p. 71, has termed the 'architectural mnemonic' set out in pseudo-Cicero's *Rhetorica ad Herennium*.

19 See Elizabeth Salter, *Nicholas Love's 'Myrrour of the Blessed Lyf of Jesu Christ'*, *Analecta Cartusiana* 10 (1974): 24–9.

and that besily, likyngly, and abidynge; as theyh thou herdest hem with thy bodily eeres or seie hem with thyne eiȝen done; pyttynge awey for the tyme and leuynge alle othere occupaciouns and besynesses.[20]

In the meditation for the sixth hour of Friday the reader is encouraged to act as a witness as the cross is placed in the ground:

Now ferthermore myȝt thou see whan our lorde Jesu was comen to that stynkynge hulle of Caluerie how wickedly thoo cursed werkmen bygonne to worche on alle sides that cruel werk. Take hede now diligently with all thyn hert alle thoo thinges that be now to come and make the there presente in thy mynde, beholdynge all that schal be done aȝenst thy lord Jesu and that be spoken or done of hym; and so with the ynner yȝe of thy soule byholde som settinge and ficchinge the crosse fast into the erthe.[21]

Readers who followed such injunctions would meticulously visualize familiar places, people them with those they knew, and then return to these places again and again as participants in what might now be thought of as an almost cinematographic mental drama. Such deliberate composition of internal topography was a recurring feature of late medieval devotion.[22] In the privacy of their chambers, these readers were building a chamber of the mind, just as Catherine of Siena had advised them in her famous injunction: 'Make yourself a cell in your own mind from which you need never come out'.[23]

We have a number of accounts of the lives of pious lay people at this time which show how closely prayer and reading were connected in both private and public devotion. Cicely, duchess of York and mother of Edward IV and Richard III, rose at seven each morning, and with one of her chaplains recited the matins of the day followed by the matins from the Little Office of Our Lady. She then heard a low mass in her chamber, and after that she breakfasted. When breakfast was finished she entered the chapel, where part of her household would be assembled, and here she assisted at the Office of the day and two low

20 Lawrence F. Powell (ed.), *The Mirrour of the Blessed Lyf of Jesu Christ* (Oxford, 1908), p. 12.

21 Ibid., p. 237.

22 Marrow, *Passion Iconography*, p. 12, traces the injunction to 'make oneself present' to the *Meditationes passionis Christi per septem diei horas libellus* of the thirteenth-century pseudo-Bede.

23 Raymond of Capua, *The Life of St. Catherine of Sienna*, trans. G. Lamb (London, 1960), p. 71. On the history of the image of the human mind or heart as a spiritual cell, cloister or chamber see Wolfgang Riehle, *The Middle English Mystics*, trans. Bernard Standring (London, 1981), p. 16 and n. 26; and John W. Conlee, 'The *Abbey of the Holy Ghost* and the *Eight Ghostly Dwelling Places* of Huntington Library HM 744', *Medium Aevum* 44 (1975): 137–44, esp. 138. For the association of reading and domestic privacy, see also Diana M. Webb, 'Women and Home: The Domestic Setting of Late Medieval Spirituality', in W. J. Sheils and Diana Wood (eds.), *Women in the Church: Papers read at the 1989 Summer Meeting and the 1990 Winter Meeting of the Ecclesiastical History Society* (Oxford, 1990), pp. 159–73.

masses. Leaving her chapel, she passed straightaway to dinner. The meal was accompanied by the reading aloud of some pious work, such as Hilton's *Contemplative and Active Life*, pseudo-Bonaventure's *Blessed Lyf of Jesu Christ*, the apocryphal *Infancy of the Saviour*, or the *Golden Legend*. After dinner she would give audience, rest for a quarter of an hour and then turn to her private devotions. At supper she repeated to those around her what she had heard at dinner.[24]

The daily regime of Lady Margaret Beaufort, mother of Henry VII, as described by her confessor, John Fisher, is remarkably similar. She rose soon after five, and after certain devotions recited the matins of Our Lady with one of her gentlewomen; then recited the matins of the day with her chaplain in her closet; then she heard four or five masses (presumably in her chapel); then followed prayers and devotions until dinner, which was at ten in the morning on 'eating days' and eleven on fasting days. After dinner she would go to her 'stations' to three altars daily. She recited daily 'her dyrges & commendacyons' (the Office of the Dead);

> And her euensonges before souper both of the daye & of our lady, besyde many other prayers & psalters of Dauyd thrugh out the yere. And at nyght before she wente to bedde she faylled not to resorte vnto her chapell, & there a large quarter of an hour to occupye her in deuocyons ... As for medytacyon she had dyuers bokes in Frensshe wherwith she wolde occupy herselfe whan she was wery of prayer.[25]

For these women, daily life had taken on both the discipline and the ritual dignity of the liturgy; it had been apportioned, with due hours for business and for honest recreation, its divisions marked off by a regular sequence of prayers, followed with only minor variations from day to day. Reading played a vital role in these devotions. Elegant private Books of Hours allowed the Duchess of York and Margaret Beaufort to participate in the lengthy daily liturgy, almost as if they were in orders. Nor, when Margaret Beaufort turned to private meditation, did she do so unaided; she took up a book. For such pious

24 'Orders and Rules of the House of the Princess Cecill, Mother of King Edward IV', *A Collection of Ordinances and Regulations for the Government of the Royal Household* (London, Society of Antiquaries, 1790), p. 37. The passage has been much discussed; see, in particular, C. A. J. Armstrong, 'The Piety of Cicely, Duchess of York: A Study in Late Mediaeval Culture', in Douglas Woodruff (ed.), *For Hilaire Belloc: Essays in Honour of his 72nd Birthday* (London, 1942), pp. 73–94; and William Abel Pantin, 'Instructions for a Devout and Literate Layman', in J. J. G. Alexander and M. T. Gibson (eds.), *Medieval Learning and Literature: Essays Presented to Richard William Hunt* (Oxford, 1976), p. 412.

25 John E. B. Mayor (ed.), *The English Works of John Fisher*, EETS, es, 27 (London, 1876), I, pp. 294–5.

lay women, devotional reading was a source of personal solace and relaxation, as well as an edifying accompaniment to dinner. Even when private prayer or meditation did not directly take place as a form of reading, it remained part of a cultural practice in which bookishness, privacy and piety were intimately connected.

These accounts tell us where and how often these women read, and they partially suggest how they may have read, but they still leave us a long way from the lived experience of the medieval book by a specific historical reader. For that, it seems, we must turn to the books themselves.

Margaret Beaufort had 'diverse books in French' for her meditation, but by 1400 most of the English of all classes preferred books in their native language, and clerks across the land were busy producing them. The result is a mass of late Middle English religious verse and prose, still largely uncharted, most of it preserved in plain utilitarian volumes. Its intended readership comprised those who were not fully *literati*: lay readers, but also nuns, novices and many of the secular clergy.[26] Being neither high literature nor high theology, the vernacular devotional collections and religious miscellanies which proliferated from the fourteenth century onwards have as yet received little scholarly attention, but they provide one possible entrance to this inner world.[27]

A study of this material might begin with empirical questions of production and dissemination. Unlike school texts or romances, which often circulated in a marketplace of strangers, many devotional books circulated along well-established lines of patronage, friendship and kinship.[28] For those like the Lollards who repudiated ecclesiastical authority, this could entail the creation of an underground network for

[26] As one version of *The Mirror of St Edmund* in the Vernon manuscript puts it: 'Þis may be ȝor halyday werk, / Hit wol avayle boþe lewed and clerk,' C. Horstmann and F. J. Furnivall (eds.), *Minor Poems of the Vernon MS*, EETS, os, 98 (London, 1892), p. 269.

[27] For attempts to map this vast field see W. A. Pantin, *The English Church in the Fourteenth Century* (Cambridge, 1955), pp. 220–43, 247; P. S. Jolliffe, *A Check-List of Middle English Prose Writings of Spiritual Guidance* (Toronto, 1974); and A. I. Doyle, 'A Survey of the Origins and Circulation of Theological Writings in English in the Fourteenth, Fifteenth and early Sixteenth Centuries with a Special Consideration of the Part of the Clergy Therein', unpublished Ph.D. dissertation, University of Cambridge (1953), 2 vols. On their manuscript circulation, see Vincent Gillespie, 'Vernacular Books of Religion', in Jeremy Griffiths and Derek Pearsall (eds.), *Book Production and Publishing in Britain, 1375–1475* (Cambridge, 1989), pp. 317–44.

[28] Some religious manuscript publication, however, such as that of Books of Hours, was approaching the commercial scope of the early printing press. See Nicholas John Rogers, 'Books of Hours Produced in the Low Countries for the English Market in the Fifteenth Century', unpublished M.Litt. dissertation, University of Cambridge (1982).

distributing and reading the Bible.[29] In this case, lay literacy did indeed constitute a direct challenge to the established religious institutions and can be understood as a form of lay militancy and as a competition between two clearly distinct social orders.[30] But many pious gentlefolk, who could exercise considerable control over their personal religious advisers, relied on the extensive collaboration of the clergy both to provide them with books and to teach them how to use them.

In particular, in late medieval England the pure and socially exclusive order of the Carthusians and the allied order of the Brigittines appear to have played an influential role in developing the devotional literacy of their lay patrons.[31] The techniques of meditation for the purposes of affective piety were developed to an unusually high degree by the Carthusians, whose virtual vow of silence and semi-eremitic life required unusual mental discipline.[32] The transmission of the art of meditation, as a technique and as a way of understanding the human soul, would have been facilitated by class lines and family relations, which bound together the clergy and the laity, by interzones, such as guest houses where they could meet, and by intermediaries, such as the Brigittines, who channelled Carthusian meditative piety into the broader world.

One of the earliest known owners of a copy of Nicholas Love's *Lyf of Jesu Christ*, for example, was Joan, countess of Kent, whose brother, Thomas de Holand was one of the co-founders of Mount Grace in 1397/8.[33] Similarly, Symon Winter, one of the earliest members of Syon Abbey, the English house of Brigittines founded by Henry V in

29 See Norman P. Tanner (ed.), *Heresy Trials in the Diocese of Norwich, 1428–31* Camden Fourth Series, 20 (London, 1977); and Margaret Aston, 'Lollards and Literacy', *History* 62 (1977): 347–71.

30 As K. B. McFarlane puts it in *Lancastrian Kings and Lollard Knights* (Oxford, 1972), p. 204, 'the literate laity were taking the clergy's words out of their mouths'.

31 See George R. Keiser, '"Noght How Lang Man Lifs; Bot How Wele": The Laity and the Ladder of Perfection', in Sargent (ed.), *De cella in seculum*, pp. 145–59; Vincent Gillespie '*Cura pastoralis in deserto*', in Sargent (ed.), *De cella in seculum*, pp. 161–81, esp. pp. 172–81; Michael Sargent, 'The Transmission by the English Carthusians of Some Late Medieval Spiritual Writings', *Journal of Ecclesiastical History* 27 (1976): 225–40; and Roger Lovatt, 'The *Imitation of Christ* in Late Medieval England', *Transactions of the Royal Historical Society*, 5th ser. 18 (1968): 97–121. Doyle, 'Survey' I, 291–5, discusses the paradox of this reclusive order playing such a role in the distribution of material to the laity.

32 On the social background and traditions of the English Carthusians, see David Knowles, *The Religious Orders in England* I (Cambridge, 1961), pp. 129–38; David Knowles and W. F. Grimes, *Charterhouse: The Medieval Foundation in the Light of Recent Discoveries* (London, 1954); and E. Margaret Thompson, *The Carthusian Order in England* (London, 1930).

33 Salter, *Nicholas Love's 'Myrrour'*, pp. 7–8, 12, 24–9. This copy, known as the Saumarez manuscript, was in private hands as of 1964.

1415, composed a life of St Jerome for Thomas's sister, Margaret, duchess of Clarence. Symon Winter may have been Margaret's personal confessor and she bought the brothers of Syon a Bible (British Library, Add. 400006) at his request. While he served as her personal religious adviser, she acted as his patron and also, in effect, as his publisher, encouraging others to read the work and have copies made.[34] Margaret Beaufort's reading and her patronage of book production similarly took place within a small circle of aristocrats and their religious advisers.[35] In these pious circles, writer and reader collaborated.

The laity had to be taught not only how to read, but how to read in specific ways, and here too the clergy taught them. Those enlisted as writers, translators or copiers of devotional material were often already religious counsellors or confessors for the intended readers, and it was therefore natural that in writing they should continue their pastoral guidance and provide specific instructions on how the works should be used.[36] Thus the apparatus, the compilation and the *ordinatio*, all reflect efforts to inculcate specific habits of reading, and these features offer the modern historian a second approach to the experience of medieval readers.[37]

Many of the devotional manuals contain detailed instructions on how to locate material, when to read it, and even at what rate. One example, the *Talking of the Love of God*, a treatise contained in the massive late fourteenth-century Vernon manuscript, actually sets out in its preface the pace at which it should be read:

Hit falleþ to red it. esyliche and softe. So as men may mest in Inward felyng and deplich þenkyng sauour fynden. And þat not beo dene. But bi ginnen and

34 See G. R. Keiser, 'Patronage and Piety in Fifteenth-Century England: Margaret, Duchess of Clarence, Symon Winter and Beinecke MS 317', *Yale University Library Gazette* 60 (1985): 32–46 and Josephine Koster Tarvers, ' "Thys ys my mystrys boke": English Women as Readers and Writers in Late Medieval England', in Charlotte Cook Morse *et al.*, (eds.), *The Uses of Manuscripts in Literary Studies: Essays in Memory of Judson Boyce Allen*, *Studies in Medieval Culture* 31 (Kalamazoo, 1992), pp. 311–12 on Lambeth Palace MS 432, which expands on Wynter's instructions for copying.

35 Ann Hutchinson, 'Devotional Reading in the Monastery and in the Late Medieval Household', in Sargent (ed.), *De cella in seculum*, pp. 215–28. Susan Groag Bell, 'Medieval Women Book Owners: Arbiters of Lay Piety and Ambassadors of Culture', in Mary Erler and Maryanne Kowaleski (eds.), *Women and Power in the Middle Ages* (Athens, GA, 1988), pp. 149–87.

36 Although, as A. I. Doyle notes in his 'Survey' I, 282–3, it was in the normal order of things for works to circulate far beyond their original primary readership.

37 The classic study of the implications of *ordinatio* is M. B. Parkes, 'The Influence of the Concepts of *Ordinatio* and *Compilatio* on the Development of the Book', in *Medieval Learning and Literature*, pp. 115–41.

leten in what paas. so men seoþ. þat may for the tyme ȝiuen mest lykynge. And whon men hath conceyued. þe maters wiþ redyng. Inward þenkyng. and deoplich sechyng. wiþouten eny redyng vppon þe selue maters. and of such oþere þat god wol senden. Hose wole sechen. schal ȝiuen in ward siȝt and felyng in soule. And swetnes wonderful. ȝif preyere folwe.
[It is proper to read it calmly and slowly so that one can best find delight in inward feeling and deep thinking. And that not right through, but begin and finish at such a pace that, as one sees, can for the occasion give most delight. And when one has understood the matter by reading, then earnest thinking and deep searching – without any reading – of the same or other similar subjects that God will send, if one chooses to seek, will give inward sight and feeling in the soul and wonderful sweetness, if prayer follow.][38]

Such apparatus indicates the devotional practice that a contemporary writer expected of an intended reader.

Finally there are personal markings and signs of use including underlinings, marginal jottings and *nota benes*, which are the physical traces of a specific reader's interest and habits. Sir Edmond Roberts (d. 1585), for example, left numerous traces of his life and his religious interests in his books. In a fifteenth-century devotional manual, Bodleian Library, Rawlinson C 894, he specifically recommends 'Rede well the iiijth chapiter [of] þe disse mori' (fol. xiv) and adds to the *Scala perfectionis* the comment 'heer begennethe a vere good mat[e]r' (fol. 57^r). In a family Book of Hours (Cambridge, University Library, Ii. vi. 2) he has added numerous Latin and English hymns on the blank verso sides of the full-page illuminations. In both books he has also entered extensive lists of the births and deaths of members of the large Roberts family.[39] Unfortunately, such traces are not common. Books, particularly handsome ones, were treated with respect, especially by lay readers. Marginal annotations in English are rare and on occasion they have been rubbed out.[40] Writing in a book implied a certain authority, one that as a rule those who were not *literati* seem to have been reluctant to claim. A copy of the Benedictine Rule in Middle English that probably comes from Lyminster priory warns the sisters that when they borrow books they are not to leave them lying around or leave

38 *A Talkyng of þe Loue of God*, ed. and trans. by M. Salvina Westra (The Hague, 1950), pp. 2–3. The manuscript contains a variety of material, some for reading aloud and some for reading privately, much of it intended for a mixed readership of clerics or lay people. See Derek Pearsall, *Old English and Middle English Poetry*, *The Routledge History of English Poetry* (London, 1977), I, pp. 140–3, and A. I. Doyle's introduction to the recent facsimile edition.

39 I would like to thank Dr Eamon Duffy for bringing this example to my attention.

40 See, for example, Huntington Library, EL 26 A 13, a copy of Hoccleve's *De regimine principum* that belonged to John Shirley.

them open 'neither kitte out of no book leef ne quaier, neyther write therinne neyther put out, without leve'.[41] The young nuns, like most of the laity, were not encouraged to make their contribution to the ongoing commentary.

As an instance of what a single book can tell us about its reader, let us consider in some detail British Library, Harley 1706, a composite manuscript of two sections, containing a variety of religious prose and poetry. It was the devotional manual of Elizabeth de Vere, countess of Oxford, who died in 1537, and bears her signature as both Elizabeth Beaumont and as the Countess of Oxford.

Elizabeth Scrope, daughter of Sir Richard Scrope of Bolton and Eleanor Washbourne, was twice married, first to William, Viscount Beaumont, who died in 1507, and then to John de Vere, 13th Earl of Oxford, who died in 1513. De Vere, a prominent Lancastrian, was an old companion of William Beaumont and took care of him during his madness. His father and brother had been executed by Edward IV in 1462 and although briefly in Edward's service he spent most of the next two decades in exile in France or in prison in England. His fortunes changed with the triumph of Henry Tudor at Bosworth in 1485, where he was Henry's captain general. Loaded with honours, he served as privy councillor, and was made high steward of the Duchy of Lancaster.[42] De Vere was a patron of Caxton, although not, apparently, a liberal one.[43] He and his father may have been among the early

41 Library of Congress, 4, fol. 36^r, cited in Tarvers, 'English Women as Readers and Writers', p. 310.

42 This account is based on H. W. Lewer, 'The Testament and Last Will of Elizabeth, Widow of John de Veer, Thirteenth Earl of Oxford', *Transactions of the Essex Archaeological Society* ns 20 (1933): 7–16; A. I. Doyle, 'Books Connected with the Vere Family and Barking Abbey', *Transactions of the Essex Archaeological Society* ns 25 (1958): 222–43; Nicholas H. Nicolas, *Testamenta Vetusta: Illustrations from the Wills of Manners, Customs etc. from the Reign of Henry II to the Accession of Elizabeth*, 2 vols. (London, 1826), esp. 1, 675; John Burke, *A Genealogical and Heraldic History of the Extinct and Dormant Baronetcies of England*, 2nd edn (London, 1844); Harris Nicolas, *The Historic Peerage of England*, revised by William Courthope (London, 1857); Bernard Burke, *Genealogical and Heraldic Dictionary of the Peerage and Baronetage*, 55th edn (London, 1893); and the *Dictionary of National Biography*. Doyle, 'Books', p. 234, notes that the Scropes were also major book collectors and that Ann, wife of John, Fifth Lord Scrope of Bolton, was probably the original owner of British Library, Harley 4012. See further Edward Wilson, 'A Middle English Manuscript at Coughton Court, Warwickshire, and British Library MS. Harley 4012', *NQ* 222 (1977): 295–303, esp. 301–2.

43 At the Earl's request Caxton undertook a translation of the life of Robert of Oxford, one of his ancestors (the book does not survive) and printed *The Four Sons of Aymon*, for which, as he complained in the prologue of 1489, he had as yet received no payment. Oxford also delivered to Caxton a copy of Christine de Pisan's *Feats of Arms*, to be translated and printed at the command of Henry VII. See N. F. Blake, *Caxton: England's First Publisher* (London, 1976), p. 50 and *Caxton and His World* (London, 1969), pp. 97–8.

owners of the Ellesmere manuscript of the *Canterbury Tales*,[44] which raises the tantalizing possibility that Elizabeth de Vere may have been one of its readers.

Elizabeth outlived de Vere by twenty-four years, dying in June 1537. On May 30, 1537, she drew up a lengthy and meticulous will. The will gives a considerable indication of her religious interests, stipulating precisely which masses are to be said, viz. 'fiftye of the Trinytie, fiftie of the holy gooste, fiftye of the five wounds, and fifty of Requies', and specifying numerous bequests to various orders, beginning with the Abbey of Barking and the church of Syon in London, each of which received four marks. She bequeathed three books, including 'a boke of golde of the valew of Cs. w*it*h the picture of the Crucyfix and the Salutacion of our ladye, to be newly made' to Lady Anne de Vere and 'a boke of golde having dyvers leffys of golde w*it*h the Salutacion of our Lady att the begynnyng' to the Countess of Surrey, both sisters of John de Vere, her nephew and godson and later the sixteenth earl. She asked to be buried with her first husband, and for masses to be said for her father, mother and husband, and she bequeathed to various relations a number of personal items, including embroidered tapestries of the story of Solomon and a quantity of religious jewellery such as a 'Jesus of diamonds sett in golde' and a 'Ring w*it*h the five Joyes of our ladye'. To her sister-in-law she bequeathed 'my Image of our lady of Pitie, to hang at her beades, to pray for my soule'. To her nephew, Edmond Jerningham, she bequeathed 'a goblett of Silver and gilte' and fifty pounds.[45] Her will makes no mention of giving him a book, but his signature appears on fol. 3^r of Harley 1706. Elizabeth also bequeathed five pounds in ready money to Elizabeth Rukwood, whom she identifies only as 'one of my maydens' and who has signed her name on fol. 37^r.

The first section of Elizabeth's book is copied by one fifteenth-century secretary hand and laid out in two ruled columns. There are some decorated initials but the work is plain. The text is generally accurate and is free from corrections. This section was copied, probably directly, from another devotional manual, Bodleian Library, Douce 322, which belonged to one Pernelle Wrattisley, a nun at the Dominican convent at Dartford in Kent (see plate 3). It was given to

44 For the suggestion that the Ellesmere Manuscript belonged to de Vere and that he inherited it from his father, see John M. Manly and Edith Rickert, *The Text of the Canterbury Tales* (Chicago, IL, 1940) I, 156–9.

45 Lewer, 'Testament and Last Will of Elizabeth, Widow of John de Veer', pp. 9–16. The will is also printed by Nicholas Harris Nicolas in *Testamenta Vetusta* but with numerous silent omissions.

Plate 3 Devotional manual of Pernelle Wrattisley, *c.* 1460–80. Oxford, Bodleian Library, Douce 322, fol. 27[a]

her by her grandfather, Sir William Baron, possibly when she took her vows.[46] The two manuscripts have been the subject of careful study by A. I. Doyle, and his summary of their relation bears repeating:

> Douce 322 is a collection of ME. prose and verse copied by one professional scribe, c. 1460–1480, for William Baron, a gentleman of Reading (Berkshire) who however lived in St Bartholomew's Close, London, and was buried in the nearby Charterhouse (c. 1484). The volume was probably made in a shop in the same vicinity, and was given (and perhaps designed) by Baron for the use of his grand-daughter in the Dominican nunnery of Dartford (Kent).
>
> The first half of Harley 1706 is a simple but hasty copy of the contents and lay-out of Douce (or of another possible lost replica, which is less likely), with a second half of similar interest, both perhaps intended for the Benedictine nunnery of Barking (Essex), on the other side of the river Thames from Dartford, or for a patroness of the metropolitan religious houses, Elizabeth Lady Beaumont and (later) Oxford, who acquired the volume sometime between 1486 and 1509 and kept it till her death in 1537.[47]

As Doyle makes clear, we cannot know quite when Harley 1706 was copied or when it came into the hands of Elizabeth Beaumont (see plate 4). But it is probably no coincidence that Pernelle was a distant cousin of Elizabeth, or that the prioress of Dartford from 1442 to 1458 was the aunt of Elizabeth's first husband, or, for that matter, that Dartford offered a spiritual refuge for aristocrats, including Bridget of York, fourth daughter of Edward IV, who retired here and became Prioress. It was the custom of the house to allow 'well born matrons, widows of good repute' to dwell there indefinitely, without necessarily taking the veil.[48] The custom provides a good example of how easily the distinction between laity and clergy could be elided. The dissemination of the first section of Harley 1706 appears, then, to have followed family ties and lines of patronage after the pattern traced out above.

The second section of Harley 1706 is composed of a number of religious treatises, including two remarkably popular pieces of pseudo-Rolle, *The Contemplacyons of the Drede and Loue of God*, which survives in

46 George Wrottesley, *History of the Family of Wrottesley, Co. Stafford* (Exeter, 1903), p. 240. See further Doyle, 'Books Connected with the Vere Family', p. 228. For a history of Dartford priory, see David Knowles and R. Neville Hadcock, eds. *Medieval Religious Houses, England and Wales*, rev. edn (London, 1971), p. 285; and John Timbs and Alexander Gunn, *Abbeys, Castles and Ancient Halls of England and Wales*, 3 vols., 2nd edn (London, 1872), I, 312.

47 A. I. Doyle, 'A Text Attributed to Ruusbroec Circulating in England', in A. Ampe, ed. *Dr. L. Reypens-Album*, Studiën en Tekstuitgaven van Ons Geestelijk Erf, 16 (Antwerp, 1964), p. 160, expanding and re-emphasizing the discussion in Doyle, 'Books Connected with the Vere Family'. For further evidence of Baron's association with book production in St Bartholomew's Close, see Doyle, 'Survey', II, 154, 200–2, 205, 226–8, 231–2.

48 See further Eileen Power, *Medieval English Nunneries* (Cambridge, 1922), p. 573.

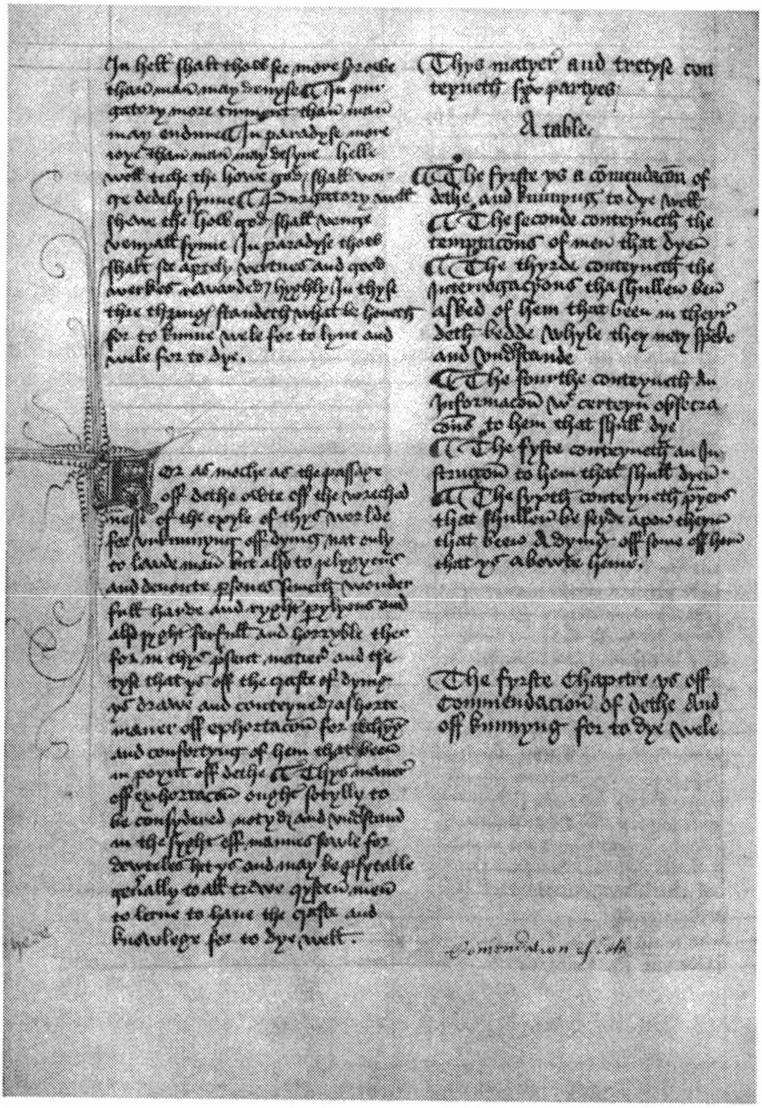

Thys matyer and tretyse con
teyneth syx partyes
A table.
The fyrste ys a comendacion of
dethe and kunnynge to dye well
The seconde conteyneth the
temptacions of men that dyen
The thyrde conteyneth the
interrogacions that schullen ben
asked of hem that been in theyr
deth bedde whyle they may speke
and vnderstande
The fourthe conteyneth an
informacion w[ith] certeyn obsecra
cions to hem that schall dye
The fyfte conteyneth an in
struccion to hem that schall dye
The syxeth conteyneth prayers
that schullen be seyde apon them
that been a dyinge off some off hem
that ys abowte hem.

The fyrste chapetre ys off
commendacion of dethe and
off kunnynge for to dye wele

Plate 4 Devotional manual of Elizabeth de Vere, Countess of Oxford. London, British Library, Harley 1706, fol. 25v

sixteen manuscripts and was printed by Wynkyn de Worde in 1506 and again later, possibly in 1525, and the *Remedy ayenst the Troubles of Temptacyons*, which survives in fourteen manuscripts and was printed by de Worde in 1508 and reprinted by him in 1519.[49] Although both may well be the work of professional scribes, the first half of the manuscript shows more clearly the process of personal circulation, while the second evokes the world of commercial copying and wide dissemination.

Like the Vernon manuscript, Harley 1706 is a book that demands to be read in a number of different ways and this is reflected in both the texts and in their presentation.

The book begins with a calendar in verse, composed by John Lydgate, that lays out the devotional programme for the entire year, noting suitable subjects for veneration for each day; but after this there appears to be no particularly significant order to the contents, let alone any sense that in reading the book one is guided along a predetermined spiritual itinerary. There is little to suggest that the compilers of either Harley 1706 or Douce 322 expected their books to be read in sequence or in a regular cycle or that they were to form a unified spiritual progress, like that laid out in the Books of Hours or copies of the *Blessed Lyf of Jesu Christ* or Lydgate's *Lyf of Our Lady*.[50] In this regard, Harley 1706 is not uncommon. As Vincent Gillespie notes, 'Miscellany manuscripts are frequently governed by an inscrutable internal logic and even more often by the random acquisition of material'.[51]

What does seem to have been envisaged by the compilers is regular consultation. The treatise, *The Book of the Craft of Dying*, for example, is a practical guide on how to assist someone on their death-bed. It contains general advice on the spiritual dangers of the last hours of life. Model dialogues or 'interrogations' are designed to lead the dying man through an affirmation of the basic articles of his faith, and model prayers are provided for the dying man or his friends to recite. These models are not intended to be repeated verbatim:

49 See M. B. Hackett, 'William Flete and the *De Remediis Contra Temptaciones*', in J. A. Watt *et al.* (eds.), *Medieval Studies Presented to Aubrey Gwynn, S. J.* (Dublin, 1961), pp. 330–48 and Doyle, 'Books Connected with the Vere Family', p. 231.

50 See further, Shearle Furnish 'The *Ordinatio* of Huntington Library, MS HM 149: An East Anglian Manuscript of Nicholas Love's *Mirrour*', *Manuscripta* 34 (1990): 50–65; and George R. Keiser, '*Ordinatio* in the Manuscripts of John Lydgate's *Lyf of Our Lady*: Its Value for the Reader, Its Challenge for the Modern Editor', in Tim William Machan (ed.), *Medieval Literature: Texts and Interpretation, Medieval and Renaissance Texts and Studies* 79 (Binghamton, NY, 1991), pp. 138–57, with important reservations on p. 154.

51 'Vernacular Books of Religion', p. 325.

And yeff he that ys seeke cannat all thyse prayers or may nat say theym for greuessnes of hys sekenes late som man that ys aboute hym sey hem before hym as he may clerely here hym/fol. 33^r sey [hem] ther chaungyng that wordes that ought to be chaunged in hys seying.

The treatise, in other words, is a manual on how to stage the ritual of pious death, and death, as it warns, comes when we are least ready. The reader must therefore 'take hede besyly and studye and lerne dylygently hys crafte off dyinge and the disposicions theroff aboue sayde whyles he ys in hele' (fol. 34^v). The reader must study the treatise in advance, just as if it were a handbook of first-aid, to be ready for the emergency when it comes.

This purpose is reinforced by the *ordinatio*, which is copied from the more lavish Douce 322 and closely resembles that in British Library, Add. 10596, a pocket-sized book which was produced for the nuns of Dartford and which contains another copy of *The Book of the Craft of Dying*. Throughout the first section there is extensive use of rubricated titles and chapter headings, and the first section ends with a table of contents (fol. 95^r). To further facilitate consultation, the compilers include indices. On folio 25^v, for example, we find a table for *The Book of the Craft of Dying*:

Thys matyer and tretyse conteyneth syx partyes (rubricated)
A table
The fyrste ys a commendacion of dethe and kunnyng to dye well
The seconde conteyneth the temptacions of men that dyen
The thyrde conteyneth the interogacyons tha[t] shullen ben asked of hem that ben in theyr deth bedde whyle they may speke and vnderstande (etc.)

Each of these descriptive headings is then repeated at the beginning of the appropriate part. Frequently these headings are written larger (e.g. folio 54^v, the account of the six masters who discussed tribulation).

Because such paratextual devices were still not taken for granted, the compilers also provide guides to their use, as in the following directions for the use of the alphabetical index to the short alphabetical treatise on loving God:

Thys schorte epistole þat foloweþ is devydyd in to sundry maters. eche mater by hymselfe in tytelys as þys kalender scheweþ. and ȝe mowe soone fynde what mater you pleseþ. þerfor ben þise tytelles in þis epystole marked *with* dyu*er*se letters of the abce in maner of a table.

A Whi eche man shulde loue gode
B Howe men sumtyme loueden god. and howe hyely sum were vysyted *with* loue (rubricated) (fol. 154^v).

Like the elaborately marked subdivisions of a modern technical manual, these devices suggest a book intended for repeated consultation but neither for sequential reading nor for meditation. This was not, however, the only way in which the book was designed to be used. The last set of prayers in *The Book of the Craft of Dying*, for example, invites a direct and emotive response. As the reader begins the lengthy invocation 'For þat loue þat made þe to be wounded' (fol. 35r), he or she is no longer studying in preparation for a future role as stage manager of a pious death but praying directly. Here reading becomes a form 'of preysynge and preyynge to god' as the compiler of the second section says it should be (fol. 212v).[52]

Like many devotional manuals and religious miscellanies, Harley 1706 is largely unadorned, but it does provide one half-page illustration of Death to serve as a *memento mori*, copied from Pernelle Wrattisley's manual (fol. 19v). The illustration accompanies, or is accompanied by, verses by Lydgate, beginning 'Syth that ye lyst to be my costes and in youre boke to sett my ymage Wake and remembre *with* gret auyses how my custome and mortall vsage ys for [to] spare nether olde ne yong of age'. This picture would seem to function as an aid to meditation, after the fashion of the mnemonic icons in contemporary *Arma Christi* collections, collections of hymns, which provide a full series of pictures of the instruments of the Passion interspersed with devotional verse.[53] Guided by such devices, reading slows and becomes a sustained exercise in affective piety.

Did Elizabeth de Vere actually read in these different ways, carefully studying the protocols of dying, crying out the prayers, or lapsing into reverie at the descriptions of the Passion? If only she had left notes, like Sir Edmond Roberts, we might have some idea. Unfortunately Elizabeth, like most lay readers, had too much respect for the text to soil it. She signed the book seven times,[54] but the only other place at

52 The passage is reproduced in Doyle, 'Books Connected with the Vere Family', p. 231.

53 Some examples of the *Arma Christi* are Huntington Library, HM 142, fols. 7r–10v and the roll HM 26054, which is devoted exclusively to the *Arma Christi*, and London, British Library, Add. 22029 and Royal 17 A xxvii, all dating from the fifteenth century. An emblematic treatment of Christ's wounds can be seen in Bodleian MS Douce 1, fols. 71r–76v, and the lost British Library, Harley Roll T 11, a copy of William Billyng's *The Five Wounds of Christ*, preserved in William Bateman's facsimile (London, 1814). See further Douglas Gray 'The Five Wounds of Our Lord' *NQ* 208 (1963): 50–51, 82–89, 127–34, 163–68 and R. H. Robbins, 'The *Arma Christi* Rolls', *Modern Language Review* 35 (1939): 415–21. Gray suggests that the large Harley roll may have been intended for public display in church and the tiny Douce manuscript for private devotion (p. 164).

54 As Elizabeth Oxford or Oxynford on fols. 3r, 93v, 95r and 214v, as Elesebeth Ver on fol. 4r, and as Elizabeth Beaumont on fols. 11r and 216r. Her hand is large, awkward and idiosyncratic.

which I can identify her hand is on one of the flyleaves, where she wrote the first line of a salve for gout (fol. 214^{v}).[55] Even this silence tells its story. For Elizabeth de Vere the book, which she had kept much of her life, was an heirloom, although not such a valuable one as to merit explicit mention in her will. Edmond Jerningham and Elizabeth Rukwood were equally restrained and a later owner, Mistress Margaret Otwell, who adds the odd line, only slightly less so.[56]

There were, however, four readers of Harley 1706 who did leave traces. The first two added short glosses in Latin.[57] It seems most likely that these were early additions, perhaps made by the male clerics who prepared or used the book before it passed into women's hands.[58] Then there are two readers who have left only their marks, one drawing in small *nota bene* hands, the other small hatch marks, like the number sign on a modern typewriter. Whoever they were, these two knew the book well. Both left scores of marks dispersed throughout the entire book, but always written lightly and restricted to the margins. Often the interests of these two readers overlapped. Both left a heavy concentration of marks in the last chapters of *The Profits of Tribulation* (fol. 55^{r} ff). Both seem to have sought reassurance. A passage describing the role of the Virgin as mediator is marked with two hands and three hatches (fol. 101^{v}). Both the readers marked a passage that begins 'I sey not þat þou schalte flee bodelye from þe worlde or from þi worldly goodys' (fol. 199^{r}); but the passage that most struck them is on fol. 21^{r}: 'O why had nat I beware in my youthe of thys that falleth me in my last dayes when I was clothed in strengthe and w*ith* beawte and had many yeres before me to come that I myght haue knowen the euelles that haue sodanly fallen apon me in thys oure'. On this page alone there are five *nota bene* hands and four hatches. There seems no way of identifying these readers, but they obviously used the book extensively

55 The flyleaves are largely devoted to medical recipes of this kind. They are the work of some eight different hands, the least elegant of which might possibly also be that of Elizabeth.

56 In addition to noting her name, Mistress Margaret Otwell, twice (fols. 191^{v} and 211^{v}) Margaret adds the following notes: 'of man mynde' (fol. 141^{r}); 'my wyfe gayme is . . . ' (fol. 156^{v}); 'I praye you of your charret [i.e., charity]' (fol. 172^{r}); 'Owre owne flesshe wol be be oure froo [foe]' (the opening line of the poem on the incommodities of old age) and on the lower margin 'I praye you of your charte/ In your prays thenke' (fol. 213^{v}). A. I. Doyle, 'Books Connected with the Vere Family', pp. 238–9, notes that her name also appears on British Library, Cotton Vespasian B. IX, a book belonging to St Bartholomew's Hospital.

57 'Item pius nota. Nota. Nichil p*ro*dest ho*minini* ieuinare et orare et alia religionis op*era* agere n*isi* mens ab i*n*iquitate revocet*ur*' (fol. 18^{r}) and 'Item e*st* ideo/ [peccatum] volu*n*tariu*m* q*uia* [id quod] no*n* sit volu*n*/[tarium] no*n* e*st* pe*ccatum*' (fol. 116^{v}, drawing on Doyle's reconstruction).

58 Doyle, 'Books Connected with the Vere Family', p. 233.

and sought consolation from it. Elizabeth de Vere could perfectly well have been one of them; this, at any rate, is how she might have been expected to read.

Harley 1706 was intended to be read in a number of ways: as a source of moral instruction, as a manual on how to die, as a stimulus to private and emotionally charged meditation, and perhaps as a collection of edifying material for general reading at dinner or with pious company. It may have been read by Elizabeth in her chamber alone or with her chaplain or with an inner circle of relatives and dependents. For all its mysteries, it provides one example of how wide a range of activities fall under the general rubric of private reading.

CHAPTER 4

The place of reading in the English Renaissance: John Dee revisited

William H. Sherman

In recent years the study of the place of reading in present and past cultures has emerged as one of the central projects of theory and research in the humanities. This project, in its most general formulation, focuses on the interaction of texts and readers and places it within not just an intellectual but a broadly cultural context. Studying the place of reading means attending to the roles of readers in concrete practices, as manifested in their artifactual traces; for example, marginalia, library catalogues, and the devices and strategies by which authors and readers influence each other – all of which are the subjects of a rapidly growing body of scholarship. But it also means attending to two interconnecting spaces: the physical place in which readings are carried out, and the cultural place of readers within their particular social and professional matrices.

My concern in this essay will be limited to the techniques and institutional profiles of early modern scholarly readers – those readers, that is, who were trained and employed in a scholarly capacity – and of one reader in particular, the Tudor polymath John Dee (1527–1609).[1] As we shall see, an attention to the place of reading offers the means to reassess one of the most misrepresented careers in early modern history. Readers who are familiar with Dee will most likely know him as England's great magus, the philosopher-magician who embodied the Hermetic, Neoplatonic Renaissance at

I want to thank the editors for inviting me to participate in the conference from which this volume grows: it proved an important step in the conversion of my doctoral dissertation into a book. That book has since been published (by the University of Massachusetts Press as *John Dee: The Politics of Reading and Writing in the English Renaissance*) and I am grateful to my publishers for permitting the duplication of some material. In turning my spoken paper into a printed essay I have benefited not only from the guidance of the editors but from conversations with Lisa Jardine, Warren Boutcher, Lorna Hutson, Christy Anderson and Alan Stewart.

1 See Nicholas Clulee, *John Dee's Natural Philosophy: Between Science and Religion* (London, 1988); and Sherman, *John Dee*.

Queen Elizabeth's court.[2] But treating him as creator of one of Elizabethan England's largest libraries, and as one of the period's most active readers, produces a different perspective on Dee, if not a different Dee; one who was not an isolated wizard but a well-connected scholarly adviser. Dee, for his part, brings into focus some important and often overlooked features of the early modern textual and cultural landscape. To recover his reading practices is to go some way toward appreciating the ways early modern readers gathered and processed textual information and applied it in activities which implicated them in not only literary and philosophical but social and political economies. Perhaps most usefully – and this is the point toward which this essay moves – the place of Dee's reading forces a reassessment of some deeply rooted assumptions about the 'private' nature of both the library and the act of reading.

As in the prologues and choruses which Renaissance dramatists used to introduce drastic leaps of time and space, the reader must lend some imaginative indulgence as we travel back over four hundred years for a brief tour of Dee's library. Before we enter the building in which it was housed we should pause to note its location. Dee's residence, during a period which roughly corresponds to the reign of Queen Elizabeth I, was in Mortlake, in the western suburbs of London. This was conveniently situated on England's main waterway, the Thames, near the hubs of government and commerce.[3] It was separated from the Queen's palace at Richmond by less than two miles, and the path between the two saw regular traffic in both directions.[4] Mortlake's proximity to both Court and City naturally brought Dee into contact with illustrious neighbours: these included the Controller of the Royal Household (and Irish projector) Sir James Croft, his associate William Herbert of St Julians, and Henry Maynard, an agent of William and Robert Cecil. From early in his career Dee was associated – and associated himself – with London and Mortlake. He became known as 'Joannes Dee Londinensis' and

2 The classic study to cast Dee in this form is Peter J. French, *John Dee: The World of an Elizabethan Magus* (London, 1972), but see also the works of French's principal influence, Frances A. Yates. R. W. Barone's 'The Reputation of John Dee: A Critical Appraisal', unpublished Ph.D. dissertation, Ohio State University (1989), offers a good account of Dee's place in recent historiography; see also the introductory chapters of Clulee and Sherman.

3 E. W. Brayley, *A Topographical History of Surrey*, (*Victoria County Histories*) 4 vols. (London, 1902), III, 188.

4 J. O. Halliwell (ed.), *The Private Diary of Dr. J. Dee, and the Catalogue of his Library of Manuscripts* (London, 1842), provides vivid glimpses of these visits to and from the court.

often dated his writings with the phrase, 'At my poor house [or study, or museum] at Mortlake.'

Turning from the setting to the contents of the *Bibliotheca Mortlacensis* (as it was known), we find not only a massive but an encyclopedic collection of books and manuscripts.[5] A look around what Dee called his 'library room' – and this does require imagination, since no contemporary picture survives and the building itself was long ago buried under a tapestry works – reveals at least three thousand volumes, in twenty-one languages, representing virtually every aspect of classical, medieval and Renaissance learning. As we know from its 1583 catalogue, and even more so from Roberts's and Watson's assessment of it, the library was rich in scientific and historical manuscripts, and was unsurpassed in its mathematical, navigational, Paracelsian and Semitic collections. The sheer number of books was impressive – indeed, almost certainly unparalleled in Elizabethan England. But their visual impact would be quite different from the show-piece library established by Samuel Pepys and preserved in Magdalene College, Cambridge: the books were not bound in distinguished bindings (and, in fact, many remained unbound, as they would have been purchased), nor were they stored according to any consistent method.[6]

But in Dee's library we see much more than shelves stuffed with books. As Dee informs us in an autobiographical account, his library was furnished with reading equipment such as tables and cases, and had four 'appendixes'.[7] The first was a collection of 'rare and exquisitely made instruments mathematicall', including globes, compasses, and tools for astronomical observation and calculation. The second was a cabinet full of charters, seals and coats of arms. The third

5 All students of Dee – and, indeed, of early modern texts – are indebted to R. J. Roberts and A. G. Watson for their monumental edition of *John Dee's Library Catalogue* (London, 1990) which assembles virtually all known data pertaining to the creation, contents and provenance of Dee's collection. Another invaluable tool is currently being produced by Adam Matthew Publications. Under the editorial guidance of Elisabeth Leedham-Green, Adam Matthew is releasing a series of microfilm facsimiles of the reconstructed libraries of Renaissance scholars. The project's first subject is John Dee, and the first volume of books from his library has already been published (Marlborough, 1993). The series is the more important because it includes the manuscript annotations which are often removed from facsimiles. Subsequent volumes are under preparation.

6 Roberts and Watson, *John Dee's Library Catalogue*, introduction. For further comparisons see Anthony Hobson, 'English Library Buildings of the 17th and 18th Century', in *Wolfenbütteler Forschungen* (Bremen, 1977), II, pp. 63–74.

7 See the 'Compendious Rehearsall', in James Crossley (ed.), *The Autobiographical Tracts of Dr. John Dee, Chetham Miscellanies Vol. I* (Manchester, 1851).

was a motley assortment of mirrors and natural wonders. And the fourth was what Dee interestingly termed the 'appendix practical' – a large laboratory for chemical and alchemical exercises, built as an annex to the library.[8]

In the 'library room' we would find not only Dee himself but a considerable number of resident and visiting associates. Dee's household was a bustling one, and his *familia* was on the order of his great humanist predecessors: aside from his eight children and household servants it is possible to trace over twenty people who spent extended periods in his house, as students, scribes or laboratory assistants – several of whom went on to become accomplished in their own right.[9] The library was also frequented by some of the period's most eminent scholars and politicians. It was such an attractive and accessible site that in 1592, when he found it necessary to advertise its status, Dee referred to his house as 'the Mortlake hospice for wandering philosophers' [*Mortlacensi Hospitali Philosophorum peregrinantium*].[10] Indeed, if we timed our visit well, we could bump into the young Francis Bacon, on a day-trip from the court with Sir Thomas Wilkes; Abraham Ortelius, who discussed with Dee the geography of Cathay; Richard Hakluyt, whom Dee told about King Arthur's discovery of Friesland; the Governors of the Muscovy Company, who were planning a series of voyages in search of a Northern Passage; or – on the occasion of an extraordinary governmental field-trip – the Queen and her entire Privy Council.[11]

This description of the *Bibliotheca Mortlacensis* begs a series of questions. How did Dee finance the library's creation and maintenance, despite being of modest birth and having no ostensible source of income? What did he do there? What did visitors, friends, and patrons expect from Dee and his books? What was the position of such a scholarly reader who lived and worked outside of the universities?

Dee's library was the centre of his life and livelihood. It was the site not just of his reading and teaching but of chemical experiments and a fascinating range of astrological and medical consultations in which he determined the most fortuitous date for Elizabeth's coronation, conversed with angels, counselled his suicidal wetnurse, and treated his

8 Almost nothing is known about Dee's *devotional* books and spaces – they are conspicuously absent from Dee's own accounts – but I agree with Roberts and Watson that they would probably form another significant 'appendix' to the library.

9 See Roberts and Watson, *John Dee's Library Catalogue*, pp. 42–5, and Dee's *Diary*.

10 Dee, 'Compendious Rehearsall', p. 40.

11 These episodes are recounted in the diary and the 'Compendious Rehearsall'.

accident-prone children – one of them fell into the Thames at the local boat-landing, another tripped and stabbed his eye with a stick he was carrying, and a third 'wownded his hed by his own wanton throwing of a brik-bat upright, and not well avoyding the fall of it agayn'.[12] Judging by the extensive traces of his reading and writing, however, Dee must have spent the majority of his time gathering information, processing it and preparing it for transmission. He pursued texts from dissolved monasteries, retail booksellers and continental libraries; and he carried out rural 'itineraries' in which he combed archives, registered monuments and recorded folklore. He made manuscript copies of books he was unable to purchase, and he performed rigorous textual comparisons of multiple copies or conflicting editions of important works. One of the most extreme cases is Euclid's *Elements of Geometry*, for the first English translation of which he wrote an influential preface. Dee seems to have had twenty printed copies of nineteen editions as well as seven manuscripts of this text.[13] Even more remarkable is Dee's collection of the works of Aristotle – which, considering his reputation as Elizabethan England's greatest representative of Platonism and Neoplatonism, is a surprising and chastening example. He owned four copies of the *Opera* as well as multiple copies of fifteen separate works. His textual transactions also involved borrowing and lending arrangements. Among the more intriguing of these connections is that which involved him in the famous case of demonical possession known as 'the Seven in Lancashire.' Dee himself was consulted and, prudently refusing to take part in the proceedings, sent in his place (to the local justice) several books on demonology.

He digested his textual acquisitions actively and thoroughly: of the roughly 500 volumes that survive from his library, well over half contain underlinings and marginal notes. These amount to a textual processing system which, although in many ways similar to those of his colleagues, was employed and is documented on a grander scale than any other contemporary reader in England. Through these notes, as well as loose-leaf jottings and what must have been a prodigious memory, Dee created a map to a huge body of material which could meet his, and others', present or future needs. He put this information

12 Dee, *Diary*, p. 38.

13 See Roberts and Watson, *Library Catalogue*. My '"A Living Library": The Readings and Writings of John Dee', Ph.D. dissertation, University of Cambridge (1992), contains an appendix listing Dee's extensive holdings of multiple copies of works.

at the disposal of a range of governmental, commercial and scholarly interests – usually upon request and sometimes with an explicit commission. These 'knowledge transactions'[14] were either oral – sometimes taking place within the walls of the library itself – or written, in the form of letters, reports and treatises. They were the means by which Dee mediated between textual traditions and contemporary needs. They must have been the basis both for his service, by which he earned a living, and for his social interaction, by which he forged and maintained links with a wide range of contacts. Noticing these transactions over fifty years ago, F. R. Johnson described Dee's library as a 'public amenity';[15] but Dee's library might be more suggestively (if perhaps anachronistically) described as an early modern think-tank, and Dee as one of Elizabethan England's leading intelligencers or consultants.

Late in his life, in 1597, Dee performed what was possibly his most striking piece of service in this capacity. In the summer of that year he received a letter from Sir Edward Dyer, who was representing a Privy Council deep in negotiations over the troubled trade with the Hanseatic League. In response, on September 8th, Dee penned a brief treatise entitled, 'THE BRITISH SEA-POWER; or, an Extemporaneous Miscellany, on the Sea-Jurisdiction of the British Empire'.[16] Its main purpose was to prove 'her Majesties Title Royall and Sea Sovereigntie' in the Channel and in all of the so-called 'British Ocean' – which, Dee argued in a bold anticipation of Selden's *Mare Clausum*, extended all the way to the Northwest coast of Europe. Dee's tract, in the form of a letter, began by giving Dyer what he termed a 'directed reading' of the text he had written at Dyer's request twenty-one years earlier, his *General and Rare Memorials pertayning to the perfect Arte of NAVIGATION*. Sending a copy of the earlier text along with the letter, he wrote, 'There, in the 20th page of that boke, (against the figure 9, in the margent) begynneth matter, inducing the consideration of her Majesties Royall Sealimits ... And heruppon, in the 21st page, both in the Text, and allso in the Margent, is pregnant matter conteyned ...

14 This phrase was suggested by Lisa Jardine and is explained in our essay, 'Pragmatic Readers: Knowledge Transactions and Scholarly Services in Late Elizabethan England', in A. Fletcher and P. Roberts (eds.), *Religion, Culture and Society in Early Modern Britain: Essays in Honour of Patrick Collinson* (Cambridge, 1994), pp. 102–24.

15 Roberts and Watson, *Library Catalogue*, p. 42.

16 There are three known copies of this manuscript. Two are in Dee's hand: a draft, in London, British Library, Harley 249 (later owned by Sir Simonds D'Ewes), and a formal copy bound in with British Library C.21.e.12. The third, roughly contemporary, copy is British Library, Royal 7 C.XVI, fols.158–65. I cite the Harleian copy.

Afterward, you may passe over, to the 37th page: and there (in the .15th. lyne, from the ende of that page) you may begin againe, to reade ... Yet, a little more, your paynes takinge, will get you some more matter, here & there, till you comme to the end of the boke.' What these references, in fact, amount to is a collection of passages from the civil law pertaining to the question of national sea-limits. This was a characteristic way of proceeding for a man who was both a reader and a reader's guide.

Both the ideological impetus and the employment opportunities existed in Elizabethan society for professional scholarly readers like Dee to leave the Ivory Tower and enter the civic sphere.[17] In what can be considered a version of civic humanism, Elizabethan scholars were encouraged to apply academic theory in civic practice; to supplement knowledge with experience; to use their learning, generally speaking, to improve their commonwealth and the human condition. In Francis Bacon's classic formulation, from his essay 'Of Studies,' reading must be followed by communication: 'Reading maketh a full man; conference a ready man; and writing an exact man.'[18] And as Patrick Collinson has recently pointed out, Whitney's *Choice of Emblemes* of 1586 contains an emblem addressed to the Cambridge scholar Andrew Perne, entitled, 'The use, not the reading, of books produces prudent men' [*Vsus libri, non lectio prudentes facit*]. Its message is, 'Firste reade, then marke, then practise that [which] is good ... Of practise long, experience doth proceede;/ And wisedome then, doth euermore ensue:/ Then printe in minde, what wee in printe do reade,/ Els loose wee time, and bookes in vaine do vewe ...' Perne remained a university reader and it is quite possible, as Collinson suggests, that Whitney's emblem represents him as a negative rather than positive *exemplum*.[19]

Civic-minded scholarly readers, more often than not, pursued employment in non-academic sectors. They sometimes did so in visible ways, taking on high-profile positions in administrative, legal or military institutions. Take, for instance, Sir Thomas Smith, whose books survive in Queens' College, Cambridge, and are annotated in ways quite similar to Dee's. He rose to academic prominence, becoming the first Regius Professor of Civil Law; but in 1547 – just

17 Sherman, *John Dee*, and Jardine and Sherman, 'Pragmatic readers'.

18 Francis Bacon, *The Essays*, ed. John Pitcher (Harmondsworth, 1985), p. 208.

19 Patrick Collinson, 'Andrew Perne and his Times', in Patrick Collinson, David McKitterick, Elisabeth Leedham-Green (eds.) *Andrew Perne: Quartercentenary Studies* (Cambridge, 1991), pp. 1–34.

before Dee himself left Cambridge – he traded his professorship for public office, acting as a Member of Parliament, Clerk of the Privy Council, Master of Requests, Ambassador and Principal Secretary.[20] Often, though, they fulfilled less visible roles within noble households – such as Spenser and Harvey with the Earl of Leicester, or the circle of scholars around the Earl of Essex[21] – and, in exceptional cases like Dee, within their own household.

While many factors were conducive to lending certain readers consultant status and making certain libraries useful to political and private interests, perhaps the most important for our purposes was the absence of a royal library and a comprehensive state archive. Both Dee and Robert Cotton, the possessors (along with Lord Lumley) of Elizabethan and Jacobean England's most valuable libraries, began their programmes of collection only after petitioning the crown to create a national library under royal auspices, and offering their services as agents or librarians.[22] The failure of these projects meant that many of the nation's most valuable textual resources – not just books and manuscripts but maps, charters, and letters – either remained in private hands or disappeared altogether.

We leave Dee's library, then, with three general impressions. First, Dee's base of operations was his own household, and his textual activities were carried out alongside his domestic and communal duties. Second, Dee's library should also be considered, in some senses, a museum and an academy. Like most of the larger libraries of the early modern period, it was part of a general space in which the books co-existed with laboratories, gardens and cabinets of curiosities, and in which the reader interacted with students, visitors and members of his or her household. Third, it represented a place where court, city and university could meet. Ideally situated for visits from Richmond, London or abroad, and well equipped for intellectual inquiry, it offered a space where scholarship could be carried out and circulated among interested academic, commercial and political communities.

As this account of Dee and his library is intended to suggest, the term 'private library' is not one which we can afford to take for granted: we

20 Mary Dewar, *Sir Thomas Smith: A Tudor Intellectual in Office* (London, 1964).

21 Paul E. J. Hammer, 'The Uses of Scholarship: The Secretariat of Robert Devereux, Second Earl of Essex, *c.* 1585–1601', *English Historical Review* 109 (1994): 26–51.

22 Dee's remarkable 'Supplication to Q. Mary for the recovery and preservation of ancient Writers and Monuments' (1556) is reprinted by Roberts and Watson. For Cotton, see Kevin Sharpe, *Sir Robert Cotton, 1586–1631: History and Politics in Early Modern England* (Oxford, 1979).

must reconsider exactly how 'private' the early modern private library really was. While it strictly signifies a non-institutional collection of books and manuscripts, the term has taken on modern connotations that, in relation to early modern readers, are at best oversimplifying and at worst misleading. It has become, by most accounts, diametrically opposed to 'public'; it is a place of isolation, inhabited by the figure of the solitary reader retiring into repose among the books which are the means of entertainment or contemplation.

This picture depends so heavily upon the case of Michel de Montaigne that I think it is fair to call it the 'Montaigne Model'.[23] As the well-known story goes, in 1571 Montaigne renounced his public duties and returned to his country chateau, where he set about composing his *Essais*. He established a beautiful library, on the wall of which he had inscribed, 'Michel de Montaigne, long since bored with the slavery of parlement and public office but still vigorous, withdrew to lay his head on the breast of the learned Virgins in calm and security; he shall pass the remaining days of his life there. Hoping that fate will allow him to perfect this dwelling, this sweet paternal retreat, he has consecrated it to his freedom, tranquility, and leisure.'[24] This position is reinforced by his often-quoted essay, 'On the three kinds of commerce' (*Essais*, III, 3), in which he claims that the third and best kind of commerce is that of a man with his books – which is to say, with himself. He describes his library as an oasis from public obligation: ''Tis there that I am in my kingdom, and there I endeavour to make myself an absolute monarch, and to sequester this one corner from all society, conjugal, filial, and civil'.[25] In his recent account of Montaigne's library, Adi Ophir calls it a 'solitarium,' in which Montaigne's self – the mould of the modern self – was studied and reconstituted.[26] As Ophir envisions it, the early modern library was a sort of solipsistic utopia, in which books 'allow[ed] the self to meet itself without the distortion of public, social life'. And in the course of a survey of early modern textual activity Roger Chartier cites the same passages and comes to a similar conclusion: 'The hours spent in the library are hours of withdrawal in two senses, which define the essence of privacy in the

[23] This label was suggested to me by Dr David Starkey.

[24] Cited in Roger Chartier, 'The Practical Impact of Writing', in Chartier (ed.), *A History of Private Life. III: Passions of the Renaissance*, trans. A. Goldhammer (Cambridge, MA, 1989), p. 134.

[25] As cited in Raymond Irwin, *The English Library* (London, 1966), p. 200.

[26] Adi Ophir, 'A Place of Knowledge Re-Created: The Library of Michel de Montaigne', *Science in Context* 4 (1991): 163–89. Cf. Henri-Jean Martin's use of the Montaigne Model in *The History and Power of Writing* (Chicago, IL, 1994), p. 363.

modern era: withdrawal from the private sphere, from civic responsibility, from the affairs of city and state; and withdrawal from the family, from the household, from the social responsibilities of domestic intimacy.'[27] These comments are no doubt coloured by their context – they are part of a *History of Private Life* which seeks to identify the emergence of modern forms of privacy in the Renaissance period – but they do tend (unlike Chartier's other work) to reproduce the Montaigne Model as a Renaissance norm.[28]

Montaigne was not unusual in stressing his aloneness. Indeed, as Steven Shapin has shown, there is a 'pervasive topos in Western culture, from the Greeks onward, [which] stipulates that the most authentic intellectual agents are the most solitary'.[29] This has been accompanied, and articulated, by a 'rhetoric of solitude', which can be set alongside the rhetoric of civic humanism; a conflicting repertoire which 'maintained that those seeking the highest forms of knowledge must live in relative solitude'. This 'rhetoric of solitude' is one of scholarly authenticity and validity and it is significant that it flourishes particularly during 'crises of legitimation' in the professional relations of the scholar. It is therefore worth bearing in mind that our picture of Montaigne's library rests entirely upon his own accounts – on taking him at his word, that is, in texts which are concerned precisely and classically with the development of the rhetoric of scholarly self-fashioning.[30]

In Dee's case, the rhetoric of solitude has been supplemented by what can be called the 'myth of the magus', in which he is presented as an ascetic adept at plumbing the depths of nature in the shadowy secrecy of his library/laboratory. In this guise he is posited as Prospero's real-life counterpart. Even a brief visit to Dee's library,

27 Chartier, 'The Practical Impact', p. 136.

28 Chartier's *The Order of Books* (Cambridge, 1993) and his dialogue with Pierre Bourdieu, 'La lecture: une pratique culturelle', in Chartier (ed.), *Pratiques de la lecture* (Paris, 1985), are both exemplary in their attention to the social and ideological frames of reading.

29 '"The Mind is its Own Place": Science and Solitude in Seventeenth-Century England', *Science in Context* 4 (1991): 191–218. See also Shapin's '"A Scholar and a Gentleman": The Problematic Identity of the Scientific Practitioner in Early Modern England', *History of Science* 29 (1991): 279–327. These ideas have long figured in intellectual history: see, for instance, Maren-Sofie Röstvig's *The Happy Man: Studies in the Metamorphosis of a Classical Ideal, 1600–1700* (Oslo, 1954).

30 My treatment of Montaigne is indebted to Warren Boutcher, who kindly shared with me several unpublished papers on the fashioning of Montaigne. These included '"Th'Intertraffique of the minde": Montaigne's *Essays* and Trading Liberties in the Early Modern European Republic of Letters', which was delivered to David Norbrook's Renaissance Seminar in Oxford, and '"Catching the Court-Ear" in Sixteenth-Century Europe', soon to be published in Jill Kraye (ed.), *The Cambridge Companion to Renaissance Humanism.*

however, should be sufficient to question the use not only of the magus as a model for Dee, or Dee as a model for Prospero, but Montaigne as a model for the early modern reader. Montaigne's library, rather than being exemplary, was exceptional – and even, to a certain degree, fictional.

Recent work in a number of fields has begun to suggest the ways in which the early modern private/public boundary needs to be contextualized and complicated, and the ways in which attention to the place of reading can offer alternatives to the Montaigne Model. Most visibly, those fields most closely concerned with the production and consumption of books – e.g., publishing history or the history of reading – have taught us to see libraries as embedded in broader networks of textual production and dissemination. Collecting and processing the information contained in a library on the scale of Dee's or Montaigne's was not a leisurely pursuit. It was hard work, and it inevitably entailed many kinds of commerce beyond that of a man with his books.

The best way of illustrating how other 'commercial' interests intrude upon the solitary intercourse between a reader and his or her books is to give two examples from Dee's library. First, when Dee prepared his catalogue in 1583 he called upon the assistance of a man named Andreas Fremonsheim. As it turns out, his interest was not only social but economic: Julian Roberts has discovered that he was the London agent of the great Birkmann booksellers of Cologne. His motives for helping Dee to compile his inventory are not entirely clear, but when Dee left soon after on a six-year continental sojourn, he had an outstanding debt to the Birkmanns of over sixty-three pounds. The second example is Dee's practice of writing wish-lists or notices of particularly interesting holdings directly into the margins or flyleaves of his books. On the back flyleaf of one of his copies of Geoffrey of Monmouth, now in the library of Christ Church, Oxford, he listed the names and locations of six men who had 'good store of moniments' and medieval manuscripts. Among them is the historian John Stow, and a Mr Clyderall of Newcastle, who 'hath a barell full of old histories of this land'.[31]

[31] Oxford, Christ Church, Wb.5.12. Dee's copy of the 1574 *Epitome* of Conrad Gesner's *Bibliotheca Universalis* – which was recently acquired by the Bodleian Library (Arch.H.c.7) – will prove a unique source for Dee's textual commerce: in this encyclopedic guide to Renaissance books Dee made many notes of his acquisitions and interactions with authors, publishers and collectors (see Julian Roberts's comments in 'Notable Accessions', *The Bodleian Library Record* 14 (1994): 529–33).

A field which has made more surprising contributions is the history of science – or, more specifically, the historical sociology of science.[32] Recent studies by Simon Schaffer, Steven Shapin, Owen Hannaway and others have encouraged us to put scientific and scholarly activity in its context by putting it, literally, in its place:[33] by attending to what they call, simply enough, the 'place of knowledge'.[34] Work in this field has been principally concerned with the observatory, the academy, and the laboratory and – aside from Ophir's essay on Montaigne – has not yet treated the library as a place where science is carried out and where knowledge is produced. As Paula Findlen's closely related work on museums suggests, we have some way to go in recovering and assessing the range of scientific spaces in early modern Europe.[35]

What kinds of mediation took place, then, within the early modern private library? According to Ophir, and virtually all other recent commentators, 'the object that books mediate for Montaigne' is his isolated self:[36] it 'is not out there, ready for observation, reachable through voyage or experiment,' nor can books 'provide a solid frame of reference' by which external objects 'could have appeared … as an object of knowledge'. Even if this is true of Montaigne, this division between books and the material world does not apply to most readers. In early modern science – as in scholarship and politics – the book was by all means a medium of observation, voyage and experiment, which not only provided a solid frame of reference but lent (through the authority invoked in the reference) considerable argumentative force. This is most vividly represented by Dee's activities in the area of maritime expansion. Dee collected cosmographical texts and collec-

32 In fact, this second field is not exclusive of the first: for a preliminary study of their intersection, see Adrian Johns, 'Wisdom in the Concourse: Natural Philosophy and the History of the Book in Early Modern England', unpublished Ph.D. dissertation, University of Cambridge (1992); forthcoming with the University of Chicago Press.

33 Steven Shapin and Simon Schaffer, *Leviathan and the Air-Pump: Hobbes, Boyle, and the Experimental Life* (Princeton, 1985); Shapin, 'The House of Experiment in Seventeenth-Century England', *ISIS* 79 (1988): 373–404; and Owen Hannaway, 'Laboratory Design and the Aims of Science: Andreas Libavius versus Tycho Brahe', *ISIS* 77 (1986): 585–610.

34 See the special issue of *Science in Context* 4 (Spring, 1991) on 'the place of knowledge'.

35 In *Possessing Nature: Museums, Collecting, and Scientific Culture in Early Modern Italy* (Berkeley, CA, 1994), Paula Findlen discusses the early modern museum in terms which are remarkably resonant for Dee's situation. She not only agrees that museums mediated between the public and the private, but also finds intimate connections between the library and the laboratory within the museums she studies.

36 Cf. Richard L. Regosin, *The Matter of My Book: Montaigne's Essais as the Book of the Self* (Berkeley, CA, 1977).

tions of voyages and canvassed European geographers for their opinions about countries, markets and passages. These informed the services which he provided for the men who actually made the voyages: he taught them the rudiments of astronomy, drew them maps and helped them stock their on-ship libraries. They in turn brought back to him maps and accounts of their observations, as well as new world artifacts such as the obsidian mirror of Mexican origin which is now on display in the British Museum. And finally he wrote new texts to persuade the government and merchant backers to invest in new voyages, new experiments which would build on the experiences of earlier ventures.

In such a centre the interface between library and world, self and society, reading and politics, is complicated and blurred. According to the Montaigne Model there operated in the early modern library a rigid boundary, one which – in the terms of Ophir – 'distinguished the private from the public' and 'distanced the self from others'. In a library like Dee's, however, as in Schaffer's and Shapin's work on seventeenth-century scientific spaces, that boundary functioned more as a permeable membrane than a rigid boundary: it let certain people, texts and ideas in, and kept others out.

The rhetoric of solitude notwithstanding, Renaissance writings on the history and theory of libraries generally stressed their value as public commodities. Dee's contemporary, Thomas Bodley, retired from government service after being passed over for the position of Secretary of State. But, wishing to remain 'a profitable Member of the State', he resolved to establish a university library at Oxford, convinced that 'in my Solitude ... I could not busy my self to better purpose, than by reducing that Place (which then in every Part lay ruined and wast) to the Publick use of Students'.[37] On the Continent, at roughly the same time and near the end of his own career, Justus Lipsius wrote his *Bibliothecis Syntagma* (or *Brief Outline of the History of Libraries*), in which he surveyed the libraries of Greece, Byzantium and Rome. At the end of his final chapter he concluded, 'I have nothing further that seems worth saying on this subject of libraries, except for a few words about their use [*fructum*]. If they stand empty ..., if students [*homines*] do not frequent them and make use of their books, why

[37] *The Life of Sir Thomas Bodley Written by Himself* (Chicago, IL, 1906), p. 57. This text was written in 1609 and was first printed in 1703 in Thomas Hearne's *Reliquiae Bodleianae.*

were they ever established ...?'[38] When Gabriel Naud wrote his *Avis pour dresser une bibliotheque* in 1627 (translated in 1661 by John Evelyn and published as *Instructions Concerning Erecting of a Library*) he produced an updated list of notable libraries and noble librarians as a prelude to the same message: 'To ... condemn so many brave witts to a perpetual silence and solitude, is ill to understand the scope of a *Library* ...'[39] Naud, who presided over the massive collection of Cardinal Mazarin – which became, in effect, France's first public library – assured his patron that there is 'no expedient more honest and assur'd, to acquire a great reputation amongst the people, than in erecting of fair and magnificent *Libraries*, to devote and consecrate them afterward to the use of the Publick' (B4v). By collecting books meet for all purposes, 'Reformed Librarie-Keepers' (as Evelyn's contemporary John Dury described them) could become 'Agents for the advancement of universal Learning'.[40] This made them supremely valuable within both the republic letters at large and the particular commonwealths which they served.

Perhaps, to conclude, what is needed is a shift in vocabulary from 'private' to 'privy.' Scatological references aside, the primary connotations of this term in early modern England are suggested by its cognates such as 'privileged', its synonyms such as 'secret' and 'proper', and its use in such institutions as the 'Privy Council', the 'Privy Chamber', and 'Secret [or Privy] Service'. In Samuel Johnson's *Dictionary*, as in the *Oxford English Dictionary*, it implies both exclusion (in the sense of secret or clandestine) and inclusion (in the sense of 'being admitted to secrets of state' or 'to participation of knowledge'). The private, or privy, library was thus less asocial and apolitical than selectively social and political. It could only be otherwise in cases where the physical space of reading was absolutely separate from its professional and domestic status; where no interest operated except self-interest; where the reader had minimal connections or maximal privilege. Throughout the sixteenth century, at least, such situations must have been exceedingly rare, and it took Montaigne's boldness and virtuosity (as well, of

[38] Justus Lipsius, (trans.) John Cotton Dana, *Brief Outline of the History of Libraries* (Chicago, IL, 1907), p. 111. I have supplied the original Latin for some important words, from the first edition (Antwerp, 1602).

[39] Sig.G3^{v}. Evelyn was a Fellow of the Royal Society and, significantly, the author of a text entitled, *Public Employment and an Active Life Prefer'd to Solitude.*

[40] *The Reformed Librarie-Keeper* (London, 1650; repr. Augustan Reprint Society, no. 220 (1983)), pp. 16–17.

course, as his status, self-interest and privilege) to make it a model.[41] The private library and the solitary scholarly reader are less representations of early modern reality than rhetorical strategies by which early modern subjects negotiated their place in society.

[41] A final, telling example of Montaigne's highly charged manipulation of the private/privy boundary is found, once again, in the essay 'De trois commerces'. Near the end of the essay he writes, 'L'ambition paye bien ses gens de les tenir tousjours en montre, comme la statue d'un marche: "Magna servitus est magna fortuna". Ils n'ont pas seulement leur retraict pour retraitte' (Pierre Villey (ed.), *Les essais de Montaigne* (Paris, 1924), pp. 828–9). Although M. A. Screech's recent translation (Harmondsworth, 1991) is superb, his version of this passage does not quite convey Montaigne's play: 'Ambition well rewards its courtiers by keeping them always on display like a statue in the marketplace: "Magna servitus est magna fortuna". They cannot even find privacy on their privy' (p. 933).

CHAPTER 5

Reading and the technology of textual affect: Erasmus's familiar letters and Shakespeare's King Lear

Lisa Jardine

> A letter or epistle, is the thyng alone y[t] maketh men present which are absent. For among those that are absent, what is so presente, as to heare and talke with those whom thou louest?
>
> (Myles Coverdale)[1]

> They were trained together in their childhoods, and there rooted betwixt them then such an affection which cannot choose but branch now. Since their more mature dignities and royal necessities made separation of their society, their encounters, though not personal, have been royally attorneyed with interchange of gifts, letters, loving embassies, that they have seemed to be together though absent. (*The Winter's Tale*)[2]

This paper is an attempt at historicizing reading in order to reveal the textual construction of feeling in the early modern period.[3] Historical approaches to Shakespeare's plays (including my own) have so far tended to concentrate on contextualizing social and cultural practices. So, for example, we may revive the significance of a key plot point in a play, like Othello's naming Desdemona 'whore' in front of Emilia, by retrieving the sixteenth-century social historical evidence on 'defamation'.[4] We have not, to date, tried in any systematic way to contextualize the pivotal affective moments: the point at which emotion is

1 Myles Coverdale, *Certain most godly, fruitful, and comfortable letters of such true Saintes and holy Martyrs of God, as in the late bloodye persecution here within this Realme, gaue their lyues for the defence of Christes holy gospel: written in the tyme of theyr affliction and cruell imprysonment. Though they suffer payne amonge men, yet is their hope full of immortalitie*(London, 1564).

2 J. H. P. Pafford (ed.), *The Winter's Tale*, Arden edn (London, 1963), I.i.22–9.

3 This piece of work has been shaped by extensive discussion with Lorna Hutson, particularly about the links between Erasmus's textbook treatment of letter-writing and the technology of textual affect in *King Lear*. I am deeply grateful to Lorna for the intellectual support she has always given to my work.

4 See my '"Why should he call her whore?" Defamation and Desdemona's case', in M. Warner and M. Tudeau-Clayton (eds.), *Addressing Frank Kermode: Essays in Criticism and Interpretation* (London, 1991), pp. 124–53.

intensified so as to structure the audience's and the reader's allegiance, and gain our assent to the unravelling or resolving of the action.[5]

The body of writing chosen here to begin this historicizing process is Desiderius Erasmus's *Epistolae*. At first sight such a choice appears perverse. Nothing could, apparently, be less contrived emotionally than Erasmus's *Letters*. Erasmus studies, indeed, are premised on the 'authenticity' and transparent truthfulness of those letters as *the* source of Erasmian biographical information.[6] It will be argued here, however, that Erasmus's letters are crucially affective, and that they are major contributions to the Renaissance's construction of letter writing and reading as emotionally charged events. Moreover they were centrally influential in the pedagogic construction of a certain kind of reading: a version of emotionally compelling communication in the second half of the sixteenth century. So influential was this pedagogical model of reading that the exchange of familiar letters could come to stand for the efficiency with which humanistic text-skills could be used to alter an individual's social position and prospects. As discussed in Erasmian handbooks on letter-writing, the familiar letter structures and organizes feeling so as to manipulate its intensity at a distance and, in the absence of the persons involved, enabling persuasion to a desired outcome.

The project of the present piece is to set *King Lear* within this contextualized version of the controlled production of feeling.[7] *King Lear* elicits our revulsion towards such efficiency by presenting us with the prospect of a world in which real affection is deprived of

5 There are, however, some suggestive pointers, prompting inquiry into the influence of Erasmus and an Erasmian concern with the rhetorical production of feeling in Shakespeare in Emrys Jones, *The Origins of Shakespeare* (Oxford, 1977), pp. 9–13. It might be argued that all Shakespeare criticism has, until comparatively recently, been fundamentally about 'feeling', in the sense that it set out to match intensity of emotion in the Shakespearean text to the sensibility of the critic's own period. The difference between such an approach and the one I have in mind here is, of course, that such criticism was committed to the view that feeling was transhistorical – that feeling elicited by the text in the nineteenth or twentieth centuries was necessarily that feeling which it had elicited when first written and performed. I would like to thank Emrys Jones and Barbara Everett for extremely helpful suggestions made for clarifying points in a version of this piece of work delivered to their graduate seminar at New College Oxford in January 1994.

6 I have in mind the fact that the entire Erasmus literature is grounded upon P. S. Allen's monumental compilation of Erasmus's letters: the *Opus epistolarum Erasmi*. For the purposes of such work, Erasmus scholars almost inevitably treat these letters as pure content – the transparent transmission of authentic detail concerning Erasmus's life, thought and work. See my *Erasmus, Man of Letters: The Construction of Charisma in Print* (Princeton NJ, 1993).

7 In their different ways, Deborah Warner, directing the play in 1992 at the National Theatre, and Max Stafford Clark, directing it at the Royal Court in 1993, both still structured their productions around this emotional intensity. In the case of Max Stafford Clark's production,

instrumentality (the ability to influence the outcome of actions and events) precisely to the extent that a cynically operated technology of affect – of warmth and intimacy generated by letters – debases the heart's expressive resources, leaving 'nothing' to be said.

Three key concepts structure early sixteenth-century, Erasmian thinking about familiar letters. These are, friendship, effective transmission of feeling and absence made present. All three are incorporated in the definition of the *epistola* which Erasmus gives in his *De conscribendis epistolis*. Letters should be 'intimate conversations between friends' ('amicorum inter ipsos confabulationes'):

> As the comedian Turpilius aptly wrote, the *epistola* is a kind of mutual exchange of speech between absent friends.
> [Est enim (quod scite scriptum est Turpilio comico) epistola absentium amicorum quasi mutuus sermo.][8]

This idea of a form of written work which crucially makes vivid the voice of the friend from whom one is separated, so as affectively to render that friend present, is a fascinating one, particularly since I do not think it tallies closely with our own understanding of the 'personal letter' (in other words, we have lost touch with this historicized version of letter writing).[9] It has its roots in pseudo-Libanius (a source in whom Erasmus had a considerable emotional investment, as I have discussed elsewhere). And it immediately notifies us of the importance for Erasmus of the affective dimension in epistolary writing – shared feeling, textually transmitted, substitutes for the individual who cannot be present, whose absence is a cause for regret and longing on the part of both parties in the textual transaction.

But the first thing to note, as we set about reconstructing a context for the pedagogic importance of 'familiar letters', is that Erasmus's clear indication of his source takes us not to Turpilius (for whom there are no surviving works), but rather to Saint Jerome. For the attribution of that precise definition of the function of the familiar letter is to be found in a

which aspired to contemporize the play (with the divided map used to evoke the current disintegration of the nation state in the Balkans), this investment in a transhistorical emotional core was particularly striking.

8 *Opera Omnia Desiderii Erasmi Roterodami, recognita et adnotatione critica instructa notisque illustrata* (Amsterdam, 1969) (hereafter *ASD*) I-2, 225. On some of Erasmus's indebtednesses in defining letter-writing in the *De conscribendis epistolis*, see J. Monfasani, 'Three Notes on Renaissance Rhetoric', *Rhetorica* 5 (1987): 107–18; 'Two Greek Sources for Erasmus's *De conscribendis epistolis*', 115–18.

9 I suspect that nowadays we reserve the form of 'affect at a distance' which Erasmus associates with the letter for telephone communication.

key letter of Jerome's, included with a commentary in Erasmus's collected edition of Jerome's *Epistolae.* The letter opens as follows:

Jerome to Nitias – In his treatment of the exchange of letters, Turpilius the comedian said: 'It is the unique way of making absent persons present.'

The familiar letter, in other words, constructs a fiction of the affective presence of an absent individual. Jerome indicates that in this case the deception of fiction is legitimate, because it achieves a morally laudable outcome:

Nor, in so doing, does it deceive, although it achieves its purpose by means of what is not true. For what, if I may speak truly, is more present between those absent from one another, than to address and hear what you value by means of letters.

The feigned element in letter-writing is legitimate, because it is needed to elicit the right degree of intensity of feeling in the recipient (by its simulation of over-wrought feeling in the sender).[10] And he goes on to add historical and etymological material to support the fact that familiar letters have traditionally been the purveyors of humane understanding amongst men:

Even before the use of paper and parchment, those primitive Italians, who Ennius calls 'Casci', who (according to Cicero, in *Rhetorica*) wished to gain understanding of themselves almost as a way of life, repeatedly sent one another mutual epistolary exhortations, either on writing tablets of smoothed and polished wood, or on the bark of trees. Whence those who carry letters are called 'tabellarii' [tablet carriers], and copyists are called 'librarii' from the bark [liber] of trees. How much the more, then, must we avoid overlooking what they themselves excelled in – whose milieu was raw and rustic, and who were ignorant of all 'humanitas' whatsoever?

Jerome now moves to exemplify the features of familiar letter-writing which he has just identified. Notice how the tone changes:

See how Chromatius, sacred Eusebius's brother by equality of morals as much as by nature, roused me to the task of letters. But you having departed from us, rend asunder our recently formed friendship rather than dissolving it, which Laelius most prudently prevented in Cicero. Unless perhaps the east is so hateful to you that you are afraid of your letters coming here also. Awake! Awake! wake from your sleep, produce a scrap of paper, for goodness' sake. Between the delights of your native land and the journeys abroad we shared, breathe at least a word. If you love me, write I beseech you. If you have been

[10] It is this nonchalance concerning 'feigning' in order to achieve 'sincerity' which we shall see causing difficulty and anxiety in *King Lear*.

angered, you are entitled to write angrily. I will have great solace, and that which I long for, if I receive my friend's letters, even if my friend is displeased.[11]

So Erasmus's definition of the familiar letter has already taken us to a fascinating source: a letter of Jerome's which bears all the marks of being itself 'exemplary' – illustrating the very features of letter-writing which the writer identifies as those formally associated with the effective textual transmission of 'humanitas'. The letter is a text-book example of the genre, and indeed, following Erasmus's interest in it, it seems to have been used in northern classrooms on a regular basis to introduce students to letter-writing.[12]

Actually in Jerome's letter to Nitias, 'Turpilius' does not say precisely what Erasmus attributes to him. For 'Turpilius' (or should we say, Jerome?) the familiar letter 'is the unique way of making absent persons present'. Here, the familiar letter renders absence present, its written text substituting for the affective presence of a physical speaker, without the extra component of *amicitia*. The letter in its entirety, however, adds the crucial dimension of 'friendship' and intimacy performatively – the absence for which the letter itself seeks to compensate is that of a beloved friend: 'you having departed from us, rend asunder our recently formed friendship'. As Erasmus explicitly adds *amicitia* to 'Turpilius's' definition, he apparently regards the friendship aspect of epistolary communication as particularly important.

Since Erasmus himself chooses to direct us to Jerome for an understanding of the fundamental features of the familiar letter, it is appropriate to turn for further insight to the commented edition of Jerome's letters which Erasmus contributed to the Froben complete Jerome of 1516. There he summarizes Jerome's 'Letter to Heliodorus' (the opening letter in his collection) as follows:

When St. Jerome had gone to the desert he tried to keep with him his dearest friend Heliodorus, who out of a sense of duty had accompanied him, as he testifies elsewhere. Failing in this endeavour he wrote him a letter urging him to join him in the solitary life. He refutes several considerations which could either keep him from the desert or detain him in a city. And he shows him how it is not safe to undertake the office of bishop and how it is not easy to keep that office once undertaken. Then as a peroration he sings over and over the joys of the hermit life, and he portrays for him the terror of the Last

11 Erasmus, *Epistolae Hieronymi* (Basle, 1524) I, 218.

12 For example, Barlandus produced a slim manual on letter writing in the 1520s, consisting of three commented letters of Jerome's, of which the first is the letter to Nitias.

Judgment. He mentions this letter by name in the catalogue of his works and calls it a hortatory letter. He wrote this when quite young, little more than a boy, as he testifies in the next letter, adding that in this letter he had played with the flowery language of the schools, still fired with enthusiasm for rhetorical studies, youth that he was. Accordingly it abounds with metaphors, allegories, even fictitious in origin, and with the oratorical ornaments of exclamation, dilemma, and other figures of that sort. His efforts show the kind of artistry in which one can recognize a beginner, but a beginner of the highest promise. The subject-matter belongs to the hortatory genre, which we will discuss a little later.[13]

The letter itself begins as follows:

So conscious are you of the affection that exists between us that you cannot but recognize the love and passion with which I strove to prolong our common sojourn in the desert. This very letter – blotted with tears – gives evidence of the lamentation and weeping with which I accompanied your departure. With the pretty ways of a child you then softened your refusal by soothing words, and I, being off my guard, knew not what to do. Was I to hold my peace? I could not conceal my eagerness by a show of indifference. Or was I to entreat you yet more earnestly? You would have refused to listen, for your love was not like mine. Despised affection has taken the one course open to it. Unable to keep you when present, it goes in search of you when absent. You asked me yourself, when you were going away, to invite you to the desert when I took up my quarters there, and I for my part promised to do so. Accordingly I invite you now; come, and come quickly... But what is this, and why do I foolishly importune you again? Away with entreaties, an end to coaxing words. Offended love does well to be angry. You have spurned my petition; perhaps you will listen to my remonstrance.[14]

What is striking is the intensely affective tone of the Jerome letter which Erasmus (unlike other editors) selects to put first in his collection, and to which, exceptionally, he attaches two separate commentaries – a more or less standard commentary on unusual words, allusions and doctrinal points, and an *annotatio artis*, which explicates the structural and rhetorical devices which produce the letter's emotional impact. This *annotatio artis* is remarkable in a sixteenth-century scholarly commentary on a leading Father of the Church, and, in particular, one whose *vita* contained a well-known episode in which (in a dream) he was summoned before God's tribunal to answer the charge of paying too much attention to secular literary excellence, in particular to Cicero. Here, at the very beginning of his *renovatio* of Jerome's oeuvre

[13] *Collected Works of Erasmus* (Toronto, 1976–) (hereafter *CWE*), LXI, 109.
[14] *CWE* LXI, 109–10.

and reputation, Erasmus foregrounds the rhetorical and affective in Jerome's letter-writing.[15]

In fact the *annotatio artis* confirms what is already thematically clear in Erasmus's first commentary (as in commentaries to subsequent letters in the volume) – that the key criterion according to which Erasmus judges the effectiveness of Jerome's epistolary writing is its emotional intensity. As Chomarat puts it:

L'émotion est le critère esthétique décisif.[16]
[Emotion is the decisive measure of aesthetic success.]

Erasmus justifies the provision of the *annotatio artis* itself on the grounds that 'St Jerome ... confesses that in this [letter] he played with an ornate rhetoric'.[17] The following are typical passages from the 'rhetorical annotation':

When [Jerome] tells how Heliodorus had accompanied him on his journey into the desert and how in vain he had asked him to remain with him there is a narration, so to speak. Then when he says that it was the object of his letter to have Heliodorus leave the cities and come to the desert there is the proposition. And yet St Jerome does not give us a lifeless account of these details, but he is always on fire, a man, it appears, of a vigorous disposition and vehement in both praise and blame. For he ardently praises those he loves, and he vigorously attacks those who have aroused his hostility.[18]

What keeps you in your father's house? Such rhetorical figures as questions, repetitions, and short clauses make the discourse more impassioned. Metaphor or rather allegory elevates it to an even loftier and more pleasing level. Indeed he uses a well-nigh continuous metaphor. It is almost the constant practice of Jerome, however, to place at the beginning passages that are especially attractive and delightful by which to entice the reader through pleasure and induce him to read on more eagerly. For no one is inattentive to what gives him delight.[19]

This commentary is of a kind with Erasmus's discussion of the rhetorical structure of the familiar letter in his textbook, *De conscribendis epistolis*. There, too, Erasmus cites this very letter as a model example of an emphatically persuasive letter (*exhortatio*):

15 I should say here that this is the only one of the letters which has such an *annotatio artis* in addition to its primary commentary. Nevertheless, the fact that this is the first letter suggests that Erasmus attached importance to establishing the possibility of such commentaries. Characteristically, in volumes annotated by Erasmus, commentaries tail off, and become perfunctory, some little way into the edition.

16 Jacques Chomarat, *Grammaire et rhétorique chez Erasme*, 2 vols. (Paris, 1981) I, 537.

17 *CWE* LXI, 123.

18 *CWE* LXI, 124–5.

19 *CWE* LXI, 126.

Amongst Jerome's letters there is an *exhortatio* addressed to Heliodorus, which is an absolute classic of this genre.
[Est et inter Hieronymianas epistolas, exhortatoria ad Heliodorum, quae vniuersum eius generis artificium vna complectitur.][20]

Note that this letter conforms fully to Erasmus's preferred definition: it is an 'intimate conversation' between separated friends, which vividly produces the one to the other. Notice something else. The classic of the form is a piece of highly specific writing from the *vita* of St Jerome – a letter in which he implores his close friend to join him in a life of asceticism and study. And (according to the commentary which Erasmus provides for his edition) the affective power of the letter impinges with equal force on the reader who is neither the original recipient of the letter nor its author. Erasmus has something further to say on this score in his *annotatio artis*:

Writings of this kind are nothing else than Christian declamations. For when Christians saw that eloquence was something at the same time most beautiful and most useful and did not think it fitting to be occupied as the profane rhetoricians were with trifling subjects ... they made the whole theory of declamation subservient to moral instruction.[21]

The intimate conversation between separated friends makes any suggested (closely argued) proposal vividly compelling by its emotional 'presence'. The patristic familiar letter is therefore the preferred genre for exhortation to moral rectitude, which makes church teaching on behaviour vividly present to the sixteenth-century Christian reader.[22]

For the second stage in this historical contextualizing of the way Erasmian epistolary instruction develops a technology of affect to 'fabricate intimacy' I turn to the pedagogic context – not to the *De conscribendis epistolis* (Erasmus's manual on letter-writing), but to the *De copia* (his

[20] *ASD* I-2: 353.
[21] *CWE* LXI, 124.
[22] The *annotatio artis* contains a discussion of persuasive and hortatory epistolary writing which is repeated almost verbatim in the *De conscribendis epistolis*. 'And first to say something about the kind of subject, it belongs to the hortatory genre... This is so close to the persuasive kind of discourse that Aristotle did not think that there was any distinction between the two. In my judgment, however, there is some difference. For the aim of persuasion is to influence the will; the aim of exhortation is to encourage and enable. Persuasion is directed at the irresolute, exhortation at the inactive. We persuade when we show what it is advantageous to do, we exhort when we add emotion to our discourse... Exhortation has this special feature: it is more fiery and has a large admixture of the laudatory, which however Jerome does not use in this letter. For men are incited above all by two factors, praise and the fear of disgrace' (*CWE* LXI, 124).

general textbook on Latin textual production). There are a number of indications in the *De copia* that Erasmus has in mind familiar letter-writing as the generalized model for textual production which deploys ornament and amplification persuasively in order to have some desired compelling emotional impact on the reader. The most obvious signal is Erasmus's choices of phrase for virtuoso variation in Book One (*De copia verborum*) – one hundred and fifty alternative ways of expressing the sentiment:

Your letter pleased me mightily
[tuae litterae me magnopere delectarunt]

Two hundred versions of:

As long as I live, I shall preserve the memory of you
[semper dum vivam tui meminero][23]

The first of these is obviously epistolary. The second is an intense expression of friendship, and of presence evoked affectively, and as Erasmus specifies his own and Thomas More's names in the course of the variations ('as long as Erasmus lives, the name of More will never perish') the phrase involves absence across geographical distance (Erasmus in the Low Countries, More in England).[24]

The compelling reason for choosing the *De copia* to contextualize the pedagogy of affective epistolary writing is, however, a more local and specific one. It has to do (as elsewhere in my recent work on Erasmus) with a particular published volume, and one which was not a first edition. The volume in question, I shall argue, in its capacity as friendship gift in a particular geographical location, for a particular occasion, offers us the chance to respond to the texts it contains in something like the spirit in which Erasmus offered them, and (I believe) contemporary readers in northern Europe – for our purposes, in England – received them.

In 1514 Erasmus gave the second, emended edition of the *De copia* to the printer Matthias Schürer at Strasbourg, to publish together with the first edition of his *Parabolae*, or book of comparisons. Between the two pedagogic texts are printed two letters, exchanged between Erasmus and Jakob Wimpfeling – spokesman for the *sodalitas literaria* (literary society) at Strasbourg, and a collection of verses. In addition, the *De copia* carries a prefatory letter to Schürer, the printer, the *Parabolae* carries a prefatory letter to Erasmus's close friend in Antwerp,

23 *CWE* XXIV, 348; *CWE* XXIV, 354.
24 For another relevant link between the *De copia* and letters (this time Seneca's), see my *Erasmus, Man of Letters*, chapter 5.

Pieter Gilles. These four letters frame the pedagogic contents of the two treatises in a particularly interesting way. In essence, they construct a quite elaborate affective scenario – a sequence of *epistolae* which do two different jobs simultaneously. They specify the 'occasion' for the volume (providing it with a vivid biographical Erasmian setting); and they carefully exemplify and animate the pedagogic precepts in the *De copia* and the *Parabolae* manuals.[25]

P. S. Allen includes Wimpfeling's brief letter to Erasmus, and Erasmus's lengthy reply in their chronological place, in his *Opus epistolarum Erasmi*, as a genuine exchange of letters. The internal evidence of the letters, however, makes it quite clear that the second is a highly contrived, virtuoso rhetorical exercise, elicited at the request of Wimpfeling's *sodalitas literaria* following a visit to the literary society by Erasmus as he was passing through Strasbourg on his way to Basle. The presence of the Wimpfeling letter, unlike the prefatory letters, is announced on the title-page of the volume itself. The Erasmus letter should, therefore, I think, be treated as a worked example of a familiar letter, clearly offered to the reader of the volume as such.[26]

The rhetorical techniques used in Erasmus's letter to Wimpfeling consistently follow closely the rhetorical methods of amplification inventoried in the *De copia* (and metaphors from the *Parabolae*).[27] The

25 For evidence of such careful 'staging' of a text by means of the accompanying letters and verses, in which Erasmus was closely involved, see the exchanges of letters soliciting endorsements for Thomas More's *Utopia*.

26 One further piece of cross-referring by Erasmus links Jerome and familiar letters to the Schürer volume. In Book Two of the *De copia* there is a section entitled *De parabola*, which provides the structural context for the insertion of *parabolae* (comparisons) of the kind collected in the companion text in the volume. The example Erasmus chooses to illustrate this technique is Cicero's use, in the *Pro Murena*, of an extended comparison as follows: 'Those just sailing into harbour after a long sea-voyage eagerly give information to those setting out about the likelihood of storms and the pirate situation and what the different places are like, because it is natural to feel kindly towards those who are about to face the dangers which we have just escaped. What then should be my feelings, who am just coming into sight of land after a terrible tossing, towards this man who, as I can see, must go out to face dreadful storms?' (*CWE* XXIV, 621). He goes on immediately to point out that Jerome closely imitates this passage of Cicero's, in the letter to Heliodorus, and cites that passage also in its entirety (*CWE* XXIV, 621–2).

27 For example: 'It was possible, when I was with you, to see in one city the virtues of all the most celebrated city-states: Roman severity, Athenian wisdom, and the self-restraint of Lacedaemon' (amplification of place) (*CWE* II, 26); 'That incomparable young man Jakob Sturm, who adds lustre to his distinguished family by his own high character, crowns his youth with a seriousness worthy of riper years, and gives great charm to uncommon learning with his incredible modesty' (amplification of person) (*CWE* II, 27); 'Do not forget Ottmar, a man who seemed to me well read without ostentation, who with the rapid trilling on his pipes that outdid the very nightingale so ravished me that I seemed rapt in ecstacy' (amplification of person) (*CWE* II, 29).

letter, in other words, is a full *exemplum* of the kind provided throughout the *De conscribendis epistolis*. It has the added advantage, however, over those compressed, generalized examples, of being clearly addressed to specified, known individuals, at a specified, known location. Given that the invitation to write, and Erasmus's reply itself, specify that the 'familiarity' of those addressed is more courtesy than reality the tone of the affect can be very precisely placed as warm but not intimate.[28]

Beyond the detail of its rhetorical structure – the technology of its affect – the Wimpfeling letter does something further. It stages the entire volume as a textual gift, an *amicitia* – or friendship – transaction, with the intellectual community at Strasbourg. It comes complete with verse-offerings to individual members of the group, one of whom (Thomas Vogler) has previously sent laudatory verses to Erasmus:

Johann Witz, since I saw that he could hardly be torn away from me, I have consoled with a quatrain; and to make the keepsake of more value to my admirer, or more truly to one who is head over heals in love with me, I have written it out in my own hand. Here it is. I send you also what I had written on the journey to that incomparable man Sebastian Brant; for I have changed a few words in it of no importance. I have added the nonsense I scribbled rather than wrote to Vogler.[29]

All these items are printed in the physical volume, following the Wimpfeling letter, so that the material gift is as nearly as possible present to the reader.[30] The device of the 'keepsake' which Erasmus has 'written out in [his] own hand' ('meis digitis scripsi') is a favourite one of his, which teases the reader with the discrepancy between the original, and its print 'copy', deceptively 'the same'. And just as these

28 The only other letters to or from Wimpfeling in Allen are equally formal, endorsing, or seeking endorsement of, printed works. Allen I, 463 [ep. 224] (Wimpfeling defends himself against anti-Erasmian sentiments in a letter appended to Schürer's edition of the *Moriae encomium* (1511)); Allen II, 180 [ep. 382] (unpublished; Wimpfeling tells Erasmus he has mentioned him favourably in his *Cathologus* of writers); Allen II, 187–8 [ep. 385] (Erasmus's nine-line courtesy reply, published in a volume of Mantuan edited by Wimpfeling).

29 *CWE* II, 33.

30 This is inevitably the point at which a note is needed to indicate how totally the historical context of both letters and poems is lost as they are presented (or rather, not presented) in *CWE*. Allen already obscures the relationship between the four letters by reassigning them to their (effectively spurious) chronological positions within his *Opus epistolarum Erasmi*. Thus Erasmus's letter to Wimpfeling is separated from the letter which elicited it as formal response, and the preface to Schürer follows, rather than precedes these letters. Allen does, however, indicate that the poems alluded to are included with the text of the letter in the Schürer volume. *CWE* omits these notes, and instead refers the reader to Reedjik's collected edition of Erasmus's poems for the texts. It is no longer clear that they were, to all intents and purposes, produced for the volume. As far as the History of the Book is concerned, we have altogether lost the book. The book is replaced by pseudo-biography.

poems are friendship offerings, so the texts themselves – the *De copia* and the *Parabolae* – are gifts to the Strasbourg printer, Schürer.

Matthias Schürer is named as a worthy member of the Strasbourg *sodalitas literaria* in the letter to Wimpfeling:

> Besides, there is Matthias Schürer, a man to whom I am much attached on many other grounds, but still more as a son of Sélestat, that town so fertile in learned and gifted men to which I owe also Beatus Rhenanus and Johann Witz and Wimpfeling himself. And so, were I not deeply attached to Matthias, I should rightly be accused of having iron and adamant where my heart should be, such was his initiative in offering by acts of kindness to become my friend. Nor will I so act as to fall short in spirit at least and in readiness, although it was he who began it; one day I will repay what he has done for me, if only my spirit is matched by my capacity.[31]

The 'acts of kindness' Schürer has performed are editions of Erasmus's works; the suggestion is that they were no less acts of friendship for the fact that Schürer's relationship is a professional one. Erasmus's prefatory letter to the *De copia* text specifies that text and the text of the *Parabolae* as gift-offerings to a printer personally worthy of Erasmus's admiration, a man of humane learning, as emanating from a circle with whom he has (in the Wimpfeling letter) publicly associated himself in *amicitia*.

The prefatory letter to Schürer effectively refers us back to the letter to Wimpfeling. For there Erasmus offers a *narratio* in which he gives a vivid account of his movements since he left Strasbourg ('And now, since you want to know how the rest of my journey went, here is the story in few words'). That *narratio* establishes Basle – Erasmus's settled location, and the publishing centre for his major works of the next three years, the Seneca, the expanded *Adagia*, the *Novum Instrumentum*, the Jerome – as crucially situated both geographically and intellectually in relation to neighbouring Sélestat and Strasbourg (Wimpfeling's native town, and the place where he now resides). The intellectual centrality of Basle is skilfully conveyed through Erasmus's vivid account of the physical convergence of scholars from these locations upon Basle (Witz accompanying Erasmus on his journey; Beatus Rhenanus, native of Sélestat, meeting him there to take on the job as trusted editor), coupled with his equally vivid picture of a constant exchange of letters and verses between those physically separated and remaining at the three locations. All of this finally allows Erasmus to lay claim to Basle

31 *CWE* II, 29.

as 'his' native town – Germany as his intellectual motherland (*mea Germania*).

If we turn, finally, to the prefatory letter to the *Parabolae*, addressed to Pieter Gilles, it makes compellingly explicit the scenario I have been teasing out of the volume's structure and physical presentation. The letter opens on the theme of true *amicitia* (intimate friendship), and with a series of *parabolae* or emotionally stimulating comparisons, fully worthy of the textbook it proffers:

Friends of the commonplace and homespun sort, my open-hearted Pieter, have their idea of relationship, like their whole lives, attached to material things; and if ever they have to face a separation, they favour a frequent exchange of rings, knives, caps, and other tokens of the kind, for fear that their affection may cool when intercourse is interrupted or actually die away through the interposition of long tracts of time and space. But you and I, whose idea of friendship rests wholly in a meeting of minds and the enjoyment of studies in common, might well greet one another from time to time with presents for the mind and keepsakes of a literary description. Not that there is any risk that when our life together is interrupted we may slowly grow cold, or that the great distance which separates our bodies may loosen the close tie between our minds. Minds can develop an even closer link, the greater the space that comes between them. Our aim would be that any loss due to separation in the actual enjoyment of our friendship should be made good, not without interest, by tokens of this literary kind. And so I send a present – no common present, for you are no common friend, but many jewels in one small book.[32]

Here the *Parabolae* is offered as a gift (a jewel, a token) to an intimate friend, and the tone of the letter is equivalently more intense and affectively compelling.[33] Following the opening contrast between commonplace friendship, and friendship of minds, Erasmus produces a variant on a favourite *topos* – truly intellectual friendship is not cooled by separation, minds sustain their ardour even when apart.[34] Written texts are the ideal friendship-tokens for such enduring friendships.

Erasmus produces a worked example of personalized and intimate letter-writing, in which *parabolae* heighten the affective force of the (otherwise formulaic) sentiments, and in which he once again foregrounds the exemplary nature of the writing by self-consciously alluding to the effectiveness of the devices he incorporates in the very

32 *CWE* II, 44.
33 The second edition of the *Parabolae* was printed by Martens at Louvain, edited by Gilles, suggesting that this text was truly his gift.
34 Erasmus expresses closely similar sentiments to Thomas More.

act of employing them. ('Deprive the orators of their arsenal of metaphor, and all will be thin and dull'; 'this man has a pretty knack of making his work sound important'; 'Would this win no credit as an ingenious application of the parallel?'[35])

I think that it is absolutely essential that we register the 'staging' of Erasmus's epistolary technology of affect in the Schürer volume if we are to historicize appropriately the ways in which feeling is textually provoked and manipulated in writing of the period.[36] The Schürer *De copia/Parabolae* volume does much more than provide an inventory of techniques of rhetorical amplification, and itemize comparisons drawn from classical works of literature. Yet we have the greatest difficulty in seeing beyond the apparently unstructured compilation of textual material, because we tend to ignore all the physical apparatus of the book itself which provides the instructions for its reading. It is the self-conscious framing in terms of geographical place of publication (prominent on the book's title-page), the prefatory material to the publisher (selected on grounds of friendship and past gift-exchanges), the letters from and to Wimpfeling, locating the publishing 'event' in relation to Erasmus's pedagogic and publishing activities as a whole, the letter of friendship to Gilles, transforming the *Parabolae* from textbook into intellectual gift cementing *amicitia*, which together provide the school reader (teacher or student) with instructions on how to read. They frame instruction so as to convey the efficacy of the precepts compellingly by producing them in a vivid scenario of 'real life' textual transaction.

I have been arguing that Erasmus's is an extremely sophisticated version of the ability of the familiar letter to capture and communicate highly wrought emotion from absent friend to reader. At the heart of Erasmus's thinking lies some idea of *authenticity*. Whereas a textual version of a Cicero oration lacks the gesture and intonation which made it compelling in its original form, a letter of Jerome's survives in precisely its original state – every element in it preserved and available to the sixteenth-century reader. And I have been arguing that we miss the care with which, in his pedagogic treatises, Erasmus reconstructs a textual milieu within which the richness of possibility for letter-writing

35 *CWE* II, 43–6.

36 For a somewhat similar argument about textual strategies for manipulating feeling in the period, see K. Meerhoff, 'Rhetorica: creativiteit', in M. Spies and K. Meerhoff, *Rhetorica: Strategie en Creativiteit* (Amsterdam, 1993), pp. 25–53.

is 'staged' for the novice reader. Renaissance readers of the *De copia*, I am suggesting, composed their own 'occasional' letters in the engaged and rhetorically stringent way exemplified by Erasmus in the letter to Wimpfeling. It remains to show that such possibilities were recognized by Shakespeare's contemporaries in England, in particular – that those who passed through early modern English classrooms expected 'familiar letters' to convey passionate feeling, to create bonds of friendship, and to make the absent loved one (or intellectual kindred spirit) vividly present. That they, like their continental contemporaries regarded the familiar letter as a highly crafted form of communication, which could act as intermediary between separated individuals linked by bonds of shared feeling and an emerging trans-European intellectual ideal of *humanitas*.

We know that Erasmian works like the *De copia* were the staple of European schoolteaching throughout the second half of the sixteenth century, and that the persuasive potential of the Erasmian familiar letter was well understood. Erasmus's 'epistle to perswade a young gentleman to marriage' was included in Thomas Wilson's popular *Arte of Rhetorique*, as a model of the kind of discourse which could combine the affective transmission of warmth of feeling, friendship and emotional sincerity with conventional techniques of logical persuasion to produce a compelling case for a particular course of action.[37] To reassure ourselves further that such continental subtleties may realistically be associated with an English setting, a 1564 publication of Myles Coverdale provides us with a vivid context for such feelingful epistolary communication. Coverdale's *Certain most godly, fruitful, and comfortable letters of such true Saintes and holy Martyrs of God, as in the late bloodye persecution here within this Realme, gaue their lyues for the defence of Christes holy gospel* is a compilation of letters 'written in the tyme of theyr affliction and cruell imprysonment' by Protestant Englishmen persecuted under Mary.[38] Coverdale recommends to the devout reader the careful reading of the letters of those who suffered punishment and death for their faith. And he draws directly upon Erasmus to make a double case for letters as the primary resource for spiritual truth, and Christian feeling:

[37] 'I will neither wish that the love of your freends ... nor yet mine authoritie that I have ouer you, should do me any good at all, to compasse this my request, if I shall not proue unto you by most plain reasons ... to be necessary for you at this time to marry' (G. H. Mair (ed.), *Wilson's Arte of Rhetorique (1560)* (Oxford, 1909), p. 40).

[38] See n. 1 above. I am grateful to Lorna Hutson and Alan Stewart for finding this passage. Here, as always, their breadth of reading and alertness to reference has proved invaluable.

[I]t doth vs good to read and heare, not the lying legendes of fayned, false, counterfayted, and popish canonized saincts, neither ye triflyng toyes & forged fables of corrupt writers: but such true, holy, & approued histories, monuments, orations, epistles & letters, as do set forth vnto vs ye blessed behauiour of gods deare seruauntes. It doth vs good (I say) by such comfortable remembraunce, conceaued by their notable writinges, to be conuersaunt with them, at the least in spirite.

S. Hierome, writing to one Nitia, and hauyng occasion to speake of letters or epystles, maketh mention of a certain Authour named Turpilius, whose woordes (sayeth he) are these: a letter or epistle, is the thyng alone y^t^ maketh men present which are absent. For among those that are absent, what is so presente, as to heare and talke with those whom thou louest? Also, that noble Clarke Erasmus Roterodame, commendyng the booke of the Epistles or lettters which S. Augustine dyd write, sayeth thus: by some of Augustines bokes we may perceaue, what maner of man he was being an infant in Christ. By other some, we may knowe what maner a one he was being a young man, and what he was being an olde man. But by thys onely booke (meaning the booke of the Epistles or letters) thou shalt knowe whole Augustyne altogether. And why doth S. Hierome or Erasmus saye thus? No doubt, euen because that in such writynges, as in a cleare glasse, we maye see and beholde, not onely what plentifull furniture and store of heauenly grace, wisedome, knowledge, vnderstanding, fayth, loue, hope, zeale, pacience, mekenes, obedience, with the worthy fruites thereof, almighty god hath bestowed vpon the same his most deare children: but also what a fatherlye care he euer hadde vnto them.[39]

The first idea here – that saints' letters are a more valuable source of spirituality and insight into sanctity than legend and fiction – is taken from Erasmus's *Vita Hieronymi*, which prefaces his edition of Jerome's letters.[40] The second, that letters provide the affective presence of the absent loved one, complete with its reference to Turpilius and Nitias, comes, as we saw, from the beginning of Erasmus's *De conscribendis epistolis*, referenced to the first Jerome letter in Erasmus's collection of the saint's letters.

Erasmus's subtle, and doctrinally complex version of affective Christian feeling, transmitted through the familiar letter, is here invoked as definitive, at the pulse-point of Elizabethan protestantism. And the easy way in which Coverdale makes the assumption that the reader will take the Erasmian point allows us, I think, to infer that the familiar letter, for the Christian Englishman, carried a freight of Erasmianism concerning its capacity to transmit feeling – to make the

39 Ibid., sig.a.ii.^r-v^.
40 See Jardine, *Erasmus, Man of Letters*, pp. 60–2.

absent friend present, and to make the effects of intimacy and friendship work at the level of persuasion.

In Act 4, scene 3 of *King Lear*, a gentleman describes to Kent the effect upon Cordelia of letters he brought her:

> KENT Did your letters pierce the queen to any demonstration of grief?
> GENT Ay, sir; she took them, read them in my presence;
> And now and then an ample tear trill'd down
> Her delicate cheek; it seem'd she was a queen
> Over her passion; who, most rebel-like,
> Sought to be king o'er her.
> KENT O! then it mov'd her.[41]

The gentleman goes on, prompted by Kent, to specify the intense way in which Cordelia responded:

> KENT Made she no verbal question?
> GENT Faith, once or twice she heav'd the name of 'father'
> Pantingly forth, as if it press'd her heart;
> Cried 'Sisters! sisters! Shame of ladies! sisters!
> Kent! father! sisters! What? i' th' storm! i' th' night?
> Let pity not be believ'd!' There she shook
> The holy water from her heavenly eyes,
> And clamour moisten'd, then away she started
> To deal with grief alone.[42]

This passage is often used as the most intensely affective presentation of Cordelia in the play. Indeed, I have argued myself that this portrayal of Cordelia, iconically grieving, passively suffering on behalf of her father, provides the moral justification for her active participation in warfare, a scene later. It now strikes me somewhat differently. The gentleman recounts an exemplary response to a familiar letter – a textbook example of the production at a distance of intense emotion and passionate feeling. The letters in question are, surely, from Kent: in Act 2, scene 2, Kent, in the stocks, comforted himself with a letter from Cordelia;[43] in Act 3, scene 1, Kent sends a gentleman to Dover with letters and a token for Cordelia.[44] Now the gentleman tells Kent how

41 Arden edn, 161. This scene is not in the 1623 folio.
42 Ibid., 162–3.
43 Ibid., 79: 'Approach, thou beacon to this under globe, / That by thy comfortable beams I may / Peruse this letter. . . . I know 'tis from Cordelia, / Who hath most fortunately been inform'd / Of my obscured course.'
44 Ibid., 102–5: 'If you shall see Cordelia, – / As fear not but you shall – show her this ring.'

Cordelia received 'his letters' – letters of *amicitia*, vividly making absence present ('Kent! father! sisters! What? i' th' storm! i' th' night?'), transmitting passionate feeling ('O! then it mov'd her').[45]

But most of the many epistolary transactions in *Lear* are not so securely morally admirable. Feeling and attendant action are manipulated by letters not to connote the bonds of intense personal commitment, but rather to mislead and distort. The most obvious examples of this are the forged letter Edmund uses to persuade Gloucester that his son Edgar is treacherous, and the adulterous letter from Goneril to Edmund, whose interception brings about hers and Edmund's downfall. In between, letters which Gloucester receives secretly from France, the existence of which Edmund betrays to Cornwall, lead to Gloucester's mutilation. Clearly something un-Erasmian, or possibly anti-Erasmian is at stake here.

Let us look first at the two letters which are sent in haste towards the end of Act 1, the receipt of which provides a plot crux in Act 2. 'I'll write straight to my sister / To hold my very course', resolves Goneril in Act 1, scene 4, as she determines to insist on Lear's reducing the number of his followers and curbing their riotousness. At the end of the scene, after her confrontation with Lear and his precipitate departure, Goneril dispatches her letter at the hands of her household servant Oswald:

> GON. What he hath utter'd I have writ my sister;
> ...
> How, now, Oswald!
> What, have you writ that letter to my sister?
> OSW. Ay, madam.
> GON. Take you some company, and away to horse:
> Inform her full of my particular fear;
> And thereto add such reasons of your own
> As may compact it more.[46]

Oswald is here involved with the letter, not simply as trusted

[45] Leo Salingar has suggested to me that the letter Macbeth sends to Lady Macbeth in Act 1, scene 5 of the play, informing her that the witches' prophecy has already begun to come true also conforms to this Erasmian model. The audience experiences the full emotional intensity of the incident for *Macbeth* by watching the histrionic and rhetorical response of his wife to the *letter* ('Glamis thou art, and Cawdor ...'). It is also worth noting that the most familiar type of such a letter (to which, in a sense, Macbeth's letter conforms) is the intimate love letter. In the sixteenth century it was already customary for a love letter to be a particularly significant 'gift' from a lover (see Alan Macfarlane, *Marriage and Love in England 1300–1840* (Oxford, 1986), pp. 301–3).

[46] Arden edn, 54–5.

messenger, but as rhetorically expert co-author of the text – should the persuasive technology prove inadequate he is authorized to 'add such reasons of [his] own / As may compact it more'. By contrast, Lear too resolves to send letters to Regan, informing her of his ill-treatment at Goneril's hands, and requesting lodging at her house. His messenger is the disguised Kent, who has specified his suitability for such message-carrying as part of his recommendation for Lear's service:

LEAR What services canst thou do?
KENT I can keep honest counsel, ride, run, mar a curious tale in telling it, and deliver a plain message bluntly; that which ordinary men are fit for, I am qualified in, and the best of me is diligence.[47]

Kent, in other words, is not the kind of servant to employ fancy rhetoric and pen his master's letters, nor add to their arguments if they fall short.[48] When Lear sends his letters he specifies that Kent will be the mere carrier of his message:

LEAR Go you before to Gloucester [i.e. the place] with these letters. Acquaint my daughter no further with any thing you know than comes from her demand out of the letter. If your diligence be not speedy I shall be there afore you.
KENT I will not sleep, my Lord, till I have delivered your letter.[49]

For Lear, letters are mere messages, sent by the fastest carrier to anticipate his own arrival. Or, put rather more closely in Erasmian terms, Lear does not trust the letter to convey the arguments of his love and authority, persuading for him in his absence; he simply dispatches it to herald his imminent arrival in person, which he assumes will be an argument irresistible in itself.

What happens to the letter sent, and to its messenger, conforms to the spirit in which it was dispatched: Lear's 'blunt' missive is repelled, its carrier clapped in the stocks; Goneril's messenger and message insinuate themselves into favour. As Kent describes it, after the event, to Lear:

KENT My Lord, when at their home
I did commend your Highness' letters to them,
Ere I was risen from the place that show'd

47 Ibid., 38.
48 It would be attractive to argue that the exemplary letter received by Cordelia, and written by Kent, in Act 4, scene 3, which exists only in one text of the play, was an addition for dramatic effect, which, however, is actually not strictly in character with Kent's 'bluntness' elsewhere.
49 Ibid., 56.

My duty kneeling, came there a reeking post,
Stew'd in his haste, half breathless, panting forth
From Goneril his mistress salutations;
Deliver'd letters, spite of intermission,
Which presently they read: on whose contents
They summon'd up their meiny, straight took horse;
Commanded me to follow, and attend
The leisure of their answer.[50]

Because the contents of the letters are never revealed to the audience (they are never 'read aloud'), their dramatized reception stands in for the contrast between their epistolary techniques.

On her arrival at Gloucester's Castle, Regan describes the way in which her sister's letter has prompted Cornwall's and her removal from their home to seek Gloucester's advice. They have come

REG. Thus out of season, threading dark-ey'd night:
Occasions, noble Gloucester, of some prize,
Wherein we must have use of your advice.
Our father he hath writ, so hath our sister,
Of differences, which I best thought it fit
To answer [away] from our home; the several messengers
From hence attend dispatch.[51]

Effectively, this is a contest for affective impact between the two letters, a contest which apparently Goneril and the persuasive technology of Oswald's crafted letter win: Kent is clapped in the stocks, his message unanswered; Gloucester is persuaded to give shelter to Goneril, Cornwall and their cause, allowing Lear, on his arrival, to be turned out into the storm. Dramatically, the contest is displaced on to the messengers – their brawl physically reproduces the differing terms of the communications they bear. The insults Kent heaps upon Oswald all characterize him as a manipulator of language and forms, 'a lily-livered, action-taking, whoreson, glass-gazing, super serviceable, finical rogue'; 'you come with letters against the King, and take Vanity the puppet's part against the royalty of her father'.[52] As for Kent himself, on the contrary, ''tis my occupation to be plain'. Or, as Cornwall puts it:

CORN. This is some fellow,
Who, having been prais'd for bluntness, doth affect

50 Ibid., 84.
51 Ibid., 67.
52 Ibid., 70.

> A saucy roughness, and constrains the garb
> Quite from his nature: he cannot flatter, he,
> An honest mind and plain, he must speak truth:
> And they will take it, so; if not, he's plain.[53]

It is this plain truth which (as in the morality plays) ends up in the stocks. It is the smooth-tongued rhetorician who carries the day.[54]

What we seem to have here is the demonization of the persuasive technology of affect. We recall that the rhetorical 'feigning' of the epistolary transaction, though sanctioned by Jerome (and Erasmus) nevertheless implies an 'insincerity' to which some commentators drew attention.[55] In this play, bastard sons and unnatural daughters conduct epistolary transactions which convince; plain folk and close kin are misled by letters, or betrayed by them.[56] The most striking contrast here is that between the intimate letters which are exchanged between Kent and Cordelia in private (through the trusted intermediary of the gentleman), and the mirroring exchanges of letters which bring about Gloucester's downfall. In the first scene of Act 3, Kent sends letters to the French camp; in the third scene, Gloucester tells Edmund he has received letters thence:

> GLOU. Go to; say you nothing. There is division between the Dukes, and a worse matter than that. I have receiv'd a letter this night; 'tis dangerous to be spoken; I have lock'd the letter in my closet.[57]

Challenged by Cornwall – 'Come, sir, what letters had you late from France?' – Gloucester tries to establish that these are familiar letters, not espionage:

53 Ibid., 74–5.

54 Lorna Hutson points out that in the earlier chronicle play, *King Leir* (registered in 1605) letters already structure the contest for authority here between Goneril and Lear. But in *King Leir* Goneril *intercepts* letters intended to warn Lear, and *substitutes* letters addressed to her sister 'which contayne matter quite contrary to the other: ther shall she be given to understand, that my father hath detracted her, given out slanderous speeches against her; and that hee hath most intollerably abused me, set my Lord and me at variance, and made mutinyes amongst the commons'. And she instructs the messenger to lay false oath if necessary, to ensure that her letters are accepted as true: 'These things (although it be not so) / Yet thou must affirme them to be true, / With othes and protestations as will serve' (Geoffrey Bullough, *Narrative and Dramatic Sources of Shakespeare* 7 (London, 1973), pp. 360–1). Here it is plotting by means of letters (instrumentally), rather than rhetorical effect through letters which secures the desired outcome.

55 Tony Grafton points out to me that Justus Lipsius stressed this misleading quality as potentially exploitable in familiar letters.

56 I owe this insight to Lorna Hutson.

57 Arden edn, 112.

GLOU. I have a letter guessingly set down,
Which came from one that's of a neutral heart,
And not from one oppos'd.[58]

But in the economy of this play, letters are written and received to incite mendaciously to action and to pervert the truth.[59]

The two most vital exchanges of letter for the plot, however, are of course those which involve the treachery and duplicity of Edmund. At the beginning of the play, it is the forged letter, supposedly from Edgar to his brother Edmund, which convinces Gloucester that his legitimate son is a traitor to him. In the final act, the intercepted letter from Goneril to Edmund, reminding him of their 'reciprocal vows', and inciting him to murder her husband, leads to the discovery of Edmund's general treachery. These are also the only two letters whose contents are discovered to us – both are banally instructive, without any kind of rhetorical embellishment. For Shakespeare's dramatic purposes, persuasive affect is located elsewhere. It is in the mouths of Regan and Goneril, contradicting their marriage vows in order to swear total love and duty to their father, and the mouth of Edmund, assuring his father of his trust at the moment he betrays him.

For the final section of this paper I want to argue that this is significant: that *Lear* severs affect from its epistolary setting where it could be controlled, and leaves it circulating at large – on the Heath. Affect, let loose from its civilized setting in the familiar letter, is demonized as the trigger for social disruption and disturbance.

CORD. Unhappy that I am, I cannot heave
My heart into my mouth: I love your Majesty
According to my bond; no more nor less.
LEAR How, how, Cordelia! Mend your speech a little,
Lest you may mar your fortunes.[60]

True blood kin, in *Lear*, are distinguished by their reluctance to commit their feelings of obligation and love to any contrived form of words. Cordelia loves 'according to [her] bond', but refuses to enhance that bond's immediate value by giving it rhetorical expression.

Neither Cordelia nor Edgar is prepared to manipulate expressions of feeling within the setting of court and household to match the complex

58 Ibid., 140–1.
59 The same letter is sent on from Cornwall to Albany at the beginning of Act 3, scene 7, as evidence that the French have landed (138).
60 Ibid., 9.

version of 'service', as technical command of language transactions, manifested by Regan, Goneril and Edmund.[61] These latter, unlike the 'natural kin', held in place by innate, unexpressed emotional bonds, are problematically placed in relation, in particular, to first-born sons. Rather than being held in place by locally specific bonds of emotional and economic dependency, they become threateningly mobile as a result of their capacity to 'study' to create affection and compel belief.[62]

Exchanges of letters in *Lear* seem to draw attention to their disturbing efficiency as instruments for effecting social mobility. Just those features of the familiar letter which Erasmus values for their ability to create intense feeling at will, to concoct *amicitia* and its associated binding emotional intensity are shown to be capable of loosening existing bonds of affection and creating new alliances where expedient. Letters transform old affections, persuade friends to new courses of action and, finally, make the reader of the printed text (the audience) morally complicit. With each alteration in the configuration of alliances in *Lear*, fresh letters redefine the bonds of affection amongst the remaining protagonists. The news of Cornwall's death, and the putting out of Gloucester's eyes, is brought to Goneril and Albany accompanied by urgent letters for Goneril from her sister:

> MESS. This letter, Madam, craves a speedy answer;
> 'Tis from your sister. [*Presents a letter.*]
> GON. ... I'll read, and answer.[63]

In Act 4, scene 5, Regan knows that there is some reorganization of the bonds of affection as soon as she hears that Oswald carries a letter from Goneril to Edmund:

> REG. Why should she write to Edmund? Might not you
> Transport her purposes by word? Belike,
> Some things – I know not what. I'll love thee much,
> Let me unseal the letter.[64]

[61] For a full version of this argument see Lorna Hutson, *The Usurer's Daughter* (London, 1994).

[62] At the very beginning of the play, when Kent is not known to Edmund, Gloucester instructs Edmund, 'remember him heareafter as my honourable friend': '*Edm.* My services to your Lordship. *Kent* I must love you, and sue to know you better. *Edm.* Sir, I shall study deserving. *Glou.* He hath been out nine years, and away he shall again' (4–5). In other words, Edmund has to build the bonds of kin and service with learnt knowledge of affect.

[63] Ibid., 159–60.

[64] Ibid., 7.

Her remedy is herself to send a note, by the same bearer, to Edmund, to persuade him to turn his affections towards her.

Which brings us, finally, to that almost intolerably powerful emotional effect which we as audience experience on the Heath with Lear, and on Dover cliffs with Gloucester and Edgar. For if the persuasive technology of familiar letters has been demonized in this play, where does that leave the true *amicitia* between friends and close kin, and its possibilities for expression?

Cordelia's consternation at the play's opening already answers the question:

> LEAR what can you say to draw
> A third more opulent than your sisters? Speak.
> CORD. Nothing, my lord.
> LEAR Nothing?
> CORD. Nothing.[65]

Equally unjustly accused of unfilial conduct, Gloucester's 'true' son Edgar also finds himself incapable of confecting the kind of plausible utterance which would restore him to his father's favour: '*Edg.* Edgar I nothing am.'[66] So strong is their resistance to 'feigned' sentiment of the kind so adeptly marshalled in the play's familiar letters, that each child is reduced to inarticulateness and verbal helplessness before the spectacle of their father's misfortune in the last two acts of the play. There is, within the play's ambit, no scope for 'true expression', to set against the sentimental contrivedness of Edmund and Oswald, Goneril and Regan.

For Erasmus, the beauty of the familiar letter lay in its structuring and controlling emotional transactions, so that their moral value was enhanced. In *Lear* such controlled expression of feeling is apparently not available – it has been banished from the scene, and replaced by a version of epistolary artifice which distorts and misleads because it is in the wrong hands (always a risk the rhetorician is aware of). In consequence, I suggest, the only emotional transactions to which true kin have access are uncontrolled and unstructured – are technically out of control. Cordelia cannot 'heave her heart into her mouth' to order, for her father, she can only pant out verbal ejaculations of distress to represent her true feelings:

65 Ibid., 9.
66 Ibid., 82.

GENT. Faith, once or twice she heav'd the name of 'father'
Pantingly forth, as if it press'd her heart.[67]

Throughout his companionship with Lear on the Heath, and his compassionate guiding of his blinded father, Edgar utters not one word of comfort or consolation to either. Instead he contributes a sense of surreal dislocation of speech and action, which produces an almost intolerably emotionally meaningless commentary on the events as they unfold.

Such emotional dyslexia is meant, I think, to be a terrifying prospect. Lear and his party on the Heath, and Gloucester and the disguised Edgar at Dover Cliffs, are offered as appalling manifestations of helplessly uncontrolled feeling, damagingly circulating without motive or purpose, its moral efficacy terribly out of focus. When unnatural sons and daughters have taken control of the technology of affect, for their own manipulative purposes, there is, it seems, no possibility of articulation left for the naturally caring members of the family. This is the play's catastrophe – its darkly nihilistic message, not its resolution.

Once we historicize the networks of feeling which form and reform the bonds of duty and friendship in *Lear,* around the persuasive technology of letter writing and reading, we are bound, I think, to recognize that the 'natural' and uncontained versions of passionate emotion in the play are not available as a solution to the problems raised by Lear's misconstruing his daughters' declarations of love. Raw emotion is not an attractive prospect for an audience which had placed its trust in Erasmus's promise that mastery of the familiar letter would enable humane individuals to persuade one another affectively to collaborate for a better, more Christian Europe. The spectacle of such 'civilized' technical skill working successfully on the side of deception and self-interest is disturbing and deeply pessimistic. Yet it is to precisely this vividly dramatized scenario that we, the modern audience, respond positively and intensely emotionally, because it is, of its essence, a representation of emotion unmediated by historicized social forms. The combination of horror and embarrassment with which we experience the spectacle of Edgar deluding the desperate Gloucester into casting himself down from a non-existent cliff owes nothing to Erasmus, or to humanist rhetoric, or to Renaissance philosophy. Like Gloucester and Edgar, we experience with immediacy that raw emotional intensity, in a moral, social and historical void.

67 Ibid., 162.

CHAPTER 6

The editor as reader: constructing Renaissance texts

John Kerrigan

The practice of editing literary texts was transformed, during the 1920s and '30s, by the innovative and assiduous researches of Alfred W. Pollard, R. B. McKerrow, and W. W. Greg. Between them, the New Bibliographers discovered a number of crucial facts about early modern printing, about the rules which governed 'copyright' before 1709, and about the textual status of such landmark volumes as the Shakespeare first Folio. They also formulated principles which continue to shape editorial thinking across a range of post-medieval periods. Greg's famous paper 'The Rationale of Copy-Text' (1950) is not, in fact, narrowly addressed to questions of authorship and authority, but, by encouraging editors confronted with variant texts to base their editions on sources as close as possible to authorial manuscript, Greg implied a model of literary production which became, in the work of his most gifted followers – Fredson Bowers and G. Thomas Tanselle – explicitly intentionalist.[1] For textual scholars in this tradition, it is the job of an editor to identify and strip out corruptions introduced by scribes and printers in order to recreate, as accurately as possible, the 'ideal' work intended by the author. Such an approach construes the literary text in quasi-Kantian terms, as an end in itself, free of historical contingency and the accidents of material circumstance. It also, and connectedly, pays little or no attention to the role of the reader.

Over the last twenty-five years, this approach has come under pressure. D. F. McKenzie's demonstration, in 1969, that the lucid

[1] W. W. Greg, 'The Rationale of Copy-Text', *Studies in Bibliography* 3 (1950): 19–36. See, repeatedly, Fredson Bowers, *Textual and Literary Criticism* (Cambridge, 1959), *Bibliography and Textual Criticism* (Oxford, 1964), *Essays in Bibliography, Text, and Editing* (Charlottesville, VA, 1975); G. Thomas Tanselle, 'The Editorial Problem of Final Authorial Intentions', *Studies in Bibliography* 29 (1976): 167–211, repr. in his *Selected Studies in Bibliography* (Charlottesville, VA, 1979), *Textual Criticism Since Greg: A Chronicle, 1950–1985* (Charlottesville, VA, 1987), *A Rationale of Textual Criticism* (Philadelphia, PA, 1989); and, for a discriminating overview, James McLaverty, 'The Concept of Authorial Intention in Textual Criticism', *The Library* 6th ser., 6 (1984): 121–37.

patterns of compositor behaviour posited by Bowers and his associates do not match the erratic work-schedules of actual seventeenth-century printers induced scepticism about bibliographical explanations based on the 'logic' of the printing process.[2] Editors noticed that Greg's views of authorship and copy-text were not easily reconciled with the collaborative features of those Renaissance play-scripts which most interested him.[3] More generally, changes in the discipline of literary criticism rendered intentionalism and formalism problematic. As Marxist and post-structuralist critics modified perceptions of authorship and textuality, and as reader-response and reception theory heightened awareness of the contribution made by audiences to literary meaning, the work of Bowers and Tanselle began to look like the bibliographical wing of the – increasingly discredited – New Criticism. Though a great deal of editing still takes place in the shadow of Greg, textual scholars are being tempted beyond formalism. D. F. McKenzie, for instance, has encouraged them to recognize what is lost when the literary work is construed as a self-contained object – a 'verbal icon' or '*well-wrought Urn*'[4] – and urged them to analyse such 'non-book texts' as maps, prints, music, electronic forms of data storage and film.[5] Meanwhile, Jerome J. McGann has pointed towards new ways of thinking about literature by maintaining, against Bowers and Tanselle, that textual criticism should not be cultivated for exclusively editorial ends but become part of an integrated programme of textual-historical enquiry.

McGann's work on the theory of editing first bore fruit in *A Critique of Modern Textual Criticism* (1983). This civilized polemic points up the drawbacks of an editorial practice which, wedded to false intentionalism and fixated on authorial manuscript, ignores the part played in the creation of literary artefacts by the process of publication. It urges textual critics to recover the breadth of historical and philological interest shown by the great German scholar-editors of the early nineteenth century. In *The Beauty of Inflections* (1985), McGann reconnects bibliography with historical scholarship and practical criticism, working through examples from Blake, Poe and others to demonstrate

2 D. F. McKenzie, 'Printers of the Mind: Some Notes on Bibliographical Theories and Printing-House Practices', *Studies in Bibliography* 22 (1969): 1–75.

3 See, most recently and trenchantly, T. H. Howard-Hill, 'Modern Textual Theories and the Editing of Plays', *The Library* 6th ser., 11 (1989): 89–115.

4 *Bibliography and the Sociology of Literary Texts*, The Panizzi Lectures 1985 (London, 1986), chapter 1, esp. pp. 16–17 (citing catch-phrases of the New Criticism, originally associated with W. K. Wimsatt Jr and Cleanth Brooks).

5 *Bibliography and the Sociology of Literary Texts*, chapters 2–3.

the importance of those determinants of literary meaning which lie in the circumstances of publication and reception, beyond authorial control – a claim furthered by the contextualizing commentary of his seven-volume edition, *Lord Byron: The Complete Poetical Works* (1980–93). Most recently, in *The Textual Condition* (1991), McGann has pushed his argument to extremes. On the one hand, he examines the part played by such apparently external agents as publishers, reviewers and audiences in creating the interactive 'human event' called literature, and, on the other, he shows how such inwardly bibliocentric minutiae as typeface, layout and paper quality should not be regarded as incidental features of what contains or transmits 'the authorial text' but as signifying components of the textual phenomena.

Together, McGann's books constitute the most influential contribution to editorial theory and practice since the birth of the New Bibliography. To examine them in the present context, however – in a collection of essays on reading – is to identify a grave deficiency. Given his belief that 'texts' become 'poems' only when they enter the public realm and interact with audiences,[6] McGann is damagingly indifferent to the synchronic variety and historical complexity of reading practices. It is understandable that, in the *Critique*, where he engages directly with the arguments of Bowers and Tanselle, he should replicate their neglect of the reader.[7] More troubling is the suppression of individual reading in *The Beauty of Inflections*. There is a Marxist-theoretical strain in this book which leads McGann to collectivize the literary audience. He is no more willing to privilege individual reading responses than he is to value biographical criticism of authors: both, by implication, involve a false social geography. As a result, when he finds Coleridge saying, of scripture, 'the conflicts of grace and infirmity in your own soul, will enable you to discern and to know in and by what spirit they [i.e. biblical figures] spake and acted, – as far at least as shall be needful for you, and in the times of your need', he turns a Protestant concern with personal grace and salvation into a historical materialist point about the reader being 'subject to time-specific cultural limitations'.[8] Similarly, when he quotes Tennyson's remark, 'Poetry is like shot-silk with many glancing colours. Every reader must find his own interpretation according to his ability, and according to his sympathy with the

6 *The Beauty of Inflections: Literary Investigations in Historical Method and Theory* (Oxford, 1985), pp. 114–15.

7 For undeveloped exceptions see *A Critique of Modern Textual Criticism* (Chicago, IL, 1983), pp. 48, 60.

8 *Beauty of Inflections*, p. 149.

poet', he glosses away the subjectivism with a faintly Stakhanovite (and certainly Bakhtinian) account of *The Princess*: 'Tennyson worked hard to fashion a poetic vehicle that was not merely designed to accom[m]odate different views and alternate readings, but that actively anticipated those differences – that (as it were) called out to them, and that offered Victorian readers a place where they would find their differences reconciled.'[9] For McGann, the contexts of poetry work together with the words on the page to 'enforce' reader-responses. This is the verb he uses when, discussing an Emily Dickinson lyric as it appears in two different editions and an anthology, he insists that the 'bibliographical environments . . . enforce very different reading experiences'.[10]

The same impulse to deny the agency of readers by finding their responses hard-wired into (and so 'anticipated' by) the literary work in its material setting remains apparent in *The Textual Condition*. Here, McGann invokes reader-centred theories of interpretation only to reject them. Reacting against the idealism which he finds in both Tanselle and the post-structuralist Paul de Man, he yokes these unlikely bed-fellows with the most dexterous of reader-response critics, Stanley Fish,[11] and sets them against his own position. There is no question of a McGann-accredited reader construing, say, an advertisement as a lyric poem. To do so would constitute a mistake, or an illicitly creative act. Nor, apparently, should we think of responses to the 'shot-silk' of poetry taking shape in pre-verbal fields of irridescent neurological activity; that would lead to talk of minds, and compromise materialism. 'Reading appears always and only as text', McGann insists, 'in one or another physically determinate and socially determined form. This is not to deny either the reality or the importance of silent and individual reading. It is merely to say that textuality cannot be understood except as a phenomenal event, and that reading itself can only be understood when it has assumed specific material constitutions.'[12] The ambiguities of this are inordinate. 'Physically determinate', for instance, lends 'socially determined' a hint of mere definition while leaving its late-Marxist determinism intact. And is it the case that what cannot be 'understood' cannot be 'understood' as having happened?

McGann's belief that literary texts are characterized by an ability to

9 Ibid., p. 178; cf. p. 180.
10 Ibid., p. 85.
11 See, e.g. Stanley Fish, *Is There a Text in This Class? The Authority of Interpretive Communities* (Cambridge, MA, 1980).
12 Jerome J. McGann, *The Textual Condition* (Chicago, IL, 1991), pp. 4–5.

'anticipate' or 'call out' different 'readings' allows him to short-circuit historical change when explaining the emergence of new meanings. His model of reading, that is, impoverishes his historicism. 'Every text', he asserts, 'has variants of itself screaming to get out, or antithetical texts waiting to make themselves known. Various readers and audiences are hidden in our texts, and the traces of their multiple presence are scripted at the most material levels'.[13] Behind the mystificatory notion of 'readers ... hidden in' texts lies an unwillingness to admit that, because of broadly based historical developments to which the 'variants ... or antithetical texts' of, say, *Clarissa* contribute remarkably little, eighteenth-century approaches to Richardson are quite different from nineteenth- or twentieth-century ones. In other words, McGann's neglect of the active individual reader is compatible with his residually formalistic views about the changing significance of particular texts. For as long as he is thinking about reading acts, his account of the evolution of literary meaning hardly looks beyond the 'readings' already coded into the text.

In this essay I want to show how unfortunate these limitations are, and to suggest that, by supplementing McGann's work, it might be possible to arrive at a more generously defined alternative to the weakened but still dominant mode of formalist-intentionalist editing. Because his literary interests are mostly nineteenth-century, McGann's thinking about textual criticism has concentrated on Romantic, Victorian and modernist poets. I want to inspect, by contrast, Renaissance texts, partly because the influence of Greg and Bowers remains particularly strong among editors working in that period, but also because early modern writers are revealingly explicit about the variety of responses which they expect from readers. The business of engaging with and managing such responses is so firmly built into their writing that it seems to me impossible to think about how to edit them without attending to 'the practice and representation of reading'.

In 1572–3 Henry Bynneman and his associates printed, for the publisher Richard Smith, an unusually interesting quarto. George Gascoigne's *Hundreth Sundrie Flowres* offers virtually a conspectus of Elizabethan literature. Starting with translations of Ariosto's comedy *I Suppositi* and (also through Italian) of Euripides' *Phoenician Women*, it includes an experimental novella entitled 'a pleasant discourse of the

[13] Ibid., p. 10.

aduentures of master F.I.', a gathering of lyrics, all composed by Gascoigne but presented as 'diuers excellent deuises of sundry Gentlemen', plus 'certayne deuises of master Gascoyne', before ending with a set of poems which record 'the dolorous discourse of Dan Bartholmew of Bathe'.[14] Within this heterogeneity, there is further local variety. Although 'the aduentures of master F.I.' is predominantly a prose work, it is organized around a series of lyrics supposedly penned by 'F.I.', while the section called 'diuers excellent deuises of sundry Gentlemen' resembles one of those manuscript or print miscellanies which were so popular during the sixteenth century. In themselves, these features are editorially unremarkable. But they are associated with bibliographical irregularities which heighten the impression of diversity: inconsistencies in typeface, end-of-text arrangements printed long before the end of the book and, most strikingly, a break in pagination, from 164 to 201, between the plays and the *Adventures*. It would seem unwise to edit Gascoigne without analysing these traits.

The still-standard *Complete Works*, however, edited by John W. Cunliffe in two volumes (1907–10), side-steps the problem by using as its copy-text a later version of the *Flowres* material, *The Posies* (1575). This book (also published by Richard Smith) is of great interest because it shows Gascoigne reordering and revising his work in response to criticisms of *A Hundreth Sundrie Flowres*, and confirming his authorship of the poems previously ascribed to 'sundry Gentlemen'. At many points, however, *The Posies* is unsatisfactory, because the text has been weakened by self-censorship. The poet's desperate search for patronage led him to alter his work[15] in ways which are of major significance in the history of its reception, but which, editorially, make a preference for the 1575 text over that of 1573 unacceptable. As a result, when C. T. Prouty came to edit Gascoigne in 1942, he used the 1573 edition as copy-text. Following classically post-Greg principles, he set out 'to provide a text of *A Hundreth Sundrie Flowres* which would represent as accurately as possible the author's final intention'.[16] Unfortunately the search for that elusive psychological commodity led Prouty into biographical speculations which were filled out by reading

[14] 'The contents of this Booke', A1^{v}.

[15] See, e.g. Richard C. McCoy, 'Gascoigne's "Poëmata castrata": The Wages of Courtly Success', *Criticism* 27 (1985): 29–55.

[16] *A Hundreth Sundrie Flowres*, University of Missouri Studies 17:2 (Columbia, MS, 1942), p. 221; cf. p. 17.

back from presumed confessions, boasts and riddles in the *Flowres* themselves, so that an historical romance about the author – fitfully documented in the 'Critical Notes'[17] – was produced to provide an intentionalist framework within which the edition could take shape.

The consequences of this approach are most alarming in respect of the plays. Confronted by the jump in pagination which follows them in 1573, Prouty decided – without documentary evidence – that Gascoigne had been driven abroad by financial and legal difficulties during the printing of the *Flowres* and that Bynneman had used the opportunity provided by his absence to include the commercially 'more attractive' play-texts. This explains, apparently, why the book was printed in two sections (though not why the second unit, which starts with 'the aduentures of master F.I.' should not be numbered from page 1). Prouty admits that 'It cannot be said with assurance that Gascoigne was unaware of the printer's intention to include the plays',[18] but the uncertainty does not hamper his editorial decisiveness. Swayed by a New Bibliographical prejudice against publication itself – as a process which contaminates and corrupts authorial intentions – Prouty resolved to right a possible wrong, and entirely excluded the plays.

An edition of *A Hundreth Sundrie Flowres* which cuts about forty per cent of *A Hundreth Sundrie Flowres* has to be problematic. As it happens, recent research by Adrian Weiss has shown that the irregularities in Bynneman's quarto were caused by the sharing of work with another printer (Henry Middleton), by the piecemeal provision of copy over a production period which lasted at least eight months, and (it may be) by the poet's failure to complete 'Dan Bartholmew of Bathe' to schedule – since, when the fifty-four stanzas added to that work in *The Posies* are included, it is the only text in the Gascoigne canon which runs to a length which would fill the gap between the plays and 'the aduentures of master F.I.'[19] The claim about 'Dan Bartholmew' is hard to prove, of course, because the poet might have withdrawn another, now lost text, rather than failed to deliver at the promised time one which was subsequently and incompletely added to the end of the *Flowres*. But it is

[17] For example, the comments on 'the aduentures of master F.I.', 57 (lines 26–30), 'deuises of sundry Gentlemen', nos. 8, 38. Prouty was unduly influenced by the rage for interpretation *à clef* which afflicted his unscholarly predecessor B. M. Ward. The latter's edition of the *Flowres* (London, 1926) has been updated and expanded by Ruth Loyd Miller (Port Washington, 1975) to illuminate the early career of that well-known author of Shakespeare's works, Edward de Vere, 17th Earl of Oxford.

[18] Ibid., p. 18.

[19] 'Shared Printing, Printer's Copy, and the Text(s) of Gascoigne's *A Hundreth Sundrie Flowres*', *Studies in Bibliography* 45 (1992): 71–104.

clear that, the more we learn about the process of publication in 1573, the more reflective of evolving authorial intentions, hopes and compromises the quarto appears. The result of such information, however, cannot be a more fully Gregian, or Bowersian, edition, because the principle of changing intent opens the text up to its reception and later history in *The Posies*. To edit Gascoigne in a way which is sensitive to the formation of the 1573 text, it is necessary to look far beyond 'the author's final intention'. This means, first, starting from the McGannish principle that we should reproduce the entirety of the text (including the plays) as it reached print, and, secondly, resolving that relations between the *Flowres* and *The Posies* should be foregrounded by the editor, because how the work was received is essential to its evolution, not just between 1573–5, but within the 1573 edition, given the spectrum of responses which Gascoigne – as I shall presently show – expected to meet when he published the *Flowres*.

The reception of the *Flowres* refutes the idea that 'readings' are lodged inside an Elizabethan text and 'called out' to those who peruse it, not least by showing that responses which go against the grain of the text (as we or the poet might see it) can be potent enough to disgrace the author. *The Posies* begins with no fewer than three addresses: 'To the reuerende Diuines', 'To al yong Gentlemen' and 'To the Readers generally'. All three concede that the *Flowres* has been criticized for immorality, but stress that an author cannot be held responsible for his readers' responses. Gascoigne does not collectivize his audience. After dividing divines from gallant gentlemen, he goes on, when addressing the latter, to discriminate 'curious Carpers, ignorant Readers, and graue Philosophers' (¶¶2^{v}). While the curiosity of the former makes them variously wayward, the folly of the ignorant renders them equally unpredictable. In every case, a text will be interpreted by different individuals according to their natures. 'As the industrious Bee may gather honie out of the most stinking weede, so the malicious Spider may also gather poyson out of the fayrest floure that growes' (¶¶3^{v}). His book resembles a garden, Gascoigne says, planted with flowers, herbs and weeds. Even weeds may be medicinable, and the author should not to be blamed 'if the Chirurgian which should seeke Sorrell to rypen an Vlcer, will take Rewe which may more inflame the Impostume'. In short, 'it is your using (my lustie Gallants) or misusing of these Posies that may make me praysed or dispraysed for publishing of the same' (¶¶3^{v}).

These claims would be familiar to Gascoigne's admirers not least because they recycle remarks made by 'The Printer to the Reader' in the *Flowres*. Bynneman (ostensibly) tells us that, 'as the venemous spider wil sucke poison out of the most holesome herbe, and the industrious Bee can gather hony out of the most stinking weede: Euen so the discrete reader may take a happie example by the most lasciuious histories'. In this book, we are assured, 'you shall not be constreined to smell of the floures therein conteined all at once ... But you may take any one flowre by itselfe, and if that smell not so pleasantly as you wold wish, I doubt not yet but you may find some other which may supplie the defects thereof' (A2^{v}). These assertions are highly conventional, based on commonplaces derived from Seneca and Horace. They may indeed be the work of Bynneman. But Gascoigne scholars generally agree that 'The Printer to the Reader' was scripted by the poet, extending the editorial role which he plays elsewhere through the figure of that 'G.T.' who (via the agency of one 'H.W.') conveys the story and writings of 'F.I.' to the reader, and through the 'reporter' who frames the tale of 'Dan Bartholmew'. Repeatedly, in the *Flowres*, the editorial presence of the author impinges, recommending responses but conceding that readers cannot be constrained. 'This is but a rough meeter', 'G.T.' will say (of the poem 'A cloud of care ...'), 'yet haue I seene much worse passe the musters'; 'This Ballade ... percase you will not like, and yet in my iudgement it hath great good store of deepe inuention ... leauing it to your and like iudgements'; and again, 'This Sonet treateth of a straung seede, but ... let it passe amongst the rest, & he that liketh it not, turn ouer the leaf to another, I dout not but in this register he may find some to content him, unlesse he be to curious'.[20]

Gascoigne is far from unique in his attempt to manage reader-responses editorially. To run down a scale from indubitably external commentary to authorial self-annotation, the same practice recurs in Antoine de Muret's glosses on Ronsard's *Amours* (1553), 'E.K.''s remarks on *The Shepheardes Calender* (1579), and Thomas Watson's notes to his *Hekatompathia* (1582). But Gascoigne's case is especially instructive because we know how actual readers responded to the author's prompting, not just from the addresses which preface *The Posies* but from remarks in George Puttenham's *Arte of English Poesie* (1589) and Gabriel Harvey's marginalia. The latter, for instance, glossed the tale

[20] D1^{v}, E3^{v}, G1^{r}. On G.T.'s limitations as a reader, and Gascoigne's manipulation of them, see George E. Rowe, Jr, 'Interpretation, Sixteenth-Century Readers, and George Gascoigne's "The Adventures of Master F.J."', *ELH* 48 (1981): 271–89, esp. pp. 278–9.

of 'F.I''s frustrated adulterous affair in *The Posies* with a remarkably pragmatic moral:

> The discouerie of his mistres, a false Diamant. His sicknes, & Jealosie did not help the matter, but did marre all. Woomen looue men: & care not for pore harts, that cannot bestead them. Especially at the returne of his riual, her Secretarie; it imported him to emprooue himself more, then before; & not to languish like a milksopp, or to play the pore snake vpon himself. Ladie Elinor woold haue liked the man that woold haue maintained his possession by force of armes, & with braue encounters beat his enimie owt of the feild.[21]

This is typical of Harvey's habit of annotating his books with *aide-mémoires* in summary form, and, in terms of application, of his emphasis on patterns of behaviour. He studied Gascoigne, as he studied Caesar and Livy, 'for action',[22] looking for strategies which would advance his own career in the courtly world inhabited by 'F.I.', but also seeking the means of such advancement by identifying exemplary instances of wise or fruitless conduct which could be retailed to those noblemen (such as Philip Sidney) who employed him as an intelligencer. Harvey's closing remarks about 'force of armes, & ... braue encounters' are particularly characteristic, since they point to a deep identification with the ideology of Leicester's war party. What *this* reader deduces from Gascoigne, somewhere down the line, is that firm and courageous dealing with Spain is the only way to success.

Puttenham, by contrast, is interested in verbal texture. He repeatedly quotes Gascoigne to show how rhetoric operates, and how epithets, periphrasis and alliteration can be abused.[23] But his style of 'close reading' differs from that of a twentieth-century formalist. He cites 'A cloud of care ...', for instance, to exemplify 'mixt' allegory, to show the kind of poem which 'discouers withall what the *cloud*, *storme*, *waue*, and the rest are, which in a full allegorie should not be discouered, but left at large to the readers iudgement and coniecture'.[24] This interest in what critics now call 'the reader's share' is symptomatic. Citing a Gascoigne poem which begins 'This tenth of March when *Aries* receyud, / Da[n] *Phœbus* rayes, into his horned head', Puttenham objects to the redundancy of expression and proposes an improvement:

21 G. C. Moore Smith (ed.), *Gabriel Harvey: Marginalia* (Stratford-upon-Avon, 1913), p. 167.

22 On Harvey's reading in the classics, see Jardine and Grafton, 'Studied For Action'. For a suggestive attempt to extend this analysis to prose fiction, see Lorna Hutson, 'Fortunate Travelers: Reading for the Plot in Sixteenth-Century England', *Representations* 41 (1993): 83–103.

23 Gladys Doidge Willcock and Alice Walker (eds.), *The Arte of English Poesie* (Cambridge, 1936), pp. 182, 212, 221, 236, 254, 255, 258–9.

24 Ibid., p. 188.

'The month and daie when Aries receiud, / Dan Phœbus raies into his horned head.' This is better, he says, because 'there remaineth for the Reader somewhat to studie and gesse vpon, and yet the spring time to the learned iudgement sufficiently expressed'.[25] Puttenham's mind then passes to Surrey's melancholy pastoral, 'In winters iust returne ...' Perhaps Gascoigne prompted the association, for in *The Posies*' address 'To al yong Gentlemen' the poet cites as an example of 'ignorant' reading those whose literalism is such that they interpret Surrey's 'pleasant dittie' of rustic life as 'made indeed by a Shepeherd' (¶¶3^r). Puttenham's remarks are less robust; they make an early contribution to the subtleties of reader-response theory. Quoting Surrey's opening lines – 'In winters iust returne, when Boreas gan his raigne, / And euery tree vnclothed him fast as nature taught them plaine' – he worries at the problem of imputing a sense to 'winters iust returne' which is more than circumlocutionary. Once taken as 'the time which we call the fall of the leafe' (rather than a roundabout way of saying 'winter'), the phrase becomes apt and poignant. If the reader finds this meaning in the text, Puttenham says, he 'may ... iudge as I do, that this noble Erle wrate excellently well and to purpose'.[26]

Gascoigne was peculiarly alert to the mixed nature of his audience, and to the danger of encountering spiders. But an awareness of reader diversity was widespread among his contemporaries, almost a condition of authorship in the expanding market for print. In the addresses 'To the Reader' printed with early modern literary texts there is a recurrent stress on division. Authors set 'fond curious, or rather currish back-biters' against 'courteous Readers', separate the 'captious' from the 'vertuous', the 'Pretender' from the 'Vnderstander'.[27] They castigate 'scornefull and carpynge Correctours' and 'trust the indifferent Reader'.[28] Sometimes the division is by gender. Lyly, for instance, starts *Euphues and His England* (1580) with epistles 'To the Ladies and Gentlewomen of England' and 'To the Gentlemen Readers'. The former are invited to sport with the novel in between playing with their lapdogs, to nibble at it 'as you doe your Iunckets, that when you can

25 Ibid., p. 194.
26 Ibid., pp. 194–5.
27 Robert Greene, *Pandosto: The Triumph of Time* (1588), A1^v; Thomas Lodge, *Prosopopeia: Containing the Teares of the Holy, Blessed, and Sanctified Marie, the Mother of God* (1596), A6^v; Ben Jonson, *The Alchemist* (1612), A3^r.
28 Barnabe Googe, *Eglogs, Epytaphes, and Sonettes* (1563), A5^v; William Painter, *The Palace of Pleasure* (1566), ¶¶¶1^v.

eate no more, you tye some in your napkin for children' (¶1^{v}). Their reading experiences will evidently be quite unlike those of the gentlemen. For though the latter are, like the women, welcomed to variety, being invited (as though by Gascoigne) 'into a Gardeine, some [to] gather Nettles, some Roses, one Tyme, an other Sage', they are expected to show a more commanding involvement with the text: 'Faultes escaped in the Printing, correcte with your pennes: omitted by my neglygence, ouerslippe with patience: committed by ignoraunce, remit with fauour' (¶3^{v}).

When authors discuss their audiences at length they tend to distinguish ever more groups and sub-categories, approaching the atomism remarked by Robert Greene: 'no book so yll but some will both reade it and praise it; & none againe so curious, but some wil carpe at it. Wel, so many heades, so many wittes'.[29] Thomas Dekker, for instance, observes:

> He that writes, had need to haue the Art of a skilfull Cooke; for there must be those *Condimenta* (seasonings) in his pen, which the other caries on his tongue: A thousand palats must bee pleased with a thousand sawces: and one hundred lines must content fiue hundred dispositions. A hard taske: one sayes, it is too harsh[:] another, too supple: another too triuiall: another too serious.[30]

It does not diminish the force of Dekker's complaint that it elaborates a commonplace. When Burton, for example, uses the same topoi as Greene and Dekker to characterize the audience of *The Anatomy of Melancholy*, his dependence on classical authority does not make his account of the mixed nature of his readership any the less solidly compatible with his ruling perception, in the *Anatomy* as a whole, of the quirkiness of mankind. 'To say truth with *Erasmus*', he writes,

> *nihil morosius hominum iudiciis*, theirs naught so peeuish as mens iudgements, yet this is some comfort, *vt palata, sic iudicia*, our censures are as various as our Palats.
>
> *Tres mihi conuiuæ prope dissentire videntur*
> *Porcentes vario multum diversa palato, &c.* [Hor.]
>
> Our writings are as so many Dishes, our Readers Guests; our Bookes like beautie, that which one admires another reiects; so are wee approued as mens fancies are inclined.
>
> *Pro captu lectoribus habent sua fata libelli,*
>
> That which is most pleasing to one is *amaracum sui*, most harsh to another. *Quot*

29 *Mamillia: A Mirrovr or Looking-Glasse for the Ladies of England* (1583), A3^{r}.
30 *A Strange Horse Race* (1613), A3^{r}.

homines, tot sententiae, so many men, so many minds: that which thou condemnest he commends.[31]

Though Renaissance authors knew that readers' responses could be as various as the readers themselves, they were wary of abandoning their works to misconstruction. That could lead to imprisonment, or worse. It was partly for temperamental and aesthetic reasons that Ben Jonson sought to constrain readers by deploying prefaces, marginal annotation and author-critic figures in his works;[32] but in the case of *Sejanus*, an apparatus was introduced (in quarto) to refute those ingenious readers – 'those common Torturers, that bring all wit to the Rack' – whose detection of treason in the tragedy was responsible for having its author investigated by the Privy Council.[33] Thomas Nashe could joke about contemporaries who read political allusions into everything: 'Let one but name bread, they will interpret it to be the town of Bredan in the low countreyes; if of beere he talkes, then straight he mocks the Countie Beroune in France.'[34] Others had to worry, though, when reader-responses created a scandal. In *A Free and Offenceles Ivstification, of Andromeda Liberata* (1614), George Chapman protests that, in choosing such an ancient subject for his poem, he had thought himself beyond allusive reading, and 'presum'd, that the application being free, I might *pro meo iure* dispose it (innocen[t]ly) to mine owne obiect: if at least, in mine owne wrighting, I might be reasonablie & conscionablie master of mine owne meaning' (*3^{r}). If a troublesome meaning is brought to the text by a reader, what blame should the author bear? 'Doth any Law therfore cast that meaning vpon me?' Chapman asked, 'Or doth any rule of reason make it good, that let the writer meane what he list, his writing notwithstanding must be construed *in mentem Legentis*? to the intendment of the Reader?' (*4^{r}). It is a question which modern reader-response theory is no closer to resolving.

These notes of dissent are significant, but the general view, fostered by such sources as Plutarch's 'How a yoong man ought to heare poets, and how he may take profit by reading poemes',[35] was that the reader

31 *Anatomy of Melancholy*, 4th edn (1632), B1^{r}.

32 See, e.g., Timothy J. Murray, *Theatrical Legitimation: Allegories of Genius in Seventeenth-Century England and France* (Oxford, 1987), chs. 3 and 4, Joseph Loewenstein, 'Printing and "The Multitudinous Presse": The Contentious Texts of Jonson's Masques', in Jennifer Brady and W. H. Herendeen (eds.), *Ben Jonson's 1616 Folio* (Cranbury, NJ, 1991), pp. 168–91.

33 ¶2^{v}; cf. *Volpone* (1607), ¶2^{v}. On the editorial implications, see John Jowett, '"Fall before this Booke": The 1605 Quarto of *Sejanus*', *TEXT* 4 (1988): 279–95.

34 *Christs Teares ouer Ierusalem*, reissue with new prelims. (1594), **1^{v}.

35 *The Philosophie, Commonlie Called, The Morals*, tr. Philemon Holland (1603), pp. 17–50.

should be allowed considerable latitude in pursuit of the traditional goal of extracting moral benefit from even unpromising texts. Marion Trousdale has written well about Erasmus's skill in moralizing the death of Socrates, drawing from the tale a whole series of mutually incompatible but equally valid axioms. For Erasmus and his followers, the meaning of a fable was neither singular nor defined by the narrative but produced (ultimately from a common store of wisdom) by the reader.[36] This attitude was the more tenaciously held because supported by ancient testimony. Summarizing the message of Plutarch's essay, John Wallace writes:

> The reader's profit lay in his powers of discrimination, so that at all times he knew whether to feel raised by the sentiments he encountered or to inoculate himself against their dire effects. Immunity could be obtained by studying the implicit commentary within a work on the bad deeds and characters, by remembering better statements made elsewhere by the author, by paying careful attention to etymological niceties, and so on. If a passage remained impervious to a favorable (i.e., a moral) construction, then it was advisable to tamper with the text or to recall good moral dicta from quite different sources.[37]

These obligations and liberties were widely recognized by early modern writers. The objects of a reader's enquiry were general: truths accessible (and for the most part already familiar) to all. But the means of extracting them were particular, indeed personal. Wallace is right to conclude that, for Renaissance commentators, 'once the explicatory process had begun, then the reader was involved for his own good, and it was immaterial (or only occasionally material) whether one reader's interpretations were the same as another's, or identical with the author's aims.[38]

We should not be surprised, then, to find a poet like Giles Fletcher the Elder refusing to determine for 'the Reader' what the mistress of his sonnet sequence, *Licia* (1593), stands for: 'it may be shee is Learnings image, or some heavenlie woonder ... it may bee some Colledge; it may bee my conceit, and portende nothing: whatsoever it be, if thou like it, take it' (B1^r). Such interpretative generosity was commonplace. Occasionally, it is true, reader-responses are envisaged which seem

36 'A Possible Renaissance View of Form', *ELH* 40 (1973): 179–204; cf. John Wallace, '"Examples are Best Precepts": Readers and Meanings in Seventeenth-Century Poetry', *Critical Inquiry* 1 (1974): 273–90, p. 284.

37 'Examples are Best Precepts', p. 277.

38 Ibid., p. 275.

closer to the phenomenology of Georges Poulet[39] than the discrimination urged by Plutarch. The Beaumont and Fletcher Folio, for instance, begins with the claim: 'You may here find passions raised to that excellent pitch and by such insinuating degrees that you shall not chuse but consent, & go along with them, finding your self at last grown insensibly the very same person you read, and then stand admiring the subtile Trackes of your engagement.'[40] But this degree of self-loss was rarely proposed. Where identification with the 'person you read' was regularly encouraged, in devotional literature, the aim was to improve, by double involvement, the reader's reading of himself. In this respect, Bunyan's prefatory verses to *Pilgrim's Progress* are orthodox:

> Wouldst read thy self, and read thou know'st not what
> And yet know whether thou art blest or not,
> By reading the same lines? O then come hither,
> And lay my Book, thy head, and heart, together.[41]

The puritan writer joins hands here with the secular strain of reading-theory which descends from Plutarch. Bunyan would have understood McGann's notion of 'readings' being 'called out' to readers, but his own model was more individualized. In his early modern way, he is describing 'the reader's share', a share which, as he interprets human nature, could only ever be particular to that one reader's grace and salvation.

Where does this leave editing? We can return to the issues which began this essay by pondering Plutarch's advice about amending unacceptable text, and Lyly's request that 'Gentlemen Readers' correct 'Faultes escaped in the Printing' while exercising patience and judgement. In both cases the reader has an incipient editorial function – one which, elsewhere, becomes explicit. When Thomas Lodge, for example, introduces 'the Reader' to the 1620 edition of his *Workes of Seneca* ($b1^{r-v}$), he promises – conventionally enough – 'a Garden, wherein ... thou maiest find many holesome Herbes, goodly Flowers, and rich Medicines'. He then adds, however:

> yet can it not be but some weedes may ranckly shoote out, which may smoother or obscure the light and lustre of the better. Play the good Gardner

39 See, e.g., his 'Criticism and the Experience of Interiority', in Richard A. Macksey and Eugenio Donato (eds.), *The Structuralist Controversy: The Language of Criticism and the Sciences of Man* (Baltimore, MD, 1972), pp. 56–72.

40 *Comedies and Tragedies Written by Francis Beaumont and John Fletcher* (1647), $A3^{v}$.

41 *The Pilgrim's Progress from This World to That Which is to Come*, 2nd edn (1678), $A6^{r}$.

I pray thee, and pulling vp the weedes, make thy profit of the flowers. If thou wilt Correct, bee considerate before thou attempt, lest in pretending to roote out one, thou commit many errors.

The editing reader should be prudent, lest he multiply error. But the text is his to use, to modify and select from. 'What a Stoicke hath written', Lodge advises, 'Reade thou like a Christian.' If the reader doubts a passage, he should 'haue recourse to the sacred Synod of learned and pious Diuines; whose iudgement will select thee out that which is for thy Soules profit'. When Lodge encourages his reader 'to Correct with thy pen, that which other men lesse aduised, haue omitted by ouer hastie labour', textual emendation is only one aspect of an enterprise in which reading and editing go together. Such promptings are ubiquitous. Nathaniel Whiting, for instance, asks his readers,

> ... where the faultes but whisper, use thy pen
> With the *quod non vis* of the Heathen men.
> And if the crimes doe in loud Ecchoes speake
> Thy sponge ...[42]

The task of correcting faults involves more than the removal of printer's errors: it implies expunging authorial infelicities, extirpating chunks of text. It is a short step from this to, say, Father Sankey, in the mid-seventeenth century, going through a Shakespeare folio and deleting unacceptable passages.[43] What looks to us like a monstrous assault on the integrity of a master-text belongs to a set of practices which would have been recognized in the period as normal.

An unfamiliar nexus of relations between writing, reading and editing begins to come into view. It constitutes a field of textual activity very different from that which took shape in the long century (from Coleridge to Pound) which most interests Jerome McGann. Instead of an author producing a text, inflected by publication, which 'calls out' responses to readers, we have materials rendered 'profitable' by the editorial reading-interventions of writers (e.g. Phineas Fletcher's notes to *The Purple Island*), their annotators (e.g. Selden's commentary on Drayton's *Poly-Olbion*), their printers (e.g. the marginal summaries added by Thomas Snodham to *The Rape of Lucrece*), and, of course, individual readers. The reader might take up his pen in response to nothing more exciting than a list of 'Faultes escaped' – the Renaissance

42 *Le hore di recreatione: Or, The Pleasant History of Albino and Bellama* (1637), A4^v.
43 For an account of his expurgations see Roland Mushat Frye, *Shakespeare and Christian Doctrine* (Princeton, NJ, 1963), pp. 275–93.

equivalent of an errata slip – but one kind of emendation quickly ran into others. Harvey's correction of typographical errors is not readily separable from his inspection of what is being corrected, his glossing it with marginal comments, his production of 'readings' for action.[44] And if commentary is generated by correction, rewriting follows from both. Drayton was right (at least in spirit) when he assured those readers who amended the printer's errors in their copies of *The Muses Elizium* (1630) that 'the Muses themselues ... shall in their thankefulnesse inspire thee with some Poeticke rapture' (A4^r). The level of textual variation in seventeenth-century manuscripts is too high for us not to conclude that what was transcribed was often corrected in the sense of 'improved'. Suckling's 'A Supplement of an imperfect Copy of Verses of Mr. Will. Shakespears, By the Author' provides just one instance of rewriting growing out of editorial activity by a reader. The poem begins with some (reworked) verses from *Lucrece* before rising to the chance provided, at least fictively, by a torn leaf in the poet's copy to attempt Shakespearean pastiche. What Suckling creates is of a piece with what went on when less talented sixteenth- and seventeenth-century gentlemen transcribed verses into commonplace books and miscellanies[45] and rewrote them in the process, transforming other men's flowers through their interests and aptitudes as readers.

Though Suckling's 'Supplement' looks odd to modern eyes, it is highly indicative. The very fact that its opening might derive not from a contemporary edition of *Lucrece* but from a corrupted or 'corrected' slice of the poem printed in the miscellany *Englands Parnassus* (1600)[46] is a reminder of how user-inflected the reception of Shakespeare's poetry was. Recent work on the *Sonnets* has shown that the adaptation of text was widespread once verses got into manuscript. John Benson's repackaging of most of the sonnets, to resemble Cavalier-poet epistles, in his *Poems: Written by Wil. Shake-speare* (1640), looks less perverse when

44 For a short guide to books corrected and annotated by Harvey, see Virginia Stern, *Gabriel Harvey: A Study of his Life, Marginalia and Library* (Oxford, 1979), pp. 198–241.

45 The study of commonplace books has hardly begun, but see Hilton Kelliher, 'Contemporary Manuscript Extracts from Shakespeare's *Henry IV, Part I*', *English Manuscript Studies 1100–1700* 1 (1989): 144–81, 'Unrecorded Extracts from Shakespeare, Sidney and Dyer', *English Manuscript Studies 1100–1700* 2 (1990): 163–87; and Peter Beal, 'Notions in Garrison: The Seventeenth-Century Commonplace Book', in W. Speed Hill (ed.), *New Ways of Looking at Old Texts: Papers of the Renaissance English Text Society, 1985–1991* (Binghamton, NY, 1993), pp. 131–47. On miscellanies and transcription see, e.g. Mary Hobbs, *Early Seventeenth-Century Verse Miscellany Manuscripts* (Aldershot, 1992) and Arthur F. Marotti, 'Malleable and Fixed Texts: Manuscript and Printed Miscellanies and the Transmission of Lyric Poetry in the English Renaissance', in Hill (ed.), *New Ways of Looking at Old Texts*, pp. 159–73.

46 Thomas Clayton (ed.), *Sir John Suckling: The Non-Dramatic Works* (Oxford, 1971), p. 228.

we find Sonnet 106, for instance – apparently addressed to a 'lovely youth' in the 1609 quarto – appearing in one manuscript entitled 'On his Mistris Beauty',[47] and, in another, 'conflated with the text of a lyric that is found also, in slightly different form, in the 1660 poetical anthology pretending to be an edition of the poems of Pembroke and Rudyerd'.[48] One reason why modern editors cannot provide a stable text of the *Sonnets* is that Shakespeare, it seems, revised them. But how far do the variants found in manuscript, or in *The Passionate Pilgrime* (1599), derive from editorial rewriting by readers? We can never be sure. Manuscript texts of Sonnet 2 club together closely enough for their divergence from the 1609 quarto to suggest that traces of two 'authorial' versions survive.[49] But to think of only two forms of the sonnet is to diminish the significance of, for instance, the text in Cambridge, St John's College, MS s.23, which transcribes (for the most part) the quarto wording of Sonnet 2 but transposes its meanings by transferring it to another medium (script not print), by placing it between poems by Ben Jonson and Thomas Carew (rather than between Sonnets 1 and 3), and by employing a pattern of punctuation which – varied from the quarto – amounts to a 'reading' recorded by the slow-motion of transcription.

All this should make us more aware of the reader in the modern editor. A textual scholar who corrects, amends and (in his or her own eyes) 'improves' the 1609 version of the *Sonnets* is doing what Shakespeare's contemporaries did: producing a more or less personalized, or personally adaptable, text, out of already mediated textual evidences, not simply 'getting the text right'. Every practising editor is familiar with the experience of drafting commentary – that is, producing readings – as a way of explaining the text to him or herself, and then reconstructing the exploration by putting together annotation which provides what other readers might need to reach related ends more swiftly. It is through that process of individual but self-consciously communicative reading that corruptions are identified and textual emendations proposed, not (and certainly not primarily) from thoughts

47 On this text (in a *c.* 1630s miscellany from Saffron Walden) and other sonnet versions in manuscript, see Peter Beal, comp., *Index of English Literary Manuscripts*, vol. I (1450–1625), (London, 1980), pt 2, pp. 449–63.

48 Arthur F. Marotti, 'Shakespeare's Sonnets as Literary Property', in Elizabeth D. Harvey and Katharine Eisaman Maus (eds.), *Soliciting Interpretation: Literary Theory and Seventeenth-Century English Poetry* (Chicago, IL, 1990), pp. 143–73 (p. 149).

49 Cf. Gary Taylor, 'Some Manuscripts of Shakespeare's Sonnets', *Bulletin of the John Rylands Library* 68 (1985–6): 210–46.

about the print-shop, or the physical oddness of a word on a page. Editions of the *Sonnets* differ because they are produced by particular readers, with different thoughts about other readers. This obvious point is repressed in editorial theory, dominated as it is by the legacy of New Bibliography, while McGann and his followers, striving to collectivize audiences and to present 'readings' as functions of the text, have done little to redress the balance.

This is not the place in which to explore the consequences of this suppression of the reader. Nor is there room to do more than gesture towards what would follow if editors took reading more seriously. One current reaction to methodological distress, represented by Randall McLeod's advocacy of un- or anti-editing, can, though, be bracketed off. Random Cloud or Clod (as he calls himself) has produced some erudite and stimulating pieces of bibliographical description,[50] but the texts which would trickle down to readers from editors following his principles could only be more or less in facsimile, with all the problems of accessibility which that entails, and with the questions which it begs about the 'already mediated' yet historically deracinating claims of photographic reproduction. Moreover, Randomness has the paradoxical effect of fixing in textual concrete that which it regards as contingent; it fetishizes what a Gregian would regard as incidental by insufficiently respecting the relational qualities of editions. To promote facsimile, in other words, is to Cloud the scene by neglecting the ultimate lack of historical privilege which attaches to a text's being early, or first, or simply in a particular place, in the chronological run of a 'work''s printings, and, not unrelatedly, it is to underestimate the extent to which the uniqueness of a given edition (what makes it part of an unrepeatable, yet variably renewable, literary phenomenon) is a function of reading practices. There is, of course, no way in which a facsimile text can remain faithful to the dispositions of its source while reordering its material to convey to a modern reader how it struck contemporaries. Yet, as should be apparent by now, Renaissance books have the traits which they possess not simply because of authorial or print-shop peculiarities, but because they have certain designs upon, or hopes of interacting with, readers. McLeod's bibliocentrism discounts the extent to which the

[50] McLeod's more editorially directed work has mostly related to Shakespeare. See, e.g. Randall McLeod, 'Unemending Shakespeare's Sonnet 111', *Studies in English Literature* 21 (1981): 75–96, 'UNEditing Shakespeare', *Sub-stance* 33/4 (1982): 26–55, and Random Cloud, 'The Marriage of Good and Bad Quartos', *Shakespeare Quarterly* 33 (1982): 421–31.

characteristics of, say, Harington's Ariosto, need to be referred to the kinds of reader whom the translator had in mind – considerations which led him, to the confusion (at times) of the printer, to enrich his pages with guides to responses.[51]

Another, more practical reaction to the breakdown of Gregian approaches, and the difficulties which inhere in McGann's work, might have us move towards modernized editions. Given that past reading-styles can be hard to recover, never mind inhabit, would not more be gained than lost by concentrating on the responses of the present generation of Shakespeare's 'great Variety of Readers', instead of seeking to reconstitute editorially the reading habits of those who bought his *Workes* in 1623?[52] Unfortunately, modernizing is no solution, because so many determinants of the meaning of a text – and thus of its likely textual readings – are timebound that it is impossible to separate the editorial (and any other adequate) reading process from the composition and reception of the text in its historical moment. The scale of the difficulties involved can be gauged by the results. When Stephen Orgel, for instance, is led by the conventions of the Yale Ben Jonson to squeeze the poet's commentary out of the margins of his masques, so that the layout of his 1969 edition can be modernized to match the modernization of his spelling, the result is a massive erasure of attempts to inform and direct reader-responses which are so characteristic of the poet that, without them on the page before us, we are simply not reading Jonson.

A more appealing prospect is offered by the hope of mediating between Renaissance and modern reading experiences. As it happens, this is what Stephen Booth attempted in his valuable edition of *Shakespeare's Sonnets* (1977). Using facing pages, he set a facsimile version of the 1609 quarto opposite a semi-modernized text which compromised between 'the punctuation and spelling of the Quarto text ... and modern directive spelling and punctuation (which often

51 Representatively lively observations by McLeod, taking in Harington's Ariosto (1591), can be found in, e.g. Random Clod, 'Information on Information', *TEXT* 5 (1991): 241–81. On the translator's plans for the book, and its readers, see Simon Cauchi, 'The "Setting Foorth" of Harington's Ariosto', *Studies in Bibliography* 36 (1983): 137–68, esp. pp. 143–5, Judith Lee, 'The English Ariosto: The Elizabethan Poet and the Marvelous', *Studies in Philology* 80 (1983), 277–99, and Evelyn B. Tribble, *Margins and Marginality: The Printed Page in Early Modern England* (Charlottesville, VA, 1993), esp. pp. 92, 95.

52 John Heminge and Henry Condell address this 'great Variety' in the first Folio: 'From the most able, to him that can but spell: There you are numberd' (A3^r^).

pays for its clarity by sacrificing a considerable amount of a poem's substance and energy)'.[53] Punctuation is a particularly important and, until recently,[54] under-examined system of cues and interpretative options which helps individuals produce distinctive readings, and there is no doubt that the tactful lightness of Booth's pointing does free his readers from the constraints which tend to be imposed by modernizing editors. But his commentary damages his attempt to 'give a modern reader as much as I can resurrect of a Renaissance reader's experience of the 1609 quarto',[55] because its polysemic perversity implies that early modern readers, so far from studying for action, or admiring rhetorical schemes, or seeking moral axioms, were post-structuralists eager to find more ambiguities in the text than could be sustained in any conceivable response. Predictably, Booth neglected the manuscript tradition of the *Sonnets*, despite the listing, collating and printing of texts from miscellanies by such editors as Tucker Brooke (1936) and H. E. Rollins (1944). The diluted historicism of his semi-modernizing policy is bound up with a late-formalist attitude to the text which, when translated into attitudes to reading, would have considerable difficulty in registering the deflection of the reading-experience created by the expectations which Shakespeare's contemporaries carried to poems recorded in script as well as print,[56] and thus to print in a context of script.

Perhaps the best hope for scholarship lies in critical old-spelling editions produced not along Gregian lines but by developing McGann's method of editing in order to bring out the formative role of individual reading acts in the creation of historically specific meanings. The editor of a post-Romantic author, persuaded of the value of such a venture, might be over-provided with the testimony of readers and have to codify rules of relevance. For those working in earlier periods, the problem would more often be that of deciding how to maximize scarce information. A good edition of Gascoigne, for example, would include, in *A Hundreth Sundrie Flowres*, the plays cast out by Prouty as well as the poems and prose. It would give a full, preferably on-the-page representation of the 1575 changes, and link Gascoigne's revisions to reader-responses by pointing up the significance of *The Posies*' three

53 *Shakespeare's Sonnets* (New Haven, CT, 1977), p. ix.

54 See, now, Lennard, *But I Digress*, Parkes, *Pause and Effect*.

55 *Shakespeare's Sonnets*, p. ix.

56 For a stimulating attempt to characterize such differences in reader assumptions, see Love, *Scribal Publication*, esp. ch. 4; cf. D. F. McKenzie, 'Speech-Manuscript-Print', *The Library Chronicle of the University of Texas at Austin* 20 (1990): 87–109.

addresses. Recognizing the importance of manuscript circulation, not just as a source of variants but as a means of audience division and enabler of varying responses in individual readers with access to the same texts in both script and print, the edition would notice manuscript recensions of Gascoigne's poems and prose[57] with the same scrupulousness as the 1575 reworkings. The reactions of Puttenham and Harvey would be woven into the commentary, but also be foregrounded in an introduction. Their reading techniques would be compared with those of other Elizabethans, and attention would be paid to Puttenham's apparent tendency to engage in Sucklingesque editing/rewriting while producing his readings of Gascoigne – not just when announcing improvements but when quoting, as it were, direct.[58] The editor would have to think hard about 'G.T.''s remarks on 'F.I.''s lyrics, and about the curtailment of that editor-in-the-text's observations in *The Posies*, while pondering the role of the marginalia added in the later book. What meanings do these devices facilitate? How did Gascoigne's readers relate text and gloss?[59] To annotate a literary work always requires historical tact – an awareness of what early readers would *not* have understood, as well as what they would.[60] Where modern annotation has to mesh with Renaissance glosses, these difficulties are compounded, both by the need to establish appropriate hierarchies of commentary and by the theoretical and practical problems contingent on deciding where and how to indicate what is obscure, misleading or false in notes contemporaneous with the text.

The researches involved in preparing such an edition would be at least as contextual as those associated with McGann's seven-volume *Byron*, for they would add to his attention to socio-historical circumstance and the publishing history of works a wide-ranging analysis of Elizabethan attitudes to manuscript, editorial role-playing by writers,

57 The sources range from poems in unremarkable miscellanies to presentation texts given to Queen Elizabeth (references to her in gilt, pen and ink drawings of Gascoigne handing over his book, &c.). See Beal, *Index of English Literary Manuscripts*, I.ii, pp. 99–100.

58 The first six lines of 'A cloud of care . . .' , for instance, are given in a form both elegantly accomplished and markedly variant from *Flowres* and *The Posies* (see *Arte*, p. 188). Manuscript influence is possible, even though Puttenham's quotations generally appear close to the 1575 edition.

59 For relevant observations see William W. E. Slights, 'The Edifying Margins of Renaissance English Books', *Renaissance Quarterly* 42 (1989): 682–716, '"Marginall Notes That Spoile the Text": Scriptural Annotation in the English Renaissance', *Huntington Library Quarterly* 55 (1992): 255–78, and Tribble, *Margins and Marginality*, pp. 68–70.

60 Cf. Ian Small, 'The Editor as Annotator as Ideal Reader', in Ian Small and Marcus Walsh (eds.), *The Theory and Practice of Text-Editing: Essays in Honour of James T. Boulton* (Cambridge, 1991), pp. 186–209.

and the function of marginal notes. This would mean (life being short) that the editor would need to draw on the not-yet-existing body of 'Historical Reader-Response Criticism' which Robert D. Hume has called for in another context.[61] But then, so integrally connected are editorial constructions and reader-responses that criticism of that sort will not be produced until textual scholars apply their skills to assessing those features of early books which manage readers' reactions. For the sake of their editing, certainly, but also to help complete what McGann has called 'a finished programme of historicist textual criticism',[62] editors should start thinking harder about 'the practice and representation of reading'.

61 'Texts within Contexts', pp. 80ff.
62 *Beauty of Inflections*, p. 82.

CHAPTER 7

Popular verses and their readership in the early seventeenth century

Adam Fox

Reconstructing the reading practices of men and women at the lower levels of early modern English society is an enterprise frustrated by lack of evidence and problems of method. Recent scholarship has suggested the likely existence of a significant popular readership in England from at least the sixteenth century. Both quantitative calculations based upon signatures and qualitative testimony derived from anecdotal sources indicate that some degree of literacy was not uncommon relatively far down the social order by this time.[1] Moreover, analyses of extant specimens of cheap printed material from the period have demonstrated the diverse and expanding range of ephemeral literature available for just a few pence.[2] Despite the likelihood of a quite widely dispersed ability and opportunity to read, however, direct examples of the humble reader in action remain scattered and occasional. Few references exist to anyone in the process of actually enjoying a broadside ballad or a pamphlet, an almanac or a newsbook, and there is little opportunity to gauge the responses which such texts may have evoked.[3]

This essay seeks to capture people from the lower and middling

1 Schofield, 'The Measurement of Literacy', in Goody (ed.), *Literacy*; David Cressy, *Literacy and the Social Order: Reading and Writing in Tudor and Stuart England* (Cambridge, 1980); R. A. Houston, *Scottish Literacy and the Scottish Identity: Illiteracy and Society in Scotland and Northern England, 1600–1800* (Cambridge, 1985); T. W. Laqueur, 'The Cultural Origins of Popular Literacy in England, 1500–1850', *Oxford Review of Education* 2 (1976): 255–75; Spufford, 'First Steps in Literacy'; Keith Thomas, 'The Meaning of Literacy in Early Modern England', in Gerd Baumann (ed.), *The Written Word: Literacy in Transition* (Oxford, 1986), 97–131.

2 See for example, Louis B. Wright, *Middle-Class Culture in Elizabethan England* (Chapel Hill, 1935); Victor E. Neuburg, *Popular Literature: A History and a Guide* (London, 1977); Bernard Capp, *Astrology and the Popular Press: English Almanacks, 1500–1800* (London, 1979); Margaret Spufford, *Small Books and Pleasant Histories: Popular Fiction and its Readership in Seventeenth-Century England* (London, 1981); Bernard Capp, 'Popular Literature', in Barry Reay (ed.), *Popular Culture in Seventeenth-Century England* (London, 1985), pp. 198–243; Watt, *Cheap Print*.

3 'John Bunyan is the only specific example of the humble reader being influenced by this cheap print who can be produced': Spufford, *Small Books and Pleasant Histories*, pp. 7, 45–6. See the critical points made in Barry Reay, 'Popular Literature in Seventeenth-Century England', *Journal of Peasant Studies* 10 (1983): 243–9.

ranks of early seventeenth-century English society in the act of reading. It does so, not by an examination of commercially produced print, but by recovering some of the scurrilous verses which were commonly invented, written down by hand and read aloud in local communities at this time. Such compositions sometimes appeared in legal records when they involved the mockery or derogation of a particular individual or group who subsequently sued the authors for libel, and in so doing was required to produce a copy of the offending material as evidence in court. From the documentation generated in such cases, it is possible to discover the producers, distributors and readers of this form of literature and to gauge the reactions which it inspired amongst its audiences. Such libellous rhymes and songs may not be a representative contemporary genre, but their identification in these sources does at least provide the opportunity to observe the milieux in which popular texts circulated and to see some of the ways in which they were read.[4]

The common practice of concocting scandalous verses is well illustrated by some internal evidence from a piece of popular print. In *Dobsons Drie Bobbes* (1607), a jestbook set in late sixteenth-century Durham, the story is told of a group of townspeople who compose and publish some home-made ballads based on a piece of neighbourhood gossip. When the cuckolding of a local haberdasher was made public by a case before the ecclesiastical courts, communal jokes and extempore versifyings on the subject were rife. 'Heereupon such poeticall braines as were resident in the Citty, to whome intelligence was giuen of the circumstances, rymed vpon the Haberdashers fortune, and his wifes behauior, the Schoole-boyes sung ballads thereof in euery streete, and for nine dayes there was no talke in request, but to discourse how the Haberdasher was knighted.' As literate members of the community, some Durham school boys were able to write out an eight-stanza ballad on a piece of parchment. In order to provide that element of pictorial representation so important for communicating messages in a partially literate environment, they also had painted a 'pageant' depicting a man in his shop selling hats and a local butcher with his

4 For a more detailed analysis of this genre and some of the material discussed here, see Adam Fox, 'Ballads, Libels and Popular Ridicule in Jacobean England', *Past and Present* 145 (1994): 47–83. See also, C. J. Sisson, *Lost Plays of Shakespeare's Age* (Cambridge, 1936); Martin Ingram, 'Ridings, Rough Music and Mocking Rhymes in Early Modern England', in Reay (ed.), *Popular Culture in Seventeenth-Century England*, pp. 166–97.

arm around a woman. This production was then, together with a pair of bull's horns, fixed above the victim's front door. The next day, being the Sunday of assizes week, the town was bustling with people from outlying areas. As intended, 'no man passed but hee surueighed the ignominy of the poore Haberdasher, reading the verses vnderset so many as could, others that had no skill in letters got them perused by such as could, and as they vnderstoode the contents, euery man blessed his forehead from the Haberdasher and his hattes, laughing apace, and making good sporte at the conceit of the ieast'. When the object of this ridicule realized what was happening, he rushed outside and 'in furious and most terrible manner assaulting the hornes, hee all to batterd and cut them from the doores, and tearing off the scrowle, he rent it into peeces: at which spectacle the people were ready to die with laughing'.[5]

This fictional example points to the way in which texts could be invented within a community in response to a live and current issue, could be read out in specific situations, and might evoke a number of measurable responses ranging from hysteria to hilarity. At a time when reading aloud was commonplace, giving many texts a communal quality, even those people who 'had no skill in letters' had access to the written or printed word. The verses on the haberdasher became a fluid and dynamic composition, one which slipped in and out of oral and written forms, coming from the people and speaking back to them, both reflecting common opinion and helping to shape it. The impression given here is of an interaction between text and readers or hearers of a kind which is not often retrievable at this social level. There is a sense of that dialogue between author and audience which is facilitated by reading.

The description of these events represented no mere literary trope nor recorded simply an isolated incident. It may be compared with many similar accounts which can be reconstructed from the records of courts before which the objects of this kind of ridicule prosecuted their detractors for defamation of character. One such case, preserved in the records of the Star Chamber, involved some townspeople from Evesham in Worcestershire who decided, in December 1605, to versify the scandalous gossip that a local attorney, George Hawkins, had fathered an illegitimate child by a prostitute. In order that their composition might be read they persuaded Lancelot Ratsey, a

5 *Dobsons Drie Bobbes: Sonne and Heire to Skoggin* (London, 1607), sigs. D1–D2.

tradesman from Coventry who happened to be lodging at the Swan Inn kept by Edward Freme, to set them down on paper. This he did together with a drawing of 'three seurall pictures or images decyferinge and notefyinge one of them to be the pyctuer of [George Hawkins], one other to be the picture of one whoe was supposed to be a whore and had had the bastarde, the thirde and other to be the picture of the bastarde ytself'. Multiple copies of this production were then made out and dispersed. Some were plastered up in the Swan 'uppon wales and doares in the sayde howse to the intent that all persons might take notice thereof', while others were given to Freme's servant, George Hooke, to distribute in neighbouring hostelries. At the Swan the authors were reading aloud and singing their ballad while pointing out the displayed texts to the locals as to the many strangers who passed through. They 'did laughe and jeste att the said pictures', inviting everyone to participate in the entertainment and succeeding in eliciting the general ridicule of Hawkins.[6]

These hand-written publications were not necessarily any less widely disseminated than pieces of cheap print, therefore. Indeed, they might enjoy an even larger distribution at the local level, as authors always had multiple copies made and took vigorous steps to disperse them. Many texts which circulated in seventeenth-century England did so in manuscript rather than in printed form.[7] Popular literature was no exception to this. The broadsides and chapbooks to which scholars have looked for insights into plebeian tastes and mentalities comprised just one part of a much larger range of production, and that perhaps the most conventional and conservative part, given the restrictions imposed by censorship from Church and State.

In what could be a largely oral world at this social level, songs and rhymes were ubiquitous, a principal medium for the communication of information and an essential vehicle for instructional and recreational material. Even villagers and townspeople who were unable either to read or to write were perfectly capable of composing their own ballads and tales and regularly did so. Most of them probably never entered the written realm to be fixed in text; on the other hand, the value of propagation via reading was already sufficiently appreciated for considerable efforts to be made to commit a message to paper. People

6 These details are based upon Public Record Office, London (hereafter PRO), Proceedings in the Court of Star Chamber for the reign of James I (hereafter STAC8), 178/20, and PRO, STAC8/178/37.

7 McKenzie, 'Speech-Manuscript-Print'; Love, *Scribal Publication.*

seemed to know where to go to get their thoughts versified and their verses transcribed. When in October 1601, for example, Thomas Chitham, a schoolmaster from Boreham in Essex, called at the house of Hugh Barker, a barber of Chelmsford, he was asked if he would compose a ballad from some tit-bit of neighbourhood gossip: 'It is nothing (quoth Barker) but to have you pen a few verses for me upon a pretty jest which I shall tell you.' Joseph Turpin and his accomplices were capable of inventing their own verses as they sat drinking at a tavern in Rye, Sussex, one day in June 1632. But they too wanted their verses to be read, for Turpin proclaimed 'that he would give a pott of beear to see them'. Fortunately a man called Spirling offered to write them down in return for a quart of wine as payment (for a typical example of this penmanship, see plate 5).[8]

Many of those to whom these texts were directed, of course, could not themselves read handwriting. Typical was Richard Jerard, a serving-man from Beckington in Somerset, who, when he came across a scripted ballad displayed in the common field at Berkley in September 1611, 'folded up and sealed with wax in the manner of a lettre', was 'not able to reade it (for he cannot reade a written hand)' and took it back to his master's house where someone who 'could reade a written hand took the writing from [him] and opening the seale reade from parte of it in [his] hearing'. Jerard may have been one of those contemporaries whose understanding extended to some form of the printed word, 'print hand', but who had difficulty deciphering hand writing, 'written hand'. Thomas Mumby, a yeoman from Marshchapel in Lincolnshire, may have been of similar capacity. Apparently, when handed two wax-sealed ballads found in his yard in July 1621, he 'opened the same and indeavoured to read [them] but could not, but here and there a part'.[9]

It was precisely because of such widespread inability to read that verses were such an important means of disseminating information and entertainment in this environment. For they were as much an oral medium as a written one, a mnemonic communicator easily imbibed, easily retained and easily repeated. It was for this reason that when a group of villagers from Jacobstow in Cornwall wanted to broadcast some parochial scandal in September 1616, they decided 'to reduce the

8 F. G. Emmison, *Elizabethan Life: Disorder* (Chelmsford, 1970), p. 74; Samuel Rawson Gardiner (ed.), *Reports of Cases in the Courts of Star Chamber and High Commission*, Camden Society, ns, 39 (London, 1886), pp. 149–55.

9 PRO, STAC8/92/10, m. 3; PRO, STAC8/114/12, m. 1.

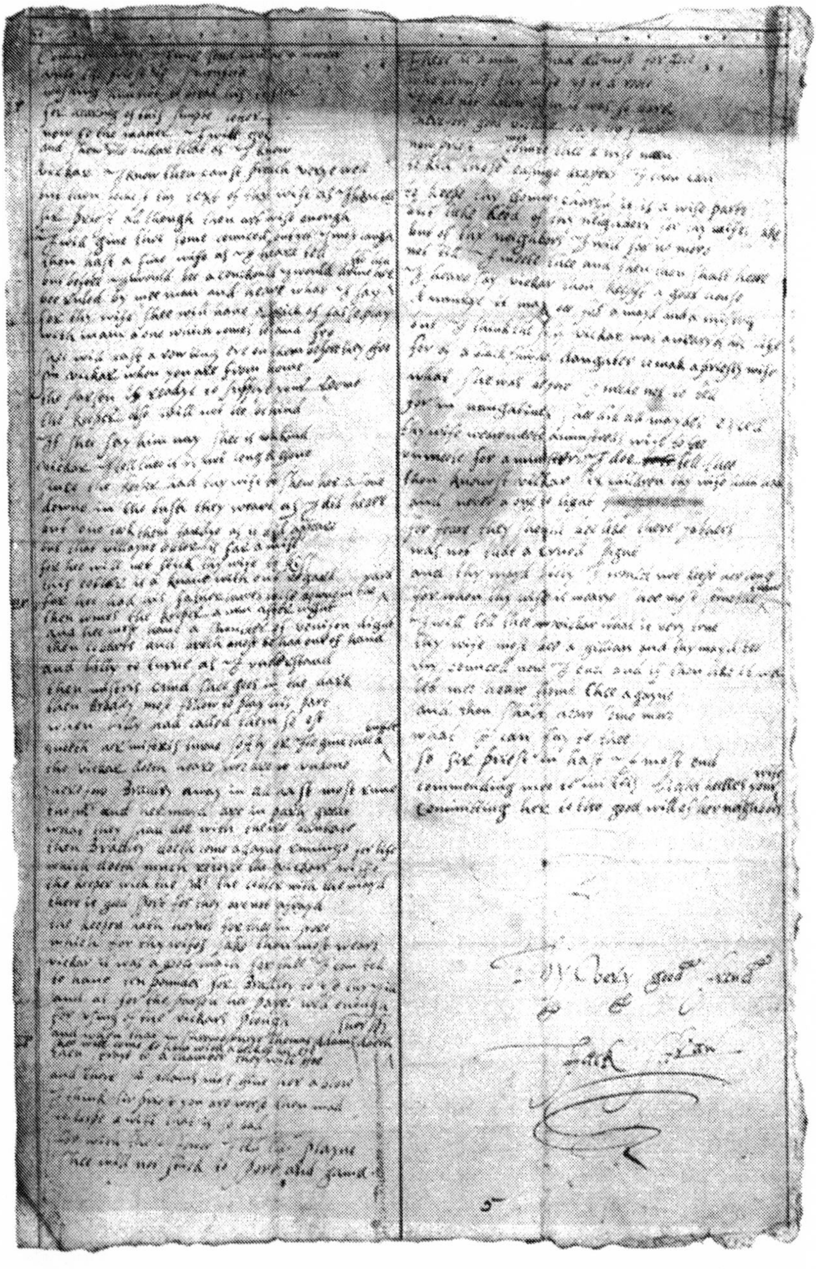

Plate 5 A copy of the libel allegedly composed in August 1604 by Thomas and John Browne against Henry Cunde, the vicar of Montford in Shropshire and his wife Joan. It is signed pseudonymously, 'Thy very good frend, Jack Straw.' Public Record Office, STAC8/100/18, m. 5.

same into rimes' so that the point 'might take the deeper roote and impression in the myndes of the comon and vulgar sorte of people within the said parish'. Equally, it was the importance of illustrations and drawings that they spoke to all, whether readers or not. One sketch made on the back of a ballad written on 'a longe rolle of paper' and attached to the market cross at Petworth, Sussex, in August 1608, was said to have conveyed its message 'even amongst the baser sort of people who doe the better remember and take a greater apprehension ... bye signes and pictures then by the bare report, seeing, reading or hearinge of the same'.[10]

For many, therefore, the ability to 'read' images and remember rhymes was a crucial skill. But the fact that writings of all kinds were habitually articulated aloud also mitigated the disadvantage of being unable to read at first hand. Reading was not the individual and largely silent process which has become the more familiar experience of subsequent generations. These sheaves of verse, in particular, were as much oral as they were textual. Something which began in the verbal realm found its way into the written before passing back again into speech and song. The following instance from Lancashire depicts this norm. One night in February 1619 a group of people from Newton in Makerfield, including Thomas Yewley, a chandler, and Margaret his wife, Thomas Stirroppe, a glover, and his wife Cecily, James Travis, Roger Rothwell and his son Edward, all yeomen, secretly pinned a verse to the town stocks. There it remained for most of the next day 'to be openly seene and redde of all that came nere'. Its purpose was the ridicule of the local bailiff, John Wood, and the authors announced to all that 'there was a lettre of newes uppon the whipstocke ... and wished them to goe and see what it was. Whereby there was presently a great concourse of people gathered together ... insomuch that the whole towne was in uprore.' Furthermore, for those people unable to read it for themselves, they did 'reade and singe the said libell as a ballate with a lowde voyce so that all the rest of the companie might heare it' and on many subsequent occasions they 'repeated and sunge the same and taught their children and boyes to singe [it] in the streets in scoffinge manner'.[11]

Another ballad, of typical broadside length and divided into the conventional two parts, was directed against a customs official from the harbour at Lyme Regis in Dorset. It was similarly fastened 'uppon a

10 Ibid., STAC8/8/27/10, m. 2; STAC8/146/27, m. 48.
11 Ibid., STAC8/307/9, m. 2.

board under the pillory standing in the most eminent, conspicuous and open markett place of [the] towne' on 6 March 1608. The opening stanza proclaimed the intention that it should be read or sung out loud.

> Give eare a while,
> And listen unto this newes I shall you tell.
> Of a long meeching fellow,
> Which in the towne of Lyme doth dwell.
> His name in breef I will you tell,
> With two syllables you may it spell.
> A rope and a halter,
> Spells Robin Salter.[12]

Many examples suggest the manner in which authors endeavoured to read their work in the most public and populous places so as to reach the widest possible audience. A verse composed at Droitwich, Worcestershire, during the spring of 1615 was published by 'reading, singing and repeating the same in alehowses, taverns and other places of resort and by coppying, lendyng and deliveringe the same to others to read and coppie out'. In July 1622 William Wood, an ironmonger of Derby, could be heard with his accomplices not only pronouncing some verses 'in the open marketts and elsewhere ... in words in the hearing of greate multitudes' but also giving copies 'in writing unto others and did give and offer [them] monie to reade and publish the same abroad in the open marketts'. Sometimes the records convey a sense of the performance involved in these public readings, an insight into the way exponents would render their compositions in order to draw a crowd, to entertain and to court complicity. William Burton, a yeoman of Ladbroke in Warwickshire, wrote a number of 'lewd and injurous books, pamphletts, rymes and libells' at the time of the Midland Revolt of 1607, which he was to read out 'with a highe and lowde voyce' at a tenants' meeting called in the village smithy. There, 'in the presence and hearing of above an hundred severall persons', he delivered his polemic, 'usinge manie scornfull jests and countenances and speeches'.[13]

The responses of readers and hearers to this literature often depended upon the success of such performances, and reactions might vary greatly according to the quality and content of the material involved, the sensitivity of the issues upon which it touched and the attitudes of people towards both the authors and their subjects. Those

12 Ibid., STAC8/258/15.
13 Ibid., STAC8/160/15, m. 4; STAC8/221/21, m. 7; STAC8/159/6, m. 2.

verses which came before the courts had by definition been perceived as scandalous and defamatory and were likely to have evoked strong opinions. When Daniel Steward, a yeoman from Sutton in Surrey, composed a variety of ballads against his vicar Robert Cordell, he earned the reputation of 'being a comon sclanderer and backebiter of his neighbours' and was presented as such before the ecclesiastical authorities, the quarter sessions at Kingston and finally the Star Chamber of Westminster. His wares ranged from full ballads, like 'Hay downe a-downe go downe a-downe/This was Hollore Cole of Carsholton towne', to this bawdy little jingle:

> The parson of Sutton
> Loves last mutton
> Venison is soe leene,
> He was burnt with a whore
> And therefore he swore
> He would come noe more there.[14]

Most ridiculing ballads seem to have elicited the general mirth which was intended or hoped for by their composers. 'There was good laughing at the ... readinge', remembered Christopher Horder, a West Country husbandman, of a ditty he had the benefit of hearing in 1603. On other occasions it is possible to detect a reader response much more hostile to scandalous material. When, for example, Christopher Auncell, an apprentice tanner from Wimborne Minster in Dorset, found a copy of a salacious verse in his master's back yard in August 1622 he 'read the same' to various people declaring, or so he claimed, that 'it was a fowle piece of worke and that he would not have been the contriver of it for forty pounds'.[15]

In terms of style, these spontaneously created compositions were usually much cruder and less polished than their printed equivalents and, at their worst, they were little more than semi-literate pieces of doggerel. Such characteristics suggest their generation in an environment unaccustomed to the standardized forms of print culture. Not all of these verses were quite so basic, however. Enough of them reproduced the style and the subject matter of more conventional popular literature to suggest that there could be a degree of overlap between the two forms. Much material which ended up in print clearly had its origins in stories or songs long known to oral or manuscript

[14] Ibid., STAC8/90/24, m. 2.
[15] Ibid., STAC8/190/7, m. 13; STAC8/153/29, m. 1.

tradition. Equally, the vernacular and the hand written repertoires drew upon and refashioned many influences stemming from the London presses. It is sometimes difficult to establish which of the canonical titles and tunes passed down were first known in print, and which were merely made famous by it.

Thus, a number of people who composed their own ballads set them to tunes which were familiar from contemporary broadsides. 'Better to be sung than to be redd, to the tune of Bonny Nell', was the advice given by one verse which appeared in Nottingham in 1617. Thomas Aldred, a local apothecary, certainly thought it was highly amusing 'in regarde of the strangness and conceyted tune sett to it'. Joseph Turpin of Rye and his fellows decided to set their drinking song of 1632 to the famous catches 'Watch Currants' and 'Tom of Bedlam'. The equally celebrated melody 'Take thy old Cloak about thee', made famous by Shakespeare in *Othello*, was one of several accompaniments to a splendid jig set down by Francis Mitchell, servant of Edward Meynell of Hawnby in Yorkshire, in December 1601, that he and his friends 'might bee merrie in Christmas withall'. Another jig composed in Shropshire two decades later was set, in part, 'to the tune of A:B:C:'.[16]

Popular productions were much more likely to be set to tunes known from print if they were taken up and performed by professional performers such as town waits, minstrels or ballad singers. In some cases, extemporized songs and rhymes became so successful that they were adopted by commercial musicians and added to their repertoire; in other instances, the authors of such material might solicit the services of players in order to enhance the quality of its performance and heighten the extent of its exposure. The Nottingham version of 'Bonny Nell' was hammered out in the streets to the rough music of candlesticks, tongs and basins, played in taverns by professional pipers, and 'prickt in 4 parts to the vyalls' in gentlemen's houses. In 1621, George Thomson, the vicar of Aberford in Yorkshire, employed various ballad-mongers and those 'profesing of pipeinge and fidling, running and ranginge upp and downe the countrie from place to place to gett their livings at fayres, marketts and idle meetings and merrements' in order to have his compositions played before audiences 'in diverse and sundrie alehouses and innes and in diverse and sundry companies drawne together of purpose to heare the same songs, rithmes and

[16] Sisson, *Lost Plays of Shakespeare's Age*, pp. 135–40, 199, 201, 206–8; Gardiner, *Reports of Cases*, p. 152. For these tunes see William Chappell, *Popular Music of the Olden Time*, 2 vols. (London, 1853–9).

libells and to reioyce and laugh thereat in scornfull, derideinge and infamous manner'.[17]

It was not only at the musical level that the scripted and the printed, the amateur and the professional, might borrow from each other. Stories and characters could also be appropriated, recycled and passed between the two realms just as regularly. Some of the tropes and figures familiar to cheap print might turn up in an extemporized ditty sung by local people in their villages and towns, just as a version of such a ditty could appear, in turn, at the shop of a London printer to be set in black letter. Thus in 1588 the inhabitants of Earls Colne in Essex were regaled with a rhyme from a tailor, John Brande, which appears to have been a direct antecedent of verses printed in *Tarltons Jests* a few years later. In much the same way, a mock sermon delivered by John Cradock the elder, a yeoman of South Kyme in Lincolnshire, as part of some summer games in August 1601, involved 'a collaudation of the ancient story of *The Friar and the Boy*', which had first appeared in ballad form in 1586. A song contrived in 1608 by James Cowarne and Morris Attwood, mercers, and distributed at 'innes, taverns, tipling howses and other places of assembly' throughout Gloucester, included references to the great fictional characters Pasquil and Reynard the Fox and contained a version of the famous *A Moste Strange Weddinge of the Frogge and the Mowse*. The latter was first noted to be in oral circulation in 1549; it was registered by the Company of Stationers as a broadside in 1580; and it remains familiar today in its nineteenth-century form as *A Frog He Would A-Wooing Go*. The Gloucester adaptation included,

A frogg longe wooed a jolly mouse,
To have his will within her sheene.
She first denyed and said she scorned,
A frogg should haue authoritie there.
But it at length she graunte him jurisdiction,
This, Dion saith, is noe fiction.[18]

Sometimes those accused of inventing or rendering libellous items protested that they were doing no more than repeating orthodox compositions. Edward Seede, the son of a Somerset squire, for example, claimed when thus indicted that he had been simply singing 'manie old songs and rymes' remembered from his youth, including

[17] Sisson, *Lost Plays of Shakespeare's Age*, p. 198; PRO, STAC8/275/22, m. 2.

[18] Ingram, 'Ridings, Rough Music and Mocking Rhymes', p. 180; N. J. O'Connor, *Godes Peace and the Queenes: Vicissitudes of a House, 1539–1615* (London, 1934), p. 120; PRO, STAC8/285/27, m. 8.

'the daunce called the *Jew of Malta* and thereunto singing one ditty or tune, secondly dauncing the *Irish Daunce*, singing to that another, with diverse such like'. When George James, a servant from Lutterworth in Leicestershire, was charged with having rendered a jig defamatory to his mistress in 1616 he went so far as to argue that it had not only been performed by comedians before Henry VIII but that it had also been 'seene, approved and allowed by the right worshippfull the Maister of the Revells to his Majestie'.[19]

In this way, print culture could feed into and inspire the creative skills of ordinary people. This relationship could be mutually influential, moreover, as some authors sought to have their rough compositions polished up and put into print, perhaps in the belief that in so doing they might reach a nationwide audience. Among such people were three Worcestershire men, John Rotton and his brother Richard, both from Moseley, and William Pretty of Yardley. In March 1607, they composed three versions of a ballad alleging the adultery of Richard Nightingale, a yeoman of Tipton in Staffordshire, with a local girl, Anne Bellamie. Richard Rotton, a weaver, sang one of them in his shop and at the alehouse of John Tomlinson in Moseley to a tune which a number of the patrons recognized as 'Jamey'. Not content, however, the authors also conspired to have their works typeset for they were later 'Imprinted at London at the signe of the woodcocke in Paules Churchyarde'. It seems likely that the printer employed a professional ballad writer at some stage in order to improve the quality and standardize the form. Two of the versions were now entitled 'A pleasant new history/declaring of a mysterie/Of Richard Nightingale by name/and Anne Bellamie of Dods Lane/You may sing it to a merry new tune' and couched in a dialogue between Peter and Solomon. The third was set 'To a pleasant new tune called Marcus Tullius Cicero'. No such titles were entered in the Stationers' Company register and, almost certainly, they would not have been approved because of their defamatory nature. Perhaps, like other illicit literature, they never came before the authorities at all. No printed copies of these ballads are extant but the complete texts survive in the records of the court of the Star Chamber, transcribed by the clerk.[20]

The dissemination of these libellous verses, therefore, affords some insight into the practice of reading at the least literate levels of society in early modern England. From descriptions in the legal records of the

19 PRO, STAC8/98/20, m. 27; STAC8/59/4, m. 1.
20 Ibid., STAC8/220/31.

ways in which such material was created and broadcast, it is possible to gain an impression of how one variety of popular literature was actually communicated and received. In isolation, the surviving text of a ballad or verse in manuscript or print can reveal little about who read it or about how it was read. By recovering something of the context in which these particular compositions operated, however, insight may be gained into that reciprocal relationship between text and audience which is allowed by reading.

CHAPTER 8

The physiology of reading in Restoration England

Adrian Johns

While he was still at school, the great natural philosopher Robert Boyle later recalled, he had once contracted a tertian ague. All physic failed. Reduced to a melancholic state, Boyle returned from London to Eton in the hope that the change of air and diet might help ease his condition. But his mentors also had other remedies in mind. To 'divert his melancholy', they made their charge 'read the state adventures of *Amadis de Gaule*, and other fabulous stories'. Their treatment was by no means a success. Far from curing Boyle, he later testified, the stories 'prejudiced him, by unsettling his thoughts', and thereby exacerbated his complaint. Meeting in him with 'a restless fancy, then made more susceptible of any impressions by an unemployed pensiveness', they 'accustomed his thoughts to such a habitude of roving, that he [had] scarce ever been their quiet master since'.

Boyle's advisers should have read their Burton. *The Anatomy of Melancholy* had endorsed the reading of learned books to counter melancholy, not that of romances. But then, even such a well-attested remedy was prone to be counterproductive. The unhappy patient might all too easily 'make a *Skeleton* of himselfe', Burton attested, eventually coming to resemble those 'inamoratoes' who read nothing but 'play-bookes, Idle Poems, Jests' – and, to be specific, *Amadis de Gaule* itself. Far from being cured, Boyle risked ending up 'as mad as *Don Quixot*'.[1]

Luckily for him, in the end no such traumatic outcome came to pass. As he later acknowledged, after much effort Boyle did eventually manage to 'fix his volatile fancy'. He did so by subjecting himself to a rigorous intellectual regime. In particular, he found that mathematics

I am grateful for discussions with Alison Winter, Rob Iliffe, Mark Jenner, James Raven, Simon Schaffer, Steven Shapin, Helen Small and others during the writing of this piece.

1 Robert Burton, *The Anatomy of Melancholy*, ed. Nicolas K. Kiessling, Thomas C. Faulkner, Rhonda L. Blair, 2 vols. (Oxford, 1989–90), II, 90.

provided the best tool 'to fetter, or at least to curb the roving wildness of his wandering thoughts'. The most effective way to restrain his meandering mind was to concentrate on 'laborious operations of algebra'.[2] Nevertheless, the harmful effects of his experience could not be eradicated entirely. Years later Boyle would still find himself leaving his manor at Stalbridge to wander alone in the fields, there to 'think at random, making his delighted imagination the busy scene, where some romance or other was daily acted'. This odd behaviour was regularly imputed to his melancholic humour; but Boyle himself knew better. It was in reality nothing but 'his yet untamed habitude of roving, a custom (as his own experience often and sadly taught him) much more easily contracted, than destroyed'.[3] The effects of reading those romances had proved permanent, and Boyle simply had to live with them.

Evidently, if one wished to retain reliability and independence of mind then one must be careful what one read. In Oxford in the 1650s, at the time when he, Wren, Wilkins and others were pursuing the discussions of experimental philosophy which would eventually lead to the creation of the Royal Society, Boyle applied this hard-earned knowledge well. This, he noted, was the time when 'the *Cartesian* philosophy began to make a noise in the world', and he could hardly avoid hearing about it. But Boyle resolved to 'acquiesce in no single man's hypothesis'. Accordingly, by a publicly declared self-denying ordinance, 'for many years he would not read over *Des Cartes*'s *Principles*'. He even refused to read Bacon's *Novum Organum*, 'that I might not be prepossessed with any theory or principles'.[4]

To the historian, these declarations are remarkable. A typical account of the intellectual history of the period would make Descartes and Bacon the most influential of all the disciples of 'the new philosophy', yet here we see the 'acknowledged leader'[5] of experimentalism denying having read either. At the same time, moreover, we see the same man claiming that the reading of romances had had

2 Robert Boyle, *Works*, ed. Thomas Birch, 6 vols. (London, 1772), I, xvi-xvii (composed *c.* 1647–8, when Boyle was about 22). Steven Shapin, *A Social History of Truth: Civility and Science in Seventeenth-Century England* (Chicago, IL, 1994), chapter 4, is essential for understanding the importance of such biographical statements.

3 Boyle, *Works*, I, xix-xx.

4 Boyle, *Works*, I, 299–318, esp. 301–2. Cf. similar passages in, for example: I, 317, 355–6; II, 289, 327; III, 8–9, 11, and see also John T. Harwood (ed.), *The Early Essays and Ethics of Robert Boyle* (Carbondale, IL, 1991), pp. 192–7.

5 *Dictionary of National Biography*, s.v. 'Boyle, Robert'.

a permanent unhealthy effect on him. Clearly, Boyle must have thought that reading exercised a remarkable power over body and mind alike.

Boyle was by no means isolated in this appreciation of the power of reading. Many of his contemporaries attested to similarly impressive encounters with books at an early age. Perhaps the most disquieting of such accounts is that of Abraham Cowley, who concluded that reading Spenser in his mother's parlour had 'made [him] a Poet as immediately as a Child is made an Eunuch'.[6] Experiences like these were widely credited, and led many to declare that they had refused to read important books for fear of their irreversible effects.[7] Moreover, Boyle's successful treatment, too, was well warranted. Francis Bacon himself had said that there was no 'impediment in the wit' which could not be 'wrought out by fit studies: like as diseases of the body may have appropriate exercises'. 'So if a man's wit be wandering', he had advised, 'let him study the mathematics.'[8] In short, Boyle knew what he was talking about. Both his condition and its cure were well-recognized. The historian would therefore be unwise to dismiss his testimony too hastily as simply erroneous. Instead, such testimony can be put to use, to help us understand more about the cultural history of reading practices in his period.

In describing such powerful effects, Boyle's cautionary statements directed attention to what he thought actually occurred, physically, at the decisive moment of face-to-face confrontation between reader and read. Historians have remained strangely reticent about this moment of confrontation, perhaps because it seems to embody so self-evident, so natural an act that there appears little they could usefully say about it. Yet it ought perhaps to be central to an account of the history of reading, if only because, as a matter of fact, descriptions of it have varied widely in different periods. What is it that passes from page to mind when someone reads, and how does it have an effect? We must now address such a fundamental question, not in our own terms but

6 *The Works of Mr. Abraham Cowley*, 8th edn (London, 1684), pp. 143–4.

7 Other examples are provided in Conal Condren, 'Casuistry to Newcastle: "The Prince" in the World of the Book', in Nicholas Phillipson and Quentin Skinner (eds.), *Political Discourse in Early Modern Britain* (Cambridge, 1993), pp. 164–86.

8 Francis Bacon, 'Of Studies', in James Spedding, Robert Leslie Ellis and Douglas Denon Heath (eds.), *The Works of Francis Bacon*, 14 vols. (London, 1858–61), VI, 497–8. Thomas Willis, too, suggested mathematics as a remedy: Thomas Willis, *Two Discourses Concerning the Soul of Brutes, which is that of the Vital and Sensitive of Man*, trans. Samuel Pordage (London, 1683), p. 194.

as it was represented in late seventeenth-century England.[9] What follows aims to reconstruct, in short, a Restoration physiology of reading.

As an initial strategy, one can try interpreting Boyle's words at face value. 'Prejudice', 'fancy', 'impressions', 'habitude', 'thoughts' – to an informed early modern reader these were readily recognizable terms, originating in a variety of sciences relating to perception and the workings of the mind. They should perhaps be read literally, then, to refer to processes of the mind and body. Knowledge of such processes was widely available in the Restoration, through a number of sources ranging from everyday medical and casuistical advice to highly specialized anatomical practice. People felt able to use such resources to describe their experiences of perception and reasoning, including those involved in reading, and to act on those descriptions. The following discussion attempts in small measure to recover something of their knowledge and its uses.

There is a fundamental question with which to start: that of perception. How, exactly, did one see letters on a page? What was it that passed through the air and into the eye, and how did it have an effect? The most influential single treatment of these issues was to be found in the work of René Descartes. According to his account, light was a pressure transmitted through a plenum of 'very subtle and very fluid matter' existing in the space between an object and the individual. On hitting the eye, this pressure caused an effect similar to the imprinting of an impression on wax by a seal.[10] Its impact was transmitted to the retina at the back of the eye, and there constituted as an image (see plate 6).

In discussions of how this image was formed, the eye was conventionally represented as the natural equivalent of a *camera obscura*.[11] This was a well-known device – by 1655, Meric Casaubon could assume that most people 'that have any curiosity' would have seen one. It consisted of a darkened chamber with a pinhole in one wall; light admitted

[9] Robert Darnton calls in passing for such an approach in his 'The History of Reading', esp. p. 152. See also his 'Readers Respond to Rousseau' in Darnton, *Great Cat Massacre*, pp. 215–56.

[10] *The Philosophical Writings of Descartes*, trans. John Cottingham, Robert Stoothoff, Dugald Murdoch and Anthony Kenny, 3 vols. (Cambridge, 1985–91), III, 39–40, 152–6.

[11] Johann Kepler, *Ad Vitellionem Paralipomena* (Frankfurt, 1604), pp. 176–7; Isaac Newton, *Opticks* (London, 1704), pp. 9–11; cf. John Locke, *An Essay Concerning Human Understanding*, ed. P. Nidditch (Oxford, 1975), pp. 162–3. See also Svetlana Alpers, *The Art of Describing: Dutch Art in the Seventeenth Century* (Chicago, IL, 1983), pp. 50–1.

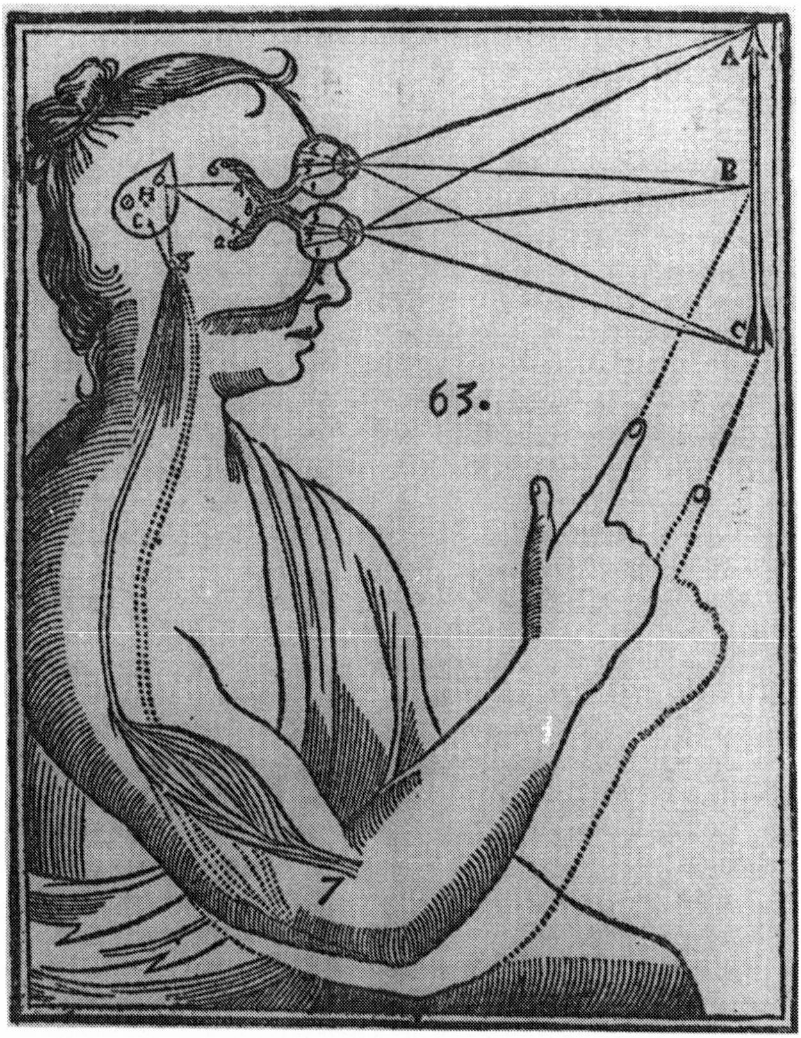

Plate 6 The Cartesian mechanism for perception and action, 1st French edn of Descarte's *Treatise on Man* (1644). Cambridge, University Library, M.3.40

through this hole formed an inverted image on the opposite wall.[12] In the eye, correspondingly, an image was thought to be 'imprinted' or 'painted' (both words were used) on the retina – a process anatomists were able to reconstruct using specimen eyes from cadavers. From

12 Giambattista della Porta, *Natural Magick* (London, 1658), pp. 363–5; Meric Casaubon, *A Treatise Concerning Enthusiasme, as it is an Effect of Nature* (London, 1655), p. 43.

thence, the image was transmitted instantly to the brain through 'spirits' channelled in the optic nerves. There it was again 'impressed' onto 'something . . . called the *sensus communis*', where it was perceived by the mind.[13] This *sensus communis*, whatever it was, was thus imprinted at the same instant as the eye, and in a manner determined by the structure of the human body. Descartes himself placed it at the pineal gland.

Such a *camera obscura* model provided a convincing account of correct perception. But the impressions on the *sensus communis* need not come from the eyes. They could equally be produced from the senses of smell, taste, hearing or touch. Or they might not derive from outside the body at all. In fact, images produced by the imagination were apprehended by the same process of imprinting. Whenever the mind either imagined or perceived an object, then, it was really considering an image traced on the surface of the *sensus communis* – and it could not always be sure which it was doing. Descartes insisted that the term 'idea' must therefore be applied to any such 'impressions', whether imaginative or perceptive in origin. Such ideas then resulted in physical actions, transmitted by the self-same nervous system which mediated perception.[14]

This meant that *camera obscura* models of vision could not be as simple as their proponents had perhaps hoped. Far from having been rendered regular and even mechanical, in such schemes vision was liable to be corrupted or counterfeited either by the imagination or by physiological conditions. Qualifications to *camera obscura* models accordingly became routine. Indeed, Isaac Newton himself endorsed them, in the most influential of all accounts. Only in the proper circumstances, and only if the perceived phenomena were not 'produced or altered by the power of imagination', he reckoned, could knowledge of colours be considered a Newtonian mathematical science. This he had actually verified on himself, managing solely through the exercise of his 'fantasie' to create an illusory perception of the Sun in his rooms at Trinity College, Cambridge.[15]

Acceptance of a *camera obscura* model therefore meant that to account for the construction of knowledge from perceptions one needed some appreciation of the 'affections' internal to the human constitution. The physical structure of the brain and nervous system played an essential

13 Cottingham, Stoothoff and Kenny (eds.), *Philosophical Writings of Descartes*, I, 41–2, 166–7; Johann Kepler, *Dioptrice* (Augsburg, 1611), pp. 23–5.

14 Cottingham, Stoothoff and Kenny (eds.), *Philosophical Writings of Descartes*, I, 42, 105–6.

15 Newton, *Opticks*, pp. 9–11, 48, 135–7; Richard S. Westfall, *Never at Rest: A Biography of Isaac Newton* (Cambridge, 1980), pp. 93–5. For similar cases, see Simon Schaffer, 'Self Evidence', *Critical Inquiry* 18 (1992): 327–62.

part in the reception and manipulation of ideas. This part could not be gainsaid, since it was built into the human frame. On the contrary, it must be confronted and understood.

For the most authoritative account of this subject we can go to Oxford, where worked the most renowned neurological anatomist of his time: the Sedleian Professor of Natural Philosophy, Thomas Willis. In the early 1660s Willis undertook a series of detailed dissections of the brain, accompanied by Richard Lower, who probably did much of the more grisly work, and by Christopher Wren, who drew the results.[16] 'Hecatombs' of cadavers were dissected – not only humans, but horses, sheep, calves, goats, hogs, dogs, cats, foxes, hares, geese, turkeys, fish and even a monkey. In London Boyle was kept informed of their labours, Walter Charleton repeated them, and Henry Oldenburg, Secretary of the Royal Society, spread news of their findings across Europe.[17] Together these workers created the most important and best-known work on neurology and brain structure to be produced before the nineteenth century. As several historians have indicated, this work was of central importance to representations of reading during that whole period.[18]

It is important to convey some impression of Willis's project, since it was a specific and unusual one. He was not engaged in routine, didactic morbid anatomy. Rather, Willis aimed to provide knowledge of the soul. (Himself a convinced Anglican, he had held Common Prayer services *incognito* during the Interregnum, and his works were dedicated to his patron, the Archbishop of Canterbury.) He began from a belief in an at least twofold division of the soul in the human body, into a

16 Thomas Willis, 'The Anatomy of the Brain' and 'The Description of the Nerves', in *The Remaining Medical Works of that Famous and Renowned Physician Dr. Thomas Willis*, trans. Samuel Pordage (London, 1681), pp. 55–136 and 137–92. For the circumstances surrounding this work, see Kenneth Dewhurst, *Thomas Willis's Oxford Lectures* (Oxford, 1980), pp. 37–49 and 52ff, Robert G. Frank, Jr, 'Thomas Willis and his Circle: Brain and Mind in Seventeenth-Century Medicine', in G. S. Rousseau (ed.), *The Languages of Psyche: Mind and Body in Enlightenment Thought* (Berkeley, CA, 1990), pp. 107–46, and W. F. Bynum, 'The Anatomical Method, Natural Theology, and the Functions of the Brain', *Isis* 64 (1973): 444–68. The main source for anatomical work in the period is Robert G. Frank, Jr, *Harvey and the Oxford Physiologists: A Study of Scientific Ideas* (Berkeley, CA, 1980).

17 Thomas Birch, *The History of the Royal Society of London*, 4 vols. (London, 1756–7), I, 416, 421–2, 436, 444; A. Rupert Hall and Marie Boas Hall (eds.), *The Correspondence of Henry Oldenburg*, 13 vols. (Madison, WI, 1965–86), II, 141–5, 300–9, 631–3.

18 G. S. Rousseau, 'Nerves, Spirits, and Fibres: Towards Defining the Origins of Sensibility', *Studies in the Eighteenth Century* 3 (1976): 137–57; Rousseau, 'Science and the Discovery of the Imagination in Enlightened England', *Eighteenth-Century Studies* 3 (1969): 108–35; John Mullan, 'Hypochondria and Hysteria: Sensibility and the Physicians', *The Eighteenth Century: Theory and Interpretation* 25 (1984): 141–74; Christopher Lawrence, 'The Nervous System and Society in the Scottish Enlightenment', in Barry Barnes and Steven Shapin (eds.), *Natural Order: Historical Studies of Scientific Culture* (Beverley Hills, CA, 1979), pp. 19–40.

rational component, which was immaterial, immortal and intellectual, and a sensitive one, which was corporeal and mortal. The former could not be subjected to physiological study, but the latter could. This 'sensitive soul' conducted all the physical processes of perception and movement, acting through the vehicle of 'animal spirits' sublimed from the blood and channelled through the nervous system. Among other things, these were the spirits which transmitted perceptions to the *sensus communis*. They were like internal 'Rays of Light', Willis declared: 'For as light figures the Impressions of all visible things, and the Air of all audible things; so the Animal Spirits, receive the impressed Images of those, and also of Odors, and tangible Qualities.' Imagination and perception were thus difficult to distinguish precisely because they depended on this same vehicle. It was a vehicle not confined to any particular organ, let alone to the mind, but 'Co-extended to the whole Body'; and Willis wanted his anatomy to elucidate its workings to the full. His true subject, he announced, was therefore 'Psycheology', or the 'Discourse of the Soul'.[19]

Believing that the sensitive soul functioned by the flow of animal spirits through material channels, Willis thought it possible to reveal those channels by anatomical practice. In so doing, he hoped to identify in the brain physical features associated specifically with such functions as memory, imagination and the appetites.[20] But this required a novel method of dissection. He advocated 'a new way of opening ye Brains', observers reported. It was a method that, rather than producing horizontal sections through the head, uncovered the brain layer by concentric layer, thereby revealing 'the order of Nature'.[21] It is important to stress this practical novelty, for it was their embodiment in skill and practice which lent such legitimacy to Willis's views. His anatomical works were not just *texts*: they were representations of actual practical procedure, performed before real audiences, and it was this which gave them their unique authority.[22]

19 Willis, *Two Discourses*, sigs. [A3]^v-[A4]^v, pp. 5, 18, 38ff.

20 Willis, *Remaining Medical Works*, pp. 91, 95–7; Willis, *Two Discourses*, pp. 23–5. For Willis's treatment of vision as analogous to the *camera obscura*, see *Two Discourses*, pp. 33, 75–86.

21 Willis, *Remaining Medical Works*, pp. 55–62; Hansruedi Isler, *Thomas Willis, 1621–1675: Doctor and Scientist* (New York, 1968), p. 25.

22 For the importance of practice and audience in establishing knowledge claims, see Steven Shapin and Simon Schaffer, *Leviathan and the Air-Pump: Hobbes, Boyle, and the Experimental Life* (Princeton, NJ, 1985), David Gooding, Trevor Pinch and Simon Schaffer (eds.), *The Uses of Experiment: Studies in the Natural Sciences* (Cambridge, 1989), for example, pp. 10–11, 191–3, and Jan Golinski, *Science as Public Culture: Chemistry and Enlightenment in Britain, 1760–1820* (Cambridge, 1992), pp. 1–10.

Briefly, Willis's technique revealed two membranes enveloping the brain. The first of these membranes was loose, and in four places it formed cavities called 'bosoms'. Blood flowing into the brain collected in these bosoms, whence vessels carried it into the interior of the head. Beneath lay the second membrane, tightly fitting the three inner structures of *cerebrum*, 'oblong marrow' and, to the rear, *cerebellum*. Its purpose was to distinguish these parts of the brain one from another, and thereby to act as a 'fence' to restrain the animal spirits in their respective 'cells and orbs'.[23]

All physicians and anatomists knew that the animal spirits had their origin in the blood. But Willis could now observe where, and hence how, they were manufactured. He could see within each of the bosoms a matrix of strong 'Fibres' which, like 'flood-gates', controlled the flow of blood into the brain. Additional ligaments traversing the bosoms controlled their expansion and contraction, thereby acting to manifest certain passions in the body as a whole (it was because of the contraction of these ligaments, for example, that 'fear and great sadness' caused the blood to accelerate so noticeably to the heart).[24] When full, the bosoms acted as heat sources, gradually warming blood flowing in tiny vessels beneath. Eventually, 'as if it were a certain Chymical operation', this blood underwent a distillation. Its subtle extracts were then channelled towards the brain by vessels in the inner membrane – vessels which, when injected with an ink solution, resembled 'little serpentine chanels hanging to an alembic'. Like this alchemical apparatus, the vessels served as extra 'distillatory Organs', rendering the refined blood still more 'subtil and elaborated' as it proceeded along them. At length, only the finest 'Chymical Elixir' was admitted into the inner brain, in the form of animal spirits.[25]

Once manufactured, the animal spirits circulated 'as in a publick *Emporium* or Mart' in a 'free and open space' at the base of the brain. This was the 'common Sensory' – the *sensus communis* – where the 'Strokes of all sensible things' were registered. It was here that impressions from the senses and the imagination were combined, and remembered ideas received. It was also the centre from which the animal spirits were 'directed into appropriate Nerves' for all responsive actions.[26]

23 Willis, *Remaining Medical Works*, pp. 56–9, 81–4.
24 Ibid., p. 80.
25 Ibid., pp. 79, 82–3, 87–8.
26 Ibid., pp. 93, 96; Dewhurst, *Willis's Oxford Lectures*, pp. 54–6, 65–7.

The *sensus communis* was a space of open exchange, where the spirits mingled. But some differentiation of functions nevertheless remained. Most importantly, while the *cerebrum* was the site of imaginative and ratiocinating actions, the *cerebellum* directed all those functions which did not rely on imagination, memory or reason: that is, all the regular motions necessary for life. So the nerves controlling respiration, nutrition and similar functions derived their spirits from there. It seemed essential, indeed, that they did so, for otherwise the most basic life-preserving activities of the body would have been vulnerable to 'the winds of Passions and Cogitations'.[27] Yet even separated in this way they were not immune, for a mechanically transmitted 'sympathy' existed between the spirits in the *cerebellum* and those in the *cerebrum*, so that any passion excited in the latter could still produce physical symptoms. In fact, whenever 'a violent passion, as Joy, Sadness, Anger, [or] Fear' arose, its 'impression' would produce 'notable mutations in the Organs'. Hence someone subject to a fit of rage, say, experienced changes in body temperature, heart rate and stomach functions.[28] A 'fountain' of animal spirits continuously flowed out from the *sensus communis*, through the spinal cord, to all parts of the body, there to 'irradiate' it and cause such symptoms.[29]

So perception was part of a single, continuous process. Seeing an object, imagining one and reasoning with the resulting ideas and memories could never be separated from the circulation of the blood and the movements of the body.[30] Willis had shown that a skilled anatomist could do much, despite the impossibility of actually seeing the spirits in action, to elucidate their nature, routes and purposes. His findings were readily applicable to a wide range of fields, including that of reading. The following sections will convey some idea of the scope of such applications.

Almost unavoidably, Willis's anatomical work led him to discuss the nature of the passions. The mutual dependence of mind and body, he found, guaranteed that every 'passion of the sensitive Soul' implicated both the physical body and its perceptions, 'whether we will or no'. He was now joining a large contemporary literature, treating a popular

27 Willis, *Remaining Medical Works*, pp. 110–13, esp. p. 111; Dewhurst, *Willis's Oxford Lectures*, pp. 145–50.

28 Willis, *Remaining Medical Works*, pp. 96, 108, 114–16.

29 Ibid., p. 95.

30 Willis, *Two Discourses*, pp. 55–60; Dewhurst, *Willis's Oxford Lectures*, p. 100; Frank, 'Thomas Willis', p. 134.

subject: Descartes had anticipated that by its title alone his own account of the passions would sell better than any of his other books.[31] Descartes, royal physician Walter Charleton and others helped create a market for such discussions which was still going strong well into the eighteenth century.[32] Such writers, in particular Charleton, often drew on Willis's brain anatomy as the best available.

Strictly speaking, passions were 'Apprehensions, resentments, or emotions of the Soul, ... caused, fomented, and fortified by some motion of the spirits'.[33] That is, they were responses excited by the senses and other stimuli, such as the imagination: *passiones* correspondent to the *actiones* of motions impinging on the brain. Such a wide definition meant that some things counted as passions which we would not now recognize as such, the desire for knowledge being a crucial example. Their study, accordingly, was reckoned to be extremely important. The philosophy of the passions, wrote Catholic priest Jean Senault, might be less formally prestigious than other branches of learning, but in reality it was fundamental to them all. 'For it is she that makes *Philosophers*, and which purifying their *understanding*, makes them capable of *considering* the wonders of *Nature*.' Such learning was 'to *Philosophy*, the same as *Foundations* are to *Buildings*'. Someone possessing adequate knowledge of – and thereby control over – the passions was in a good position to become 'an *honest man*, ... a good *Father* of a *Family*, a wise *Politician*, and an understanding *Philosopher*'. Those without such knowledge would soon be forced to confess that 'our Passions are chains, which make us slaves to all such as know how to manage them well' (see also plate 7).[34]

What made the passions problematic was the postlapsarian state of humanity. Before the Fall, everyone agreed, human apprehensions had been in perfect accord with nature. The senses had 'made no false reports', and, being 'uninterressed', had been in conformity with Reason. All that had now changed. Corrupted, 'rather *Faulty* then *Innocent*', the senses of a representative Restoration reader were thought

[31] René Descartes, *The Passions of the Soule* (London, 1650), sig. B3[v].

[32] See, for example: Thomas Wright, *The Passions of the Minde in Generall* (London, 1604); Edward Reynolds, *A Treatise of the Passions and Faculties of the Soule of Man* (London, 1640); Descartes, *Passions of the Soule*; J. F. Senault, *The Use of Passions*, trans. Henry, Earl of Monmouth (London, 1649); [W. Charleton], *Natural History of the Passions* (London, 1674); Bernard Mandeville, *A Treatise of the Hypochondriack and Hysterick Passions* (London, 1711); Francis Hutcheson, *An Essay on the Nature and Conduct of the Passions and Affections*, 3rd edn (London, 1742).

[33] Descartes, *Passions of the Soule*, p. 23.

[34] Senault, *Use of Passions*, sig. c[v], p. 163. See also Richard W. F. Kroll, *The Material Word: Literate Culture in the Restoration and the Early Eighteenth Century* (Princeton, NJ, 1991), pp. 219–23.

Plate 7 Reason and the Passions. Engraved title page from J. F. Senault, *The Use of Passions*, tr. Henry, Earl of Monmouth (1649). Cambridge, University Library, sss.2.6.

to be 'subject to a thousand illusions'. Guided by the passions generated from such illusions, the mind was almost certain to go wrong.[35] Charleton, for example, declared that 'most commonly *false Opinions* are occasioned ... by our *Passions*'.[36] In short, the problem posed by the passions was a problem of knowledge. What was at stake was the discrimination of truth from falsity, and the propriety of actions resultant upon such discrimination, in the particular situation of a postlapsarian subject.

It was impossible to enumerate all the passions which could affect one's knowledge: the variety of impressions constantly arriving at the brain made their number simply too great. But writers like Charleton, Descartes, Senault and, indeed, Willis himself nevertheless did frame a standard 'genealogy' in terms of which their effects might be discussed. By common consent the first stage in generating a passion occurred when the senses presented a '*new* and *strange* object' to the soul. Instantly the soul '*admire*[d]' this new image. This admiration was the primary of all the passions. The soul then entertained an 'appetite' to know the object better – an appetite called '*Curiosity* or desire of Knowledge'. Curiosity thus constituted the second passion. On it depended all further intellectual inquiry. It was nothing less than 'the mother of knowledge': 'all natural *Philosophy*, and *Astronomy* owe themselves to this passion'.[37] Typical genealogies then went on to recognize five more simple varieties of passion: love and hatred, desire, and joy and grief. All others were best regarded as compounds or species of these.[38]

The motions of the spirits concomitant to these passions, reported Charleton, 'change the very countenance, gestures, walking, and ... all the actions'. Writers were accordingly able to link a wide variety of visible symptoms, through the physiology of the passions, to processes of perception and imagination. The primary passion, admiration, for example, caused the animal spirits to be called into the brain to hold the image in place for consideration. Simultaneously they were also directed into the muscles holding the body in position and the eyes focused, so as to keep the organs in contact with the object. By such symptoms could it be recognized. In extreme cases, though, the spirits could produce '*Stupor*, or *Astonishment*' – perhaps even catalepsy. Such

35 Senault, *Use of Passions*, sigs. c2^r-c4^r, pp. 61, 105.

36 [Charleton], *Passions*, sig. A3^r; a similar point about the Fall is made in Reynolds, *Passions*, pp. 5–6, 27–8.

37 [Charleton], *Passions*, pp. 87–9. For Willis on taxonomies of the passions, see Willis, *Two Discourses*, pp. 45–55.

38 [Charleton], *Passions*, p. 164. Cf. Descartes, *Passions of the Soule*, pp. 47–55.

'immoderate' admiration could not but be harmful to the health. Physical symptoms were therefore revelatory of one's passionate state in normal circumstances, but actively harmful in extreme ones – a pattern common to the other passions. Physicians above all were familiar with the complaints accompanying such intense states. Symptoms included 'leanness, a defect of Nutrition, Melancholy, the Scurvy, Consumption', rheumatism, lameness, bloated faces, swollen limbs, amenorrhoea, green sickness, fevers and death. Excessive reading could bring on such conditions, many of them experienced by women: they complained of insomnia, breathlessness, trembling, upset stomachs, vertigo, headaches, ringing ears, 'rising' sensations and swooning.[39]

Among other things, by discriminating between madness and sanity in cases like these physicians were producing everyday solutions to the problem of knowledge posed by the passions. However, it is important to stress that that problem also had a much wider, political significance. The conflicts of seventeenth-century Europe were so disturbing, it could be argued, because the human body itself was constantly fighting a civil war between competing candidates for knowledge, based respectively in the sensitive and rational souls.

Ideally, the faculty producing knowledge should have been the 'Understanding', which was the province of the rational soul alone.[40] However, the sensitive soul mediated between this and the body which provided its raw materials, and was the main seat of the imagination and the passions. By consequence a highly unstable entity, it was subject to both diseases of the body and 'impressions of sensible *Objects*'.[41] All reasoning was thus liable to be subjugated to such phenomena. In effect, human beings contained two distinct 'faculties of *Knowing*': the understanding and the imagination. A constant '*intestin war*' raged between the two, as Willis himself testified. The 'twofold Knowing Power' in every subject, he declared, led necessarily to

39 [Charleton], *Passions*, pp. 89–92, 109–10, 141–3; Wright, *Passions of the Minde*, pp. 61–3; Michael Macdonald, *Mystical Bedlam: Madness, Anxiety, and Healing in Seventeenth-Century England* (Cambridge, 1981), pp. 174, 181–3, 185–92, 288 n. 59; cf. Kenneth Dewhurst (ed.), *Willis's Oxford Casebook (1650–52)* (Oxford, 1981), pp. 145–6 for a case involving Willis himself as physician. Images of faces in various passionate states were provided by Charles Le Brun in 1698: John Williams (trans.), *A Method to Learn to Design the Passions* (London, 1734). Jacques Revel remarks that such works provided 'an alphabet of the passions that everyone had to learn to read': 'The Uses of Civility', in Chartier (ed.), *A History of Private Life*, III, 167–205, esp. 170.

40 [Charleton], *Passions*, sigs. A3^{v}-A4^{r}, 2–3. For the divisions of the soul, see Katharine Park, 'The Organic Soul', in Charles B. Schmitt, Quentin Skinner and Eckhard Kessler (eds.), *The Cambridge History of Renaissance Philosophy* (Cambridge, 1988), pp. 464–84.

41 [Charleton], *Passions*, pp. 9–10, 22–5.

'wicked Combinations, troublesom Contests, and more than Civil Wars'. It was a vital struggle, on the outcome of which rested the fate of every individual human being, and hence that of the polity as a whole. If the sensitive soul won, then the 'divine *Politie*' of the rational soul would be lost forever to 'the brutish lusts of the insolent usurper', and hence to its appetite for 'triumphs of libidinous carnality'. In Willis's terms, the sensitive appetite 'seduces in us the Mind or Chief Soul, and snatches it away with it self, to role in the Mud of Sensual Pleasures'. Charleton for one considered this the more likely outcome, 'for, it is from the *Imagination* alone that [the soul] takes all the representations of things, and the fundamental *ideas*, upon which she afterward builds up all her *Science*'.[42]

Small wonder, then, that proposals to solve – or rather contain – this problem lay at the heart of attempts to reconstruct some sort of social and moral order out of the chaos of the British civil wars and, more widely, the Thirty Years' War. In their various ways, Charles I, Thomas Hobbes and even the notorious republican Algernon Sidney all aimed at producing polities which could successfully discipline humanity's inescapably passionate nature, and channel it to correct ends.[43] Their answers depended on proper forms of self-discipline, social organization, literary representation and communication. As that implies, reading and writing were profoundly implicated.

The significance of the material presented thus far for the subject of this chapter is consequently dramatic: for according to contemporary analysts, reading was an important element – perhaps *the* important element – in this civil war of the microcosm and macrocosm. The reason, again, lay in the very fundamentals of the practice, beginning with vision. Visual perception often worked in a way that seemed simply natural, as when one just 'saw' a block of wood. This was the effect successfully encapsulated in the *camera obscura* model. But even in such straightforward cases, vision necessarily functioned as part of the natural economy of the passions. Moreover, there were other instances in which it seemed that some active conditioning of that natural economy must be involved. Reading was one such instance. In such cases, 'habits' had grown up in each individual, by which the motions of the animal spirits and imagination in response to particular stimuli

42 Ibid., sig. A4^{v}ff, pp. 48–50, 54–9, 64; Willis, *Two Discourses*, sig. A2^{v}, pp. 42–3.
43 Kevin Sharpe, *The Personal Rule of Charles I* (New Haven, CT, 1992), pp. 189–91, 227–30; Thomas Hobbes, *Leviathan*, ed. Richard Tuck (Cambridge, 1991), pp. 37–59, 483–91; Jonathan Scott, *Algernon Sidney and the English Republic, 1623–1677* (Cambridge, 1988), pp. 35–8.

had been regularized. In learning to speak, for example, one habituated the motions of the spirits so that one only had to imagine what one wished to say, not the individual movements of the body which together produced vocal speech. Only a similar habituation allowed us to read words 'by the figure of their letters, when they are written'.[44]

This concept of habituation was crucial to representations of the body and its political significance in general. 'Habits' were held to be the best hope one had of countering immoral, unhealthy or erroneous passions. While the rational soul could not simply remove such passions, it could perhaps habituate the individual to physiological responses taming them. There were two principal means by which this might be effected, both of which rested substantially on the anatomical revelation of labyrinthine matrices of vessels in the brain. First, the rational soul could imagine objects producing a contrary passion to the one experienced. This could eventually produce a habit separating the motions of the blood and spirits from the impressions to which they would naturally be consequent, by accustoming them to passing through alternative channels. And secondly, one could learn to delay judgement of an impression. This would allow the spiritual turbulence to recede, permitting the rational soul a more detached interpretation.[45] Contrariety and hesitation: these were the routes to virtue. The habituation process reckoned so fundamental to reading was the same as that held up as the solution to the political problem of the passions. That was why John Locke, for one, reckoned it 'the great Thing to be minded in Education'.[46]

This issue was most prominently confronted in efforts to combat 'enthusiasm'. As defined by two of its key antagonists, Henry More and Meric Casaubon, enthusiasm was 'nothing else but a mis-conceit of being *inspired*'. That is, it was the conviction, held especially by some of the Interregnum's more notorious religious radicals, that God was at certain crucial moments in direct communication with them, and would vouchsafe them privileged knowledge by direct personal revelation.[47] Such a belief clearly warranted drastic action on the part of its holder,

44 Descartes, *Passions of the Soule*, pp. 35–6, 43–4.

45 Descartes, *Passions of the Soule*, pp. 36–7, 171; [Charleton], *Passions*, pp. 182–5.

46 [John Locke], *Some Thoughts Concerning Education* (London, 1693), pp. 18, 175–89.

47 [Henry More], *Enthusiasmus Triumphatus, or, A Discourse of the Nature, Causes, Kinds, and Cure, of Enthusiasme; written by Philophilus Parresiastes, and prefix'd to Alazonomastix his Observations and Reply* (Cambridge, 1656), pp. 1–2; Casaubon, *Treatise Concerning Enthusiasme*, pp. 3, 17. These characterizations, of course, were polemical and contested: Nigel Smith, *Perfection Proclaimed: Language and Literature in English Radical Religion 1640–1660* (Oxford, 1989) is the best attempt to recover 'enthusiasts'' own perspectives.

and therefore threatened social upheaval. After the Restoration, in particular, it was commonly blamed for the Great Rebellion and its consequences. More and Casaubon in the 1650s, and the Royal Society thereafter, were prominent in the struggle against it.

The method these antagonists adopted was to allege that an experience of apparent inspiration was in fact a 'distemper'. It was a physiological condition, needing to be cured rather than exorcized or idolized.[48] In short, it had natural causes. More knew Cartesian philosophy better than anyone else in the country at this time – he it was who introduced it into English intellectual culture, in the context of this very struggle against enthusiasm – and he singled out Descartes's *Passions* as an influential work. So it is unsurprising that, like Descartes, More placed the passions at the centre of his analysis.[49] According to his treatment, enthusiasm was nothing more than the consequence of an excess of 'ecstatical passion', which had created an 'illusion of the imagination'.[50]

While his own proffered physiology did not agree with Willis's, which he regarded as too materialist, More agreed with the Sedleian Professor that in practice reasoning could never be separated from corporeal perceptions. It therefore must always be prey to 'Phantasmes'. 'Thoughts', he believed, 'offer or force themselves upon the mind, . . . according to the nature or strength of the complexion of our Bodies'.[51] In some individuals, and in certain circumstances, the images thus presented in the imagination were as strong as those sensed in the outside world – and in such a case the party concerned could not fail to confuse the two.[52] Here was the real source for alleged experiences of inspiration. In their dreams, enthusiasts attained a state of '*Extasie*', in which the imagination was able to dominate the *sensus communis* to such an extent that the memory was 'as thoroughly sealed

48 Casaubon, *Treatise Concerning Enthusiasme*, pp. 28–9; [More], *Enthusiasmus Triumphatus*, sigs. [A5]^v-[A6]^v, pp. 2–20; Meric Casaubon, *Of Credulity and Incredulity, in things Natural, Civil, and Divine* (London, 1668), pp. 29–30.

49 Henry More, 'The Immortality of the Soul', in *A Collection of Several Philosophical Writings of Dr Henry More*, 4th edn (london, 1712), sig. [Ll4]^v. For More's appropriation of Descartes in the fight against enthusiasm, see Alan Gabbey, '*Philosophia Cartesiana Triumphata*: Henry More (1646–1671)', in Thomas M. Lennon, John M. Nicholas and John W. Davis (eds.), *Problems of Cartesianism* (Kingston, 1982), pp. 171–250.

50 Casaubon, *Treatise Concerning Enthusiasme*, p. 211.

51 [More], *Enthusiasmus Triumphatus*, pp. 2–4. For conflicts between More and Willis, see John Henry, 'The Matter of Souls: Medical Theory and Theology in Seventeenth-Century England', in Roger French and Andrew Wear (eds.), *The Medical Revolution of the Seventeenth Century* (Cambridge, 1989), pp. 7–113.

52 [More], *Enthusiasmus Triumphatus*, pp. 4–5.

therewith, as from the sense of any external Object'.[53] In an enthusiast, then, the sensitive soul was well on the way to winning the microcosmic civil war: the '*Imaginative* facultie has the preheminence above the *Rationall*'.[54] Moreover, since enthusiasts effectively surrendered their reason to their passions, far from being emancipated by their 'visions', as they themselves claimed, they were in fact delivering themselves up to merely mechanical reflexes. The body of such a person became 'perfectly *Cartesius* his *Machina*'.[55] More and his friend Ralph Cudworth had a name for such individuals. They called them '*Neurospasts*': marionettes or 'meer Puppets'. In a technical sense, since they had let the sensitive soul dominate completely, they had reverted to the status of mere beasts.[56]

More's problem was that in the 1640s he himself had published Platonic poems which had expressed what looked very like ecstasies. Was he then, as his opponent Thomas Vaughan claimed, 'sick of that Disease I would pretend to cure others of'?[57] More could see the point. He himself confessed that he had 'a natural touch of Enthusiasm in my complexion'.[58] To illustrate the difference between his own experiences and the professed inspirations of the enthusiast, though, he now recounted a dream he claimed to have had at around the time of the outbreak of the Civil War. He dreamt that he was at a friend's house on the road between England and Scotland. Leaving this house on a bright moonlit night, More saw a series of huge figures in the sky, most prominent among them that of an old man with a long beard. Lying on his side in the heavens, this figure made a number of gestures with his arm; and finally, as More re-entered the house, he intoned, 'There is indeed love amongst you, but onely according to the flesh.' Back indoors, More was able to tell his companions the import of the vision, 'expounding the generall meaning of my dream in my dream'. He interpreted the movements of the old man's arm as 'an Embleme of the proceedings of God when he chastises a nation', adducing 'reasons out

53 Ibid., p. 27.
54 Ibid., pp. 40–1, 43–6, 50–1, 294–5.
55 More, 'Immortality', pp. 132–3.
56 Ralph Cudworth, *A Discourse Concerning the True Notion of the Lord's Supper. To which are added Two Sermons*, 3rd edn (London, 1676), p. 64; Nathanael Ingelo, *Bentivoglio and Urania, in Six Books*, 4th edn (London, 1682), p. 91; [More], *Enthusiasmus Triumphatus*, pp. 315–16. See also Alan Gabbey, 'Cudworth, More, and the Mechanical Analogy', in Richard Kroll, Richard Ashcraft and Perez Zagorin (eds.), *Philosophy, Science and Religion in England 1640–1700* (Cambridge, 1992), pp. 109–27.
57 [More], *Enthusiasmus Triumphatus*, p. 309.
58 More, *A Collection of Several Philosophical Writings*, p. x.

of *Aristotles* Mechanicks, which I had very lately read', for the precise nature of the movements. It appeared to have been a true vision, then, with a valid message. But then More recalled that 'the *Vision* (as I may so call it) in this dream' had a terrestrial origin after all. He had been reading Ptolemy's *Geographia* the evening before, and, seeing a particular iconographic figure on the engraved frontispiece, 'my fancy it seems having laid hold on his venerable beard, drew in thereby the whole scene of things that presented themselves to me in my sleep'. One's 'Fancy' could evidently be imprinted entirely naturally by an image on the frontispiece of Ptolemy during waking hours, and without one being aware of any unusual effects.[59] It could happen to anybody, and could produce a seeming vision of utterly convincing reality.

Similar effects could also be generated by reading words. In his own attack on enthusiasm, Meric Casaubon thus concentrated on what he called 'the strange, but natural effects' produced by words on the soul. Metaphors, for example, provided 'representation of shapes and images' to the imagination.[60] Classical rhetoricians had observed that it was 'When by a kind of Enthusiasme ... you think you see what you speak of, and so set it out by words to those that hear you, that you make it in a manner visible.' Casaubon himself was able to testify that whenever he read a passage from a classical poet, 'I do not only phancy to my self, that I see those things that they describe; but also find in my self (as I phansy) the very same content and pleasure, that I should, if my eyes beheld them in some whether coloured, or carved representation of some excellent Artist'.[61] The error of the enthusiast lay in attributing to such natural reading experiences the status of certain, even divinely warranted, truth; such an error was at its most dangerous, needless to say, when what was being read was Scripture itself.

Casaubon and More thus used accounts of the effects of reading texts and images in order to characterize and attack enthusiasm. Enthusiasts were those who did not habituate their reading and their passions properly. Knowledge, civility and the physiology of reading intersected here, as More and Casaubon put their ideas of the nature and effects of reading to work in the most controversial of circumstances, to discriminate true from false knowledge, safe veneration from

59 [More], *Enthusiasmus Triumphatus*, pp. 309–12. See also pp. 312–35, for another dream which More describes as the nearest he ever came to experiencing a '*Vision* or *Enthusiasme*'. His reading of '*Aristotle's* Mechanicks' played a central part in this dream, too.

60 Casaubon, *Treatise Concerning Enthusiasme*, pp. 135ff, 150–1, 170, 175–6, 182.

61 Casaubon, *Treatise Concerning Enthusiasme*, pp. 182–4.

rebellious sectarianism. As the greatest of all anatomists, William Harvey, had put it, whoever 'read the words of Authors' and did not 'by the aid of their own senses abstract therefrom true representations of the things themselves as they are described in the authors words, [could] not conceive in their own minds aught but deceitful eidola and vain fancies and never true ideas. And so they frame for themselves certain shadows and chimaeras, and all their theory and contemplation, which none the less they count knowledge, represents nothing but waking men's dreams and sick men's fantasies.'[62]

Harvey was by this time revered by a certain group of men as providing something which they, at least, definitely 'counted knowledge'. The Restoration saw the establishment of a new, 'experimental' philosophy, designed, as Steven Shapin and Simon Schaffer have famously shown, to overcome precisely the problem of knowledge which was thought to have fostered the turmoil of the Great Rebellion. At the forefront of this effort stood the victim of passionate reading already introduced, Robert Boyle, and the institution he substantially embodied: the Royal Society.[63]

Many sources could be used to illustrate the Royal Society's involvement with issues of knowledge and the passions. There is not space here to attempt a comprehensive survey. However, by common consent the most impressive single document produced during the first decade of the Society's existence was Robert Hooke's *Micrographia*, and it is therefore appropriate to concentrate on this work. Moreover, while the spectacular engravings for which it has been remembered were indeed unprecedented, contemporaries also recognized in the volume a prescriptive model for the practice of natural philosophy itself, and therefore for the safe and reliable attainment of knowledge.[64]

Hooke began by expressing similar concerns to those of Casaubon and More, pronouncing it no wonder that existing knowledge was imperfect, since 'the *forces of our own minds* conspire to betray us'.

62 William Harvey, *Disputations Touching the Generation of Animals*, trans. Gweneth Whitteridge (Oxford, 1981), p. 16, cited in Andrew Wear, 'William Harvey and the "Way of the Anatomists"', *History of Science* 21 (1983): 223–49, esp. p. 240.

63 Shapin and Schaffer, *Leviathan and the Air-Pump*; Simon Schaffer, 'Godly Men and Mechanical Philosophers: Souls and Spirits in Restoration Natural Philosophy', *Science in Context* 1 (1987): 55–85.

64 John T. Harwood, 'Rhetoric and Graphics in *Micrographia*', in Michael Hunter and Simon Schaffer (eds.), *Robert Hooke: New Studies* (Woodbridge, 1989), pp. 119–47; Michael Aaron Dennis, 'Graphic Understanding: Instruments and Interpretation in Robert Hooke's *Micrographia*', *Science in Context* 3 (1989): 309–64.

However, he then asserted a way to circumvent this problem, 'by rectifying the operations of the *Sense*, the *Memory*, and *Reason*'. He proposed to do this, significantly, by using instruments. He believed that the senses could give false information for two reasons. They might be disproportionate to the objects of interest, and thus unable to perceive them at all (as was the case, for example, with atoms); or they might err in their perception of those things which they could pick up. As a result, many of the most 'solid' notions of philosophers were 'rather expressions of our own misguided apprehensions then of the true nature of the things themselves'. The remedy had to reach to the essential cause of the problem. For Hooke this meant 'the adding of *artificial Organs* to the *natural*'. If the organs of perception could thereby be standardized, then the reformation of knowledge at which he professed to aim could be achieved with no more reliance on the 'strength of *Imagination*', but simply by 'a *sincere Hand*, and a *faithful Eye*'. The 'Science of Nature' had been for too long 'only a work of the *Brain* and *Fancy*', and it was time for his artificial organs to rectify them. Hooke was thus proposing nothing less than a 'universal cure of the Mind'. And if his approach proved fruitful, it might even be possible to recapture the original '*unpassionate*' knowledge which had existed before the Fall.

Micrographia began as if it were a work of geometry. Instead of a mathematical point, though (the classic starting element of that science), Hooke began with its physical equivalent, the tip of a pin. Under his microscope this sharpest of material points was revealed to be blunt and pitted.[65] Hooke then turned the microscope onto 'a *point* commonly so call'd': 'that is, the mark of a *full stop*, or *period*'. Through the microscope any such character, printed or written – and Hooke had examined 'multitudes' of each – appeared 'like *smutty daubings* [made] on a matt or uneven floor with a blunt extinguisht brand or stick's end'. By a combination of irregularity of type, uneven cloth-based paper and rough use of ink, the result was reminiscent of nothing so much as 'a great splatch of *London* dirt'. The microscope likewise revealed some much-vaunted tiny writing as barely readable without 'a good *fantsy* well *preposest* to help one through'. All letters, Hooke reported, were like this. The postlapsarian disproportion of the senses to nature, and their alliance with the imagination, were precisely sufficient to allow human beings to read under normal circumstances.[66] Since the 'Imaginations'

65 This point was stressed in the review in the *Journal des Sçavans*: Betty T. Morgan, *Histoire du Journal des Sçavans depuis 1665 jusqu'en 1701* (Paris, 1928), pp. 162–3.

66 Hooke, *Micrographia*, pp. 1–4; cf. Della Porta, *Natural Magick*, p. 363.

we had of objects were not decided by 'the Nature of the things themselves' so much as by 'the peculiar Organs, by which they are made sensible to the Understanding', different organs would have produced different perceptions. Hooke had himself been able to read letters in what would otherwise be reckoned darkness, thanks to one of his artificial organs contrived from 'an ordinary double Convex Spherical Lens'.[67]

If perception varied with the senses, then this obviously seriously prejudiced one's knowledge: in the brain, the understanding was 'apt to be sway'd to this or that hand, according as it is more affected or prest by this or that Instance'.[68] However, Hooke now pointed out a still greater implication. There existed fundamental causes of prejudice particular to individuals, he maintained, by virtue of 'every Man's own peculiar Structure'. Every philosopher was born to 'a Constitution of Body and Mind, that does more or less dispose him to this or that kind of Imagination or Phant'sy of things'. This affected the sort of philosophy he produced: 'some kind of Constitutions of Body does more incline a Man to Contemplation, and Speculation, another to Operation, Examination, and making Experiments'.[69] This had been true in the history of natural philosophy above all. Previous philosophers, Hooke indicated, had become 'habituated' against 'any thing that offered it self as a Novelty or New Discovery', and they had embraced dogmatism – the Royal Society's professed antithesis, and a sign of enthusiasm. Hooke could even provide real examples, relating some of the most eminent schools of philosophy to the mental physiology of their founders.

Just as a Man that is troubled with the Jaundice, supposes all things to be Yellow, and all things he eats, till otherwise prevented, serve to augment his Choler, by being chang'd into it: Or a melancholy Person, that thinks he meets with nothing but frightful Apparitions, does convert all things he either sees or hears into dreadful Representations, and makes use of them to strengthen his Phant'sy, and fill it fuller of such uneasy Apprehensions, so is it in Constitutions of Mind as to Philosophy. Thus *Aristotle*'s Physick is very much influenced by his Logick: *Des Cartes* Philosophy savours much of his Opticks: *Van Helmonts*, and the rest of the Chymists of their Chimical Operations: *Gilberts* of the Loadstone: *Pythagoras*'s and *Jordanus Brunus*'s,

67 Richard Waller (ed.), *The Posthumous Works of Robert Hooke* (London, 1705), pp. 8–9, 13.
68 Ibid., pp. 5–6.
69 Ibid., pp. 9, 47. Cf. Reynolds, *Passions*, pp. 6–7.

Kepler's, &c. of Arithmetick and Harmony of Numbers ... and indeed every one according to the things he most fancies naturally.[70]

If Hooke was right, then there was no way, even in principle, to produce true knowledge on one's own, and the history of philosophy was a catalogue of demonstrations of that fact. Knowledge must be produced collectively, as exemplified by the practice of the Royal Society.

Such a recommendation, since it valued social processes of legitimation so highly, necessarily returned Hooke to the issue of the proper recording and transmission of knowledge. Experiments must be 'registered' as soon as they had been conducted, in as much incidental detail as possible. They should be written down on 'a very fine piece of Paper', and entered in a large book called a 'Repository'. Just as the quality of the lens in a microscope was all-important, moreover, so was the visual layout of this register. Its contents must be 'ranged in the best and most Natural Order', so as to be 'manifest to the Eye'. Throughout, everything must be expressed in as few words as possible, perhaps even in shorthand, so as to be 'the more obvious, and ... thereby the less disturb the Mind in its Inquiry'. It was best to write in different inks, with consistent colour-coding to aid immediate perception. It was not the mere fact of registration which Hooke thought important, then, but the detailed way in which information was traced on the page. Only if disciplined in this correct manner could experimental matters of fact help to 'rectify the Mind'.[71]

Hooke took the provisions of this recipe very seriously. He emphasized these very factors, for example, in championing projects for publication. Moses Pitt's *English Atlas*, which he strongly supported, was thus designed to present 'a plaine simple cleer and uncompounded Representation of the Object to the Sense', to 'more easily imprint that idea the Deeper in the memory, which is the Principall use of such a work'.[72] That he maintained this view so strongly is hardly surprising, since Hooke based it on principles of mind and body which he felt to be of universal applicability. As he declared in a lecture on geometry, given these principles it was essential to follow his mechanisms for

70 Waller (ed.), *Posthumous Works of Robert Hooke*, pp. 3–4, 9–10. Cottingham, Stoothoff and Kenny (eds.), *Philosophical Writings of Descartes*, I, 47.

71 Waller (ed.), *Posthumous Works of Robert Hooke*, pp. 18–19, 24, 34, 36, 42, 63–5, 138–48 (esp. pp. 139–40); Lotte Mulligan, 'Robert Hooke's "Memoranda": Memory and Natural History', *Annals of Science* 49 (1992): 47–61, esp. pp. 50–3.

72 London British Library, Sl. 1039, fols. 1^r-2^r.

'furnishing the Mind with the true grounds of Knowledge'. Adherence to them was not just necessary for experimental philosophy, moreover – *all* knowledge must be communicated in such a fashion. 'We see it necessary, and practised in many other things where a good habit is to be acquired', he insisted – 'as in Reading, Writing, Musick, Drawing, and most other Manual Operations'.[73]

This chapter has used contemporary accounts of anatomy, the passions, philosophical method and perception, in order to encourage a widening of the terms in which we view the practices and representations of reading in the Restoration. The fact that uses of this material were so various in the period, so that the treatment offered here has at times departed from a narrow concentration on reading itself to consider issues of knowledge and politics, only reinforces its salience. Such uses remind us, moreover, that the history of reading should seek to have an impact on more general issues in cultural historiography. Indeed, its importance in this respect derives not only from modern historiographical debates, but from simple attention to the words of historical characters themselves. For example, John Dryden insisted upon the importance of reading history because 'it informs the understanding by the memory'. Since mankind was 'the same in all ages', he explained, and 'agitated by the same passions', nothing could come to pass unless 'some Presedent of the like nature has already been produc'd'. It was a view shared by many.[74] That this was so rested largely on assumptions about the natural economy of the passions – an economy which Dryden and his contemporaries assumed to be universal and sempiternal. Yet if the purpose of reading history was based on this economy, then what about the purposes of reading literature, philosophy and other fields of knowledge? They too were to be assessed in terms of the repertoire of processes adumbrated by Dryden. So in turn were any *actions* they could be taken as warranting: actions perpetrated in the realms of society and politics. If the widening of terms proposed by this chapter is accepted, then, the implications should extend beyond the historiography of reading *per se*. Meanwhile, historians of reading should continue asking themselves what theirs is a history *of*, and what it is *for*.

[73] Waller (ed.), *Posthumous Works of Robert Hooke*, p. 70.
[74] Joseph M. Levine, *The Battle of the Books: History and Literature in the Augustan Age* (Ithaca, NY, 1991), p. 274.

CHAPTER 9

'In the even my wife read to me': women, reading and household life in the eighteenth century

Naomi Tadmor

The image of the passive female reader recurs very often in eighteenth-century historiography and literary criticism. This image is fed from various directions. One of its main sources of sustenance is a theory of social and economic change. Alice Clark, in her path-breaking book *The Working Life of Women in the Seventeenth Century*, published in 1919, says: 'At the beginning of the seventeenth century it was usual for the women of the aristocracy to be very busy with affairs – affairs which concerned their households, their estates, and even government.'[1] But 'once the strong hand of necessity' has relaxed, due to the rise of capitalism, 'there has been a marked tendency in English life for the withdrawal of married women from all productive activity, and their consequent devotion to the cultivation of idle graces'.[2] Clark does not specify what these idle graces were, but her reference at this point to Mary Astell's *A Serious Proposal to the Ladies* can suggest to the reader that the consumption of novels and romances was among the vices of the age.[3]

Nearly sixty years later, this argument was extended in Lawrence Stone's *The Family, Sex and Marriage*. 'Wives of the middle and upper

I am grateful to the participants at *The Practice and Representation of Reading in Britain from the Fourteenth to the Nineteenth Centuries* for their questions and comments. I would especially like to thank David Feldman, James Raven, Helen Small, Miriam Tadmor and Amanda Vickery for their help in preparing this essay for publication.

1 Alice Clark, *Working Life of Women in the Seventeenth Century*, ed. A. L. Erickson (1919; London, 1992), p. 14.

2 Clark, *The Working Life of Women*, pp. 295–6, 38–41. A recent development of a similar theory, can be found, for example, in Susan D. Amussen, *An Ordered Society: Gender and Class in Early Modern England* (Oxford, 1988), p. 187: '... the family was changing as women in wealthy families gradually withdrew from work, and as poorer families became increasingly dependent on wages'.

3 Mary Astell, *A Serious Proposal to the Ladies for the Advancement of their True and Greatest Interest* (1694; London, 1697). See, for example, her following recommendation on p. 51: 'since the *French Tongue* is understood by most Ladies, methinks they may much better improve it by the study of Philosophy (as I hear the *French Ladies* do), *Des Cartes*, *Malerbranche* and others, than by reading idle *Novels* and *Romances*'.

classes', says Stone, 'increasingly became idle drones. They turned household management over to stewards, reduced their reproductive responsibilities by contraceptive measures, and passed their time in such occupations as novel-reading, theatre-going, card-playing and formal visits ... the custom of turning wives into ladies "languishing in listlessness" as ornamental status objects spread downwards through the social scale.'[4] Stone sees novels and the female novel reader not only as manifestations of empty-headed idleness, but also as potential agents of social change. Novels have stimulated romantic notions in the hearts of young women, taught them to fall in love, vent their feelings in unrestrained ways, and make imprudent and unhappy choices of marriage partners. Fiction reading also set impossible expectations of marital bliss, which were doomed to failure. The result was that idle and frustrated women threatened to undermine the social cohesion of the nuclear family.[5]

Other historians, such as J. H. Plumb, describe the eighteenth-century female reader as a woman of leisure. She is located in the expanding middling ranks – the dynamic core of the growing consumer society – which had more money to buy and borrow books, more booksellers and libraries from which to buy and borrow, and more time to indulge in these activities.[6] The growing 'middling' readership, and the female reader are also described by historians of the book. Influential early historians of the novel, most famously Ian Watt, connected these new phenomena to the growth of individualism, and particularly to the influence of Protestantism, with its emphasis on private reading, introspection and thought.[7]

The image of the passive and idle female reader has had a significant impact on feminist literary criticism as well. The emergence of the novel as a distinct form of entertainment which was to be enjoyed in private is perceived as one of the milestones in the rise of a new form

4 Lawrence Stone, *The Family, Sex and Marriage in England, 1500–1800* (London, 1977), pp. 396–7.

5 See Stone, *The Family, Sex and Marriage*, pp. 282–8, 396–7.

6 J. H. Plumb, 'The Public, Literature and the Arts in the Eighteenth Century', in P. Fritz and D. Williams (eds.), *The Triumph of Culture: Eighteenth-Century Perspectives* (Toronto, 1972); Plumb, 'The Commercialization of Leisure in Eighteenth-Century England', in Neil McKendrick, John Brewer and J. H. Plumb (eds.), *The Birth of a Consumer Society* (London, 1982). See also James Raven, *British Fiction 1750–1770: A Chronological Check-List of Prose Fiction Printed in Britain and Ireland* (Newark, DE, 1987), pp. 31–2.

7 Watt, *Rise of the Novel*; Altick, *The English Common Reader*. For the role of the woman of leisure see, e.g. Watt, *Rise of the Novel*, pp. 43–4, and J. J. Richetti, *Popular Fiction Before Richardson: Narrative Patterns, 1700–1739* (Oxford, 1969), pp. 125–6.

of femininity.[8] Nancy Armstrong describes how the domestic woman was given dominance over private life, while her desire was crushed by domestic fiction.[9] Kathryn Shevelow sees the domestic woman as being constructed 'in and by print'.[10] The woman's undervalued and unwaged labour in the home is at times recognized, but on the whole the reading woman tends to be associated with leisure, if not with boredom and idleness: 'the fantasies of heroism ... accurately register the boredom of a well-reared female's life', says Patricia Meyer Spacks in a recent work.[11]

One possible reason for this enduring image of the female reader is an underestimation of the household work that was performed by women – even gentlewomen – in both practical and managerial capacities.[12] Another reason is the belief that eighteenth-century moralists held in the impressionable nature of women, and particularly young women.[13] Related to it is the faith in the power of example: 'the power of example is so great' that 'care ought to be taken that, when the choice is unrestrained, the best examples only should be exhibited', said Samuel Johnson in

8 See, for example, the summarizing view in Rosalind Coward, 'The True Story of How I Became my own Person', in Catherine Belsey and Jane Moore (eds.), *The Feminist Reader: Essays in Gender and the Politics of Literary Criticism* (London, 1989), p. 36.

9 Nancy Armstrong, *Desire and Domestic Fiction: A Political History of the Novel* (Oxford, 1987), pp. 1–2. Compare, for example, Ruth Bernard Yeazell, *Fictions of Modesty: Women and Courtship in the English Novel* (Chicago, IL, 1991); Catherine Belsey, *Critical Practice* (London 1980). See also Amanda J. Vickery's illuminating analysis of historiographical categories such as 'separate spheres' and 'public and private', in her 'Golden Age to Separate Spheres? A Review of the Categories and Chronology of English Women's History', *The Historical Journal* 36 (1993): 383–414.

10 Kathryn Shevelow, *Women and Print Culture: The Construction of Femininity in the Early Periodical* (London, 1989), p. 5. Shevelow's main argument, however, also highlights the important paradox between women's increasing participation in print culture and the restrictive ideology that this culture advertised.

11 Patricia Meyer Spacks, *Desire and Truth: Functions of Plot in Eighteenth-Century English Novels* (Chicago, IL, 1990), p. 16. On the leisure of women in periodicals, see Shevelow, *Women and Print Culture*, pp. 53–7, and references there in n. 27 to Clark, *The Working Life of Women*, and n. 31 to J. H. Plumb, 'The Commercialization of Leisure in Eighteenth-Century England', and to Terry Lovell, *Consuming Fiction* (London 1987), pp. 38–9: ' "the relationship of women to leisure time is notoriously problematic" because of the difficulties women's household labour raises for Marxist discussions of work and production and for discussions of relationship between the hallmarks of leisure – "free time," "consumption," and pleasure – and women's position within the home'.

12 See Vickery, 'Golden Age to Separate Spheres?', pt 2 and especially pp. 409–10.

13 See Michael McKeon, *The Origins of the English Novel, 1600–1740* (Baltimore, MD, 1987), p. 22. Note McKeon's important critical comment on p. 52: 'From Dante on, the fear that women's morals will be corrupted by reading romances is quite conventional, and its articulation may provide evidence less of the rise of the reading public than of the persistence of anxiety about women.'

the *Rambler*.[14] The pages of eighteenth-century periodicals, sermons and other instructive texts are filled with warnings against the malign influence of novels, 'the literary opium that lulls every sense into delicious rapture'.[15] Self-deprecation is also a recurring theme in eighteenth-century novels: novelists frequently strove to assert the value of their own writing by condemning the genre. Henry Fielding, for example, followed Jonathan Swift in describing pastry cooks using the pages of idle romances for lining pie-dishes.[16] The image of the impressionable and idle female reader, however, remains with us. It seems, indeed, that the rebukes of eighteenth-century moralists have been elevated to the status of an historical fact.

This essay examines the ways in which reading was conducted in two eighteenth-century households: the household of Thomas and Peggy Turner, and the household of Samuel Richardson. The argument presented here is that the practice of reading in both these households was connected not to idleness, listlessness or frivolity but to a routine of work and of religious discipline. The essay also seeks to show that in both households reading was a private experience in the sense that it was done in the home, but it was often a sociable rather than a solitary experience and this was especially manifested in the regular habit of reading aloud. The link that allows us to associate these two households – the Turners' and the Richardsons' – is a novel, *Clarissa: The History of a Young Lady*. *Clarissa* was planned and written, read and debated, edited and re-edited within the walls of Samuel Richardson's household.[17] In 1755–6 it was also read by Peggy Turner and her husband Thomas.

Thomas Turner was a mercer and draper in the village of East Hoathly, Sussex. He was born in 1729, and it is not known whether and

[14] Samuel Johnson, *Rambler* 4 (31 March 1750), quoted in Meyer Spacks, *Desire and Truth*, p. 22. The great impact of literary example on the female mind is also a recurring theme in contemporary medical treatises. I am grateful to Helen Small for drawing this to my attention.

[15] *The Universal Magazine* (1772), quoted in Stone, *The Family, Sex and Marriage*, p. 284. See reference there, p. 396 to Oliver Goldsmith's lament: 'How delusive, how destructive, are those pictures of consummate bliss.'

[16] *The History of Tom Jones*, ed. R. P. C. Mutter (1749; Harmondsworth, 1978) pp. 151 and 879, n. iv. Generic self-deprecation is the main theme of Charlotte Lennox, *The Female Quixote* (1752; Oxford, 1989). See also Jane Austen, *Northanger Abbey* (written 1788–9, published 1817; Oxford, 1987), p. 1: 'No one who had ever seen Catherine Moreland in her infancy would have supposed her born to be a heroine.'

[17] This process started around 1742, heightened with the publication of *Clarissa* in 1748–9, and possibly continued until Richardson's death in 1765, see T. C. Duncan Eaves and Ben D. Kimpel, *Samuel Richardson, A Biography* (Oxford, 1971).

where he may have received regular schooling.[18] In his teens he probably served as an apprentice, to a shopkeeper, and at the age of twenty-one he set up his business in East Hoathly. He married at twenty-four. Margaret [Peggy] Turner was the daughter of a farming couple. Nothing is known of her education. At the time that she met Thomas Turner she was living as a servant in Lewes. Soon after their marriage, Thomas Turner started keeping a diary, which he continued to write for eleven years.

Both Thomas and Peggy Turner read. The list of books mentioned by Thomas Turner in his diary amounts to over seventy items.[19] It is possible to suggest four main points for considering the practice of reading in the Turner household. First, reading was part of a daily routine which consisted mostly of hard work. Secondly, reading was part of a religious discipline. Thirdly, reading was part of a social life, and, fourthly, reading was done intermittently: that is, texts were read in combination with other texts and genres and texts were also read in combination with – or while doing – other things.

Both Thomas and Peggy Turner worked in their house and the adjoining shop. Their reading time was usually in the evening, at the end of a day's hard work. For example, on Saturday, 18 September 1756 Thomas Turner reported: 'In the even T. Davy brought a p[ai]r Shoes for my Nephew and stayed and Supp'd w[i]th us and I read him the 4th of Tillotsons Sermons. Very busy all day'. On Friday, 7 May 1756 he wrote: 'my wife read to me in the Even 4 No. of the Freeholder'. And on Monday, 21 March 1757 he reported once again that 'Thomas Davy sate with us an hour or two in the even to whom I read part of the newspaper.'[20] Daytime reading was practised most

[18] This short summary is based on David Vaisey's introduction to the Oxford edition of *The Diary of Thomas Turner* (Oxford 1985), xvii-xxxix. See references there to baptism, marriage and burial registers of Thomas Turner and members of his family. See also Thomas Turner's 'Notes on family history', printed in G. H. Jennings (ed.), *The Diary of a Georgian Shopkeeper* (Oxford, 1979), pp. 79–84. The following references to Thomas Turner's diary cite Thomas Turner Papers, Manuscripts and Archives, Yale University Library. Diary entries are mentioned by date. I am grateful to Yale University Library for allowing me to reproduce quotations from the diary.

[19] See Vaisey, *Diary*, Appendix D 'Thomas Turner's Reading', and references there.

[20] See also other references on Thursday, 25 September 1755; Saturday, 3 January 1756; Wednesday, 14 January 1756; Saturday, 24 January 1756; Wednesday, 28 April 1756; Thursday, 29 April 1756. The way in which reading was embedded in a routine of work created interesting juxtapositions in many diary entries between the intellectual and the mundane. For example, 'In reading the Odyssey last night among many curious passages these two lines I think applicable to the present times, Viz, "why cease ye then ye wrath of Heaven to stay; Be humbled all & Lead ye great the way" ... Paid for brooms 6*d*', Saturday, 21 February 1756.

regularly on Sundays and holidays. On Sunday, 22 May 1756, for example, Thomas Turner read three of Tillotson's sermons, four more were read on the following Sunday, 30 May. On Christmas day of 1756 he read seven of Tillotson's sermons during the day and the evening, and seven more sermons on the following Sunday.[21] Daytime reading on weekdays was also practised, at times extensively, but it seems to have been a sign of slow trade rather than prosperous leisure. During the months of November–December 1756, for example, Thomas Turner makes a number of complaints such as the following: 'what Will becomes of me I cannot Imagine, my trade being so bad ...'[22] Around that time he also spends daytime hours in reading. On Thursday, 26 May 1757 he moans once again: 'nothing to do in the Shop, a prodigious Melancholy time'. At the start of June he spends daytime hours reading Locke's treatise on Education.[23]

Reading was also part of a religious discipline. Thomas and Peggy Turner were frequent attendants at the Sunday services in the East Hoathly parish church. Their shared religious sentiments were also expressed in reading: 'in the Even my Wife Read one of Tillotsons Sermons';[24] 'in the Even my Wife & I read part of the Sermon preach'd ... at the opening of St Peters Cornhill 1681.'[25] Indeed, a large part of the reading time at the Turner household was devoted to religious books and sermons. Tillotson's sermons were the most favoured and were read again and again, not only by Peggy and Thomas Turner but also by friends who visited their household: 'Mr Elles and I read 3 of Tillotsons Sermons'.[26] 'Joseph Fuller Jun. & Tho. Durrant drank Some Coffe with me ... to whom I read One of Tillotsons Sermons.'[27]

Reading involved social transactions and was also part of sociability. This was expressed in mainly three ways. Firstly, purchasing, lending and borrowing of books were closely connected with other social

21 Saturday and Sunday, 25–6 December 1756.

22 This particular complaint was made on Thursday, 16 December 1756.

23 For example, Thursday, Friday and Saturday, 9–11 June 1757.

24 Thursday, 23 September 1756.

25 Monday, 1 November 1756. It should be noted that Thomas Turner was also engaged in the reading of intellectual and scientific texts, which, apparently, he normally read on his own. Sometimes he combined these with the reading of devotional texts: it is tempting to think that the combination was intentional. The reading of Locke's *Essay of Human Understanding* during the daytime was counterbalanced by two of Tillotson's sermons in the evening, Saturday, 27 November 1756. Locke's *Thoughts Concerning Education* was read with Tillotson's sermons on Thursday, Friday and Saturday, 9–11 June 1757. Part of *The Whole Duty of Man* and part of the *Medical Essays* were read on Friday, 10 February 1758.

26 Friday, 17 December 1756.

27 Sunday, 4 December 1763.

networks. On Saturday, 10 July 1756, for example, when Thomas Turner went to visit his brother in Tunbridge Wells, he also bought two books on behalf of two of his close companions. He subscribed to *Martin's Magazine* together with one of them, but agreed to pay a larger share so as to keep the issues.[28] On Friday, 9 January 1756 a volume of *The Guardian* was lent to a female neighbour. On Saturday, 24 January Peggy Turner's father borrowed a volume of plays, and on 18 February the gardener at Halland House, the Duke of Newcastle's mansion, borrowed *The Whole Duty of Man.* Secondly, reading was often done in company. Thirdly, much reading was done aloud. Thomas Turner and his wife read together, and to each other. It is likely that their servant-maid or nephews, who lived in their house during these years participated in at least some of these exchanges and, as we have seen, guests who came to the house also took part in reading and listening: 'Tho. Davy Spent the Even & Supp'd at our House and read 2 of Tillotsons sermons to us', [29] 'in the Even Tho. Davy at Our House to whom I read the 4th Book of Miltons Paradise Lost',[30] 'in the Even my Wife read Part of Salmon on marriage to me'.[31]

Finally, reading was also done intermittently. Parts of texts were read on one evening and parts of other texts were read on the next. The reading of many texts stretched over months and was entwined with reading of other texts from various genres. Many volumes were not read in a linear way from beginning to end, or were not read throughout.[32] This practice of intermitted reading could have been a matter of personal preference. But the habit of evening reading was also interrupted by various social activities, or simply by long hours of work. This was lamented by Thomas Turner in the following journal entry: 'Mr and Mrs Burgess and their Children drank Tea at our House. Mr Burgess and his wife stay'd and plaid at Cards (my Wife & I lost 6*d*) and Suped at our House on the remains of to days Dinner. this is not that pleasure as if I had spent the even in reading.'[33]

This was the setting in which *Clarissa* was read in the Turner household in 1755–6. On the evening of Thursday, 25 September 1755

28 Wednesday, 21 January 1756.
29 Sunday, 10 October 1756.
30 Saturday, 20 May 1758.
31 Thursday, 7 September 1758.
32 A similar point was made by John Barrell and Harriet Guest with regard to poetry, see 'On the Use of Contradiction: Economics and Morality in the Eighteenth-Century Long Poem', in Felicity Nussbaum and Laura Brown (eds.), *The New Eighteenth Century: Theory, Politics, English Literature* (New York, 1987), pp. 121–43.
33 Wednesday, 5 December 1756.

one neighbour came to visit and stayed and smoked a pipe, and Peggy Turner read aloud from *The Guardian.* On Sunday, 5 October Thomas Turner read from *The Whole Duty of Man.* On Wednesday, 15 October Peggy Turner read to Thomas part of *Clarissa Harlowe.* During this autumn Thomas Turner also read part of 'The Jews Antiquities',[34] *Voyage into the Levant,*[35] *The Recruiting Officer*[36] and *The Yeoman of Kent.*[37] On the evening of Monday, 1 December he was writing letters to his suppliers in London; on the same evening he also read a part of the 7th volume of *Clarissa Harlowe.* On the following day he returned to *Voyage into the Levant.*[38]

During the rest of December, evenings were spent in various activities such as reading,[39] a supper at a neighbour's house, card-playing[40] and entertaining Peggy Turner's father who came to visit.[41] The evenings of January were spent in similar ways. On Monday, 26 January Peggy and Thomas Turner lost money at cards and went to bed drunk. At the start of February they spent two evenings working together preparing tobacco papers.[42] On Tuesday, 10 February they had a bitter argument: Peggy Turner went alone to the house of a female friend, won twopence at cards and did not return until one in the morning. But on Monday, 23 February she again read *Clarissa Harlowe* to her husband and this time, too, household reading was combined with work: 'in the even I wrote my London Letters ... also read the News paper ... as I was a writing all the even my wife read Clarissa Harlowe to me'. The reading aloud of *Clarissa* continued, as did work: the 'moving Scene of the Funeral of Miss: Clarissa Harlowe' was read while Thomas Turner was doing his accounts. Nonetheless he was deeply affected: 'Oh: may the Supreme Being give me Grace to lead my life in such a manner as my Exit may in some respect be like that Divine Creatures ...'[43] On Saturday, 28 February Thomas Turner reported that Peggy Turner 'finished reading of Clarissa

34 Sunday 26 October 1755.
35 Friday, 21 November 1755; Thursday, 27 November 1755.
36 Monday, 24 November 1755.
37 Wednesday, 26 November 1755.
38 He continued reading it on Thursday, 4 December.
39 Reading from *The Guardian,* Tuesday, 23 December 1755; from William Derham, *Psycio-Theology: or, a demonstration of the being and attributes of God, from his works of creation,* and reading poems by Smart together with a friend, Thursday, 25 December 1755.
40 Monday, 29 December 1755.
41 Entertaining Thomas Davy and Mr Slater, Wednesday, 31 December 1755.
42 Tuesday, 3 February; Thursday, 12 February 1756.
43 Wednesday, 25 February 1756. See also his comment on Friday, 27 February 1756.

Harlowe'. He commented that it is 'a very well wrote thing tho it must be allowed it is to[o] prolix'.[44]

It may be that this diary does not detail all the different reading practices within the Turner household. But at the very least it is possible to see that there is enough evidence to suggest that the reading of *Clarissa* did not turn Peggy Turner into an idle drone, a frenzied consumer or a domestic angel. Following entries continue to reveal her strong will and hard work: 'My Wife at home very busy to day in putting up the goods for the Audit',[45] 'my Wife very Busy at home all day ...';[46] 'my Wife a Picking of hops for Joseph Fuller in the Afternoon ...'[47] Nor did Peggy Turner 'languish in listlessness as a decorative object'. Indeed, she never recovered her health after her early pregnancy and the death of her only child. In the years following the reading of *Clarissa* she was often unwell, but she still continued to work in the house and shop. At the age of twenty-seven she died after a painful illness.

The Richardson household was more highly placed socially than that of the Turners, all the more so after the publication of Samuel Richardson's first novel. This household was deeply engaged with the world of books. This is how one of the women who lived there in her youth described the impact of her happy days in Samuel Richardson's family: 'The piety, order, decorum, and strict regularity that prevailed in his family, were of infinite use to train the mind to good habits, and to depend upon its own resources. It has been one of the means which, under the blessing of God, has enabled me to dispense with the enjoyment of what the world calls pleasures, such as found in *crowds*, and actually to relish and prefer the calm delight of retirement and books.'[48]

The practice of reading – the 'calm delight of retirement and books' – is described in this passage as a private activity, as opposed to public 'pleasures, such as found in *crowds*'. But this domestic retirement did not necessarily imply a solitary communion of reader and text. In present-day terms we would probably say that reading in the

44 He did, however, approve of its ending: 'as to the manner of its ending I like better than if it had terminated in more happy consequences', Saturday, 28 February 1756.

45 Monday, 24 October 1757.

46 Tuesday, 25 October 1757.

47 Wednesday, 30 August 1758.

48 Anna Letitia Barbauld (ed.), *The Correspondence of Samuel Richardson*, 6 vols. (London 1804), I clxxxv-vii. The italics are mine. Eaves and Kimpel identify the writer as Mary Pool Way, see Eaves and Kimpel, *Samuel Richardson*, p. 475.

Richardson household was not done in private. Rather, it was a sociable activity. It was also part of a religious and moral discipline. The day started with Mrs Richardson reading aloud from the Psalms, her four daughters standing around her in a circle. After breakfast, the younger ones read to Mrs Richardson the lessons for the day.[49] At various times these gatherings probably included at least one niece, as well as other girls and women who stayed in the house as part of the family. Samuel Richardson believed that 'domestic usefulness' was very important for 'Girls of middle families, middle life', such as his own, and the girls were therefore allowed little public diversion, 'once, twice, thrice in the season; and not so often as *thrice* if I saw that they were likely to be drawn from domestic usefulness by the indulgence'.[50] During the day they were employed in activity in the house and after dinner they sometimes went for a walk. The convention was that 'nobody must read or be read to until the walkers return' – note that in this phrase 'reading' potentially encompasses both silent reading and reading aloud.[51]

In the evening reading sessions, sociable reading-aloud was combined with work. The evenings were spent around the table in Mrs Richardson's parlour, 'where the practice was for one of the young ladies to read, while the rest sat with mute attention around the large table, and employed themselves in some kind of needle-work'.[52] Sometimes Mr Richardson himself would be asked to do the reading, as in his following description: 'The honest man who is to be taken up and laid down, as they please, is asked if he will not *read* to them by-and-by? ... At last ... they assemble at one large table: one goes to ruffle making; one to border making; one to muslin flowering; one to drawing; and the passive man is called to his lesson'[53] (see also plate 8).

Theirs was a strict upbringing. The same observer, who described the reading practices in the household noted that Mrs Richardson 'had high and Harlowean notions of parental authority': she kept the young ladies in order and at a distance. Consequently, they 'acquired a

49 *Correspondence of Samuel Richardson*, I, clxxxvi-clxxxvii.

50 *Correspondence of Samuel Richardson*, II, 214, to Miss Highmore, 26 November 1749.

51 *Correspondence of Samuel Richardson*, III, 224, to Miss Mulso, 15 August 1755.

52 *Correspondence of Samuel Richardson*, I, clxxxvii.

53 *Correspondence of Samuel Richardson*, III, 224, to Miss Mulso, 15 August 1755. 'Drawing' in this case could refer to a purely artistic activity, or to the drawing of patterns for various forms of needlework. When describing his own upbringing, Richardson mentions similar sessions of reading and work: 'I was an early favourite with all the young women of taste and reading in the neighbourhood. Half a dozen of them, when they met to work with their needles, used ... to borrow me to read to them', *Correspondence of Samuel Richardson*, I, xxxix.

Plate 8 Mr. Richardson, reading the Manuscript of Sir Charles Grandison in 1751, to his Friends. Cambridge, University Library, Nn.49.2

certain degree of fastidiousness and delicate refinement'.[54] But on the whole, it seems that they also acquired a good degree of individual competence by the standards of their own society. Most of the young ladies who resided at the house became mistresses of households and mothers of children. This was the lot of three of Richardson's own daughters, who became mistresses of 'middling' families.[55] A more privileged devotee, young Mrs Scudamore, née Westcomb, had a household of twenty-three under her care.[56] These women no doubt participated in leisure activities, such as formal visits or theatre-going, and they most probably employed servants. But they probably also devoted a substantial amount of their time to the management and accomplishment of various tasks, including childcare and home-based schooling, the production of clothes and personal and household linen, nursing the sick, preparing and preserving food and drink and administering the family accounts.[57] Some of the women who were connected with the house also struggled with conditions of domestic and financial hardship. This, for example, was the lot of Susanna [Suky] Richardson, Samuel Richardson's niece, or Hester Mulso, later Mrs Chapone.[58] Some of them revealed impressive intellectual ability and critical judgement. In fact, some of them used their judgement to challenge the patriarchal voice of the author of *Clarissa*. Miss Mulso, Mrs Chapone senior, Miss Highmore or Miss Talbot, for example, disputed Mr Richardson's views on issues such as filial duty and women's independence.[59]

To be sure, the economic and social differences between the Richardsons and the Turners contributed to the different upbringing and life experience of the women of these households. Nevertheless the examples of reading in the two homes bear important similarities.

54 *Correspondence of Samuel Richardson*, I, clxxxix. This view was also shared by Miss Highmore: Eaves and Kimpel, *Samuel Richardson*, p. 485, and reference there.

55 See references in Eaves and Kimpel, *Samuel Richardson*, to Mary [Polly] Richardson, later Mrs Ditcher, Martha [Patty] Richardson, later Mrs Bridgen, and Sarah [Sally] Richardson, later Mrs Crowther. Anne Richardson, who remained single is said to have 'lived out her life in genteel comfort', ibid., p. 484.

56 *Correspondence of Samuel Richardson*, III, 324.

57 See Vickery, 'Golden Age to Separate Spheres', pt 2.

58 Eaves and Kimpel, *Samuel Richardson*, p. 471; *The Works of Mrs Chapone*, 4 vols. (London, 1807), I, i-ii.

59 See Eaves and Kimpel, *Samuel Richardson*, e.g. pp. 344–9, 352–64, and references there especially to *Correspondence of Samuel Richardson*, *Works of Mrs Chapone*; *The Posthumous Works of Mrs Chapone: Containing her Correspondence with Mr. Richardson*, 2 vols. (London, 1807), and *A Series of Letters between Mrs Elizabeth Carter and Miss Catherine Talbot* (London, 1808). See also Sylvia Harcstark Myers, *The Bluestocking Circle: Women, Friendship and the Life of the Mind in Eighteenth-Century England* (Oxford, 1990), e.g. pp. 78–9, 140–7.

Sociable reading, devout reading, intermittent reading and the combination of reading, discipline and work, formed part of the encounter of readers and texts in both cases. This essay, then, not only has implications for the way in which we understand eighteenth-century practices of reading, and the practice of household reading in particular, but it also has implications for the way we assess the period's conceptions of femininity. The practices of reading in the Turner and Richardson households present an interesting discrepancy between the ways in which these women read, and images of the female novel reader. The analysis presented here is not meant to suggest that texts had no role in constructing ideologies of femininity and domesticity. But it does suggest we should be cautious before re-inscribing as history the eighteenth-century fantasy of supine femininity induced by reading.

CHAPTER 10

From promotion to proscription: arrangements for reading and eighteenth-century libraries

James Raven

There was a library revolution in eighteenth-century England. Commercial circulating libraries, developed from the lending services of booksellers, were first established in the 1740s. The twenty circulating libraries operating in London by 1760 had increased to more than 200 nationwide by 1800. In 1821 the *Monthly Magazine* calculated that some 1,500 fiction-lending libraries were 'supplying with books at least 100,000 individuals regularly and another 100,000 occasionally'.[1] With parallel success, subscription libraries were founded in large towns and cities, although the designation 'circulating' or 'subscription' disguised growing indistinction between the types of service offered. Many of the smaller libraries sent out catalogues to members rather than encouraging them to visit the collection in person. Larger libraries housed their stock in newly designed or refurbished buildings. The library at Liverpool, opened in 1758 and with claims to be the first of its kind in Britain,[2] advertised its services for 'Gentlemen and Ladies who wish to promote the Advantage of Knowledge'. By the end of the century there were more than a hundred such libraries.[3] Their example inspired the modest libraries of scores of debating clubs and gentlemen's societies,

1 *The Monthly Magazine; or, British Register*, 51, pt 1 for 1821.

2 The Library Company of Philadelphia was founded as a subscription library in 1731.

3 Accounts of library development in this period are led by Hilda Hamlyn, 'Eighteenth-Century Circulating Libraries in England', *The Library* 5th ser. 1 (1947): 197–218; Frank Beckwith, 'The Eighteenth-Century Proprietary Library in England', *Journal of Documentation* 3 (1947–8): 81–98; Paul Kaufman, 'English Book Clubs and their Role in Social History', *Libri* 14 (1964): 1–31; Paul Kaufman, 'The Community Library: A Chapter in English Social History', *Transactions of the American Philosophical Society* ns 57, pt 7 (1967); Paul Kaufman, *Libraries and their Users* (London, 1969); Devendra P. Varma, *The Evergreen Tree of Diabolical Knowledge* (Washington, 1972); M. J. Jannetta, 'Footnotes on Circulating Libraries', *Factotum* 5 (Apr. 1979): 15–16; Victor A. Berch, 'Notes on Some Unrecorded Circulating Libraries of Eighteenth-Century London', *Factotum* 6 (Oct. 1979): 15–18; K. A. Manley, 'The London and Westminster Libraries, 1785–1823', *The Library* 6th ser. 7 (1985): 137–59; and M. Kay Flavell, 'The Enlightened Reader and the New Industrial Towns: A Study of the Liverpool Library, 1758–1790', *British Journal for Eighteenth-Century Studies* 8 (1985): 17–35.

but bibliomania also markedly advanced in the homes of the propertied classes. An unprecedented number of domestic libraries were built in the last two-thirds of the eighteenth century. Amongst these were dozens of grandiose buildings designed or commissioned by the very wealthy, translating the idea of the monumental library to the city residence and the country house.

The characterization of many of these libraries as either 'private' or 'public' is ambiguous.[4] The new domestic libraries, like the visitable commercial and proprietary libraries, created appropriate places for the enjoyment of print and for sociability in the setting of literature. Many apparently private libraries were designed for display and for use by friends and neighbours. The supposedly 'public' commercial libraries restricted entry by fee or membership to rooms designed to suggest privacy and even domesticity. All the larger libraries provided space or books for the individual, silent reader, and yet supported, in different ways, the social celebration of books and the communal reading performance. Similarly, all such libraries fostered selection, browsing and the part-reading of a variety of books, but also encouraged concentrated reading, either silently or, as in the case of many domestic libraries, aloud to company. Few were places of distinctive, exclusive activity. Many were favoured arenas for conversation and business. Many domestic libraries supported teaching, needlework, painting, dramatic and musical performance, gaming and drinking.

What all these libraries also had in common was their promotion, in varied ways and with varied deliberateness, of statements about what a library represented. This, in turn, offered particular messages about the purpose and consequences of reading and the characteristics and qualifications expected of readers. At the more humble level such messages were conveyed by the type of books collected and the manner in which they were treated and housed. At their most grand, ideas about the book were embodied in the architectural features of large subscription libraries and the even larger commissions of those wealthy enough to indulge in extensive domestic library building and refurbishment. Enthusiasts emulated the recent designs and decorations of noble or collegiate libraries. Others pursued more original, not to say eccentric, concepts and embellishments. Within the libraries there was

[4] Contrasts between 'private' and 'public' are, of course, the subject of long-standing discussion. A recent view of Habermas, Koselleck, Chartier and others is given by Dena Goodman, 'Public Sphere and Private Life: Toward a Synthesis of Current Historiographical Approaches to the Old Regime', *History and Theory* 31 (1992): 2–20.

even greater freedom to give physical expression to notions of the relationship between reading, knowledge and civilization, as well as to provide practical comforts and aids to study and literary enjoyment. For inspirational models one only had to turn to some of the books shelved in such libraries. Many frontispieces illustrated idealized library interiors, complete with classically draped readers and students surrounded by muses, Minervas, cherubs and iconographic 'geniuses' of learning, literature, science and wisdom.[5]

The following discussion of library reading explores the ways in which libraries were used, and the political and cultural statements they presented. It argues that what particularly shaped eighteenth-century concern about reading environments was a conflict between support for the increased production and circulation of print, and moral and political misgivings about the extension of reading. The tension was not novel, but it was refocused by the arrangements for reading, real and imaginary, offered by the many new libraries. The essay considers, therefore, the accessibility of different types of library, the activities within them, and the meaning intended by their internal and external design. Because of limits of space, it concentrates on larger commercial circulating libraries and libraries in aristocratic and middle-class households. Commercial and domestic libraries will be taken in turn, with examples of each examined against surviving evidence of their appearance.

The examples given are, of course, highly selective, but so too is the evidence that we have of what libraries looked liked, of how they were arranged, and even of how they were used. Some of our best evidence comes from contemporary prints, and these, in turn, raise a further issue discussed below in relation to both commercial and domestic libraries: how did library owners intend their libraries and readers to be represented publicly? It will be argued that the attempt to promote the commercial library as private, select and well-ordered, and the statements made by the design and depiction of domestic libraries, were both responses to the diversity of social practices within libraries, and fears about the social composition of readers.

In the first instance, such statements, emphasizing exclusiveness and social boundaries to reading, were reactive to the expansion of the book trades. The commercial changes to the printing, publishing and

5 Broader themes in library iconography are discussed in André Masson, *Le decor des bibliothèques* (Geneva, 1972), and André Masson, trans. David Gerard, *The Pictorial Catalogue: Mural Decoration in Libraries* (Oxford, 1981).

distribution of books, including the development of circulating libraries, raised alarms about improper reading. From just before mid-century, shifting consumer tastes and innovations in book trades business techniques combined to promote book-reading on an unprecedented scale. Unlike many other contemporary industries, expansion within the book trades was not related to major technological change. New literature was produced in response to a demand created by the changing incomes and literary interests of the propertied classes, and assisted by new financial organization, by developments in transportation, and by a breakdown of restrictive legislation and informal monopolistic control. In addition, wholesale publishers and retail booksellers became more professional in production and promotion, many setting up as specialist distributors, librarians or publishers of particular types of work. For many fiction publishers, the most heavily targeted audience was not library-owners but library-users. These were the ladies and gentlemen who supported the pioneering circulating libraries of Samuel Fancourt, Thomas Wright, Francis and John Noble, Thomas Hookham, Thomas Lownds, John Bell and William Lane.

Commercial booksellers and lenders prospered by promoting fashionable literature and by encouraging emulative buying and the extension of reading. Many boasted smart establishments with distinctive frontages and carefully dressed windows. Their addresses and their specialities were broadcast by the stylish trade directories issued regularly from the 1770s. Many of the streets to which the works of genteel authors were sent were models of the new and fashionable commercial district. The Leadenhall Street of the circulating novel librarian, William Lane, was, for example, the subject of George Dance's ambitious architectural plans for new shops and arcades. The trial stories and chapbooks sold by pedlars and chapmen still streamed from the presses, but by the end of the century they were quite distinct from the advertised respectability of number publications by Bew, Bell, Harrison, Cooke, Hogg and others. *De luxe* subscription and special editions were marketed to specific custom and to those who had the money to aspire to learning, position and gentility. The book became the focus of broader industry supplying the social accoutrements of print, including furniture for the parlour and library and even the design of the house itself.[6]

As a result, this expanding book industry contributed not only to

6 A more detailed discussion is given in James Raven, *The Commercialization of the Book* (Cambridge University Press, forthcoming).

greater literary enthusiasms and the wider circulation of print, but also provoked alarmist reaction which required defensive emphasis on the exclusiveness and significance of reading. From the outset, circulating libraries claimed to be both fashionable and selective. The commercial efforts of writers, compilers, booksellers and the proprietors of circulating libraries were directed towards increasing sales amongst those for whom the book was no longer an expensive luxury but a social necessity, while at the same time much paper and ink was exhausted in determining the proper limits which should be set for reading and book acquisition. This tension between promotion and guardedness, between commercialization and exclusivity, was a recurrent theme in statements, architectural as well as literary, about the use of books.

The central concern was arbitrary or irresponsible reading attributable to the uneducated and ruder classes, but also to the young, impressionable and ill-informed. Much has been written about opposition to circulating libraries in this period, to novels and allegedly seditious literature, and to the whole idea of the lower orders reading.[7] A single example can stand for dozens and dozens of hostile review notices. In 1772 the anonymous *Virtue in Distress ... By a Farmer's Daughter in Gloucestershire* suffered a common fate in the *Critical Review*:

> When a farmer's daughter sits down to *read* a novel, she certainly misspends her time, because she may employ it in such a manner as to be of real service to her family: when she sits down to *write* one, her friends can have no hope of her. The rustic authoress of this volume ... has totally mistaken the use of her hands: we have never seen her hands indeed, but we will venture to say, that she may turn them to a better account by making butter than by making books.[8]

The *Catalogue of the Books of the London Library* in 1786 declared in its preface that 'the young of both sexes too frequently suffer from a deprivation of morals as well as taste from the indiscriminate reading of common circulating libraries'. It was a comment on popular reading typical for the next half century or more. Twenty years later, in his *Essay on Light Reading*, Mangin warned that 'there is scarcely a street of the metropolis, or a village in the country, in which a circulating library may not be found: nor is there a corner of the empire, where the English language is understood, that has not suffered from the

7 John Tinnon Taylor, *Early Opposition to the English Novel: The Popular Reaction from 1780 to 1830* (New York, 1943); and W. F. Gallaway Jr, 'The Conservative Attitude Toward Fiction, 1770–1830', *Proceedings of the Modern Language Association* 55 (1940): 1041–59.

8 *Critical Review* 33 (London, 1772): 327. I am grateful to Stephen Bending for this reference.

effects of this institution'. He went on to denounce the 'tribe of illiterate and rapacious miscreants, who earn a livelihood by infusing immorality and absurdity into the general mind, and accumulate not only wealth, but celebrity, by writing novels'.[9] As Mangin himself noted, Sheridan's gibe against the circulating library as 'an evergreen tree of diabolical knowledge' was as fresh and relevant in 1805 as it had been in 1775.

Reports criticized readers for reading in unsuitable places or for reading badly, quickly, insensitively, or too much. Candle wax in books, as a result of reading in bed, was one complaint. It was famously voiced by Hannah More in tracts condemning slovenly reading. It was also noted in advertisements by fire insurance companies. The late eighteenth-century *Lady's Magazine* repeatedly noted that reading was a favoured occupation during hairdressing, but that as a consequence too many library books were full of hair powder. It was not appropriate to read in the boudoir while having your hair done. At the very least, so the association went, if you did read in inappropriate places, then it was likely that your reading material was worthless.[10]

Such educated reservations about reading sharply contrasted with the excitement expressed by artisan and humbler readers. Thomas Turner, shopkeeper and diarist, recorded an imposing list of books, whether or not he fully read them all.[11] The autodidact bookseller, James Lackington, not only commented on his own entrancement by reading, but left in his *Memoirs* some of the most frequently quoted passages about peasants taking *Pamela* under their arms back to their hovels to read. Jeremiads on reading were also contradicted by those like Leigh Hunt who recalled in later years his excitement about the availability of new types of pocket books and cheap reprints in the final decades of the eighteenth century.[12] For Hunt and Lackington the availability of print was the liberating force of the age, and according to the accepted authority on working-class reading of the period, Richard Altick, 'the history of the mass reading audience is, in fact, the history of English democracy'.[13] This statement should not be misunderstood, however. Enthusiasts like Leigh Hunt and Lackington

9 Rev. Edward Mangin, *An Essay on Light Reading, as it may be Supposed to Influence Moral Conduct and Literary Taste* (London, 1808), pp. 12–13, 22.

10 Hannah More, *Works*, 6 vols. (London, 1834), I, 49–51, III, 122–4, 187 (amongst many similar passages); 'Hints on Reading', *Lady's Magazine* 20 (1789): 79–81, 177–8; Albinia Gwynn, *The Rencontre* (Dublin, 1785) preface.

11 See above, p. 166.

12 J. E. Morpurgo (ed.), *The Autobiography of Leigh Hunt* (London, 1949), p. 142.

13 Altick, *The English Common Reader*, p. 3.

were in the minority. As this account of actual and idealized arrangements for reading in eighteenth-century libraries will suggest, the history of reading is not self-evidently a history of the spur to improvement and enlightenment, of progress from lesser to greater literacy, from ignorance and barbarism to democracy, humanitarianism and virtue. Rather, from the contradiction between market promotion and market alarm, reading was carefully presented as a privileged activity, to be guarded by protectors and modulated by codes of conduct. The connection between reading and democracy underpinned the response, more than the impulse, to reading in the first century of the popular library.

The commercial circulating libraries were a particular focus for these dual considerations of literary promotion and proscription. The promotional efforts, necessary for commercial success, were very obvious. Although many London as well as country circulating libraries were small, and, like that of Samuel Clay in Warwick, operated with no more than a small shop, counter and store,[14] many proprietors advertised widely and claimed extensive stocks and services. Francis Noble's catalogue of *c.* 1759 boasted 20,000 volumes. John Bell's 'British Library' claimed to house 10,000 volumes in 1771, 31,000 in 1776, 50,000 in 1778 and 150,000 in 1793.[15] In 1774 Lane's Leadenhall library 'contained over ten thousand items' and from his Minerva Press he offered to stock and equip all those who wished to start a circulating library in town or country.[16] Almost all circulating libraries distributed catalogues for subscribers to place orders, and many libraries – often little more than the shelves of a bookseller's room – did not offer or anticipate open access. The larger of the early commercial librarians did, however, also allow their clients browsing access to the books. Thomas Lownds, in his 1755 catalogue, advertised his library as 'kept in a Spacious Room', drawing attention, it seems, to the circumstances in which holdings could be inspected as well as stored. Bell proudly advertised a regularly updated manuscript register of new publications for the use of subscribers to his library.[17] By 1780 librarians such as

14 As I have discussed elsewhere, civic and taxation records confirm that many libraries were kept in small, confined bookshops, Raven, 'The Noble Brothers and Popular Publishing'. See also above, p. 11, and below, p. 206.

15 *Public Advertiser*, 30 October 1771, 26 January 1776; Bell's *Catalogue* [1778]; *The Oracle*, 23 March 1793.

16 *Catalogue of Lane's General and Encreasing Circulating Library* (Leadenhall-Street, London, 1791); Dorothy Blakey, *The Minerva Press 1790–1820* (London, 1939).

17 *Public Advertiser*, 29 January 1776. No such registers have survived.

Martha Bally at Bath and J. Hall at Margate advertised reading rooms and, in the case of Theophilus Shrimpton at Bath, provided separate rooms for men and women.[18] It was also in 1780 that Thomas Hookham moved his circulating library from Hanover Square to New Bond Street and advertised the new 'detached building' as 'commodiously fitted up'.[19]

Countering such invitations were attempts to limit library membership. Contemporary advertisements and descriptions professed quality books and readers and made it clear that only those with substantial incomes could afford to join the circulating libraries. In the early 1740s the first London circulating libraries were charging subscribers from between fifteen shillings and one guinea annually, and although this charge was reduced in the mid 1760s, it was re-imposed by the end of the decade. The annual subscription to a circulating library at a spa town at mid-century ranged between ten-shillings-and-sixpence and two guineas.[20] In November 1766 the London advertisement reducing subscriptions was issued jointly by 'The Reputable Circulating Libraries' of John and Francis Noble, William Bathoe, Thomas Lownds, T. Vernor and J. Chater, Thomas Jones and William Cooke, and drew special attention to their respectability.[21]

Contemporary illustrations of the circulating libraries further suggest the imposed boundaries. The engraving by Bonneau of the Nobles' St Martin's Court library served as the frontispiece to their earliest known catalogue published in about 1746 (see plate 9), and that by Ravenet of Francis Noble's later King Street library is from a tradecard of the mid-1750s (see plate 10). The engraving by Fulett of Thomas Wright's library at Exeter Court, off the Strand, is of slightly earlier date and probably once accompanied a printed catalogue (see plate 11). All three prints highlight large book stacks on open shelves. These rare surviving prints of early circulating libraries also reveal the attention given to access and fashion and depict a very respectable clientele. Some of those shown visiting the libraries are intended to represent servants bringing their masters' and mistresses' orders, but

18 Cited in Hamlyn, 'Eighteenth-Century Circulating Libraries', p. 220.

19 *Public Advertiser*, 10 November 1780. In the absence of much other evidence, these examples might raise doubts about the extent or continuance of the closed access suggested by K. A. Manley, 'London Circulating Library Catalogues of the 1740s', *Library History* 8 (1989): 74–9 (p. 75).

20 Hamlyn, 'Eighteenth-Century Circulating Libraries', pp. 209–10.

21 One copy of the advertisement is to be found bound in the British Library copy of the Nobles' *History of Mrs Drayton* (London, 1767).

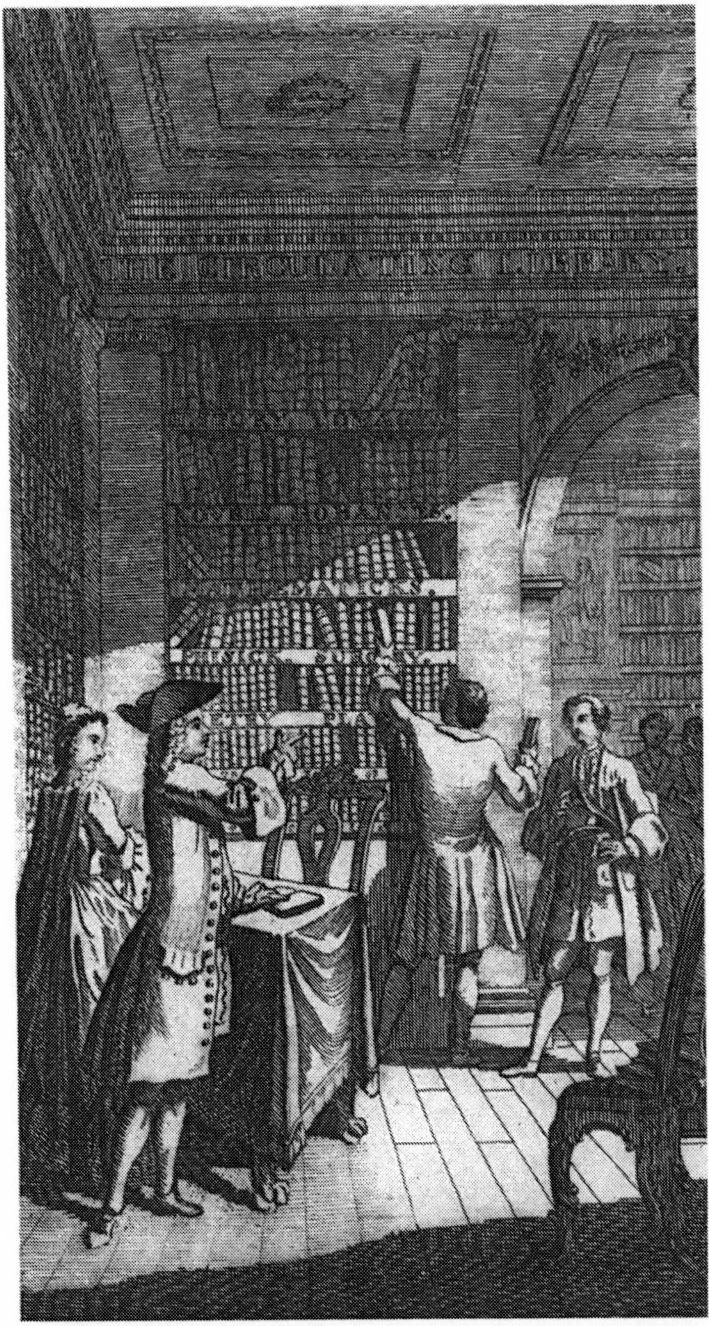

Plate 9 Interior of John and Francis Noble's St Martin's Court Library, from their catalogue, *The Yearly and Quarterly Subscriber*, *c.* 1746. Oxford, Bodleian Library, Vet.A4e.3250

Plate 10 'A View of Francis Noble's Circulating Library', tradecard, mid-1750s. London, British Museum, Heal Collection

Plate 11 Engraving of Thomas Wright's Circulating Library, Exeter Court, off the Strand, mid-1740s. Oxford, Bodleian Library, Douce Portfolio 139, no. 808

other customers are clearly of the *beau monde*. Ravenet's promotional illustration emphasizes a large and splendidly arranged stock. The St Martin's Court library is shown with chairs, table and browsing clients in the background, and in Fulett's engraving of Thomas Wright's library, subscribers sit or stand by a cloth-covered table in an almost domestic setting. Here, a screen by the window suggests a private service, comparable, perhaps, to an exclusive viewing at a fashionable couturier.

For commercial reasons these library trade cards and catalogue engravings of the interiors undoubtedly offered romanticized pictures to subscribers, many of whom lived in country parts. Whatever the reality of membership and behaviour, however, its representation to library users is itself significant. Contemporary memoirs also suggest that some prints were not entirely idealized. The party at Mr Wright's, for example, is probably acting in the same spirit as Fanny Burney's famous 1778 'frolic' to Bell's circulating library with her cousin Edward. Her greatly respected father, Dr Charles Burney, was the family's subscriber to Bell's library. Fanny and Edward visited to ask Bell's shopman about the popularity of *Evelina*, although Fanny also quizzed him about current magazines on display.[22]

Another impression offered by the illustrations is of a certain, if very subtle, emphasis on checks to untutored or irresponsible reading. All three of the early prints feature advice on reading given by the proprietor, his shopman or fellow visitors. Two customers stand by a table in the 1746 Bonneau print. The gentleman fingers the printed catalogue or separate guide kept in the library. He indicates his requirements to someone who is presumably either Noble or an assistant taking books from the shelves. This man seems, at the same time, to be serving another subscriber or servant who carries a book under his arm. The lady in the King Street library, reading what is probably meant to be the catalogue, converses with the gentleman by her side. The hat he carries suggests that he is a visitor; the bare-headed man searching the shelves might be Noble or his shopman.

[22] Charlotte Barrett (ed.), *Diary and Letters of Madame D'Arblay (1778–1840)*, 6 vols. (London, 1904), II, 214. My attention has also been drawn to the prints' curious depiction of folios stacked at the top of the bookshelves rather than at the base. For this and other points I am grateful to the audience of earlier versions of this chapter, on circulating libraries delivered in my absence by Deborah J. Leslie, at the SCSECS conference, Baton Rouge, March 1993; and on private libraries given at Freiburg in December 1992 and since reprinted as 'Modes of Reading and Writing in the Eighteenth-Century Private Library', in Goetsch (ed.), *Lesen und Schreiben*, pp. 49–60.

The scene in the Exeter Court library is more animated, with scattered books and an open catalogue on the table, and some apparent debate on the books read. To this extent, the illustration of order and discrimination contained worrying hints of their possible negation. What guidance was really offered to fashionable customers whose subscriptions financed the library? The depiction of a friendly discussion round the reading table even raises questions about the practical enforcement of the libraries' much-advertised rules about reading conditions. Stern warnings were issued against clients lending library books to friends and family, but policing was clearly impossible and the library scene here, idealized or not, suggests the likely problem when such a group returned home.

Similar tensions between the encouragement and fear of reading were reflected in representations of the domestic library. The quality of the personal or family collection was one focus of comment on the social consequences of book trade expansion. In a variety of forms, bibliomania was a passion of the propertied by the late eighteenth century. During the second half of the century the efforts of notable private collectors from Horace Walpole to Thomas Dibdin (both great self-publicists) encouraged others to embark on whimsical or cabinet collections of printed ephemera and curiosities. For the lesser purse, many volumes were bought from the well-advertised sales and auctions of complete libraries. The market in early or unusual books, however, was for the aspiring scholar, antiquarian or eccentric. Although the purchase of curios appealed to many and although many made a rare or one-off visit to grand antiquarian booksellers like James Edwards of Pall Mall, the staple supply to most domestic libraries was of recent publication. The market for second-hand books at this period does remain an important and neglected area of research, but such trade was of little consequence to the hundreds of readers like Mrs Pilkington, Mrs Thrale or Anna Larpent eagerly seeking new titles in London or the country town.[23]

Here, with the burgeoning demand for new volumes and titles, was the evidence of modish or chaotic purchasing to parallel charges against the irresponsible and indiscriminate reading by clients of circulating libraries. In reaction, booksellers took care to advertise new works as instructive and not merely entertaining, and they engaged with a certain disingenuousness in the debate about the

[23] See below, p. 229.

social consequences of the boom in print. Fashionable modern literature was more expensive to buy than most older volumes listed in the booksellers' and auction catalogues, but, paraded as exclusive and required reading, it appeared more desirable for most successful small estate-owners, tradesmen and their families. Such books ranged widely, from new social commentaries and devotional works, and reprinted classics of Cervantes or Richardson, to encyclopaedias of useful knowledge and bound collections of prints and designs. The collection of such books presented exactly the same contradictions seen in the representation of reading promoted by circulating libraries. Fashion and populism threatened to devalue the otherwise laudable endeavour to assemble and show off in suitable surroundings a collection of books and reading for self, family and visitors.

The development of the library was also recent. At the end of the seventeenth century, modest libraries had been incorporated into some English country houses, but the event, as Mark Girouard put it, was 'still rare enough to call notice'.[24] By the mid-eighteenth century the library had become a focal living and entertaining room for much of the English nobility and upper gentry. The aristocratic model established the trend. The library was a major feature of the rebuilding projects of noble families. Houses such as Wimpole Hall, Tatton Park, Stourhead and Woburn Abbey, became renowned for newly built or redesigned libraries, equipped with all the latest and most elegant library furniture.[25] In Hogarth's 1738 painting of the Cholmondeley family, the sitters are shown at rest and play in their sumptuous library (see plate 12). A large free-standing bookcase laden with beautifully bound volumes features centre-stage. Lord Cholmondeley's hand rests on a small finely tooled book as he pauses in reading aloud, while his children play games with a stack of large folios. Designed to divert both family and friends, the library has become the communal centre of the house. Stocked with chairs and busts and books, it is a perfect blend of comfort, civilization and choice taste. According to its sale catalogue, Mrs Thrale's library at Streatham Park had a hearth with a 'handsome steel cut and pierced fender' and a 'Brussels carpet planned to the room', a 'grand piano-forte, by Stodart', a 'mahogany library step ladder', and a 'mahogany library table' and two other tables. With a

[24] Mark Girouard, *Life in the English Country House: A Social and Architectural History* (New Haven, CT, 1978), p. 169.

[25] Each of these libraries is illustrated in John Cornforth, *English Interiors 1790–1848: The Quest for Comfort* (London, 1978), pp. 42–3, 76–7.

Plate 12 'The Cholmondeley Family', by William Hogarth, 1738

couch and twenty-two chairs in the library, it was clearly a room for entertaining.[26] The library hearth was, in fact, a recurrent feature of attention. Surrounded by various new-fangled apparatuses for the fire, it was often depicted as a reading area of particular significance.[27]

As a versatile social arena, the domestic library became the subject of wider debate about reading proprieties. The commercial restructuring of bookselling was paralleled by a boom in the fashioning and equipping of domestic libraries, from the palatial attempts of great and often new wealth to the emulative ventures of provincial gentlefolk and well-to-do tradesmen. Few town or country gentlemen could afford to build new library wings to their houses, like the bibliophile, William Herbert, but even modest gentry could build new libraries by buying books and new bookcases and other library furniture.[28] The reading wheel, of medieval origin, was replaced by a vast array of reading paraphernalia for use and display. The reading chairs, stands, desks, print-racks, ladders, rotating shelving, globes, busts, and miscellania, together with the actual design of library bays, windows, ceilings, wall shelving or space formerly enclosed by book-presses, all contributed to the realization of certain social ideals in reading practice and purpose.[29]

During the next hundred years, the sale catalogues of house clearances are studded by library accoutrements, all testimony to the new social importance of the domestic library. The middle classes were building more libraries than ever before, and not just for collecting books. Aspirant local gentry could now outdistance established neighbours in buying yards of literature to decorate their homes and lend visible weight to claims of rank. The production of library furniture, a growth industry by the end of the eighteenth century, pandered to

26 *Streatham Park, Surrey: A Catalogue of the Excellent and Genuine Household Furniture ... the Genuine Property of Mrs Piozzi* 1816, reprinted in A. N. Munby (gen. ed.) and Stephen Parks (ed.), *Sale Catalogues of Libraries of Eminent Persons*, 12 vols. (London, 1971–5), v, 34–5.

27 Cf. domestic praise of the fireside, Leonore Davidoff and Catherine Hall, *Family Fortunes: Men and Women of the English Middle Class 1780–1850* (London, 1987), pp. 165–6.

28 According to Dibdin, Herbert 'built one of the wings of his house expressly for the reception of books, and here he used to sit, under a circular skylight', cited in Robin Myers, 'William Herbert: His Library and his Friends', in Robin Myers and Michael Harris (eds.), *Property of a Gentleman: The Formation, Organisation and Dispersal of the Private Library, 1620–1920* (London, 1991), pp. 133–58 (p. 148).

29 There is no full published account of this, but see Myers and Harris (eds.), *Property of a Gentleman*; illustrations in Girouard, *English Country House*; and Cornforth, *English Interiors*; details in Munby and Parks (eds.), *Sale Catalogues of Libraries*; and compare the case studies offered by Clive Wainwright, *The Romantic Interior: The British Collector at Home 1750–1850* (New Haven, CT, 1989).

similar desires. A 1793 catalogue issued by the London cabinet-makers, listed with full specifications three types of free-standing bookcase, six different types of library writing table, two types of 'moving library or bookstand', and a 'library press bedstead'. In addition, prices were given for dozens of different 'extras', and an assortment of beading, mouldings, veneers and other decorative embellishments for shelves and domestic library fittings.[30] Many of the standard, production-line models offered in catalogues and trade advertisements were again modelled on the latest fancies of the rich and famous.

Such elegance and its restatement of the social elevation of books and reading was easily, if often shoddily, replicated. *The Director* contained numerous designs for library furniture executed by Chippendale and capable of being copied by imitators. Bookcases could be Gothic, Oriental or Indian. Library tables might be oval or kidney-shaped, extendible or convertible, and be provided with any number of stands for decanters and tea services, easels for sketching, stands for sheet music, and book or print rests. Plaster busts of great men of letters, both classical and English, were mass-produced to adorn library niches or rest atop library shelving in even modest establishments. The library of the peer could be recreated on an appropriate scale and to an appropriate budget in any gentleman's house. Some time before 1780, one upwardly mobile gentleman, Sir Richard Worsley of Appuldurcombe Park in the Isle of Wight, invested in a set of book-case beds, eight library busts and figurines, and '8 Mahogany Elbow Chairs, Antique Urn back, carved & inlaid, an Author's Head near the top of each back by Wedgewood'.[31]

The arrangement and display of books was debated by a greatly increased number of guides to good reading. In 1766 Whiston, Dodsley and Robson published *Directions for a Proper Choice of Authors to form a Library ... Intended for those Readers who are only acquainted with the English Language*. According to its preface, 'something of this Sort seems to have been long wanted, and the prodigious Encrease of Books, within these last fifty Years, makes it more necessary to distinguish those Writers, who have with Success, by their Merit, obtained a valuable Character, from those, who have merely by Necessity, or from lucrative Views only, commenced Authors, and taxed the Publick at too dear a Rate,

30 *The Cabinet-Makers' London Book of Prices, and Designs of Cabinet Work* (London, 1793), also reproduced in *Furniture History* 18 (1982): [23]–[349].

31 See a 1780 inventory of furniture, in L. O. J. Boynton, 'Sir Richard Worsley's Furniture at Appuldurcombe Park', *Furniture History* 1 (1965): 39–58 (p. 45, retaining original spelling).

for their trifling and ignorant Performances'.[32] The author also emphasizes, in a way which again suggests the growing social dilemma, that 'my design also, is not for a compleat library of a great expence, but to suit persons of a moderate fortune'.[33] A well-circulated piece of advice during the second half of the eighteenth century was to own a copy of the sale catalogue of a great library. Boswell said that 'notwithstanding its defects', Osborne's catalogue of the Harleian collection of books, with the preface by Dr Johnson, was 'the best Catalogue of a large Library of which we can boast. It should be in every good collection'.[34] A series of articles in *The Gentleman's Magazine* in 1788 and 1794 advocated the 'circulation of learning by catalogues'. Another contribution by Mangin, *A View of the Pleasures Arising from a Love of Books*, stated as its aim the elucidation of 'the many advantages arising from a judicious use of Books'.[35]

The resulting reaction to this commercialization can be observed from the surviving testimony of suppliers and collectors of books and of their actions and thoughts about requirements for reading. The two brief vignettes offered here are of the Rev. Dr John Trusler, publisher and publicist of Clerkenwell in London, and of Ralph Willett, Esq., gentleman and bibliophile of Merly in Dorset. Trusler, the son of the owner of the Marylebone Tea Gardens, set up as publisher in 1765 and during the next thirty-four years he penned and published dozens of practical guides, controversial essays, and whatever he thought could be marketed as novel, useful or notorious. Trusler and others claimed to offer a public service and declared that their works would benefit all in the community. In a period when book sales trebled, however, Trusler was genuinely troubled by the potential effects of the change. However much he modified his claims and stressed that he was selling to the middle classes and the educated, many of the books he produced, such as *The Way to be Rich and Respectable*, were not only bought by but also intended for those below gentility.

Trusler, doyen of commercial publishing, was in two minds about his business in the closing years of the eighteenth century. The question which preoccupied the later part of Trusler's 'Memoirs' was how to arrange limits to the reading ambitions of the poor. Trusler certainly

32 Whiston, *et al.*, *Directions*, pp. v–vi.

33 Ibid., p. 2.

34 John Nichols, *Literary Anecdotes of the Eighteenth Century*, 9 vols. (London, 1812–15; repr. edn, New York, 1966), III, 403.

35 Edward Mangin, *A View of the Pleasures Arising from a Love of Books: In Letters to a Lady* (London, 1814), p. 3.

had no aspirations as a universal educator. As he was at pains to point out, indiscriminate education was sinful. From the press, he said, had 'arisen all the evils which the World has experienced', and in the 1790s he detected in the spread of printing the origin of 'the French troubles'. In England the runaway press threatened political catastrophe: 'I am bold to say that the more untaught the labouring part of mankind are, the more humble are they and modest and the better servants they make'.[36] In the country villages all men were learning to read: 'they sacrifice the wholesome food of the body for the pernicious poison of the mind'.[37] Trusler was terrified by the prospect of any growth in the 'multitude of books on all subjects and so cheap as to be within the reach of almost every man'. He suggested a new tax on the printed sheet: 'the learned then wou'd possibly sink in number, but learning would rise in their defeat'.[38] According to Trusler, libraries should become closed institutions, books be locked away, and the display of books left for the inner sanctum of the subscription library or the library of the gentleman.

On this Ralph Willett would have agreed. Willett had inherited rich West Indian plantations on his father's death in 1740 and lived as an independent gentleman for the rest of his days. An amateur botanist, he was also an avid collector of paintings and books. The last passion was combined with keen architectural interests and resulted in the indulgence of his vision of the gentleman's library. In 1772 Willett designed and built a new library at his Merly estate near Wimborne in Dorset. The library at Merly was built with Willett's bedroom, dressing room and billiards room adjoining. It was the principal room of a new south-east wing to the house, and measured eighty-four feet by twenty-three, with a ceiling twenty-three feet high. The library stood for fifty years only. When Willett died in 1795 at the age of seventy-six, his property and his great collection of books passed to his nephew. In 1813 his pictures and his library were sold at auction in London. A few years later his great library building was pulled down.

What we know of his library is largely derived from Willett's own privately printed account. The *Description of the Library at Merly* explains the library murals, painted ceilings, and sculptures as part of the 'Plan' of Ralph Willett's library. The library ceiling displayed in twenty-one

36 John Trusler, 'Memoirs of the Life of the Revd Dr John Trusler: Volume 2', chapter 34, fol. 337, unpublished manuscripts, Lewis Walpole Library, Farmington, CT.

37 Ibid., fol. 348.

38 Ibid., fols. 343, 345.

panels representations of painting, sculpture, astronomy and geography, scenes of Otaheite, Athens, Egypt and Patagonia, and cameos of Osiris, Moses, Manco Capac (the 'hero of Peru'), Alfred, Christ and Confucius. The centrepiece was a representation of Great Britain. Below, mahogany bookcases were 'enriched with a compleat Ionick Order' and were just over thirteen feet high with space above and below the impost for the heads of twenty-four eminent men. A bust of Guttenberg was over the entrance door, and over the other door a bust of Caxton (Willett owned seven Caxtons). The other twenty-four busts over the bookcases included Socrates, Chaucer, Shakespeare, Horace, Homer, Addison, Newton and Willett himself.[39] The choice of exemplars was subjective and highly individual, as Willett openly admitted in his 'Plan'. His was an eclectic selection of men who had changed the world and had to be represented in his reading temple. 'An Englishman's Partiality, in an English Work', he noted, 'hath induced the Designer to give Alfred the Preference.'[40] He also admitted that the choice of Charlemagne was a difficult one because no likeness of the emperor survived. Likewise, the figure of Confucius was taken from Du Halde, 'who', comments Willett, 'says it is an exact Portrait of that great Man, though it looks more like a French missionary dressed *à la Chinoise*'.[41]

For both Trusler and Willett the ideal domestic library made a social statement to set against the turbulent background of an apparent democratization of print. Few could afford to emulate Willett, but for those building their own library there were opportunities to mould a collection according to a plan, and, as in the Merly case, to acknowledge a particular heritage and to offer a vision of the library as the guardian of knowledge and civility.[42] The modest gentleman's library, with its appropriately selected titles and furnishings, as much as the grand Merly or Wimpole or Houghton, might be regarded as a shrine requiring the recognition and appreciation of a particular tradition and visual vocabulary. On the grand scale, Willett's Merly reflects the attempts to signal particular messages about usage that were made by hundreds of contemporaries. Willett's 'Plan' with its ceiling murals, its busts, its imposing bookcases and fitments, describes the library of an

39 Sketches and MSS notes pasted in the Cambridge University Library copy of Ralph Willett, *A Description of the Library at Merly* (London, 1776).

40 Ibid., pp. 11, 12.

41 Ibid., p. 13.

42 For a discussion of this point in relation to scholarly book collecting, see McKitterick, 'Bibliography'.

Enlightenment gentleman, an archive of knowledge but also an assertion of the perfectability of man (or at least of certain men). It contains a record of reassurance about the permanence of the advance of knowledge. For Willett, the library was to become a protector of civilization, the bulwark against Hobbesian Man in his state of Nature.[43] It was to be an emblematic representation of Knowledge and Human Achievement and a cell for private reflection. It was a vision of book collection which drew an absolute division between the civilized and the primitive who could not be trusted. 'Superior Distinction' as Willett described it in his Plan of his Library, 'will call for superior external Decoration; the Savage must be, and is, satisfied with his Hut; but the Man elevated by Abilities or Fortune above his Fellow-Citizens, in larger Societies, will soon be shewing that Superiority by such outward Marks as proclaim it to the World'.[44]

What Willett was doing on the grand and eccentric scale was not untypical of the impulse behind many library arrangements. Just as circulating libraries were censured for indiscriminate custom and stock, so social considerations were addressed in the design of domestic and proprietary libraries and the placement of books and book furniture within. The good ordering of books was to maintain efficient use of space, but also to enable the reader to find information in the right way and to ensure proper respect for what was important. Recent work offering an architectural reading of eighteenth-century libraries has explored the creation of a key division between a zone of shelving (the worldly) and a brightly lit ceiling (the Heavens) from which the light of God illuminated the readers. Statues of great authors above the shelves mediated between the realm of the reader and that of the divine.[45] Such allegorical fittings of the library, grand or humble, were designed to reassure as well as to impress. The many prints and pictures in Dr William Dodd's library included two framed prints of Rubens, '4 medallions, fram'd and glaz'd', 'a whole-length Vandyke in Plaister, three others bronz'd', '23 fine Heads, fram'd and glaz'd', 'an elegant china figure of Milton' and four china figures of 'the 4 Quarters of the World'.[46]

Like the engravings of the circulating libraries, contemporary

43 Willett, *Description*, p. 2.
44 Ibid., p. 17.
45 James Campbell, 'A Place for Books: Textuality and the Radcliffe Camera', unpublished BA dissertation, University of Cambridge (1990), pp. 23–4.
46 *A Catalogue of all the Genteel and Fashionable Household Furniture ... of the Rev. W. Dodd D.D.*, repr. in Munby and Parks (eds.), *Sale Catalogues of Libraries*, v, 359.

illustrations of other library settings offer a suggestive iconography linking ordered interiors and classical references with the exclusiveness and self-awareness of respectable reading. Frontispieces of successive editions of the *Female Spectator*, paralleling the prints of the Nobles's and Wright's libraries executed during the same years, depicted the active use of books in the home. The library, or the parlour with its collection of books, was represented as a domestic and exclusive temple. The Parr engraving to the first edition of 1745, presents the three young women and the matron seated in front of two shelves of books, two busts and an emblematic painting (see plate 13). In the Bonneau engraving to the third edition of 1750 the number of books has increased, large glass-fronted bookcases and a reading lectern have been added, and an imposing bust and urns have been elevated above the scene (see plate 14). There is an air of self-conscious intimacy about the piece, in which the women, behind closed library or parlour doors, listen, read, learn and write as part of a wider, privileged community. It invites similar responses from the readers of the *Female Spectator*, anxious to recognize marks of value and distinction in their own reading and writing. For such readers, happy to be counted as discerning in their care and use of books, the *Lady's Magazine* offered its 'Hints on Reading': 'Some books may be hurried over, for they contain nothing worth retaining ... In reading your deep, grave, and learned authors, it is necessary to make many a pause and consider how far what he says concords with your own opinion and experience, for your grave, deep, authors are very apt to lead you astray, because you adopt their conclusions without examining their arguments.'[47]

By recovering a sense of the internal arrangements of these libraries, we gain more clues about the cultural significance of reading, including what has been called 'la posturologie de la lecture'.[48] Roger Chartier has drawn attention to Etienne-Louis Boullée's grandiose design for the Royal Library in Paris in 1785, projected as the greatest reading room in Europe and adorned in the architect's drawing with toga-clad readers. Here, remarks Chartier, 'study is like a voyage among books punctuated by advances and halts, by solitary reading, and by erudite conversation'.[49] A similar expedition in the late eighteenth-century English domestic library was more likely to include collision with mock

47 *Lady's Magazine* 20 (1789): 81.
48 Georges Perec, 'Lire: esquisse socio-physiologique', *Esprit* 44:1 (Jan. 1976): 9–20 (p. 14).
49 Roger Chartier, trans. Lydia G. Cochrane, *The Order of Books: Readers, Authors and Libraries in Europe between the Fourteenth and Eighteenth Centuries* (Cambridge, 1994), p. 63.

Plate 13 Library of the *Female Spectator*. Frontispiece to the 1745 London edn. Cambridge, University Library, T900.d.62.1

Plate 14 Library of the *Female Spectator*. Frontispiece to the 1750 London edn. Cambridge, University Library, Ely.d.89

Chippendale library clutter, but the conception is similar: a parade room, a literary browsing room, corners to read in, hearths to read by, steps leading to books, desks to sit at, spaces in which to pause and discuss.

One particular form of experience suggested by this recreation of library space – and one which reinforced the notion of the select social intimacy of the library – was shared reading. Although complementing rather than rivalling solitary study, communal reading in such settings has received little attention. Michel de Certeau, for example, in writing of the deterritorializing of the reader, emphasized the primacy of the silent, modernized, internalized reader.[50] By contrast, certain domestic library arrangements reflected the demands of performance, and the library and parlour as arenas for communal, performative reading appeared in various late eighteenth-century magazine articles and essays about reading. Reading in company, as well as solitary reading, was assessed in pieces ranging from 'The Ill Effects of Reading without Digesting', to a 'Humourous Method of Reading the News-papers' and complimentary descriptions of women reading to their husbands from judiciously chosen libraries.[51] The passion for play readings in the family circle also contributed to the popularity of play book publication in the late eighteenth century, and popular periodical publications, such as the *Lady's Magazine*, *Town and Country Magazine*, *European Review* and many others, included items suitable in length and variety for reading in turn in a group.[52] Several reviews of novels suggest their being read aloud, while at least one deems this a standard by which they were to be judged. In 1773 the *Monthly Review* condemned indecent passages in the newly published translation of Wieland's *Reason Triumphant* over Fancy, noting that 'no man should read a novel, or any book of entertainment, which a gentleman cannot read aloud in a company of ladies'.[53]

These reading performances attracted theoreticians of varying pomposity. In 1775 William Cockin published his *Art of Delivering Written Language; or, An Essay on Reading* in which he defined reading as 'the Art

50 de Certeau, *The Practice of Everyday Life*, pp. 175–6, on silent reading as a modern experience.

51 *Town and Country Magazine* 19 (1787): 355–57; *Annual Register* 9 (1766): 220–1; *Lady's Magazine* 6 (1775): 489–91.

52 More elaborate play performances were often attempted, as in the Burney circle in the 1770s, Annie Raine Ellis (ed.) *The Early Diary of Frances Burney 1768–1778*, 2 vols. (London, 1907), I, 127–30, II, 164–79. See also Richard Cumberland, 'Remarks upon the Present Taste for Acting Private Plays', *European Magazine* 14 (1788): 115–18.

53 *Monthly Review* 48 (1773): 126–29.

of Delivering written language with propriety, force, and elegance'.[54] In the same year Thomas Sheridan published his *Lectures on the Art of Reading*, the most reprinted of all such directories by the end of the century.[55] The guides emphasized that practice was as necessary as careful instruction, and that good reading was within the range of everyone who might perform regularly to family, friends, colleagues or neighbours. Readers, in Cockin's words:

> have their forte, and fail a good deal in the rest; – some only shining in gay and humourous subjects, others in the solemn and majestic, and others again in the tender and plaintive, &c. But it is lucky enough that the most common and generally entertaining books (as of religion, science, history, &c) are of a kind which require only such abilities in delivering as are in the possession of almost every one.[56]

A warning by John Armstrong against more confining reading was reprinted in the magazines:

> Deem it not trifling while I recommend,
> What posture suits, to stand or sit by turns,
> As nature prompts, is best; but o'er your leaves
> To lean for ever, cramps the vital parts,
> And robs the machinery of its play.[57]

In posture, as in access to reading, freedom jostled with constraint in the contradictory notions of reading which accompanied the development of the library in the eighteenth century. Library-using and building, book collecting and arranging contributed both to prescriptive concepts of a reading 'Public' and to initiatives to expand the market for print. The commercial efforts of most eighteenth-century literary compilers and booksellers were directed towards increasing sales amongst those for whom books had become social and ornamental necessities. As literary audiences expanded, many book merchants and those engaged in the wider book-related industry attempted to forge more intimate links between readers and producers by defining more precisely their intended readership and even the

54 William Cockin, *Art of Delivering Written Language; or, An Essay on Reading* (London, 1775), p. 140. He also urged (opening up a subject too large to be treated here) that 'a reader must be supposed either actually to personate the author, or one, whose office is barely to communicate what he has said to an auditor' (p. 6).

55 Thomas Sheridan, *Lectures on the Art of Reading*, 2 vols. (London, 1775), reprinted 1775, 1781, 1782, 1787, 1790, 1794, 1798, and spawning numerous commentaries.

56 Cockin, *Art of Delivering Written Language*, p. 148.

57 'Reading', *Town and Country Magazine* 13 (1781): 601, taken from lines 68–83 of John Armstrong, 'The Art of Preserving Health: Book IV The Passions', *Miscellanies*, 2 vols. (1770), I, 87–112.

intended reading environment. They did so from both ambition and defensiveness. Emphasis upon discrimination and responsibility avoided the otherwise head-on conflict between encouragement for a print boom and fears both of a devaluation of literature and of educating the poor beyond their station.

Attempts to resolve these tensions could never be entirely successful. Precisely because definitions of 'private' and 'public' were indistinct and complicated, the popularity of the library was viewed with suspicion. For many commentators the most appropriate representation of the library was that of a sanctuary. In a library, even at its most domestic, the book was housed within a symbolic and designated environment. Whether in silent study or in shared performance, reading locations were to be selected with discrimination. For, as both radicals and conservatives emphasized, knowledge was power. Print and books and book furniture and libraries were the protectors of that power – a power not to be abused and not to be widely shared.

CHAPTER II

Provincial servants' reading in the late eighteenth century

Jan Fergus

Despite increasing interest in the history of reading in eighteenth-century England, the experience of individual readers in this period remains for the most part elusive. Although in notable instances men and women did record their reading and their responses to it,[1] little evidence remains of the broader social spectrum of reading: the kinds of reading matter selected by people in different ranks and occupations, particularly those in service. One source exists, however, which does provide important information and which has, to date, been insufficiently tapped. The records of eighteenth-century booksellers offer a unique record of the purchases of numerous individuals who left no other trace of their reading preferences. Clearly, booksellers' records cannot disclose how, or even whether, the books were read, but – in the case examined here – they can offer a suggestive insight into the 'cultural diet'[2] of useful and entertaining works which prevailed among a small group of provincial servants.

The bookselling records of the Clays of Daventry, Rugby, Lutterworth and Warwick reveal the print orders and purchases of fifty servants, who in the more than twenty-one years covered by records that extend between 1746–84 (see Table 1) bought, bound or ordered seventy books or pamphlets, including two serialized Bibles (see Table 2). Useful works were the most popular, taking up almost three-fifths of the totals, as Tables 2 and 3 indicate. Together, guides and reference works, including books on how to write letters (29 per cent) and religious works, from Bibles to a catechism (21 per

The research for this paper was funded by a fellowship from the National Endowment for the Humanities; I would like to express my gratitude to the Endowment for its support. I would also like to thank James Raven and Naomi Tadmor for much help in improving this article.

1 See the Introduction, pp. 14–15, and chapters by John Brewer and Naomi Tadmor.
2 Rose, 'Rereading the English Common Reader', p. 51.

cent), come to just half the purchases or orders, and almanacs and pocket books (7 per cent) make up the rest. But entertaining works follow closely: plays, fiction and *belles lettres* (20 per cent) were almost as popular as religious works, and a few jest books sold as well (4 per cent). Significantly, however, orders for entertaining literature appear in quantity only from 1770; before then, a servant ordered just one such work, a book of verse. Even cheaper forms of entertaining literature were rarely obtained before 1770: one of the three male servants who subscribed to magazines began his subscription in 1759, and one of the two male servants who borrowed odd volumes of Samuel Richardson's novel *Clarissa* did so in 1769. Because servants tended to pay small sums in cash, however, purchases of the cheapest forms of print, such as chapbooks, almost never turn up in the records unless a customer wanted to buy a work that the Clays did not stock. In this case, the Clays would record the order.

These results are not surprising, except perhaps for the relatively slight interest that these provincial servants show in long prose fiction: Samuel Hutchins, the servant who borrowed volumes of *Clarissa* in 1769, also ordered Fénelon's *The Adventures of Telemachus, the Son of Ulysses*, a two-volume novel,[3] and the manservant of Mr Carpenter of Stowe ordered John Bunyan's *The Pilgrim's Progress*. Both eighteenth-century observers and literary historians have shown great interest in speculating about the audience for the novel, particularly among the lower ranks. But it is likely that both authorities have for different reasons exaggerated servants' devotion to novels. As Richard D. Altick noted nearly forty years ago,

> If we are to believe the constant burden of contemporary satire, domestic servants attended [circulating libraries] in great numbers on their own account, not merely to exchange books for their mistresses; but it is possible that they were singled out for blame because the effects of novel-reading were most irritating when errands went unfulfilled, a roast burned on the spit, or an imperiously pulled bell rope went unanswered.[4]

Writing at the same time, Ian Watt, whose specific remarks about the audience for fiction were as a rule carefully qualified, probably overstated the interest of servants. He first pointed out, quite reason-

[3] This order, made in 1774, may have been for the two-volume set with French and English texts printed side by side. The third edition was published in 1767 by T. Osborne, J. Beecroft, J. Rivington, *et al.*

[4] Altick, *The English Common Reader*, p. 62.

ably, that servants had more of the necessary leisure, light and funds for reading,[5] as well as greater access to books, than other members of the lower ranks, who were also less likely to be literate; later studies support these views.[6] But Watt later remarked without any further evidence that 'Servant girls, as we have seen, constituted a fairly important part of the reading public.'[7] More recent students of the English novel-reading public are cagier. J. Paul Hunter, for instance, writes of that audience as urban, ambitious, mobile and young, without attempting to specify class or occupation.[8]

The use of class terminology in the eighteenth century is a contested matter. The status of servants is particularly hard to determine, partly because the term covered such a very wide range of occupations during this period: clerks, journeymen, apprentices, secretaries, tutors, footmen, chambermaids, servants in husbandry and so on, with very different duties and wages. In addition, servitude could be simply a stage in the life cycle of those of 'the middling sort'. Thus, the son of an innkeeper could become a neighbour's servant, as did David Prowett, one of the Clays' servant customers. Prowett would likely be young and less solvent than his master, and his standing might be less, but his 'class' might be the same. Impoverished gentlewomen could also

5 A footman might receive from 5 to 16 guineas a year in addition to board and livery, a housemaid from 6 to 10. See J. Jean Hecht, *The Domestic Servant Class in Eighteenth-Century England* (London, 1956), pp. 144, 147. For long-term changes in wages and their real value, see E. A. Wrigley and R. S. Schofield, *The Population History of England* (Cambridge, 1981), p. 432; J. A. Goldstone, 'The Demographic Revolution in England: A Re-Examination', *Population Studies* 49 (1986): 32–3. Craftsmen's wages, however, tended to be higher than labourers' wages, and there were also differences between London and the provinces; see Peter Mathias, *The Transformation of England: Essays in the Economic and Social History of England in the Eighteenth Century* (London, 1979), pp. 186–7, Table 9.1.

6 Watt, *The Rise of the Novel*, pp. 38–40, 47. R. S. Schofield's well-known figures on literacy in England suggest that in 1755 and 1790, 60 percent of men signed parish registers, compared with 35 and 40 per cent of women – 'Dimensions of Illiteracy, 1750–1850', *Explorations in Economic History* 10 (1973): 437–54. Literacy among provincial servants may have been close to these rates, or even higher. Admittedly, David Cressy has concluded that in the seventeenth century, 69 per cent of London domestic servants signed while in samples from the provinces (Norwich, Exeter and Durham) only 24 per cent did so – *Literacy and the Social Order: Reading and Writing in Tudor and Stuart England* (Cambridge, 1980), pp. 119–21. But whatever rate of literacy provincial servants achieved, it was likely to be higher than that of labourers. Sara Maza, for example, cites a study showing that mid-eighteenth-century French labourers in Lyon had considerably less than half the literacy rates of servants: menservants had a 57 per cent literacy rate and women servants 37 per cent, compared to 21 and 7 per cent for male and female labourers – *Servants and Masters in Eighteenth-Century France: The Uses of Loyalty* (Princeton, NJ, 1983), p. 50.

7 Watt, *Rise of the Novel*, p. 148.

8 J. Paul Hunter, *Before Novels: The Cultural Contexts of Eighteenth-Century English Fiction* (New York, 1990), pp. 75–81.

become servants in elite houses; such women could enjoy elite privileges, as did Philippa Hayes, another customer who may have been a distressed gentlewoman before she assumed the position of housekeeper at Charlcote. Although I have not included identifiable apprentices or journeymen, those servants represented in this study appear to occupy a wide range of social niches, in other words, a range perhaps as broad as that of 'the middling sort' themselves.

Studies that mention servants' reading, like those of Altick, Watt and Hunter, have worked from textual and contextual evidence, and suffer the disadvantages of attempting to reconstruct audiences from what contemporary texts say or imply about them. But to use actual records of servants' orders and purchases as evidence for their reading fiction (or failing to read it) offers no easy answers to the problems of constructing audience. Their orders and borrowings of novels certainly do not exhaust even these servants' interest in or access to fiction, which could be had in other forms, notably in children's books and magazines. Samuel Hutchins himself ordered six copies of John Newbery's *The Fairing: or, A Golden Toy; for Children* and at one point left three shillings to pay for magazines. Scepticism should inform all studies of audience through booksellers' records. Purchases and orders of print can offer only a very narrow perspective on reading. The Clay records show that servants were frequently employed to carry print back to their masters and mistresses and to place orders; some reading could accompany these tasks. Some servants evidently read to their employers,[9] and no doubt magazines, newspapers and other ephemera were available in many households, and perhaps books as well. Ann Kussmaul cites the memoirs of a servant in husbandry, Joseph Mayett, who in 1798 at age fifteen was 'sometimes allowed by the master to read books "of a religious nature ... as we sat by the fireside in the weekday evenings"'.[10] Individual servants were probably sometimes given improving reading material by their employers. For instance, John Parker, the clergyman of Newbold upon Avon, bought from John Clay in 1769 four copies of Eliza Haywood's *A Present for a Servant-Maid*, presumably to give to his own employees or parishioners.[11] And, as will be shown, limitations within the records themselves also restrict what can be inferred from them. For these reasons, perhaps the most

9 Chartier, ed., *History of Private Life*, III, p. 143.

10 Ann Kussmaul, *Servants in Husbandry in Early Modern England* (Cambridge, 1981), p. 89. The ellipsis is Kussmaul's.

11 Northampton County Record Office (hereafter NRO) D2925.

valuable use to be made of the records lies in extracting from them not simply categories of books bought or ordered but case studies of a few individual servants who made more than a single purchase or order.

The Clays' records include day books, where the credit transactions of every business day were recorded and where orders for print not in stock were noted. Cash transactions are therefore almost completely absent from the records. Customers who came to the shops, found what they wanted and paid in ready money simply do not appear. Only if a cash customer wanted a work not in stock would that order get into the records – into the bespoke sections. These bespoke sections contain far more references to servants' interest in print than do the records of credit transactions.

The Clays' main bookshop was located in Daventry between 1742 and 1781, but at various times during that period, John Clay and, after him, his son Thomas Clay operated shops in Rugby and Lutterworth. Another son, Samuel Clay, also ran a short-lived bookshop in Warwick, taking over the Rugby shop after his brother Thomas died in 1781. These towns were merely the centres of the Clays' activities, however; sales were made to customers who resided as far as ten or fifteen miles away from the nearest shops. As a result, the fairly broad geographical coverage of the Clays' records compensates in part for their incompleteness, particularly for the three decades before 1770 (see Table 1).

Purchases by servants or anyone else would be entered into these day books in three possible places. First, lists of subscribers to serial publications would appear on the endpapers; one manservant, William Brown of Yelvertoft, was listed as taking forty-two numbers of Francis Willoughby's edition of the Bible (first published in 1772–3) on the front endpaper of the records for 1777.[12] Second, monthly lists of subscribers to magazines appeared at regular intervals in the day books, approximately at the end of each month's transactions. In these lists, David Prowett, the innkeeper's son and a servant probably to a draper, subscribed to the *A la Mode Magazine* for two months in 1777, switched to the *Lady's Magazine* in March and apparently maintained this subscription beyond when the records end in 1780, much the longest subscription by any servant. Only two other servants were ever listed as subscribers, though no doubt others like Samuel Hutchins bought occasional copies and paid in cash: Mr Armstead's manservant

12 NRO D88.

subscribed to the *Royal Magazine* beginning in July 1759, and continued until the records end two months later, took the *London Magazine* for about four months in 1770–1, and bought the first issue of the new *Court and City Magazine* early in 1770. Joseph Denman, Mrs Dennet's man, also took the *Court and City* for the first issue, then cancelled, resubscribing in May 1770 for just two months. These short subscriptions were not unusual, particularly for new magazines, which often attracted their greatest number of customers shortly after they were issued and lost them very quickly. Prowett's lengthy subscription to the *Lady's Magazine* was more uncommon: for example, only twelve of the sixty-two women who subscribed to the *Lady's Magazine* did so like Prowett for two or more years.[13]

The third place in the day books where customers' purchases were entered was in the record of daily sales made on credit. If customers took away an item but did not pay ready money, or if they borrowed books, those transactions would appear among that day's records. Both short-term and long-term credit were available, but many servants' purchases seem to have been short-term: they took their purchases away from the shop and returned some time later (perhaps as soon as a week to a month or so) to pay for them, at which point the earlier entry showing their purchases would be crossed out. Generally, these payments occurred before the unpaid purchases had been 'posted' to the ledgers where long-term credit accounts were kept.[14] Such ledgers have survived only for Rugby. Customers listed in them include the more substantial members of the community: the gentry, clergymen, tradesmen, Rugby schoolboys and the like. Servants did not officially obtain the longer credit that such customers could command.[15] By default, however, long-term credit for servants and other infrequent customers did exist. If any customer of John Clay had not paid a debt in full by the time that a new day book was begun, the unpaid total was

13 Jan Fergus, 'Women, Class, and the Growth of Magazine Readership in the Provinces, 1746–1780', *Studies in Eighteenth-Century Culture* 16 (1986): 42, 56 (Table 3).

14 Some evidence for considering that servants obtained short-term credit appears in Samuel Clay's Warwick day book. Samuel Clay reserved the first few pages of D2929, labelled 'Odd Debts. 1770', for uncollected debts; he transferred the unpaid purchases of customers who did not have long-running ledger accounts to these pages every month or so, when he posted his accounts to his ledgers. Among servants' purchases, only those of Mrs Philippa Hayes, made on 7, 9 and 20 November 1771, appear among these debts. She died in January 1772; it is possible that ill-health prevented earlier payment. Her account was settled and the debts crossed off before the day book closed in March 1772.

15 For this reason, I have not been able to find any records of servants' buying or borrowing in the four bookselling ledgers of Timothy Stevens of Cirencester, whose records cover 1780–1806 and are deposited in the Local History archives of the Gloucester Library.

Table 1. *Clay business records deposited in Northamptonshire records office*

DAY BOOKS *Proprietor*	*Daventry*	*Rugby*	*Lutterworth*	*Warwick*
John Clay	D64 30 Sep. 46–25 Mar. 48			
bur. 18 Nov. 75	D2931 1 July 58–28 Sep. 59			
	ML692 5 Dec. 64–22 Mar. 66			
	D2930 26 Jan. 70–21 Mar.71	D2925 9 Apr. 68–11 Aug. 70		
	D7719 28 July 71–5 Feb. 72**			D2929 8 Aug. 70–
	ML699 11 Mar. 73–5 Jan. 74			(Proprietor,
	ML89 4 Jan. 74–16 Feb. 75			Samuel Clay)
Thomas Clay	ML88 29 Jan. 77–18 Dec. 77	D4843 1 Mar. 77–20 Mar. 77	ML694 11 Jul. 76–7 Aug. 77	
bur. 26 Jul. 81	ML10 31 Mar. 79–12 Sep. 80	D7938 7 Aug. 79–5 Aug. 80	D2926 27 Aug. 77–25 Feb 79	
		D3400 12 Aug. 80–Aug. 81	D2928 ?5 Mar. 79–22 Feb. 81	
Samuel Clay		D3400 Aug. 81–29 Oct. 81		
d. 6 Mar. 1800		ML478 29 Oct. 81–12 Jun. 84		

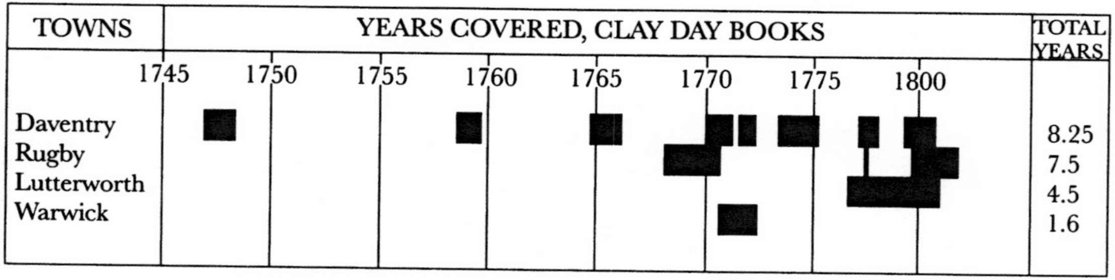

re-entered in the first pages of the new book as 'brought over' from the previous book. David Prowett's father had evidently aspired to give his son a classical education: he purchased three elementary Latin textbooks in 1765 which were delivered to his son. Nine years later, the elder David Prowett had still not paid the 4s6d owing on these texts: John Clarke's *Introduction to the Making of Latin*, the 'Eton Latin Grammar' (probably William Willymott's *Shorter Examples to Lily's Grammar Rules, for children's Latin exercises*) and *Nomenclatura: or, Nouns and Verbs in English and Latin, to be formed and declined by children of the lowest forms.*[16] Two servants' transactions are listed as long-term debts in this way: young David Prowett's purchase of *The Cheats of London* in 1773 and John Mandor's order for binding a *Book of Common Prayer*.

Orders for books not in stock would appear in the section entitled 'Bespoke' at the back of the day book. Because they tended to pay in cash rather than to establish credit, members of the lower ranks were most likely to appear not in the daily records but marginalized in the bespoke section. In these pages, the Clays listed their own notes of what to restock as well as customers' orders for items not in the shop. These undated orders would be crossed off when they were filled. If the customers then paid cash, no further record would appear in the day book. The crossing off here of orders therefore often provides the only evidence that customers received them, obviously not very satisfactory evidence. In a few instances, though, a servant's order appears in both sections because the servant first ordered a book (which was thus entered in the bespoke section), then took the book away from the shop when it arrived (so the book was entered among the daily credit transactions), and returned some time later to pay cash (so that the earlier credit entry was crossed out). This happened when Polly Atkins acquired William Leybourn's *Panarithmologia: or, The Trader's Sure Guide. Containing exact, and useful tables ready to cast up, adapted to the use of merchants*, a popular work whose fifteenth edition appeared in 1769. Although the Clays frequently made notes to restock this work, it must have been out of stock when Polly Atkins's order was placed in the undated bespoke section sometime in 1770. Later, on 12 December 1770, Polly Atkins is noted as having taken away the book.[17] Just two more of the servants' purchases are doubly witnessed in this way, however, as can be seen in Table 3. Exactly twenty other purchases appear among the daily

16 NRO ML692/ML89.
17 NRO D2930/27v/12–12–70.

transactions only, and forty-five appear only in the bespoke sections.[18] Certainly some of these bespoke orders were never received, such as that placed sometime in 1758 by the maidservant of Mrs Brooks, an innkeeper, for 'The Wanton Wife of Bath, a play'.[19] This order was never crossed out, indicating that John Clay never received it. No such play is listed in *The Eighteenth-Century Short Title Catalogue* (*ESTC*) or in the *Index to the London Stage*,[20] but a ballad of the same name does survive in printed versions throughout the century. Other bespoke orders, however, are almost certain to have been filled: for example, when Mr Chipman, coachman to Sir Francis Skipwith, ordered a six-shilling octavo Bible, he left the money to pay for it.

Although, admittedly, the bespoke records are not very satisfactory, I have included them among the totals because they offer access to some servants' intended cash purchases, even if a few of the orders were never actually delivered. Again, cash payments for items actually available in the shop would never make their way into the daily records of the day books because the books record only credit transactions. As a result, purchases of very cheap printed matter costing a penny or so almost never turn up in the records; people who bought them paid in cash. This cheap print includes ballads, penny histories and penny godly books, all of which the Clays stocked, but the only recorded orders or purchases of such material occur when a customer bought them in quantity, as did a woman in Lutterworth who appears to have been a dealer in a small way.[21] Interest in more expensive popular fiction such as children's books and eightpenny chapbooks, however, does occasionally appear among servants, lower artisans and even labourers either because the works had to be ordered or because they were so expensive that the customer could not pay on the spot. In fact, borrowings from the small circulating libraries that the Clays operated comprise the only access to cheap print that the records invariably

18 The remaining two purchases are for serialized Bibles; they are entered, undated, on the endleaves of NRO ML88.

19 NRO D2931/19^{r}.

20 *ESTC* (CD-ROM edn, 1992); Ben Ross Schneider, Jr., *Index to the London Stage* (Carbondale, IL, 1979).

21 Mrs Mary Warner is noted as having ordered fifty histories, among them 'Mother Bunch and Fortune Books' plus a half-ream of ballads, 'Godly books' and 'slipps' sometime in 1777 (NRO ML694/66^{r}). Shortly afterward (69^{r}), Thomas Clay made a note to himself in the bespoke section, 'Let the woman know as buys the histories that I can't afford them under 2/9 lb [i.e. per hundred] as 2s lb was a mistake'. Mrs Mary Warner also ordered ballads (71^{r}) and, probably in 1778, more histories by the ream, godly books in broadsheets and later five quires of godly books (NRO D2928/48^{r} and 64^{v}).

note, because the Clays needed to keep a record of who had which books. Again, however, only three servants became borrowers in all the surviving records.

Servants can be identified within the records in a number of ways. They are generally indicated by first and last names, without titles: for example, Samuel Hutchins, a servant of a Mr Wedding (who may have been a farmer in the parish of Crick[22]), appears variously in the records over about six years as 'Mr Wedding's man Samuel', 'Mr Wedding's man', 'Samuel Hutchins at Mr Wedding's', and just 'Samuel Hutchins'. Most servants, however, remain anonymous, although their position is clear, as is that of Mr Marriot's maid or Mr Armstead's man. (Mr Marriot was a clergyman and Mr Armstead a brewer who was also bailiff of Daventry). Most of these provincial servants were similarly employed in small households, headed by professional men and tradesmen. Exceptions include the two baronets' coachmen who ordered a Bible and a *Book of Common Prayer* (Mr Chipman, already mentioned, and Sir Thomas Cave's coachman), as well as a buyer of almanacs who was a groom for the Knightleys of Fawsley. Another exception was Polly Atkins, never specifically identified as a servant: in one entry she is, however, said to be 'at Mr Sawbridge's'. She is included here among the servants because she was left a legacy in the will of Edward Sawbridge, Esq., a local justice of the peace, if she remained in his service at his death.[23] Clearly, in Samuel Hutchins's and Polly Atkins's cases, the use of a first and last name without an honorific address like 'Miss' or 'Mr' suggests lower status than their employers, 'Mr Wedding' or 'Mr Sawbridge', and this distinction is largely observed throughout the records. Generally, tradespeople and some artisans and all those of higher rank are referred to by their last names, prefaced by 'Mr' or 'Miss' or 'Mrs'. But this

22 Samuel Hutchins's orders appear both in Rugby and Daventry day books. Crick was five and a half miles from Rugby and seven miles from Daventry by contemporary roads, so it is conceivable that someone living there would appear at either shop by turns. Only two men with a surname of Wedding are listed in Victor A. Hatley (ed.), *Northamptonshire Militia Lists 1777* (Kettering, 1973); both are farmers in Crick (p. 65).

23 NRO ZB/331/1, Sawbridge probate record, PCC 4 Nov. 1775, will dated 14 Nov. 1772, codicils 8 Feb. 1774 and 24 June 1774. Polly Atkins was in fact Mary Atkins and was in service with a relative, also Mary Atkins, referred to in the will as Sawbridge's 'domestic servant Mary Atkins the elder' as opposed to Mary Atkins the younger. All three servants, including Daniel Britton, were left £100 each in the will. Interestingly, the wills that Peter Earle examined earlier in the century show no instances of sums this large being left to servants: *The Making of the English Middle Class: Business, Society and Family Life in London 1660–1730* (Berkeley, CA, 1989), p. 317.

practice does not appear to be applied consistently to any particular trades or occupations.[24]

As Table 2 indicates, fourteen female and thirty-six male servants showed interest in obtaining printed matter from the Clays. They represent a small proportion of the total number of the Clays' print customers – perhaps two or at most three per cent of the one to two thousand customers who bought or borrowed print. Usually in the Clay records men far exceed women as purchasers and borrowers, reflecting disproportionate levels of income, literacy and status between men and women. Serving men are no exception. The proportion of women to men among servants as customers is, however, much more nearly equal (at fourteen to thirty-six) than it is in most subgroups derived from the records. This greater approach to equality probably occurs because women servants were, as their work required, either single or widowed; married women are always seriously under-represented in the records, most obviously because accounts tended to be in the husbands' names.[25]

These fifty servants who show interest in print certainly represent a very small proportion of those who lived in the areas served by the Clays. For example, a record exists of the masters who paid the servants' duty in Daventry in 1780; not one of the twenty-six male servants for whom they paid a guinea tax is listed as a customer for books, magazines or serials in the Clay records for 1780.[26] If these servants were interested in print, they obtained it elsewhere, perhaps from itinerant chapmen. It is not clear where else they could have bought printed matter, for no other booksellers were located nearer than Northampton. Because the servants' tax was notoriously evaded,[27] these twenty-six men probably do not represent the full complement of male servants in Daventry in 1780. Three years earlier, a more reliable record shows that in Daventry thirty-seven men between the ages of 18 and 45 named on the 1777 militia list were servants, or about 10 per cent of the 380 men listed.[28] Only one of

24 For example, five of the six butchers mentioned as customers in the Daventry records through 1772 are addressed as 'Mr' or 'Mrs'; only one, Richard Miller of Hardwick, is recorded with a first name and without the honorific 'Mr'. For some reason, his rank in 1747 seems to be somewhat lower than that of Mr Green, also a butcher, who bought books at about the same time. And Mr William Brown of Yelvertoft, listed as a subscriber to a serialized Bible in 1777, is identifiable as a servant only through the *Northamptonshire Militia Lists 1777*, p. 77.

25 See Fergus, 'Women, Class', pp. 44–5.

26 NRO 96p/136; NRO ML10.

27 Hecht, *Domestic Servant Class*, p. 33.

28 Hatley, *Northamptonshire Militia Lists*, pp. 37–44.

Table 2 *Print bought and ordered by servants*

Genres	Men (36)	Women (14)	Totals	Per cent
Guides, conduct books, etc.	14	6	20	29
Religious works	10[a]	5	15	21
Fiction, drama, *belles lettres*	10	4	14	20
Music	4	0	4	6
Almanacs, pocket books	1	4	5	7
Jest books	3	0	3	4
Miscellaneous	7	2	9	13
TOTALS	49	21	70	100

Note: [a] Includes subscriptions to two serialized Bibles

Others

Subscribers to magazines

Joseph Denman, *Court and City Magazine*, Jan. 1770 and May–June 1770

David Prowett, *A la Mode Magazine*, Feb.–Mar. 1777, *Lady's Magazine*, Mar. 1777–Sept. 1780+

Mr Armstead's man, began *Royal Magazine* July 1759, just as records end, *Court and City Magazine*, no. 1 only (Jan. 1770), and *London Magazine*, Nov. 1770–Feb. 1771

(Samuel Hutchins left 3s to pay for magazines, D2925/14-1-69)

Borrowers of novels

Samuel Hutchins, *Clarissa*, vol. 7–8 (6d to read them), 1 April 1769

Mrs. Brooke's man, *Clarissa*, vol. 7, (3d to read), 18 June 1777

Borrowers of other genres

Philippa Hayes, housekeeper, three plays (*Almida* on 2 March 1771; *The West Indian* and *Clementina* on 9 April 1771), Defoe's *Tour through the Whole Island of Great Britain* (16 March 1771)

these servants, David Prowett, is actually recorded as having obtained print from the Clay bookshop in 1777. In this sample the proportion of male servants in Daventry appears quite low. Nearby parishes probably had even higher proportions of servants, few of whom appear in the records. Throughout the county about 20 per cent of the men whose occupation was identified in the militia lists were servants.[29]

Clearly, the Clay records offer only a partial view of provincial servants' interest in print even in the areas that the Clays served. Keeping these limitations in mind, what do the seventy recorded purchases or orders by servants suggest? First, throughout the periods

[29] Ibid., p. xv.

covered, the highest proportion of servants in the records (eighteen of fifty) were prepared to spend their own money on useful works, designed to improve their positions in the world. These servants appear to have been interested, in other words, in instruction and self-improvement.

In the earliest records, the manservant of Mr Leake, an attorney, offers a good example. In 1747 he bought a dictionary with the imposing title of 'Glossographia Anglicana Nova'. The subtitle of an early edition indicates the contents: 'a dictionary, interpreting such hard words of whatever language, as are at present used in the English tongue, with their etymologies, definitions, &c';[30] this formidable tome could be had for only one shilling sixpence. The preface indicates that the book 'shou'd be useful even to the lowest sort of illiterate, yet I have chiefly consulted the advantage of such as are gently advancing to Science; and for want of opportunities of Learned Helps have the misfortune to be their own Conductors, or have not Money Sufficient to lay in the necessary Furniture of Learning'.[31] Mr Leake's man may have been interested in improving not merely his reading vocabulary but his fortune as well: he ordered in 1746 or early 1747 a copy of *Humane Prudence: or, The Art by which a Man may Raise Himself and his Fortune to Grandeur*, by William De Britaine. This enticing work, first published in 1680, had reached thirteen editions in London by 1739, and is full of such advice as 'Make choice of your Wife by the Ears, not the Eyes', a maxim that a reader of the British Library copy has highlighted in the margin – one of just two so marked.[32]

In 1768, some twenty years after Mr Leake's servant's purchases, Mr Pope's man residing near Rugby ordered Leybourn's *The Trader's Sure Guide*, as well as Daniel Fenning's *Ready Reckoner*, both of them books with tables allowing tradesmen to calculate prices of goods bought and sold in any quantity. Possibly this man was planning to set up in business for himself. He was not the only servant to show interest in the *Trader's Guide*, however. As noted earlier, Polly Atkins, who was left a total of £100 in Edward Sawbridge's will, bought a

30 See *ESTC* record T096984, the earliest listed edition, printed by Dan. Brown, Tim Goodwin, *et al.*, 1707; a 2nd edn came out in 1719.

31 From London, British Library, 1568/3629 Preface, A3^r.

32 William De Britaine, *Humane Prudence*, 12th edn (1729), p. 144. This copy (British Library, 8408.aaa.1) was signed by George Birch, 21 July 1762. The other maxim highlighted (by placing a line above and below in the margins): 'I would not advise you to marry a Woman for her Beauty; for Beauty is like Summer Fruits which are apt to corrupt and not lasting' (p. 145).

copy of Leybourne's *Guide* for 1s4d in 1770, about five years before she inherited.[33] Perhaps she wanted the guide to assist her in keeping accounts for her employer, or she may have intended to use her legacy later to go into business.

At least sixteen other instructive self-improving guides were ordered, including *Every Man his Own Lawyer* (for the manservant of an apothecary, Mr Hawkes of Lutterworth), Susannah Carter's one-shilling cookery book (for the maidservant of Mr Watkins, a draper, and for Philippa Hayes, housekeeper of Charlcote Park), Cook's *Gardener* (for Mr Cooper's man of Lutterworth, and not paid for a year after it was received in 1776), plus a book on shorthand (for a builder's manservant in 1758). The most interesting sub-category of improving works, however, is composed of conduct books, including three different guides to writing letters – precisely the sort of guide that Samuel Richardson was writing when he developed the idea for his novel *Pamela*.[34] The title of one of these works, ordered by the manservant of an attorney, Mr Harris, in 1773, outlines typical contents: *The Complete Letter-Writer; or, Polite English Secretary. Containing, familiar letters on the most common occasions in life. Also a variety of more elegant letters for examples and improvement of style* (13th edn, 1770). Such books often contained sample letters to and from servants, as did Richardson's *Familiar Letters*.

Purchasers of conduct books are especially interesting. Mr Bromwich, a joiner's man (and note the use of 'Mr'), bought *The Young Man's Best Companion* for 2s3d in 1765; in 1771, the maidservant to an attorney ordered Anne Barker's *The Complete Servant Maid: or, Young Woman's Best Companion. Containing full, plain, and easy directions for qualifying them for service in general* (printed by J. Cooke, 1770?); and the Widow Fox's manservant ordered in 1759 *Madam Johnson's Present: or, Every Young Woman's Companion, in useful and universal knowledge [with] some plain and necessary directions to maid-servants in general, and several useful tables* (by Mary Johnson, 5th edn, printed by W. Nicoll, 1769). The Widow Fox's man may have wanted the book for himself or even a daughter, to train her into service, but it is striking that a maid already in an attorney's employment should choose to obtain a book that would, presumably, improve her skills.

[33] NRO D2930/12–12–70.

[34] Col. Adams's maid ordered *The British Letter Writer* in 1771; Samuel Hutchins, Mr Wedding's man, ordered *The Polite English Secretary* in 1770; and Mr Harris's man ordered *The Complete Letter Writer* in 1773 (NRO D2930/30^{r}, 11^{v}; ML89/23^{v}).

Altogether, self-improving works account for nearly three-tenths of the servants' orders and purchases (twenty of seventy). The willingness of six (of fifty) servants to buy or order conduct books is especially remarkable when compared to the purchases of the Clay customers as a whole. I have so far recorded only about 120 instances of such purchases throughout the Clay records, although some of these represent buying in bulk by schoolmasters and schoolboys. Admittedly, all these instances include purchases only, no orders, and five of the six instances among servants consist of orders in the bespoke sections, not actual purchases. But when I examined these sections for orders by those of possible low status – that is, by customers listed by first and last names only, often a telling sign – I found only one additional order of a courtesy book: that of 'Samuel at the Swan', probably an employee at a local inn, who ordered *The Complete Letter Writer*. This result suggests that further study of the bespoke section will yield few additional orders of conduct books that do not also appear as purchases in the credit sections. Again, customers who established credit were likely to be listed by their last names and an honorific; and if they bought on credit, their purchases would appear among the daily credit transactions. Servants who were prepared to buy print thus showed a higher proportion of interest in conduct books than did other provincial customers. These figures may support common perceptions that servants during this period were attempting to be upwardly mobile,[35] or they may indicate that servants were expected by their masters and mistresses to conform to certain new norms of behaviour.

Print that served religious purposes was important to servants, though perhaps not quite as attractive as self-improving works: fifteen purchases and orders are recorded. These include four Bibles (two in serialized versions) and five books of common prayer (three of them bound only). Some hints appear that servants who were interested in print belonged to the same print universe as their masters. The two servants – a woman and a man – who ordered dissenting works such as Joseph Alleine's *Alarm to the Unconverted* lived with masters who were also dissenters. Similarly, there is some evidence that servants who showed interest in fiction lived with masters or mistresses who shared that interest, as did two of the servants of Mrs Brooke, an innkeeper's widow who carried on her husband's trade. Mrs Brooke and her daughters bought fiction in various forms – especially magazines and

35 See for instance Hunter, *Before Novels*, p. x; and Davidoff and Hall, *Family Fortunes*, p. 25.

novels, both well known (like *Robinson Crusoe*) and more obscure (like Maria Susannah Cooper's two-volume epistolary novel *The Exemplary Mother: or, Letters between Mrs. Villars and her Family* (1769).[36]

Fiction was not frowned upon in the Brooke household, although Cooper's novel itself approves only the 'best novels', those by Fielding and Richardson.[37] Cooper's novel also has much to say on the topic of reading, including servants' reading. Mrs Villars, for example, 'never refuses her servants any innocent relaxation after they have been at church ... Those who cannot read, often entreat one of us to read a chapter in the Bible or a sermon; and those who can, apply to my mother for the subject of their perusal'.[38] Mrs Brooke's maid, however, felt free to order 'The Wanton Wife of Bath', and Mrs Brooke's manservant was the second of the two servants in all the Clay records who actually borrowed fiction: he paid to read the seventh volume of *Clarissa*, although of course evidence of payment cannot be taken, here or elsewhere, as evidence for reading.[39] Richardson is thus the only novelist shown by the Clay records to have attracted servants.

In the early records, music seems to have been of interest to servants. In 1747, the manservant of Mrs Knightley, a clergyman's widow living in Charwelton, ordered *The Aviary: or, Magazine of British Melody. Consisting of a collection of one thousand three hundred and forty four songs*. The book contained lyrics, not musical notation. Other servants ordered anthems, instructions for the dulcimer, and the 'country dances' 1771.

Although the appeal of religious material and guide books remained steady between 1746 and 1780, entertaining literature increased in popularity – perhaps replacing music or songs as a diversion. This steady demand for religious works and guides, and the increasing demand for entertaining fiction, reflect what was happening in other segments of the marketplace according to the Clay records, particularly among the middling ranks. During and after 1770, servants ordered or bought thirteen entertaining works (see Table 3). Seven of these works were bought by just three frequent customers: Philippa Hayes, a housekeeper, along with David Prowett and Samuel Hutchins. Before 1770, however, as mentioned earlier, the only work of fiction, poetry, drama or *belles lettres* ordered by a servant was Nathaniel Cotton's

36 Works obscure to us were not so at the time, of course; this particular novel was read twice by Anna Larpent, according to her journal deposited in the Huntington Library; a partial transcription of the journal was kindly shown to me by John Brewer.

37 *The Exemplary Mother: or, Letters between Mrs Villars and her Family*, 2 vols. (London, 1769), I, 14.

38 Ibid, I, 13.

39 NRO ML88/6–18–77.

Table 3 *Individual servants' orders and purchases*

1 Guides, conduct books, etc. (total 20)

Customer	Title (as listed), price (if known), year ordered (if given or identifiable)	Bespoke (ordered)	Date of purchase
Atkins, Polly	Leybourn's trader's guide, 1s4d	27v	12/12/70
Bromwich, Mr	Young man's best companion, 2s3d		21/12/65
Hayes, Philippa, Warwick	Carter's frugal housewife, 1s		14/09/71
Hutchins, Samuel	Polite English secretary, 1770	11v	
Mr Watkins's maid	Carter's frugal housewife, 1s, 1774	35r	
Mrs Cadman's maid	New pocket dictionary, 1774	36r	
Col Adams's maid	British letter writer, 1771	30r	
Mr Edwards's maid	Complete servant maid, 1s, 1771	34r	
Mr Cooper's man (Lh)	Cook's gardener, 7s6d nt pd		13/06/76
Mr De Val's man	New pocket dictionary 2s, 1758	18v	
Mr Clarke's man	*2 cookery books, 4s total		04/01/66
Mr Geary's man, Warwick	New London art of gardening, 1771	15v	
Mr Hawkes's man (Lh)	Every man his own lawyer, 1779	24r	
Mr Leake's man	De Britaine's Humane Prudence, 1747	8r	
Mr Leake's man	Glossographia Anglia nova		26/08/47
Mr Pope's man (Ry)	Leybourn's trader's guide, 1769	26v	
Mr Pope's man (Ry)	Fenning's ready reckoner, 1769	26v	
Mrs Harris's man	Complete letter writer, 1774	23v	
Mr Wagstaffe's man	Book of short hand, 1758	8v	
Widow Fox's man	Johnson's every young woman's companion, 1759	33v	

* here and elsewhere, signifies that more than one book has been counted as one
Lh = customer listed in Lutterworth day books
Ry = listed in Rugby day books

2 Religious works (total 15)

Abell, Alice	bind common prayer book		29/07/47
Brown, William	Willoughby's Bible (#1–42, serial)		1777
Mr Chipman, coachman (Ry)	Bible, octavo, left 6s for it, 1768	9r	
Corey, Elizabeth	Gill on God's everlasting love, 1759	29r	
Corey, Elizabeth	Alleine's alarm to sinners, 1s		15/03/59
Hutchins, Samuel (Ry)	*2 Devout companion, 1768	19r	
Mandor, John	bind common prayer book, pre 1746	1r	
Mr Marriot's maid (Lh)	Bible with apocrypha, 6s		22/07/78
Mrs Hiorne's maid, Warwick	bind common prayer book		02/02/71
Mr Armstead's man	Fleetwood's Bible (1–2, serial)		1770
Mr Floyd's man	Dissenting gentleman's letter to White, 1s6d		13/05/47
Mr Heap's man	Catechism, 1s6d		16/03/48

Table 3 *(contd)*

2 Religious works (total 15) (contd)

Customer	Title (as listed), price (if known), year ordered (if given or identifiable)	Bespoke (ordered)	Date of purchase
Mr Clarke's man	Common prayer book with companion to the altar 4s6d		04/04/74
Mrs Williamson's man	Friendly monitor (Burgh?), 1774	4v	
Sir Thos Cave's coachman	Common prayer book with companion to the altar, 4s6d		

3 Fiction, drama, *belles lettres* (total 14)

Customer	Title (as listed), price (if known), year ordered (if given or identifiable)	Bespoke (ordered)	Date of purchase
Atkins, Polly	Love in a village, play with music, 1770	13v	
Hayes, Philippa, Warwick	Lady Mary Wortley Montagu's letters		09/11/71
Hutchins, Samuel	Fenelon, Adv. of Telemachus, 1774	36r	
Hutchins, Samuel	*6 Fairing, or golden toy, 1770	9r	
Prowett, David	Young's Night tho'ts (Bell's), 1777	22v	
Prowett, David	Thomson's works (Bell's poets), 1777	29v	
Prowett, David	Bell's poets, vol. 1–2 (Swift?), 1777	16r	
Prowett, David	The waterman, a farce, 1777	12r	
Mr Cadman's maid	Visions in verse, 1759	32v	
(Mrs Brooke's maid	Wanton wife of Bath, a play), 1758	19r	
Mr Carpenter's man	Pilgrim's progress, 1774	38v	
Mr Clarke's man	Love in a village, 1774	19v	
Mrs Williamson's man	Muse in a moral humour, 1771	1r	
Servants at Brockhall	*1 play 6d; 4 plays 2s (5 days later)		20/06/70

4 Music (total 4)

Customer	Title (as listed), price (if known), year ordered (if given or identifiable)	Bespoke (ordered)	Date of purchase
Mr Horton's man	Instructions for the dulcimer, 1747	5r	
Mr(s)? Adams's man	Country dances 1771, 1771	34r	
Mrs Knightley's man	The aviary (songs), 1747	20v	
Mr Simcock's man	Knapp's anthems (rec'd 3s6d) 1747	15r	

5 Almanacs, pocket books (total 5)

Customer	Title (as listed), price (if known), year ordered (if given or identifiable)	Bespoke (ordered)	Date of purchase
Hayes, Philippa, Warwick	Court calendar with almanac		24/05/71
Hayes, Philippa, Warwick	Ladies' pocket book (bought then returned, charged for reading it)		30/11/71
Lowell, Thomas, groom	*2 Rider's almanacs		11/12/65
Mr Adams' maid Welton	Newbery's Ladies pocket book, 1766	41r	
Mr Bradley's maid	sheet almanac, 1777	11v	

Table 3 *(contd)*

6 Jest books (total 3)

Customer	Title (as listed), price (if known), year ordered (if given or identifiable)	Bespoke (ordered)	Date of purchase
Prowett, David	Cheats of London, 1773	1v	
Prowett, David	London jest book, 1777	4r	
Mr Curtis's man	Jemmy Twitcher's jests, 1770	11r	

7 Miscellaneous (total 9)

Hayes, Philippa, Warwick	Pöllnitz's memoirs		29/06/71
Hayes, Philippa, Warwick	Wagstaffe's catalog (of black-letter books)		08/06/71
Hutchins, Samuel	Bread act, 1774	8v	
Hutchins, Samuel	Summer trials, 1766	32r	
Wykes, Richard (Ry)	Newbery book delivered to self, 6d	14r	03/10/81
Mr Armstead's man	Sessions papers	3r	18/06/70
Mr Jervis's man (Lh)	The great wall a?, 1779	15v	
Mr Parkhurst's man	Owens' fairs, stitched 1765	14r	
Widow Fox's man	Book acc. to ye advertisement, 1759	34r	

compilation, *Visions in Verse, for the entertainment and instruction of younger minds.* A clergyman's maidservant placed the order. Overall, it is striking that servants did not order or buy any English novels, despite the two borrowings of *Clarissa.*

This demand for entertainment seems to have crossed class lines. Servants were evidently interested in drama, traditionally a genre with elite and popular appeal. An unnamed group of servants at Brockhall, the country house of Thomas Lee Thornton, ordered a total of five plays, the titles unspecified. At various times, the butler at Brockhall also bought playing cards. References to servants' singing and card-playing are common in the diaries combed by J. Jean Hecht,[40] and it is quite likely that servants in a great house like Brockhall may have also bought plays to read aloud or perform among themselves. The most popular play among servants, however, and one of the most popular among the Clay customers overall, was Bickerstaffe's comic opera, *Love in a Village*, ordered by Polly Atkins in 1770 as a play with music[41] and

40 Hecht, *The Domestic Servant Class*, pp. 125–30. Hecht unfortunately does not deal with reading as a possible 'Recreation' of servants in the chapter that appears under this title.

41 NRO D2930/13v.

by the manservant of the major landowner near Daventry, Richard Clarke of Welton Place. This work, first performed in 1762, remained in the repertory throughout the century. The plot might have a particular appeal for servants. The heroine has disguised herself as a chambermaid to escape the marriage that her father has arranged. She falls in love with the gardener, who of course turns out to be the eligible young man that her father has chosen for her. The heroine's father sums up the plot as 'a romance, a novel, a pleasanter history by half, than the loves of Dorastus and Faunia; we shall have ballads made of it within these two months' (III, iv).[42] With such a plot, we need not be surprised that this work was frequently purchased by the young. Three of the seven non-servants who bought this piece were boys at the Daventry Dissenting Academy, another was a schoolboy at Rugby School who later became a clergyman, a fifth was an apprentice to a surgeon, and a sixth was a girl described as Mr Tompson's daughter. The other customer was a local squire. The work circulated among men and women of different ranks and occupations, though young customers predominated.

Another young person shows perhaps the greatest interest in entertainment. Like his father the innkeeper, who early in 1774 had not yet paid for Latin schoolbooks bought (probably for his son) in 1765, David Prowett had by 1773 obtained a book that he had not yet paid for, *The Cheats of London Exposed* (price 1s). At this time, he was employed by Mr Jeffcutt, a grocer. When young David next appeared in the records four years later, he was a servant, probably to the draper William Hickman. As noted earlier, he subscribed for two months to the short-lived *A la Mode Magazine* and for more than three years to Robinson and Roberts's *Lady's Magazine*. David Prowett also ordered a farce, a good deal of poetry and a jest book (see Table 3). His interest in the poetry of Thomson, Young and (probably) Swift as published in John Bell's *British Poets* series shows a desire to consume literature that had achieved in time a 'classic' status along with less elevated, more ephemeral works; Bell, Cooke and other inexpensive publishers of classic British literature were catering to just this desire. Prowett's purchases remind us again that Roger Chartier is right to observe:

[42] Another perhaps relevant passage in the text: Mrs Deborah Woodcock asserts that 'I never looked into a book, but when I said my prayers, except it was the complete housewife, or the great family receipt book: whereas you are always at your studies: Ah! I never knew a woman come to good, that was fond of reading' (III, viii).

To a greater extent than has been thought, widely distributed texts and books crossed social boundaries and drew readers from very different social and economic levels.[43]

Prowett's interest in obtaining fiction through magazines like the *Lady's Magazine* resembles that of other customers from all social classes in the 1770s. I have argued elsewhere that the appearance then of the *Town and Country Magazine* and above all the *Lady's Magazine* enlarged the provincial audience for fiction to include women of the middling ranks – farmers' and tradesmen's wives – who until then had not subscribed to magazines or showed much interest in other fictional forms.[44] Novellas and short stories in magazines were both cheap and easily available in the provinces, which must certainly help to account for their being much more popular than novels.

The only woman servant who ever borrowed books from the Clays was a special case: Mrs Philippa Hayes, a widow and housekeeper to George Lucy of Charlcote Park, near Stratford-upon-Avon. As housekeeper to a bachelor, she enjoyed some of the privileges of the mistress of a great house. Her letters to George Lucy read like those of a friend rather than a subordinate, and she exchanged letters with the surrounding gentry, such as the family of Sir Charles Mordaunt of Walton Hall. When Mrs Hayes was in Peterborough, about to visit Derbyshire, Miss Dolly Mordaunt wrote to her:

> ... we had a note from Mrs Dewes yesteday with the new play and entertainmt wch were sent by Miss Dewes [in London] to her Bror. I conclude you have seen both these, for I find you are Commenced a great Book worm since you left these parts. I never read the invisible spy wch I find you think worth notice a case that but seldom attends such sort of Books.[45]

It is difficult to associate servitude with the bookworm Mrs Hayes. But even she bought a guide, useful in her position, Susannah Carter's *The Frugal Housewife, or Complete Woman Cook* (1772) , along with all her other instructive and entertaining books. Although Mrs Hayes clearly read fiction, including Eliza Haywood's *The Invisible Spy*, she never borrowed any novels from Clay. Instead, she borrowed three new plays, Daniel Defoe's *A Tour through the Whole Island of Great Britain* and *A Ladies' Pocket*

43 'General introduction: print culture', in Roger Chartier, ed., *The Culture of Print: Power and the Uses of Print in Early Modern Europe* (Cambridge, 1989), p. 4.

44 Fergus, 'Women, Class', esp. pp. 43–4.

45 Warwick County Record Office (hereafter WCRO) L6/1487. Quoted in part also by Alice, Lady Fairfax-Lucy, *Charlcote and the Lucys: The Chronicle of an English Family* (London, 1958), pp. 206–7.

Book. Actually, she had bought these last two works, along with the play *Almida*, but returned them and was charged instead for reading them, a customary practice among booksellers but appearing only occasionally in the records. In addition to Carter's book on cookery, she bought Pöllnitz's four-volume *Memoirs*; these two works she evidently chose to keep.[46] Mrs Hayes's decisions – to borrow new fiction (in the form of plays), to buy ephemera and non-fictional works, and to lend books among friends – are similar to those of the gentry and professional classes served by the Clays.[47]

With Philippa Hayes we reach the highest levels of servitude, approaching social equality with the gentry. Mrs Hayes certainly had the run of George Lucy's library. Elizabeth Hands, a poet who was also a servant, possibly had equal access to her employers' library.[48] Although Hands never appears to purchase or order print in the Clay records, her employers the Huddesfords frequently did. In addition, when Hands published *The Death of Amnon. A Poem. With an appendix; containing pastorals and other poetical pieces* at Coventry in 1789, she had '1200 subscribers at 5 shillings each', thanks to the efforts of a network of patrons. These included Miss Huddesford and a former Rugby schoolboy and Clay customer, Philip Bracebridge Homer, who with his father the Rev. Henry Sacheverell Homer solicited subscriptions among his acquaintance.[49] Close to one hundred former Clay customers were subscribers, suggesting the presence of a local network of support, if not for Hands herself, then for those who chose to assist her. The Clay customers who became subscribers were drawn from among the local gentry, the professional classes and substantial tradespeople like the Clays themselves. By this time Clay was a banker as well as bookseller in Rugby, and both his wife and his sister Mrs Rowell

46 NRO D2929.

47 Jan Fergus, 'Eighteenth-Century Readers in Provincial England: The Customers of Samuel Clay's Circulating Library and Bookshop in Warwick, 1770–72', *Papers of the Bibliographical Society of America* 78 (1984): 169.

48 Hands is the most amusing and readable of several published poets who lived in the areas served by the Clays and purchased print from them: Richard Jago of Snitterfield, author of *Edge-hill* (1767) and other poems, and Benjamin West, a clergyman of Weedon, who published *Miscellaneous Poems, Translations, and Imitations* (1780), as well as the more humble William Gough, a tapster at the Globe a few miles west of Daventry, who printed some enigmas and a poem in Wheble's *Lady's Magazine* in the early 1770s (see Fergus, 'Women, Class', pp. 48–50).

49 Roger Lonsdale (ed.), *Eighteenth-Century Women Poets: An Oxford Anthology* (Oxford, 1990), p. 422. Lonsdale's information comes from W. K. Riland Bedford, *Three Hundred Years of a Family Living, Being a History of the Rilands of Sutton Coldfield* (Birmingham, 1889), pp. 112–14; cited by Donna Landry, *The Muses of Resistance: Labouring-Class Women's Poetry in Britain, 1739–1796* (Cambridge, 1990), pp. 187–8.

subscribed. Throughout the Clay records, the gentry, professionals and (after 1770) tradespeople are the principal customers for books. The only subscriber to Hands's poems whom I can identify as possibly of a lower status is Miss Plomer of Welton who may have been employed as a servant or companion in Daventry in 1789. Even so, she was connected to the gentry: she was the half-sister of John Plomer Clarke, Esq., who inherited Welton Place from Richard Clarke in 1775. Clarke's letters to his father John Plomer show that he found his father's second wife and her children rather a trial in their poverty and dependency.[50]

The Hands subscription list attests in any case to a kind of downward movement of patronage over the century. Subscribing to books provides an interesting cultural nexus: it depended upon a democratized form of patronage (or charity) and the exploitation of local networks in order to take advantage of the cultural institution of print. Book subscriptions often served as a form of charity rather than patronage because some needy authors never produced their books despite receiving the subscriptions. Those who chose to help an author obtain subscriptions approached their own friends and connections as the Homers did. Ideally it would be possible to reconstruct from the Hands list a branching network showing inter-relationships among former Rugby scholars, clergymen and professionals and their wives and the gentry, all of whom were prepared to encourage a servant who wrote. This network, while not quite like William J. Gilmore's 'transportation and communication networks that render knowledge available or unavailable',[51] operated efficiently to aid Hands, who collected some £300 from her subscribers. Although earlier humble poets like Stephen Duck relied on Queen Caroline's patronage, later in the century a community of local book buyers could usurp that privilege, joining together to support local talent in a servant who (amusingly enough) mocked the responses that she anticipated from this audience in two of her published poems.[52]

Hands was clearly exceptional. The fifty servants shown by the Clay records to have purchased and ordered print suggest, however, that those in the lower ranks were as interested as their 'betters' in making

[50] NRO Welton Box x4434.

[51] Gilmore, *Reading Becomes a Necessity of Life*, p. 163.

[52] See Lonsdale, *Eighteenth-Century Women Poets*, pp. 425–9, for 'A Poem, On the Supposition of an Advertisement appearing in a Morning Paper, of the Publication of a Volume of Poems, by a Servant-Maid' and 'A Poem, On the Supposition of the Book having been Published and Read'.

the best use of their literacy. The classic motives for reading in the period were delight and instruction, and servants' choices certainly indicate both intellectual curiosity and a desire for self-improvement. Although it would be a mistake to depend too heavily on a sample of seventy selections, the Clay records show a striking similarity between servants' choices and those of their masters, not simply within certain households, but overall. Servants' interest in print repeatedly reflects that of the middling ranks and sometimes (in the case of Philippa Hayes) even of the gentry and professional classes. With further analysis, the Clay records may indicate whether, as is sometimes argued, the middling ranks were themselves trying to imitate the gentry in their reading habits and taste, but certainly from the 1770s, tradesmen, farmers, artisans and their wives were increasingly interested in magazines and other inexpensive forms of literature, including cheap editions of well-known works as well as guides and instructive books. Servants, too, seem to have been more and more eager to spend their money on such material, as the selections of David Prowett, Polly Atkins and Samuel Hutchins reveal. Their choices, along with those of other servants and the remaining Clay customers, provide valuable evidence of an otherwise elusive subject for historians of reading: the social spectrum of readers and the kinds of reading matter valued by men and women of different ranks and occupations in late eighteenth-century England.

CHAPTER 12

Reconstructing the reader: prescriptions, texts and strategies in Anna Larpent's reading

John Brewer

This essay examines the reading of a single eighteenth-century English woman, Anna Margaretta Larpent. It is however more than an exercise in historical reconstruction, an endeavour to recover the reading of one relatively obscure person. My concern in what follows is to bring together two rather different perspectives on 'the reader' and on reading. Literary scholars are fully familiar with the complex questions raised by the reader or implied reader in a given text, though typically the texts which have been most rigorously scrutinized have tended to belong to a literary canon or, at least, to be works of imaginative literature. A few literary scholars – this is of course especially true of those who have studied the history of the novel – have also examined the sizeable body of prescriptive literature which sought to tell readers what to read and how, seeking to shape a particular sort of reader and to define the activity of reading.[1]

This literary preoccupation with the construction of the reader, whether concerned with textual strategies, reader response or the reader as 'subject' has seemed a far cry from the history of reading, as investigated by those concerned with such issues as the availability of reading matter, the institutions – like libraries, bookclubs and bookshops – that underpinned reading practices, and the recovery of what people 'really read'. Only occasionally, as in Robert Darnton's essay on the reading of Jean Ranson, the Rousseauistic merchant of La Rochelle, are the two areas of inquiry brought together.[2] Too often both literatures are content to ignore one another and, more

An earlier and rather different version of this chapter appeared as 'Cultural Consumption in Eighteenth-Century England: The View of the Reader', in *Frühe Neuzeit – Frühe Moderne? Forschungen zur Vielschichtigkeit von übergangsprozessen: Herausgegeben von Rudolf Vierhaus und Mitarbeitern des Max-Planck-Instituts für Geschichte* (Göttingen, 1992), pp. 366–91.

1 See especially Peter de Bolla, *The Discourse of the Sublime: History, Aesthetics and the Subject* (Oxford, 1989), pp. 230–78.

2 Darnton, 'Readers Respond to Rousseau'.

importantly, to ignore the voice of the reader him or herself. For if the literary scholar seems often to accept the ventriloquizing of the reader in the text, the historian and bibliographer constructs a reader who is not represented as engaged in the act of reading but as materially constituted, as if in some Swiftian nightmare, from the title pages of books and pamphlets.

My aim in this essay, then, is to restore the voice of the reader. But in doing so, I do not want to drown out the utterances of others. In giving priority to the reader's version of the reader and of reading, I do not want to claim that her account overrides all others, that it is somehow a transparent truth, where the others are obscure fictions. For, as I hope to show, the reader's reader is a fragile, imaginative construction that grows out of an elaborate negotiation between prevailing prescriptions on how to read and the desires of the reader. And, as we shall also see, the anxieties produced by this creative tension varied considerably according to the types of texts that were read.

There are many reasons why the reader so rarely represents him or herself but one of the more compelling explanations for the absence is the difficulty of finding adequate source material to be able to reconstruct their perspective. Comments on reading in letters, diaries and journals of the period are not uncommon but are notoriously perfunctory and elliptical. The inert sources for readership – inventories, library catalogues and saleroom lists – are exceptionally difficult to animate. Occasionally, however, we uncover materials in which readers illuminate their own world. Such, for instance, is the dossier of Jean Ranson used to such effect by Robert Darnton. Such, too, is the journal that is the focus of the case study that follows, the diary of Anna Margaretta Larpent.

Who was our reader, Anna Larpent? Born in 1758 at Pera in Turkey, she was the daughter of a self-educated British diplomat and fellow of the Royal Society, Sir James Porter, and of a minor European aristocrat, Clarissa Catherine, eldest daughter of Elbert, 2nd Baron Hochepied.[3] In 1782 she married John Larpent, a successful civil servant and widower, seventeen years her senior, who held the post of Inspector of Plays in the Office of the Lord Chamberlain. He acted as a censor, reading (and often altering) the manuscript texts of all

[3] George Larpent, *Turkey: Its History and Progress from the Journals and Correspondence of Sir James Porter, Fifteen Years Ambassador at Constantinople; continued to the present time, with a Memoir of Sir James Porter, by his grandson*, 2 vols. (London, 1851), I, 3–14.

theatrical performances before they appeared on the London stage.[4] Anna and her husband have a special place in theatre history, not only because of his role as censor, but because together they collected, indexed and collated all of the plays that had been submitted to the Lord Chamberlain's Office since the passage of the Licensing Act in 1737. This body of material remains one of the most important archives for eighteenth-century theatre history. Anna's collaboration with her husband was not confined to that of archivist. She is known to have censored some plays herself, and seems to have had sole responsibility for censoring Italian opera as she, unlike her husband, was fluent in the language.[5]

Anna had two children and one stepson, all of whom she helped in their studies and all of whom were to enter the ranks of the great and the good in the nineteenth century. She was a pious Anglican: she helped run a Sunday School near her country villa at Ashurst in Surrey and had a number of evangelical friends – she enjoyed going to the circus with the Bowdlers. She was well educated, knowing French and Italian; and she led, to judge from her diary, an extremely active social life.

Her diary consists of seventeen volumes, now in the Huntington Library, covering the period between 1773 and 1828.[6] Apart from the earliest volume, which is a retrospective digest – 'a methodized journal' – taken from materials that no longer survive, each diary consists of entries made every few days from scraps and notes that she kept for the purpose – she was extremely methodical – recording her daily activities in some detail. The tenor of the diary is not, except perhaps in the early years, either confessional or emotionally charged. She offers none of the excoriating self-criticism typical of contemporary conversion narratives, nor does she offer the revelations of a Rousseau. Her journal is first a record of the mind and, only obliquely, a testament of the heart. Page after page records her theatre and concert going, her visits to galleries and exhibitions and, above all, her voracious reading. The diary scrupulously, almost obsessively depicts a cerebral self, a person devoted to culture and learning, a woman who, though she never ventured into print, was a bold and stringent critic.

4 L. W. Conolly, *The Censorship of English Drama* (San Marino, CA, 1976), pp. 4–7, 34–5, 42–5, 81, 109–13, 154–9.

5 Ibid., pp. 9, 41–2, 111.

6 Huntington Library, HM 31201, hereafter HM 31201. I wish to thank the Director and Staff of the Huntington for permission to use and quote from this material.

Evidence in the diary about Anna's reading takes two forms: in the earliest journal she provides a bald list of everything that she read; in the diaries from the 1790s onwards she not only lists what she reads, but often describes the circumstances of her reading; and when she completes a work she writes an assessment of the book, rather in the manner of the *Monthly Reviews* that she scrutinized each month for new publications, distinguishing her account from the main text by placing it in quotation marks.

What did Anna Larpent read? The short answer is, a great deal: over 440 titles including books, pamphlets, plays and sermons, during the first ten years in which she recorded her reading matter. A crude breakdown gives something of the range: forty-six English novels (she preferred those by women or works of sentimental fiction); twenty-two French works of fiction, including Rousseau, Marivaux, Marmontel and Voltaire; Italian imaginative literature, especially Goldoni and Metastasio; thirty-six French plays, notably those of Corneille; thirty-eight English plays, especially Shakespeare; more than sixty works on history, biography and social science including Gibbon, Hume, Raynall, Rollin, Giuccardini, Adam Smith, Monboddo and Ferguson; sixteen books of natural philosophy, notably Fontenelle, Smellie, Goldsmith and the entire literature of the South Sea Voyages; *belles lettres* and criticism to the tune of forty-five volumes, among them Pope, Johnson, Boileau, Du Bos, Swift and Chesterfield; twenty-seven works of classics in translation, with Plutarch, Seneca, Virgil and Cicero as special favourites; a baker's dozen of advice books; forty-six collections of sermons and works of piety chiefly from latitudinarian divines but also from high churchmen and papists; the English poetic classics – Spencer, Milton, Gay, Pope, Thomson, Young and Gray – as well as a smaller body of travel literature and miscellaneous work that is difficult to identify.

Such a long shopping list conveys the breadth of Larpent's reading but gives very little sense of its place in her daily life or of its broader significance. We can see this more clearly if we reconstruct a typical day in a typical month. On 9 April 1792 Anna Margaretta Larpent rose at 7:30, a little earlier than her usual hour, 'spent some time', as she described it, 'in self-examination' and then read two chapters of that blistering critique of the British constitution, Thomas Paine's *Rights of Man*, before sitting down to breakfast. During the morning, she tutored her two teenage sons, John and George, who were on holiday from their school at Cheam. In a ritual that was to be repeated throughout the holidays, Anna and John read passages from an instructive and improving work, Sarah Trimmer's *Sacred History*, a didactic anthology from the scriptures written by the best-selling pious evangelical. George was instructed by Anna to spell, read and to learn Latin.[7]

After their morning exercise, all three left their house in Newman Street in the West End of London to see the kangaroo on exhibit from Botany Bay. It was, wrote Anna, 'like a Hare, with hind legs of immense length the front feet more like paws. It vaults six or eight feet high & gowes awkwardly in a Slower motion on the joint of the hind legs. It feeds on hay, is of horse colour, its lower tooth broad, and with the power of opening or rather clevering it in two. The meat of some shot by convicts like lean beef.' After admiring this curiosity, the family proceeded to the Polygraphic Exhibition in Schomberg House on Pall Mall. Here they saw a display of a number of mechanical reproductions of oil paintings manufactured by the portrait painter and theatrical manager, Joseph Booth.[8] Anna and her husband sat down to dinner about three o'clock. Then they both went to Covent Garden to see the evening's performance: Thomas Holcroft's sentimental comedy, *The Road to Ruin*; and an afterpiece, *Oscar and Malvina*, which Anna thought trivial but entertaining – 'A Pantomimicall Jumble of Barbarous Customs, modern Nonsense the Music Scottish. Very pretty. the Pipes and Horn very pleasing & characteristic.'[9]

This particular day, filled with diverse reading matter – piety and radical politics (what would Paine and Mrs Trimmer have thought of keeping each other's company?) – devoted to instruction and the pursuit of learning was characteristic of Anna Margaretta's life in London. In the month of April 1792 and apart from Paine's *Rights of Man*, Anna read Richardson's *Clarissa* for the second time – 'the style is prolix, the manners obsolete, & I felt fidgetted at the repetitions not being 15, yet surely it is wonderfully wrought';[10] the conservative monthly digest of new books, *The Critical Review*; a Goldoni play, probably in the original Italian; Smellie's *Philosophy of Nature* which she considered poorly organized but of sufficient value to transcribe extracts for her children; a novel by Thomas Holcroft, *Anna St. Ives*, dismissed as 'sad stuff I cannot read on';[11] her father's manuscript

7 HM 31201, I: 9/4/1792.
8 For the Polygraphic Society, see William T. Whitely, *Artists and their Friends in England 1700–1799*, 2 vols. (London [1928]), II, pp. 25–8.
9 HM 31201, I: 9/4/92.
10 Ibid., 3/4/92.
11 Ibid., 21/4/92.

memoirs; and a new opera, *Just in Time*. She also visited an exhibit of Ozias Humphry's 'crayon pictures', took in an opera, saw Sarah Siddons as Lady Randolph in Home's tragedy, *Douglas* – 'I never was more painfully delighted'[12] – attended a concert at Mrs Beaver's, and listened while her husband and stepson read aloud to her from the newspapers and Sutherland's *Tour of Constantinople*.

What can we learn from this dense narrative about Anna Larpent's taste and about her attitude towards reading? The first and most conspicuous feature of her account is that she quite clearly had different attitudes towards different sorts of reading matter. To posit a single attitude would be hopelessly reductive. Her response to reading imaginative literature differs sharply from her reading of non-fiction which, in turn, differs critically from her reading of works of piety and religion. But, I also want to argue that, although Anna responded differently to different types of literature, she also strove to construct through both the form and content of her text (the diary), a notion of an ideal reader. This was hard for her to sustain because the variety of her reading practices was difficult to contain within a stable category. Her ideal had repeatedly to be refashioned and remade and as repeatedly threatened to disintegrate. What I mean by this will, I trust, become clearer as we examine her responses to different sorts of texts.

Two features of Anna's reading of imaginative literature stand out: her confident critical judgement and her predilection for women authors and for works with female protagonists. Appropriately for a woman who helped her husband censor plays, Anna could wax lyrical but also wane indignant. She showed no doubts about her right or ability to criticize, no hesitation in expressing herself forcefully. Of Hannah More's tragedy *Percy* she writes in 1777:

> The story of Percy is simple, pathetic, distressing, 'tis worked up to the most moving height of distress; the power of virtue on the mind is well contrasted with the mad way of passion, Elwina's is an almost perfect character ... A pure love of virtue appearing throughout, & filling the virtuous heart with glowing pleasure ... the struggle in Elwina's mind between love and duty is fine, the triumph of the latter nobly painted. There is a charming delicacy, and elevation of sentiment.[13]

And on Charlotte Smith's novel, *Desmond*, she comments in 1792:

[12] Ibid., 25/4/92.
[13] Ibid., 12/12/77.

With a fine imagination, & command of Language Charlotte Smith cannot write without Interest[.] this is an odd work. She introduces in a prettily wrought novel the more early french troubles in consequence of the Revolution. she is a wild leveller. She defends the revolution. she writes with the enthusiasm of a woman and a poetess. her story is hurried has faults in the conduct & narrative, yet it interests. her descriptions are very pleasing and her characteristic conversations are somewhat forced. She writes herself out. yet her genius predominates.[14]

As these examples show, Anna was avidly interested in works by and about women. (The same was true of her taste in painting: she was a passionate admirer of Angelica Kauffman and of history paintings that made supplicant and suffering women their central figures.) But her attitudes were complex. Despite her enthusiasm for their works, Anna disapproved of women who earned their living with the pen, brush or on the stage. She expressed this loosely enforced and often breached double-standard in statements that frequently seem contradictory. She admired Sarah Siddons but was also sure that 'Acting revolts in women against female delicacy';[15] she loved Angelica Kauffman more than any other painter but believed 'being an Artist incompatible with the Duties of a good Wife and Mother'.[16] She read and praised many women novelists but reprobated 'those pecuniary wants' that led them to publish.[17] She believed that her own not inconsiderable literary powers could only be used properly in a limited sphere, one confined to the family and its circle of friends. She never ventured, to our knowledge, into print. Paradoxically, then, Anna could enjoy the cultural achievements of women only because they were prepared to act in a way that she saw as at best morally questionable and at worst thoroughly reprehensible.

Larpent reveals a similar ambivalence over the reading of novels. Despite her extensive reading of fiction – French and English novels together constitute the largest category of her reading – she adopted the conventionally censorious view of such works: 'It is not right', she recorded in 1774, 'to encourage a taste for novels – they are too seducing, too trivial, too dangerous.' But her condemnation was not wholehearted, for she added, 'but a good one sometimes, shews the World, characters &c'.[18] When educating her sister, Clara, after her

14 Ibid., 14/8/92.
15 Ibid., 7/4/90.
16 Ibid., 19/3/92.
17 Ibid., 14/8/92.
18 Ibid., 17: *Miscellaneous Observations*, 1771.

father's death in 1776, Anna insisted that her sibling read 'No novels, except Evelina & the Spiritual Quixotte'.[19] Her choice is understandable: both Frances Burney's extremely popular account of the coming of age of a virtuous provincial girl who is attracted but finally not seduced by the pleasures of the metropolis, and Richard Graves's satire on the excesses of Methodism can be read as advice manuals on how to avoid the perils of metropolitan corruption and the ranting enthusiasm of the religious zealot. They belong in that popular category of novels that profess not to be novels at all or, at least, to overcome or avoid the vices of the titillating romance. This tension between Anna's overt condemnation of novels and her desire to sneak them back into the world of legitimate reading – an ambivalence redolent of Lydia Languish's concealment of frivolous fiction beneath the covers of the edifying *The Whole Duty of Man*[20] – is, I believe, explained by Anna's desire, even while reading novels, to avoid being condemned as a particular sort of reader.

Anna Larpent was fully aware of and indeed claimed to have read the sort of prescriptive literature that represented novel reading as a dangerous activity likely to loosen the spirits and disturb the judgement of young women. She includes such popular and frequently reprinted works as John Bennett's *Letters to a Young Lady*, Hester Chapone's *Letters on the Improvement of the Mind, addressed to a young Lady* (1773) and Hannah More's *Strictures on the Modern System of Female Education* among those she studied. (As in so many other fields, she preferred works by women authors to those of men).

In these works, as in many others, she would have read admonitions against novel reading. From the likes of Joseph Robertson in his *Essay on the Education of Young Ladies* (1798) she would have learnt that, 'A young woman who employs her time in reading novels, will never find amusement in other books. Her mind will be soon debauched by licentious descriptions, and lascivious images; . . . her mind will become a magazine of trifles and follies, or rather impure or wanton ideas.'[21] This version of the world of the novel reader as private, feminized, illicit and associated with pleasure rather than instruction was one that Larpent wished to circumvent or avoid. She knew of its power but refused to accept that it applied to her own case.

This did not preclude her from reading a succession of novels, many

19 Ibid., 1778.
20 Richard Brinsley Sheridan, *The Rivals*, Act 1, scene 2.
21 Joseph Robertson, *An Essay on the Education of Young Ladies* (London, 1798), pp. 44–5.

by women, that dealt with affairs of the heart. Throughout her life she had a penchant for sentimental fiction like Elizabeth Griffith's *Lady Juliana Harley* (1773) and Charlotte Smith's *Desmond* (1792) which portrayed married women whose real affections were not for their husbands. Nor did it prevent her from representing herself as 'the transported reader'. On the contrary she could write of William Mason's play *Caractacus*: 'my soul melted into every pleasing sensation, the language charming! divine harmony, beams in every line such a love of virtue! such examples of piety, resignation, and fortitude! raise the soul to an ecstatic height. Sweet Evelinda how my heart throbbed for her!'[22]

Anna's response to imaginative literature is strongly emotional: she is 'charmed', her soul melts and her heart throbs. She feels especially for the female characters with whom she identifies. But this sentiment should not be confused with the passionate desire associated by critics with the traditional romance. Anna loved what she saw as the high-minded literature of sentiment rather than the disreputable language of love. She preferred a work in the manner of Samuel Richardson's novels, one that preached the precepts of female virtue in scenes of excruciating feeling and deep distress.[23] She enjoyed, as she put it in a revealing phrase, being 'painfully delighted'.[24] Thomas Hull's doctored version of James Thomson's *Edward and Elinora* cut no ice with the critics, but in Anna's view it was 'A most affecting Tale, pleasingly tender – fraught with virtuous sentiments'.[25] And she attributed her enthusiasm for Hannah More's tragedy *Percy* – she saw the play twice, including the night of the author's benefit, and bought a copy – to its power to represent the struggle between virtue and passion.[26]

As Anna's comments make clear, the sentiments she applauds in fictional characters are not those of romantic passion but feelings of virtue. The audience, in Anna's view, should be moved to sympathy and compassion not animated by desire. The object of their sentiment has therefore to be a victim, someone who bears misfortune with fortitude; and it was especially appropriate that the one who suffered was a woman because, as the *Essay on the Character ... of Women*, a book Anna read in 1780, put it, 'of every species of courage, the sort

22 HM 31201, 17: 7/2/77.

23 John Mullan, *Sentiment and Sociability: The Language of Feeling in the Eighteenth Century* (Oxford, 1988), pp. 61–5.

24 See n. 12 above.

25 HM 31201, 17: 1775.

26 Ibid., 12/12/77. See p. 231 above.

of which women have the greatest share, is the courage that bears affliction'.[27]

Anna read novels and plays as realms of feeling and passion but also as sites of instruction and edification. Her absorption was never so complete as to suspend her critical and moral faculties. What she sought was the opportunity to indulge what she regarded as the only legitimate pleasurable sensation, namely 'the pursuit of virtue'. When imaginative literature worked against this, either by elevating love over duty or, in the manner of the Restoration comedies that Anna especially disapproved, by failing to condemn the carnal appetites it represented, it had to be condemned. Her position is remarkably similar to that of Hannah More, who emphasized that true sentiment must be linked to principle: 'It must be the enthusiasm which grows up with a feeling mind, and is cherished by virtuous education, not that which is compounded of irregular passions, and artificially refined by books of unnatural fiction and improbable adventure'.[28]

Reading, even reading fiction, therefore becomes purposive, disciplined, a means of overcoming rather than encouraging female frivolity. In February 1779 Anna describes how she left a crowded party at Lady Mary Forbes's to take up a digest of philosophy:

> I returned home & read 4 chapters of Winn's abridgement of Lock[e] on the human understanding. the transition from such a dissipate scene to the deep reflection my study demanded was easier than I expected: how much more was I pleased with myself whilst thus exercising the faculties of a reasonable mind, in endeavoring to discover the sources of those faculties, to form them properly, to improve them, than when I was dipping a Curtesy to *one*, forcing a smile for another, hearing nonsense from a 3rd or what is worse talking nonsense to a fourth.[29]

This neat antithesis between the frivolous assembly and the studious individual provides a textbook example for the point that Hannah More makes in her *Strictures on Female Education*:

> Serious study serves to harden the mind for more trying conflicts; it lifts the reader from sensation to intellect; it abstracts her from the world and its vanities; it fixes a wandering spirit, and fortifies a weak one, it divorces her from matter; it corrects that spirit of trifling which she naturally contracts

27 *An Essay on the Character, the Manner and the Understanding of Women, in Different Ages: Translated from the French of Mons. Thomas by Mrs Kindersley. With two original essays* (London, 1781), p. 157.

28 [Hannah More], *Essays on Various Subjects, Principally Designed for Young Ladies*, 2nd edn (London, 1778), p. 101.

29 HM 31201, 17: 19/2/79.

from the frivolous turn of female conversation ... it concentrates her attention ... and thus even helps to qualify her for religious pursuits.[30]

Reading becomes a matter, as Anna frequently shows through both example and injunction, of order and clarity rather than disorderly indulgence. The transport of the reader into the world of 'irregular passions' is replaced by her elevation 'from sensation to intellect'.

Anna's critical assertiveness when discussing imaginative literature sits well with her determination to dissociate herself from the 'transported reader' or to recast the notion of readerly transcendence, but the confidence in her own voice, which balances distance and engagement in the fictional realm, declines sharply when she discusses matters of history and politics. Here again we are faced with ambivalence and paradox. On the one hand, history, society and politics are all grist to Anna's mill. She devours the long, serious histories, the theoretical works of the Scottish philosophers and, during the 1790s, a piquant but substantial diet of French history and recent politics; the last of these literatures, as she makes clear, being read in an effort to understand the aftermath of 1789. She is more than willing to tackle topics and controversies that were conventionally 'masculine'. But, on the other hand, the confident critical voice that she brings to imaginative literature is far more muted in her account of non-fictional works; her sense of herself is more as a passive recipient or receptacle of information than as an active critic. Thus, on 20 January 1792, as part of an intensive course of reading on French history and the French revolution, Anna finished James Mackintosh's *Vindiciae Gallicae* (1791), recording in her diary:

As far as I am a Judge I think this work very well understood. The author is master of his subject, & has the art of rendering others so. He is not scurrilous. He argues well, he seldom begs the question. He narrates what has passed in France traces the causes with precision – perhaps he speaks too strongly in the latter part. I gained much information from this work.

The response is complex. Her first words – 'As far as I am a Judge' – reveal her critical ambivalence, her last – 'I gained much information' – her passivity. But her remarks also imply that she has acquired a measure of critical authority, For, if Mackintosh 'is master of his subject, & has the art of rendering others so', then Anna has presumably acquired some of that mastery. She may only assert it

30 Hannah More, *Strictures on the Modern System of Female Education*, 5th edn, 2 vols. (London, 1799), II, 183.

obliquely, but her comment, however indirect, reveals her desire to gain it.

But mastery does not, in this case, seem to entail judgement. In her account of reading on the French Revolution, Anna shies away from a critical evaluation of the arguments. Instead she describes the participants in one of the most heated debates of the century as either 'just and candid' or 'partial ... and full of passion', complaining that 'It is a controversy that I cannot in its full heat form a Judgement on ... it is impossible in these prejudiced moments to determine who is right and wrong'.[31]

In the light of the conflicting reports and confused attitudes towards the revolution before the Terror of 1792, Anna's candour about her uncertainty is not surprising, but her reluctance to grapple with issues of substance was not confined to the debate about the fate of France. More often than not her remarks on non-literary topics were oblique and allusive; frequently she adopted the persona of the impartial observer. She has opinions on these subjects but feels inhibited about expressing them. Her comments mix assertiveness and delicacy, her desire to hold forth on public matters becomes tempered by partial acts of self-censorship.

This mélange of attitudes is well captured in Anna Larpent's response to Lord Monboddo's *Of the Origin and Progress of Language*. She read this controversial and much satirized work, notorious for its claim that the orang-utan was an early stage of the human species, during a summer visit to Aston House in Oxfordshire. Her diary records her usual thumb-nail sketch of Monboddo's tenor and content:

I went through that extraordinary work of Lord Monboddo on the Origin of Language. I was entertained and instructed from the singularity of the system, the many erroneous and yet plausible arguments on which it is founded, the infinite display of learning. A mind wedded to antiquity is the source together with a strong imagination easily biassed from Credulity, of the principles offered in this work. I should apprehend the criticisms to be good in many parts.[32]

Yet, no sooner does she criticize the work than she begins to qualify her powers of judgement:

There is too much classical learning in it to allow *me* to form a Judgment of it, as a learned work. Indeed it is not to be supposed I understood it in a followed manner[.] Yet I never throw aside a book because it makes me feel an ignorance I am not ashamed of from its being one belonging to my Sphere as

31 HM 31201, I: 16/5/92; 25–7/8/92; 13/4/92.
32 Ibid., 31/7/80.

a female. I read on with humble attention & often reap much information from the mere introductions to scholars.

Typically, even this self-deprecation contains a note of defiance and pride. Like many women's allusions to the masculine monopoly of classical learning, Anna's is tinged with sarcasm. And she resolutely asserts her ability to learn from the most recondite of texts.

In fact, Anna was to have the last word at Monboddo's expense. At the suggestion of another house guest she composed a fictitious letter from a professor of speech at Edinburgh University to the author who had claimed that orang-utans could acquire powers of human utterance. Having failed to teach the ape English, the professor claims that he has mastered the language of orang-utans and is happy to report to Monboddo that this particular ape is a creature of fine feelings and exquisite sensibility.

Anna's problem as a reader of fiction was to avoid the obstructive presence of a frivolous female reader. In doing so, she confronted an issue that repeatedly exercised women readers, both radical and conservative, both Wollstonecraft and More, in the late eighteenth and early nineteenth centuries.[33] Anna's task in scrutinizing history, current affairs and philosophy, on the other hand, was to confront the absence of a woman's role. Male commentators on female reading such as John Bennett condemned frivolous fiction, but they also defined women's reading in ways which confined the female reader to the realm of taste, fancy and imagination and excluded them from the province of reason and judgement. As Bennett put it:

Whilst men, with solid judgment and a superior vigour are to contrive ideas, to discriminate, and to examine a subject to the bottom, you are to give it all its brilliancy and all its charms. They provide the furniture; you dispose of it with propriety. They build the house; you are to fancy and to ornament the ceiling.[34]

How, given gendered attitudes, was it possible to give women agency, to enable them to throw off 'pretty feminine phrases' and to exercise judgement? What sort of account would permit women to be more than passive receptacles of knowledge, more than silent, decorative

33 See, for instance, Cora Kaplan, *Sea Changes: Essays on Culture and Feminism* (London, 1986), pp. 35–46.

34 John Bennett, *Letters to a Young Lady*, 2 vols. (London, 1795), I, 168–9 quoted in Jane Moore, 'Promises, Promises: Fictional Philosophy in Mary Wollstonecraft's *Vindication of the Rights of Woman*', in Catherine Belsey and Jane Moore (eds.), *The Feminist Reader: Essays in Gender and the Politics of Literary Criticism* (London, 1989), p. 158.

auditors of male discourse? Satirizing Monboddo's learning by means of an instructive fiction was a witty riposte which trounced male philosophy with female fiction, but it was no more than an answer *ad hominem*. More generally, Anna seems to have opted in her diary for the role of the dispassionate, impartial reviewer. Studied impartiality veils her predilections; her views are insinuated rather than baldly expressed. She wraps herself in a disguise that confers anonymity, using a discourse that is not obviously gendered.

Imaginative literature, history and current affairs took up much of Anna Larpent's time but they were never as constant a pursuit as her reading of pious and religious works. Every day she read either the Bible, the Psalms, or a pious text or sermon. On Sundays she devoted herself to the scriptures and to volumes of favourite sermons which she returned to repeatedly. Her reading, as I have already indicated, was ecumenical; in the manner recommended by contemporary devotional manuals, it eschewed theological controversy for personal piety. She never read current religious polemics and most of her favourite authors, like Tillotson and Clarke, were long since dead.

Though Anna studied pious works constantly, she almost never commented in her diary on her religious reading. Strange as this paradox may seem, it is the key to understanding the significance of one category of reading whose meaning was quite different from any other. Anna's daily examination of the scriptures or of a religious work was a private act of self scrutiny intended to strengthen her moral resolve and Christian faith. She read on her own, usually when she first rose in the morning. Though she often talked with her children about their pious books, especially those that they read together, she rarely mentions discussing her own religious reading with others. It was not a subject for polite conversation, like so much other material, but an act of personal devotion, an affirmation of her Christian faith. Anna read the Bible and pious texts 'intensively', returning repeatedly to her favourite scriptural passages and to the well-thumbed sermons of the divines that she most admired. In the 1790s she was still reading the sermons that she had first encountered twenty years earlier. In short, she conformed to the model of the isolated, absorbed, individual reader, cut off from the world by her immersion in the text.

Anna also undertook most of her serious secular reading when she was alone, but the significance of this isolation was altogether different. Private religious reading was truly private; it played little or no part in the realm of polite conversation and sociability. On the other hand, other sorts of reading, and particularly works of imaginative literature, were central to Anna Larpent's social identity, and to her relations with her friends and relatives. We can surmise, given that many eighteenth-century journals were kept as aids to conversation and guides to sociability,[35] that the presence, absence or character of comment in the text gives us some sense of the social significance of different sorts of reading. It may also help account for the disparity between Anna's bolder voice on the subject of imaginative literature and her more subdued tones when discussing history and politics.

Whatever the case, Anna Larpent regularly discussed her reading with friends and acquaintances and often talked with her family about books of common interest. Similarly, she was prompted to take up certain works because they were to be found in the libraries of the houses she visited, or because they were recommended by friends. Staying at a house in Kings Thorpe, Northamptonshire in 1780, Anna began reading *Les milles et une nuits* after a conversation about imaginative literature with the Bishop of Llandaff. He 'recommended the Reading these Arabian inventions as lively pictures of the government, religion, manners, prejudices of the eastern nations, & further talked on them as genuine translations from the Arabic. I own I was entertained with them in this light'.[36]

As Anna's remark indicates, she did not treat all reading with the same degree of seriousness. She made a distinction between reading 'in a followed manner' and the more superficial perusal of a text.[37] She read while a servant was dressing her hair or while out walking; she used fiction as a distraction as when, during the illness of one of her boys, she took up a novel, 'which just dissipated my Mind now and then'.[38] But for most of the time her reading was purposive. She read French history, writing digests of what she had learnt, in order to help her step-son, Seymour, while he was at school.[39] When she started attending art exhibitions in the 1780s, she ploughed her way through the works of Reynolds, Ramsay, Cozens, Akenside and Shaftesbury. An introduction to the Forsters, father and son, who, together with Sir Joseph Banks, played such an important part in the botanical investigation of the South Seas, led her to read most of the available accounts of

35 I owe this point to Amanda Vickery.
36 HM 31201, 17: 19/7/80.
37 Ibid., 31/7/80; 1: 8/10/92.
38 Ibid., 1, 4, 16/7/80; 1: 13/1/90.
39 Ibid., 3/6/90.

the voyages of Captain Cook. Her interest in flower painting nurtured her reading in botany. And, above all, the French revolution stimulated her voracious reading into French affairs in the early 1790s. Reading suffused almost everything that Anna Larpent did; it was her greatest pleasure, and it was one she always wished to share with others.

The most direct means by which reading was shared was by reading aloud. This was not, as is sometimes implied, a dying practice, increasingly confined to the barely literate, but a vital part of genteel social life. Almost every member of Anna Larpent's household read aloud to others and, when the family went on visits in the summer, they formed part of reading circles in which guests took turns to read.

Reading aloud to children and the young was, of course, a common practice, regarded as an essential part of education. Anna read aloud to her sister and her two sons; she also listened to them read. She treated this form of instruction as a way of increasing her pupil's curiosity and of opening up new paths of inquiry. Usually she and her pupil read in turn. When teaching Clara, her younger sister, about taste in the visual arts – a subject that especially interested Anna in the year or two before her marriage when she was a regular attender of art exhibitions in London – they read a number of books on aesthetics:

> We then read aloud a dialogue on taste by Mr Ramsay, a lively original book with some entertaining and instructive remarks on the progress of those arts that seem particularly to call forth the exertion of taste. I pointed out this, to carry on the pursuit in her mind though on a wholly different principle. Cozens forms beauties by Mathematical Rules: reduces all to a regular, invariable System. Ramsay makes beauty the mere result of opinion in different persons, & consequently varying with the various persons he admits of no other Standard for taste; the comparisons this difference of opinion drew and the observations that arose, the Books it led us to consult, gave us much amusing conversation.[40]

In the same way, she used passages from Defoe's *Tour Through the Whole Island of Great Britain* to prepare her two boys for a visit to Windsor Castle in 1792: 'I did it', she wrote, 'that they might have their observation raised when we carried them there. There is a great difference between *staring* and *seeing* – the one is merely Corporeal the other unites the mental to the bodily powers and lays in a stock of ideas.'[41]

But reading aloud was never confined to educating one's children. At the house party where Anna met the Bishop of Llandaff, guests took

[40] Ibid., Miscellaneous Observations, 1780.
[41] Ibid., 19/8/92.

it in turns to read to one another. On 1 July 1780, for instance, after hearing her sister Clara read Rollin's *Histoire ancienne* (a history much recommended to young women), Anna 'spent two hours in the family circle reading and working'. While her friends were engaged in different sorts of women's work – embroidering and making cushion covers – she read them a great favourite, the sentimental novel *Marienne*, by Pierre Marivaux. After dinner Anna worked while another guest read Henry Kelly's comedy, *School for Wives*; and, after supper and in mixed company, she returned to Marivaux, reading further passages from his novel.[42]

Such reading was an important part of Anna Larpent's marriage. She and her husband read the manuscripts of the plays that he was required to licence to one another. John Larpent often read to Anna while she was engaged in household work. Much of this reading was topical: the daily newspaper (usually read at the end of the day), pamphlets on the American War, the French revolution, parliamentary reform, the slave trade and religious toleration. These tracts and papers were intended to stimulate conversation. In October 1792, for example, the Larpents were reading Joseph Priestley on *The Origin of Government* 'rather to lead to conversation & observation than as a followed reading'.[43] In a lighter vein, novels and plays were read and discussed 'in the family circle', when children and servants were present.[44]

Like playing the piano, or being able to draw, reading aloud, despite the increasingly common practice of reading silently and in comparative isolation, remained an important social accomplishment of the polite classes well into the nineteenth century. It was the proud boast of Henry Austen, in his biographical note to the posthumous edition of *Northanger Abbey* and *Persuasion* that appeared in 1818, that his sister 'read aloud with very great taste and effect. Her own works, probably, were never heard to so much advantage as from her own mouth'.[45] The practice persisted because it remained one of the most important ways of sharing the pleasures of a text. Anna Larpent's journal is suffused with the warm satisfaction she feels when she settles down to read aloud or to listen to a husband, friend or relative.

What conclusions can we draw from Anna Larpent's remarkably

42 Ibid., 1/7/80.
43 Ibid., 8/10/92.
44 Ibid., 24/10/92.
45 [Henry Austen], 'Biographical Notice of the Author', reprinted in Jane Austen, *Northanger Abbey*, ed. Anne Ehrenpreis (London, 1972), p. 32.

meticulous account of her reading and its pleasures? What sort of reader and what sort of world have we (and she) constructed here?

The first and most obvious feature of Anna Larpent's universe is the ubiquity of texts. Books are everywhere: their titles are laid out in serried ranks and long lists; they are criticized and summarized. Books entertain, instruct and amuse, bind together family and friends, create a common culture and soothe sensibilities. But they also disturb and divide: they reveal depravity and passion, error and irreligion, the absence of agreement on matters of substance, and the lack of equanimity in a logocentric world that thrived on polemic and controversy. Enclosed and captured in her text, the diary, they give meaning and order to Anna's life – to a remarkable degree they constitute her experience – but they do so ambiguously, because they both reassure and question.

Of course not all books were of comparable weight or significance. Diverse texts were read in diverse manners – silently and aloud, privately and with others, as a means of encouraging good conversation or private piety or pleasure, with more or less attention. My account of Anna's reading, which emphasizes its *variety* is clearly not compatible with the view, questioned from their different perspectives by Robert Darnton and Roger Chartier, that a 'reading revolution' occurred in this period in which the manner of reading shifted from the 'intensive' and repeated scrutiny of a few texts to the 'extensive' and cursory reading of many.[46]

The case for a reading revolution is a crudely technological one. Intensive reading, it is argued, takes place in societies where there are a few books; because of their rarity and expense, such texts are treated as sacred objects, subject to repeated rereading and intense scrutiny. Read aloud, examined collectively, such texts fabricate a shared, undifferentiated culture. Extensive reading, on the other hand, is the consequence of a well developed print culture in which numerous and varied works are available to the reader. The individual book becomes less sacred, the reader more cursory, willing, as the bluestocking Frances Boscawen put it, 'not to read strictly, but *feuiller*'.[47] At the same time, the sheer diversity of literature, consumed by individuals privately, creates a fragmented cultural world.

46 Darnton, 'Readers Respond to Rousseau', pp. 219–51; Chartier, *The Cultural Uses of Print in Early Modern France*, pp. 222, 224–5, 231–3. On the 'reading revolution', see Rolf Engelsing, *Der Bürger als Leser: Lesergeschichte in Deutschland, 1500–1800* (Stuttgart, 1971).

47 Frances Boscawen to Mlle Sayer, 8 July 1788, in Cecil Aspinall-Oglander, *Admiral's Widow, Being the Life and Letters of the Hon. Mrs. Edward Boscawen from 1761 to 1805*, 2nd impression (London, 1913), p. 135.

Such a linear and undifferentiated view of changes in the nature of reading, fails to appreciate the diversity of reading practices. Anna's reading (and, in this respect, she resembled many of her contemporaries, both male and female) varied according to what she was reading (devotional literature or novels), why she was reading it (for pleasure or to instruct her children) and when she was reading. Some books – and this included fiction as well as works of piety – she read repeatedly; others she skipped through once. If we were to generalize from the case of Anna Larpent, then we would have to chart a change in which reading practices did not become more extensive but rather more diverse. 'Intensive' and 'extensive' reading were complementary not incompatible. The rise of the latter never extinguished the former, as any modern department of literature attests.

Diverse reading practices did, however, depend upon the variety of printed materials available and the ease with which readers had access to them. One of the most interesting omissions in Anna's diary is any sense of the book as an object or commodity. Unlike Jean Ranson, Darnton's La Rochelle merchant who was eleven years her senior, she rarely comments upon their physical appearance – their paper, type and binding – and she never alludes to difficulties in obtaining them. Anna took books for granted.

This enviable position was comparatively novel. It is impossible to imagine a woman in the seventeenth century, regardless of her social position, who would have been able to live the cultural and literary life of Anna Larpent. No matter how well educated and no matter how easily she had access to books, she would not have been able to obtain the number and variety of printed materials which Anna secured with such apparent ease. And, though she might have had ready access to certain sorts of literature – biblical, theological, classical, historical and polemical – others – the novel, the periodical, the 'how to' book, classics in translation, works of natural philosophy and literary criticism – would either have been unobtainable or in exceptionally short supply. Anna's ease of access to books was, of course, a function of place as well as time. She lived in a city which, together with Amsterdam, was the greatest centre of publishing in Europe. She could patronize its circulating libraries and purchase volumes from its many booksellers.

But the value of Anna Larpent's account is that it forces us to think of the reader not as another statistic, not as just another customer, and not as passive, but as having agency, as creating meaning and significance from texts. It points to the role of readers in constructing their own identity. This Anna Larpent sought to do not in but *through* an examination of literary texts. Unlike the French merchant, Jean Ranson, discussed by Darnton, Anna Larpent did not plunge herself, in the manner recommended by Jean-Jacques Rousseau, into her reading. Her judgements were more critical; her anxiety about the stigma attached to the 'transported reader' was too great. Though she often used the language of sensibility, speaking of 'the virtuous heart', she retained a highly self-conscious and sophisticated sense of herself as a reader, distinguishing, for example, between her 'speculative' and 'pure' mind when reading works that interested her, even though they caused her moral offence.[48] And, as this distinction shows, Anna was aware of the generic instability of 'the reader'. It often appears as if her repeated and almost compulsive confrontation with such numerous and varied texts marks the inexorable pursuit of an immutable literary persona which is repeatedly challenged and yet confirmed at every new reading. Her reading habits – varied and heterogeneous – repeatedly bring into question the definition of the reader, and just as frequently she returns to the task of creating a stable reading identity or, perhaps more precisely, identities.

What Anna emphasizes at every point in her account is her right to her own judgement. Her voice (except when confronted with God's word when she is obliged to be silent) is ubiquitous, even when it is muted, and even if it is only heard in her own immediate social and familial circle. To a quite remarkable degree Anna Larpent records reading – and reading with considerable care – works whose political, moral and aesthetic values she was unable to accept. The positions that she adopted, she wants to emphasize, were very much of her own making. She fashioned her diaries and journals as a record of these choices, providing a vivid account of her repeated efforts to establish her own taste, to create her own cultural identity. We should not of course fetishize Anna's undoubted agency as free will. The choices that she could make and the ways in which she could present herself as a reader were constrained by prevailing assumptions and conventions even though they are not reducible to them. For Anna Larpent's text, ostensibly modest, private and feminine, proclaims a bold, heroic enterprise, one that wrestled not only with the meaning of individual texts but with the meaning of reading itself.

[48] HM 31201, I: 4/1/92.

CHAPTER 13

Women, men and the reading of Vanity Fair

Kate Flint

Only a naive reader would believe that the representation of reading within fiction offers straightforward, empirical evidence of contemporary reading practices. Fictional depictions of what and how women and men read involve the novel's consumer in complex acts of interpretation. When such depictions are as insistent and teasing as in the novels of William Makepeace Thackeray, they directly confront the reader with the need to consider his or her own interpretive strategies whilst in the very act of employing them. Most problematically, but also most revealingly for later readers, one must acknowledge that novelists rely on their contemporary readers to bring particular associations and connotations to bear on individual texts and on specific habits of reading. Reading practices represented within fiction need to be understood in the light of contemporary ideas about the processes, the methods and the materials of reading which stretch far beyond the bounds of any one novel.

Vanity Fair is, famously, a novel in which the burden of interpretation is left up to the reader. Moreover, this fact is continually foregrounded. The narrative voice refuses to give consistent guidance as to how to interpret the events and characters depicted.[1] Questions are left unanswerably open: what *was* the 'real truth of the matter' (21)[2] regarding Mr Crisp and Miss Sharp? How much did Amelia consciously know about Becky's relationship with George? Occasionally, the reader is directly challenged, invited to determine her or his own

1 See Ina Ferris, 'Realism and the Discord of Endings: The Example of Thackeray', *Nineteenth-Century Fiction* 38 (1983): 289–303; W. Iser, *The Implied Reader: Patterns of Communication in Prose Fiction from Bunyan to Beckett* (Baltimore, 1974); and R. A. Sheets, 'Art and Artistry in *Vanity Fair*', *English Literary History* 42 (1975): 420–32.

2 Page references to *Vanity Fair* (1847–8) refer to the Oxford University Press World's Classics edition, ed. John Sutherland (Oxford, 1983). All other references to Thackeray's fiction are to the Oxford Thackeray, ed. George Saintsbury, 17 vols. (London, 1908), and will be cited in the text, e.g. (Thackeray, I, 279).

moral standards, most famously in the matter of Becky's relationship with Lord Steyne: 'What *had* happened? Was she guilty or not?' (677). At other times we are given a set of options. When Amelia weeps (Becky having given her the letter Rawdon wrote just before Waterloo): 'Who shall analyze those tears, and say whether they were sweet or bitter? Was she most grieved, because the idol of her life was tumbled down and shivered at her feet; or indignant that her love had been so despised; or glad because the barrier was removed which modesty had placed between her and a new, real affection?' (866–9). It is little wonder that Jack Rawlins, in his study, *Thackeray's Novels*, could assert that 'the reader is the subject of the tale ... That the novel appears to be about fictional characters in action proves to be an illusion; the novel begins to look like a grand rhetorical machine to bring the reader unawares face to face with himself.'[3]

What is more, *Vanity Fair* is a novel which persistently draws attention to the process of reading itself. The narrator addresses and manipulates a variety of imaginary readers engaging with a wide range of printed texts and pamphlets. The attitudes towards reading which are alluded to in the text intersect with widely circulating debates about reading in the 1840s: debates found in literary magazines and medical textbooks, in conduct manuals and religious tracts, as well as within fiction.[4] Thackeray's earlier writings make frequent use of the terms of these discussions, and a familiarity with these terms can help us to understand more about the interpretive uncertainties which today's reader of *Vanity Fair* encounters. These uncertainties are caused not just by the language of the text, but by the carefully positioned presence of allusive illustrations within it. In particular, I hope to show the significance of Thackeray's frequent distinctions between women and men readers, and to suggest that his habit of slighting the material read by women, and his assumptions about their manner of reading, are significant practices not just in relation to the presentation of women within this text, nor simply because they have important bearings on Thackeray's general attitudes towards developments in

3 See Jack P. Rawlins, *Thackeray's Novels: A Fiction that is True* (Berkeley, CA, 1974), p. 13. See also Robyn R. Warhol, *Gendered Interventions. Narrative Discourse in the Victorian Novel* (New Brunswick, NJ, 1989) for the most interesting recent sustained discussion of the relationship between narrator and reader in *Vanity Fair*.

4 See Kate Flint, *The Woman Reader 1837–1914* (Oxford, 1993). A condensed version of my argument in this book was given at the *Practice and Representation of Reading in Britain from the Fourteenth to the Nineteenth Centuries* conference, and I am grateful to the editors for allowing me the space, in this volume, to develop some of the implications of my material.

fiction, but because they become crucial to the problematics of interpreting fictional representations of reading.

Many different types of readers are designated and addressed in *Vanity Fair*. Some of these are indeterminate in gender: the 'good-natured reader'; the 'ingenious reader'; 'intelligent readers'; 'my respected reader'; 'my dear reader'. Less flattering is the 'carping reader'. When the narrator addresses the reader as 'a man and a brother' (96), or as 'my dear brethren and fellow-sojourners in Vanity Fair' (415), there are obvious pointers to his gender, but Thackeray is also simultaneously using the recognizable liberal rhetoric of the abolitionists, and reminding one, with a slightly satiric ring, that his position resembles that of a preacher in a pulpit. Nowhere is this stronger than when we are exhorted 'Oh, be humble, my brother, in your prosperity!' (725).

Beyond these generalized forms of address, one may, broadly speaking, divide the readers into two main camps. There are those whom the narrator puts on a par with himself: they are of the same generation – 'you and I, who were children when the great battle was won and lost' (405) – and they have the same habits, the same standards of judgement, and, one may infer, the same background knowledge of society on which to base this judgement. Set against these readers are those whom the narrator contemplates and addresses from a distance, and toward whom his attitude is variously amused, mocking and perplexed.

It would seem that the readers whom the narrator addresses as equals are invariably male, and with considerable exposure to life. With them, the narrator cultivates an air of knowing, if fatigued, wisdom, tinged with nostalgia for his lost youth and for certain aspects of life which are passing. This is not conveyed without a degree of literary self-consciousness. He wonders, in this age of steam, where the old coachmen now are: 'Is old Weller alive or dead?' (86), and there are echoes of Shakespeare's *2 Henry IV* when the narrator laments 'Alas! we shall never hear the horn sing at midnight, or see the pike-gates fly open any more' (87). Just occasionally, the narrator develops a paternalistic ring, addressing 'my son' as he offers advice. The tone of equality is most apparent when he uses the pronoun 'we', and, often simultaneously, enlists the male reader to his side: 'The best of women (I have heard my grandmother say) are hypocrites. We don't know how much they hide from us...' (208); or, 'We are Turks with the affection of our women', allowing them to go out smiling and fashionably dressed, with ringlets and pink bonnets taking the place of veils and yashmaks, yet insisting that their souls are only seen by one man, 'and they obey not unwillingly, and consent to remain at home as our slaves' (213–14). He asks world-weary questions: 'When don't ladies weep?'; 'Who has not seen how women bully women? What tortures have men to endure, comparable to those daily-repeated shafts of scorn and cruelty with which poor women are riddled by the tyrants of their sex? Poor victims!' (407). The tone of remarks such as these is hard to gauge: like so much of the narrative commentary in *Vanity Fair*, we can never be sure if the narrator is representative of Thackeray's own views, or if we are being asked to read with some satiric distance, or whether this attitudinizing is a masquerade of compassion with no particular didactic aim in mind. One thing is certain: we are being asked to read as men (even if male pretensions are laughed at and masculinity is teased, hardly representing a constant standard of excellence), and it is expected that we have had men's experiences: 'My beloved reader has no doubt in the course of his experience been waylaid' by someone down on his luck, but full of hopeless schemes, as Dobbin is waylaid by John Sedley (238). The narrator imagines that he and his readers will be the recipients, not the providers of comfort in their decrepit future: 'may we have in our last days a kind soft shoulder on which to lean, and a gentle hand to soothe our gouty old pillows' (726). More soberly yet, he asks his reader to imagine how his death will be received by his son and his widow. This point of assumed male complicity is reinforced by the fact that sometimes the 'we' explicitly stands for a range of men drawn from diverse social classes: 'we who wear stars and cordons, and attend the St James's assemblies, or we who, in muddy boots, dawdle up and down Pall Mall, and peep into the coaches as they drive up with the great folks in their feathers' (601).

Amelia is specifically set up as a heroine likely to appeal to the male reader. An imaginary correspondent 'with a pretty little handwriting and a pink seal to her note' writes that 'We don't care a fig for her', and the women with whom Amelia is brought into contact almost uniformly profess not to see why men find her so alluring. The narrator poses a question – 'Has the beloved reader, in his experience of society, never heard similar remarks by good-natured female friends' – before going on to note that 'the heroic female character which ladies admire is a more glorious and beautiful object than the kind, fresh, smiling, artless, tender little domestic goddess, whom men are inclined to worship' (131). Of course, as we shall see, Thackeray is partly out to educate his male reader *through* his portrayal of Amelia: falling for this type of woman is not necessarily a good thing. Some of those adjectives recur in the final description of the life-sucking Amelia as a 'tender little parasite' (871). Yet the narrator vacillates, for he acknowledges that Dobbin was not atypical in cherishing his sentimental, two-dimensional view of Amelia: 'what man in love, of us, is better informed?' (549).

Set against these relatively worldly-wise male readers are the 'fair reader', the 'mesdames', the 'ladies' who may be 'horrified' to read of the torture of corporal punishment that their own sons probably receive at public school. Such a reader may, in her turn, have fallen into the same trap as those who come into connection with Amelia, of living more in the creation of their fantasies than in reality. Indeed, she may have fallen into a *worse* trap, since her folly, like Amelia's misperception *vis-à-vis* George Osborne, will have involved, in the narrator's view, much less excusable blindness. 'Perhaps some beloved female subscriber has arrayed an ass in the splendour and glory of her imagination; admired his dullness as manly simplicity; worshipped his selfishness as manly superiority; treated his stupidity as majestic gravity, and used him as the brilliant fairy Titania did a certain weaver at Athens. I think I have seen such comedies of errors going on in the world' (148). Whilst the narrator often shows compassion for his male readers' weaknesses (they are, after all, ones which he portrays himself as sharing) his tone tends to be less sparing towards women, whom he is more given to suspect of deceit than to see being deceived: 'O ladies! how many of you have surreptitious milliners' bills? How many of you have gowns and bracelets, which you daren't show, or which you wear trembling?' (603).

One further type of reader, less obviously gendered, may be added: the 'observant reader' – the phrase Thackeray uses of the reader whom, he is confident, has picked up the hints offered in his illustrations. I want to pause, briefly, to consider how one might understand 'reading' the pictures which appeared in the first edition of *Vanity Fair*, and which notoriously have been omitted, or mispositioned, in all subsequent editions until the appearance of the Oxford World's Classics edition (1983). Thackeray's drawings, including the capital letters at the beginning of each chapter, were an integral part of his original interpretive design.[5] The surviving chapters of *Vanity Fair*'s manuscript, in the Pierpont Morgan Library in New York, show that he deliberately planned them to go just where the original printer placed them. They create dramatic hiatuses in their own right, as when Miss Sharp puts out her right forefinger to George Osborne – there follows an illustration showing her doing just that – before the sentence continues 'and gave him a little nod' (172). The typography dramatizes Becky's capacity to direct social interchange as staged drama. In his 1879 biography of Thackeray, Trollope wrote: 'looking at the wit displayed in the drawings, I feel inclined to say that had he persisted he would have been a second Hogarth',[6] and this offers a pointer to the fact that the drawings contain elements, like Hogarth's eighteenth-century scenes, which have symbolic resonance and need to be deciphered. They are not direct representations of the text's action. Thus, notoriously, in the chapter describing Becky and Jos living at Aix-la-Chapelle, a plate labelled 'Becky's second appearance in the character of Clytemnestra' (875) and showing her sinisterly lurking behind a curtain, holding something in a ready-to-stab position, gives substance to what the words merely hint at: that Jos was murdered for his insurance money. The initials which command the opening of each chapter reinforce the tone or direction of the text which follows, providing wooden sheep, shepherds and shepherdesses when pastoral is being satirized in Chapter XI ('Arcadian Simplicity'), or a mermaid strumming on a harp to introduce, in Chapter XLIV, Becky's skill in living on the surface of society (in other words, by the abuse of credit) as well as her skill in charming money out of others. Such interpretation of the illustrations obviously requires certain things of readers. It reminds them that this is a deliberately constructed text, not a transcription of real life. It obliges them, therefore, to cease – had they been so tempted – their passive reading of *Vanity Fair* and become active producers of meaning in relation to the novel.

To read actively, rather than to absorb sentiment passively like a sponge, was popularly considered, in the 1840s, to be adopting a masculine rather than a feminine style of reading – a gendered construction of reading which had been accumulating cultural force

5 See N. M. W. Pickvance, 'Thackeray and His Book Illustrations' unpublished D.Phil. dissertation, University of Oxford (1978); and Joan Stevens, 'Thackeray's "Vanity Fair"', *Review of English Literature* 6 (1965): 19–38.

6 J. Fisher, 'The Aesthetic of the Mediocre: Thackeray and the Visual Arts', *Victorian Studies* 26 (1982): 65–82 (p. 69).

since at least the mid-eighteenth century. Over-identification with the characters about whom one was reading, and a capacity to be emotionally, irrationally stirred, even to the point of imitation, by their example, were the most frequently remarked characteristics of the woman reader in the mid-nineteenth century. As I have discussed elsewhere, women, it was believed, could not help reading in this way, since they were biologically programmed for motherhood, and a capacity for sympathetic identification with the feelings of others was considered a sign of maternal worth.[7] 'The female perceptions', commented Sarah Stickney Ellis, that matriarch of advice manuals, are 'more quick, and the female character altogether more easy of adaptation, more sympathizing, and therefore more capable of identifying itself with the thoughts and feelings of others'.[8] Physiological factors conspired, it was believed, to ensure this. Thus Alexander Walker, in *Woman Physiologically Considered* (1840), argues that the organs of sensory perception are larger in a woman than in a man (he based this assumption on a comparative measurement of foreheads): thus 'the IMAGINATION, a peculiarly and strongly marked function in woman, is highly susceptible of excitement, and yields easily to every excess'.[9] Social conditions, too, particularly the amount of leisure time potentially available to women, were acknowledged to be responsible for their recourse to fiction. The co-presence of these two factors is neatly encapsulated in a review article of 1842:

> The great bulk of novel readers are females; and to them such impressions (as are conveyed through fiction) are peculiarly mischievous: for, first, they are naturally more sensitive, more impressible, than the other sex; and secondly, their engagements are of a less engrossing character – they have more time as well as more inclination to indulge in reveries of fiction.[10]

In his non-fictional writings, Thackeray demonstrates anxiety about the status of novel writing and reading. There is plenty of evidence that he enjoyed 'light reading', but he seems to have felt decidedly guilty about this enjoyment. 'I have become latterly so disgusted with myself and art ... that for a month past I have been lying on sofas reading novels, and never touching a pencil', he wrote

7 Flint, *The Woman Reader*, pp. 61–2.

8 Sarah Stickney Ellis, *The Young Ladies' Reader* (London, 1845), p. 4.

9 Alexander Walker, *Woman Physiologically Considered as to Mind, Morals, Matrimonial Slavery, Infidelity and Divorce* (London, 1840), p. 28.

10 'Moral and Political Tendency of the Modern Novels', *Church of England Quarterly Review* 11 (1842): 286–310 (pp. 287–8).

in 1839.[11] He is here aligning himself, none too flatteringly, with Mrs Shum, in *The Yellowplush Papers* (1838), who 'was such a fine lady, that she did nothink but lay on the drawing-room sophy, read novels, drink, scold, scream, and go into hystarrix' (Thackeray, I, 171). This self-disgust, whether actual or rhetorical, extended to his comments about what he wrote, continually lamenting the lack of artistic kudos involved in fiction-mongering, and putting on the pretence that he only did it out of completely mercenary, or cerebrally lazy, motives. 'I am frivolous and futile', he told a correspondent in 1855: 'a long course of idleness (wh. novel-writing is) has wasted my intellect' (*Letters* III 559). In his *Cornhill* piece, 'On a Lazy Idle Boy' (January 1860), Thackeray, in the course of an extended comparison between reading and the ingestion of food, lists those who are most given to liking novels, in phraseology which at first makes it sound as though this preference is natural and normal, and then renders it marginal, distanced and liable to make one bilious and unfit if indulged in excess. 'All people who have natural, healthy appetites, love sweets; all children, all women, all Eastern people, whose tastes are not corrupted by gluttony and strong drink . . .' (Thackeray, XVII, 354–5): such is the analogy he sets up with those who enjoy consuming novels. To read fiction is to engage in, indeed potentially to gorge upon, a particularly undiscriminating form of consumption, a form of piggery memorably practised by Mrs Shum's daughter, who 'was always on the stairs, poking about with nasty flower-pots, a-cooking something, or sprawling in the window-seats with greasy curl-papers, reading greasy novls [sic]' (Thackeray, I, 171).

Thackeray uses reading material as an important signifier of moral worth, of seriousness or frivolity, and he writes as though he is confident that his readership, or the readership which most matters, will share his assessment of the value of differing types of reading material. In the nineteenth century, as in the eighteenth, gaining knowledge about the implications of one's reading material, and the methods to be adopted when reading, was frequently written about in terms of the correct etiquette governing social introductions and interaction: 'It is said that a man or woman may be known by the company he or she keeps; a truer index to character is the books they read.'[12] Thackeray's use of books in this way is symptomatic of his whole mode of deploying material objects: as Barbara Hardy has

[11] *Letters and Private Papers of William Makepeace Thackeray*, ed. G. N. Ray, 4 vols. (London, 1945–6), I, 279; subsequent references are cited in the text in parentheses.

[12] See W. H. Davenport Adams, *Women's Work and Worth* (London, 1880), pp. 140–1.

noted, 'Thackeray's novels show people who are completely expressed by their envelope of things.'[13] Moreover, within *Vanity Fair*, printed texts are valued for reasons which go beyond their didactic or aesthetic contents, since they can be symbols both of status and of economic transaction. Thus the social *cachet* of the Reverend Veal's establishment, where Georgy is sent, is not to be judged by the learning the pupils acquire, but by the fact that on prize day even the dimmest receive 'little eighteenpenny books, with "Athene" engraved in them' (718). Reference texts, particularly, determine status: Becky and Briggs and Mrs Bute Crawley's daughters all, for their differing reasons, pore over Burke's *Peerage*, a repeated object of veneration, unsurprisingly, in Thackeray's *Book of Snobs* (1848).

The references to specific reading material within *Vanity Fair* have functions which stretch beyond the moral and social assessment of an individual, however. First, they appear to heighten the novel's mimetic realism, encouraging the reader to believe that she or he is reading about a social and cultural milieu with which she or he is, or could become, familiar. Accepting the 'naturalness' of the reading practices which are depicted is thus a device which consolidates the impression that narrator and reader share the same values. Both are caught within a 'play of cultured allusions and analogies endlessly pointing to other analogies, which, like the cardinal oppositions in mythical or ritual systems, never have to justify themselves by stating the basis of the relating which they perform'.[14] Secondly, the recognition of shared reading practices adds to a reader's sense of participation in the construction of meaning. Julia Kristeva, in *Séméiotiké*, argues that reading is a form of aggressive participation, with each reader attempting to incorporate allusions into a coherent semiotic unit.[15] Seen in this way, to encounter and recognize these allusions to other texts has implications which go beyond confirming one's confident membership of a cultural group. It alerts us to the ways in which membership of such a group is realized in the process of interpreting a text. The 'kind reader', for example, is asked to remember that this history has 'Vanity Fair' for a title, and thus is implicitly asked not only to recollect his or her knowledge of Bunyan

[13] Barbara Hardy, *The Exposure of Luxury: Radical Themes in Thackeray* (London, 1972), p. 97; see also S. Thornton, 'Icônes et Iconoclasmes dans l'œuvre de W. M. Thackeray 1837–48', *Cahiers Victoriens et Edouardiens* 35 (1992): 217–31.

[14] Pierre Bourdieu, *Distinction: A Social Critique of the Judgement of Taste* (London, 1984), p. 53.

[15] Julia Kristeva, *Séméiotiké: recherches pour une sémanalyse* (Paris, 1969), p. 120.

but to question the nature of the allusion. To see that a title has a function which strips it of its original context is to see it as metaphor, engaging a reader in interpretive activity, emphasizing that meaning and social significance must be constructed, rather than passively, unthinkingly extracted.

Furthermore, Thackeray's incorporation of references to other literary texts, like his identification of differing categories of readers, should be seen as a rhetorical exercise, in relation to his identification of the various genres of fiction which he is *not* writing – although he could be writing them if he chose. 'Jos Sedley', we are told near the opening of Chapter VI, 'is in love with Rebecca ... We might have treated this subject in the genteel, or in the romantic, or in the facetious manner' (60). Alternatively, a professional burglar might have broken into the house and carried off 'Amelia in her night-dress, not to be let loose again till the third volume, [and] we should easily have constructed a tale of thrilling interest, through the fiery chapters of which the readers should hurry, panting' (61). In the first edition, Thackeray tried out further modes at this point: 'THE NIGHT ATTACK', beginning 'The night was dark and wild – the clouds black – black – ink-black', mocks the so-called melodramatic Newgate novels, like Harrison Ainsworth's *Jack Sheppard* (1839) and Bulwer-Lytton's *Paul Clifford* (1830). Then he hypothesizes: 'Or suppose we adopted the genteel rose-water style. The Marquis of Osborne has just dispatched his *petit tigre* with a *billet-doux* to the Lady Amelia ...' But this will not do, either, and he reverts to a 'modest' preservation of his 'middle course', 'amidst these scenes and personages with which we are most familiar' (893–5). This is one further strategy to persuade the reader to believe that *Vanity Fair* is the product of observation, not literary invention. Thackeray's interest and ability in parody can be seen from his earliest writing, producing a series of burlesques in *Novels by Eminent Hands* and, in *A Shabby Genteel Story* (1840), satirizing women who derive romantic expectations from novel reading. The heroine of *A Shabby Genteel Story*, Caroline Gann, sits and reads with Becky the maid (a forerunner of Polly Clapp) 'the precious greasy, marble-covered volumes that Mrs Gann was in the habit of fetching from the library' (Thackeray, III, 307): Mary Ann Radcliffe's *Manfrone; or the One-handed Monk*, or Jane Porter's *Thaddeus of Warsaw* and *The Scottish Chiefs*. Caroline believes in the inevitability of a handsome lover appearing in her life, or what else are novels made for?

Had Caroline read of Valancourt and Emily for nothing, or gathered no good examples from those five tear-fraught volumes which describe the loves of Miss Helen Mar and Sir William Wallace? Many a time had she depicted Brandon in a fancy costume, such as the fascinating Valancourt wore; or painted herself as Helen, tying a sash around her knight's cuirass, and watching him forth to battle. Silly fancies, no doubt; but consider, madam, the poor girl's age and education; the only instruction she had ever received was from these tender, kind-hearted, silly books: the only happiness which Fate had allowed her was in this little silent world of fancy (Thackeray, III 328).

Here, Thackeray is forestalling the objections of a hypothetically censorious reader – a rhetorical strategy, for such an implicit reader is by no means likely to be equivalent to his *intended* audience. In *Vanity Fair*, Thackeray is continually concerned to defeat any conventional expectations of the workings of fiction which the reader may bring with them, and his strategies involve the incorporation of both implicit and intended readers. To do this, he relies on his actual readers acknowledging the existence of conventions, yet refusing to be entrapped by them. Of course these knowing allusions to differing types of novel imply that reader as well as narrator is familiar with these genres, and may well have experienced susceptibility to their effects.

Let us consider those who read within *Vanity Fair*. Dobbin immerses himself in the *Arabian Nights* when a boy (about the only thing which links him sympathetically with Becky in the entire novel), and in 'romantic books, with large coloured pictures of knights and robbers' (56) – an early sign that despite his eminent stock of common sense, kindness and practicality, he is not immune to losing himself in fantasy. When grown up, however, he seems to have put away childish material, in favour of serious stuff, being 'versed in the literature of his profession' (287) as a soldier, reading foreign languages (we learn in passing that he knows French and German as well as Latin), guide-books, and whatever material was necessary for composing his *History of the Punjab*. He contrasts with Rawdon: 'the only book which he studied was the *Racing Calendar*' (658). Dobbin's reading appears sober, but not as parochially bound as that of Mr Osborne, whose glazed bookcases in his study contained 'standard works in stout gilt bindings: The *Annual Register*, the *Gentleman's Magazine*, Blair's *Sermons*, and Hume and Smollett' (281),[16] or of Pitt Crawley, who makes his way through

[16] The reference is to David Hume, *The History of England, from the Invasion of Julius Caesar to the Revolution in 1688* (1754–57), and Tobias Smollett, *The History of England from the Revolution to the Death of George the Second. Designed as a Continuation of Mr. Hume's History* (1785).

pamphlets on the Corn-Laws, and, to Lady Jane's 'alarm and wonder' (575), Blue Books, recording the minutes of parliamentary commissions, and also keeps the Bible, the *Quarterly Review*, and the *Court Guide* in his study (678). Georgy, once at the Osborne's, swaggers around in a precocious imitation of adulthood, and 'after breakfast, would sit in the arm-chair in the dining-room, and read the *Morning Post*, just like a grown-up man' (715). The narrator does acknowledge that there are those 'who like to lay down the history-book, and to speculate upon what *might* have happened in the world but for the fatal occurrence of what actually did take place' (338), and such mental speculation is akin to fantasy-writing, but those lines from 'On a Lazy Idle Boy' in fact strongly echo the associations which surround Jos Sedley, the only adult male character to read fiction in *Vanity Fair*. For his journey back from India, 'he had brought a stock of novels and plays' (729). His connections with the East are emphasized not just by his enjoyment of chili peppers and curries and pilaws but by his inseparability from his hookah – another means of conveying pleasant stupefaction; his femininity underscored not just by his unmasculine disinclination to marry, but by his obsessive concern with his appearance: 'Jos was as vain of his person as a woman, and took as long a time at his toilette as any fading beauty' (728–9).

Novel-reading, or reading for emotional response alone, is, indeed, explicitly associated with women in *Vanity Fair*. Glorvina O'Dowd, in amorous pursuit of Dobbin, was constantly 'borrowing his books and scoring with her great pencil-marks such passages of sentiment or humour as awakened her sympathy' (564), a habit which Thackeray remarked on elsewhere, in 'Mr and Mrs Frank Berry' (1843):

> It is a wonder how fond ladies are of writing in books and signing their charming initials! Mrs. Berry's before-mentioned little gilt books ['half sentimental and half religious'] are scored with little pencil-marks, or occasionally at the margin with a! – note of interjection, or the words, '*Too true*, A.B.' and so on. Much may be learned with regard to lovely woman by a look at the book she reads in (Thackeray, IV, 328).

Miss Polly understands the whole story of her mother's lodger, Amelia, and Dobbin, 'as well as if she had read it in one of her favourite novel-books – *Fatherless Fanny*, or the *Scottish Chiefs*' (742): Becky writes to Amelia that 'Sir Pitt is not what we silly girls, when we used to read *Cecilia* at Chiswick, imagined a baronet must have been' (89), (and she shows a kind of continuing silliness by muddling him with a character from *Evelina* in the next sentence) although the great hall of his house, she says a couple of pages later, 'is as big and as glum as the great hall in the dear castle of Udolpho' (91). Becky's unfitness as a governess, by the standards of the mid-nineteenth century, is pointedly brought home when we learn that she and Miss Rose:

> read together many delightful French and English works, among which may be mentioned those of the learned Dr. Smollett, of the ingenious Mr. Henry Fielding, of the graceful and fantastic Monsieur Crébillon the younger ... and of the universal Monsieur de Voltaire. Once, when Mr. Crawley asked what the young people were reading, the governess replied 'Smollett'. 'Oh, Smollett,' said Mr. Crawley, quite satisfied. 'His history is more dull, but by no means so dangerous as that of Mr. Hume. It is history you are reading?' 'Yes,' said Miss Rose; without, however, adding that it was the history of Mr. Humphry Clinker (106).

He is mollified, or rather taken in, when Becky defends her choice of a volume of French plays on the grounds that this 'was for the purpose of acquiring the French idiom in conversation' (106).

For many of Thackeray's contemporaries, the mention of French literature continued to function as an instant signifier of dubious morality. The well-known critic W. R. Greg referred, for example, to 'its vile morality and its vitiated taste' in his article 'French Fiction: The Lowest Deep'.[17] These associations are played on by the narrator when delineating Miss Crawley's cultural tastes: she loved 'French novels, French cookery, and French wines. She read Voltaire, and had Rousseau by heart; talked very lightly about divorce, and most energetically of the rights of women' (112). She is also specifically mentioned as reading Pigault le Brun, writer of such infamously Gothic and *risqué* works as *The Monk of the Grotto* (1800) and *The First Night of My Wedding* (1804), published in England by the Minerva Press and, according to Montague Summers, enjoying 'a wide circulation'.[18] Nor do other women readers come off well. Fifine, Becky's maid, by making off with her *Keepsakes* and *Books of Beauty* – annuals containing sentimental short stories and poetry – both indicates that Becky is, as one might expect, a consumer of fashionable frivolity, and also condemns her, in a way that Thackeray's contemporaries would have recognized by suggesting that despite their ostensible difference in class, there was no actual difference in cultural preference between certain members of the fashionable world and those who serve them.

17 W. Greg, 'French Fiction: The Lowest Deep', *National Review* 11 (1860): 400–27 (p. 402).
18 Montague Summers, *A Gothic Bibliography* (London, 1941), p. 119.

He made a similar point in 'The Ravenswing' (1843), where the Walkers' servants realize that their employers are in financial trouble: 'The cook made the policeman a present of a china punch-bowl which Mrs Walker had given her; and the lady's maid gave her friend the *Book of Beauty* for last year, and the third volume of Byron's poems from the drawing-room table' (Thackeray, IV, 406). Becky is, of course, the person who demonstrates the most sacrilegious attitude of anyone towards books in the novel, when she hurls her copy of Johnson's 'Dixonary' out of the carriage which takes her away from Miss Pinkerton's. This may be read as a jettisoning of authority, and a violent refusal of a categorized world in which meanings and identities are fixed: these are not to be criteria by which she will proceed to live.

The narrator is quite kind to Mrs O'Dowd, reading out on Sundays from 'a large volume of her uncle the dean's sermons' (362), but this is largely because he feels sympathetic towards the talismanic, superstitious value which the volume holds for her. He is far less forgiving towards those who take their religious beliefs with proselytizing seriousness, like Mrs Kirk, another of the regimental wives, who swears by 'three little penny books with pictures, viz., the *Howling Wilderness*, the *Washerwoman of Wandsworth Common*, and the *British Soldier's Best Bayonet*' (330). Lady Southdown is similarly enthused by tracts, asking her daughter Emily to prepare *A Voice from the Flames*, *A Trumpet-warning to Jericho* and *Fleshpots Broken; or, the Converted Cannibal* for the unregenerate Miss Crawley. Her servants' hall receives *Crumbs from the Pantry*, *The Frying-pan and the Fire* and *The Livery of Sin*, 'of a much stronger kind' (416). Lady Emily, we learn, actually wrote the *Washerwoman of Finchley Common*, which becomes the narrator's catch-phrase for this type of evangelical moralizing tale. Less easy to gauge is Amelia's reading. When at Miss Pinkerton's Academy, her over-developed sentimentalism may be judged by the fact that she would cry over a dead canary, or over a mouse that the cat had caught, 'or over the end of a novel were it ever so stupid' (8); but when she has suffered loss in various forms, her reading becomes more directed. On the surface, there is nothing selfish about this: she 'read books, in order that she might tell [Georgy] stories from them' (492); she buys him the improving *Parent's Assistant* and *Sandford and Merton* as Christmas gifts. Given that she is presented as ridiculously, if affectingly over-protective and clinging, her altruistic reading does not put her in a much better light than those who disseminate improving tracts, being no more than another instance of her refusal to countenance personal change. Moreover, back again in genteel society, she cannot hold any conversation with those ladies who were very 'blue' – presumably in their stockings, who read the work of the scientist Mary Somerville and attended lectures at the Royal Institution. On this occasion her preference is not criticized by the narrator.

The anxiety about women's reading which Thackeray displays needs to be considered alongside the anxiety about women in general which he manifests in *Vanity Fair.* Women, especially attractive women, possess, like fiction, the capacity to deceive and to manipulate. 'What a mercy it is', the narrator exclaims early in the novel, 'that these women do not exercise their powers oftener! We can't resist them, if they do. Let them show ever so little inclination, and men go down on their knees at once ... Only let us be thankful that the darlings are like the beasts of the field, and don't know their own power. They would overwhelm us entirely if they did' (34). The exercise of this power is most obvious in the case of Becky, who *does* most definitely recognize her abilities in this direction. When first married to Rawdon, and honeymooning in Brighton, so as to be close to his rich aunt, she threatens to ambush her companion Briggs when she is bathing: 'I intend to dive under her awning, and insist on a reconciliation in the water' (298). The initial letter fronting Chapter XLIV has already been noted; Chapter LXIII, in which Rebecca is discovered at Pumpernickel's gaming tables, shows a woman on a seashore in a garment so flowing that it almost tapers to a tail. These images prepare us for the extended comparison which the narrator offers in Chapter LXIV:

> In describing this siren, singing and smiling, coaxing and cajoling, the author, with modest pride, asks his readers all round, has he once forgotten the laws of politeness, and showed the monster's hideous tail above water? No! Those who like may peep down under waves that are pretty transparent, and see it writhing and twirling, diabolically hideous and slimy, flapping amongst bones, or curling round corpses; but above the water line, I ask, has not everything been proper, agreeable, and decorous, and has any the most squeamish immoralist in Vanity Fair a right to cry fie? When, however, the siren disappears and dives below, down among the dead men, the water of course grows turbid over her, and it is labour lost to look into it ever so curiously. They look pretty enough when they sit upon a rock, twanging their harps and combing their hair, and sing, and beckon to you to come and hold the looking-glass; but when they sink into their native element, depend on it those mermaids are about no good, and we had best not examine the fiendish marine cannibals, revelling and feasting on their wretched pickled victims (812–13).

Amelia, too, and her type, are credited with powers of entrapment, though of a more subtle kind. Amelia may be 'kind' and 'tender', but she is also 'weak' – even if this is seen as the inevitable result of her 'martyrdom' in thankless and self-submerging servitude to men. This weakness, this desire for dependence, and this claim on men's compassion, are also seen by the narrator as a form of manipulation, albeit a necessary strategy for survival on the part of such women. Deceptive, manipulative, even treacherous, and yet compulsively attractive, women, the text suggests, are just like novels.

To isolate from *Vanity Fair* the assumed and widely circulated attributes of the woman reader of the 1840s is to do more than illuminate this novel's masculine biases. It also reveals much about Thackeray's ambivalent attitudes towards fiction, and shows that he aligns its powerful capacity to intrigue and involve the reader's emotions with the socially disruptive potential of sexuality. It is necessary, at this juncture, to reiterate that the tone and emphasis of the narrator's voice are not always easy to evaluate. Though many of the authorial pronouncements contain a degree of exaggeration or irony, it is not always easy to tell if comments such as those concerning the nature of women are ironic or not. Moreover, one should not forget that for all the suspicion with which women are treated at times, this is a novel fundamentally *about* women, and about their strategies for survival under adversity. It does not, as the narrator frequently reminds us, deal at any length with public life except in so far as it affects personal relationships. It is not, in other words, stereotypically masculine fiction, something which is acknowledged right at the start, when we are told that JONES, reading in his club, is not likely to have much interest in the fond farewells at Miss Pinkerton's. He will pronounce such scenes

> to be excessively foolish, trivial, twaddling, and ultra-sentimental. Yes; I can see Jones at this minute (rather flushed with his joint of mutton and half-pint of wine), taking out his pencil and scoring under the words 'foolish, twaddling,' etc., and adding to them his own remark of '*quite true*'. Well, he is a lofty man of genius, and admires the great and heroic in life and novels; and so had better take warning and go elsewhere (8).

On the other hand, the reader is not exactly invited to read *as* a woman, either. Thackeray, as we have noted, employs a variety of strategies to ensure that none of us reads in an identificatory manner, but rather enjoys exercising our role as interpretive spectators. Yet this, finally, is where the novel declares its distrust of femininity: identification is seen as a primarily feminine propensity in *Vanity Fair*, as it was for Victorian society. Throughout the novel, the proliferation of mirrors into which characters gaze or glance remind one of the narrator's early comment, that 'the world is a looking-glass, and gives back to every man the reflection of his own face' (15), and though the gazer here is male, vanity is a feminine and feminizing trait in *Vanity Fair*, to be avoided in reading as much as in the dressing-room.

In *Desire and Domestic Fiction*, Nancy Armstrong argues that 'domestic fiction represented sexual relationships according to an idea of the social contract that empowered certain qualities of an individual's mind over membership in a particular group or faction',[19] and that this stress on the domestic not only gave women writers authority, but ensured that the dominant form of fiction could be described as feminine. She supports her argument by reference to *Vanity Fair*. 'Thackeray's concern for Napoleonic history notwithstanding, the author's perspective in *Vanity Fair* is certainly neither on the grand scope of political events in Europe nor on the fortunes of men in love and war. His is the record of the small shockwaves felt on the home-front by two women who endeavour to keep themselves well supported by men.'[20] Yet in the end, *Vanity Fair* may best be seen as a novel about how the reading of fiction, particularly domestic fiction, in which women writers had been making such advances, may be recuperated for men. Men, it is implied, have the capacity to be far more discriminating readers than their female counterparts. Far more rarely patronized than women readers, it is men who, Thackeray suggests, have the capacity to develop the arts of self-irony and self-criticism, and to adopt the varied perspectives which the narrative tone of *Vanity Fair* encourages throughout. The accumulation of references to reading within the text point in one direction: the mode of reading which Thackeray most admires and wishes to promote is one which does not deny readerly pleasure, but which goes hand in hand with a capacity to stand back from too close, too emotional an involvement with fictional characters and situations. When one considers the references to reading within *Vanity Fair* in the context of contemporary debates and stereotypes, it becomes evident that Thackeray's early readers would easily have been able to follow his train of logic: to read well, for Thackeray, was to read as a man.

19 Nancy Armstrong, *Desire and Domestic Fiction: A Political History of the Novel* (New York, 1987), p. 30.
20 Ibid., p. 44.

CHAPTER 14

A pulse of 124: Charles Dickens and a pathology of the mid-Victorian reading public

Helen Small

> In the character of [Gray's] Elegy I rejoice to concur with the common reader; for by the common sense of readers uncorrupted with literary prejudices, after all the refinements of subtilty and the dogmatism of learning, must be finally decided all claim to poetical honours.
>
> Samuel Johnson (1781)

> A reading public of three millions which lies right out of the pale of literary civilization, is a phenomenon worth examining – ... it is perhaps hardly too much to say, that the future of English fiction may rest with this Unknown Public, which is now waiting to be taught the difference between a good book and a bad.
>
> Wilkie Collins (1858)

> ... the general public – Dr. Johnson's common reader – has now not even a glimpse of the living interests of modern literature, is ignorant of its growth and so prevented from developing with it, and ... the critical minority to whose sole charge modern literature has now fallen is isolated, disowned by the general public and threatened with extinction.
>
> Q. D. Leavis (1932)[1]

The concept of a general 'reading public' is no longer in favour with historians of the practice and representation of reading. On the contrary, opposition to the idea of a homogeneous readership is a shared assumption of current research on this subject. Reading, we know, is rarely, if ever, an undifferentiatedly collective experience. Rather, reading practices are protean, dependent upon their historical,

I am grateful to John Beer and Stefan Collini for advice about sources, and to John Kerrigan, James Raven, Naomi Tadmor and Alison Winter for helpful comments on drafts of this essay.

1 Samuel Johnson, 'Gray', in *Lives of the Most Eminent English Poets; With Critical Observations on their Works*, 4 vols. (London, 1781), IV, 485; Wilkie Collins, 'The Unknown Public', *Household Words* 18 (August 21, 1858): 217–22 (pp. 217, 222); Q.D. Leavis, *Fiction and the Reading Public* (London, 1932), pp. 21, 35.

cultural and personal contexts. Yet until recently, and for understandable reasons, the 'reading public' and its representative 'common reader' were keywords in our historical and literary critical vocabulary. It is, after all, difficult to describe such broad phenomena as the spread of literacy, or the rise of the novel, or the development of a mass market for print without invoking a 'general public'. It might be tempting to represent the avoidance of reference to the 'reading public' in recent accounts of the history of reading as evidence that the subject has moved beyond the need for broad narrative outlines to a newly pluralist interest in the social diversity of reading practices. However, to turn to the most celebrated statements about the reading public in the past is to find a lively recognition of the divided and problematic nature of that concept.

For Samuel Johnson, Wilkie Collins and Q. D. Leavis, reference to a 'common' or 'general' readership entailed the broadest of gestures toward literate society while, at the same time, admitting a distinction between different competencies within that society. The 'common' of Johnson's 'common reader' refers to a social collective, but it also marks out a less refined sub-group. It means both 'Publick; general, serving the use of all' and 'Vulgar; mean; not distinguished by excellence'.[2] More precisely, as Virginia Woolf noted, Johnson's identification of a common reader divided professional from non-professional reading.[3] The 'common reader' and the 'reading public' were terms employed by the professional critic to designate the mass of unprofessional readers whose sheer market power would nevertheless be the final and most materially effective form of criticism.

Flanked by Johnson's famous expression of his joyful concurrence with the common reader, and Leavis's forthright disgust with the 1930s reading public, Wilkie Collins's mid-Victorian uncertainty about the future looks neatly pivotal. But anxiety about the common reader's capacity for discrimination was not, of course, a product of the nineteenth century. Johnson himself was less than polite about the reading public on several occasions: his second *Rambler* essay warns those who pursue fame through writing that they solicit 'the regard of a multitude fluctuating in pleasures . . . judges prepossessed by passions or corrupted by prejudices, which preclude their approbation of any new performance'. Such distrust of the general reader was a recurrent

[2] Samuel Johnson, *A Dictionary of the English Language* (London, 1755).
[3] Virginia Woolf, *The Common Reader* (London, 1925), pp. 11–12.

theme of late eighteenth and early nineteenth-century writing on the subject.[4] One of the most vigorous warnings against the cultural consequences of increased literacy among those whose education or station in life did not equip them to be discerning readers came from Samuel Taylor Coleridge. In *The Statesman's Manual* (1816), he expressed a fervent wish that 'the greater part of our publications could be ... *directed*, each to its appropriate class of Readers ... But this cannot be! For among other odd burs and kecksies, the misgrowth of our luxuriant activity, we have now a READING PUBLIC – as strange a phrase methinks as ever forced a splenetic smile on the staid countenance of Meditation.'[5]

Nevertheless, Collins clearly saw the late 1850s as a potential turning point in the history of the reading public and in describing his anxieties and his hopes for that public he advances (as I hope to show) a specifically mid-Victorian sense of the relationship between ideas about reading and ideas about cultural, social and political cohesion. Unlike Johnson and Coleridge, Collins viewed the public as capable of a considerable advance in discrimination and his explicit hope was that, if properly educated, the mass readership would prove not a liability but a binding social force and a source of national pride. His essay on 'The Unknown Public' offers a series of comic reflections on the expansion of the mid-nineteenth-century penny journal readership. The journal-reading public Collins claims to have discovered is not only 'Unknown' but as yet unknowable, falling outside the purview of all the recognized arbiters of literary value: the established critics, the great libraries, the respected publishing houses, the distinguished writers. Collins's instinctive mistrust of the common reader's cultural credentials is undisguised: this is a readership which will remain beyond 'the pale of true literary civilisation'[6] until such time as it can be educated into literary taste and into Collins's field of social vision. But he is optimistic. The looked-for improvement of the penny-journal reader is, he concludes cheerfully, 'probably a question of time only'.

The largest audience for periodical literature, in this age of periodicals, must obey the universal law of progress, and must, sooner or later, learn to

4 On eighteenth-century critics' distrust of the taste of the general public, see Dustin Griffin, 'Fictions of Eighteenth-Century Authorship', *Essays in Criticism* 43 (1993): 181–94 (pp. 189–90); on gentility in eighteenth-century criticism, Raven, *Judging New Wealth*, pp. 138–56.

5 *The Collected Works of Samuel Taylor Coleridge*, IV, *Lay Sermons*, ed. R. J. White (London, 1972), pp. 36–7. See also the *Lectures of 1808–19*, I: 123–6 and 185–8 (*Collected Works*, V, ed. R. A. Foakes) and chapter 3 of the *Biographia Literaria*.

6 Collins, 'The Unknown Public', p. 218.

discriminate... When that public shall discover its need of a great writer, the great writer will have such an audience as has never yet been known.[7]

To many of his contemporaries, Collins's optimism about the future of the British reading public was soon to seem absolutely justified. 'The Unknown Public' was published in 1858, in *Household Words*, the journal 'conducted' by Charles Dickens, Collins's close friend and literary collaborator. That same year, Dickens began the first of several tours which would take him all over England, and to Scotland, Ireland, America, and France, for over four hundred public readings from his fiction.[8] The tours were a phenomenal success. In financial terms, they made Dickens's fortune, with earnings from the Readings amounting to over half his £100,000 fortune at his death in 1870. Dickens's performances coincided with the height of the vogue for public readings,[9] but no other reader enjoyed such extraordinary financial and popular success. The public did indeed seem to have discovered its collective need of a 'great writer' and to have proved its capacity for discrimination through him.

In the history of the reading public, Dickens's platform career holds a special place, for he succeeded in bringing together unprecedentedly large numbers of readers for a genuinely public experience of reading. Normally an invisible constituency, on these occasions the fiction reading public was to a significant degree made visible to itself as a collectivity. Moreover, Dickens's Readings were not, as might have been expected, aimed purely or even primarily at the middle classes. They were conceived and promoted as occasions which would bring together readers from widely differing social backgrounds as one reading public. In this, as I shall be arguing, the Dickens Readings form an important cultural extension of the contemporary political debate about franchise reform. The 1860s saw repeated attempts, both within parliament and outside it, to define the voting public and to determine the acceptable limits on its composition. In the extended

[7] Ibid., p. 222. On the role of critical reviews in early nineteenth-century attempts to 'forge a diverse and unstable group of the newly literate into the civic coherence of a "reading public"' see Ina Ferris, 'From Trope to Code: The Novel and the Rhetoric of Gender in Nineteenth-Century Critical Discourse', in Linda M. Shires (ed.), *Rewriting the Victorians: Theory, History, and the Politics of Gender* (New York, 1992), pp. 18–30 (p. 19).

[8] The exact number is debated. The leading authority is Philip Collins, who gives the figure of 472 performances in total. See *Charles Dickens: The Public Readings* (Oxford, 1975), pp. xxv-xxvi. Also, *Selected Letters of Charles Dickens*, ed. David Paroissien, 3 vols. (London, 1985), p. 20, n. 27.

[9] See Collins, *The Public Readings*, pp. l-li; and his pamphlet, *Reading Aloud: A Victorian Métier* (Lincoln, 1972).

and complex debate over who was to exercise the franchise, the property qualification was in a sense secondary to the consideration of what qualities were held desirable in the potential electorate. One basic determination recurred: to include only those working men who could be trusted to possess a capacity for judgement, discernment and disinterested understanding. As one parliamentary backbencher explained – articulating a hope for the Second Reform Act which crossed party divisions – the projected voting public should consist of men who would be 'honest, simple-minded (using the word in the best sense) [and] who, in exercising their vote, would look to men of respectability and character and would vote for them in preference to excitable men'.[10]

In desiring to include only those who would use their judgement to recognize the leadership of 'men of respectability and character', this speaker was articulating a recurrent ambiguity in the franchise debates: a tension between the desire to incorporate men of judgement, and the concern to ensure that their judgement would only be exercised in acknowledging the authority of others. Alarmist statements of what must be avoided in accepting working-class elements into the voting public capture exactly this anxiety about their recognition of authority. Mob radicalism was not the only fear. Opponents of the 1867 Act worried more generally that working-class men would not be *free* to exercise their judgement properly: a prominent objector to the Act, for example, warned that it would introduce 'many of the most unfit class; men dependent on their landlords and employers or open to the temptation of bribes or beer'.[11]

In the Dickens Readings, contemporary political debates about the definition of the voting public have a very revealing parallel. To a considerable extent, the political ideals of liberal reform have their cultural realization in these Readings, for, in listening to Dickens, his

10 Quoted in Maurice Cowling, *1867 Disraeli, Gladstone and Revolution: The Passing of the Second Reform Bill* (Cambridge, 1967), p. 52. For discussion of the concept of incorporation, see Francis Hearn, *Domination, Legitimation, and Resistance: The Incorporation of the Nineteenth-Century English Working Class* (Westport, CT, 1978), esp. pp. 231–65. On Gladstone's rhetoric of incorporation, see John Vincent, *The Formation of the Liberal Party 1857–1868* (London, 1966), pp. 211–35; and Peter Clarke, *A Question of Leadership: Gladstone to Thatcher* (London, 1991), pp. 11–41. On Disraeli's 'one nation' rhetoric, see Paul Smith, *Disraelian Conservatism and Social Reform* (London, 1967); P. R. Ghosh, 'Style and Substance in Disraelian Social Reform, *c.* 1860–80', in P. J. Waller (ed.), *Politics and Social Change in Modern Britain: Essays Presented to A. F. Thompson* (Brighton, 1987), pp. 59–90 (esp. p. 67). See also John Vincent, *Disraeli* (Oxford, 1990), pp. 15–16, and p. 118, with regard to Disraeli's belief that 'mass politics would require the charismatic individual'.

11 Hastings Russell, quoted in Cowling, *1867*, p. 49.

reading public was encouraged to develop and demonstrate that capacity for rational appreciation, critical discernment and moral sensibility desired in the voting public. Moreover, when working men willingly acknowledged his authority and applauded the calibre of his performances, they showed precisely that discriminating deference to 'a man of respectability and character' which the shapers of the Reform Act hoped to secure in their public. At the same time, the Dickens Readings reveal something of the attendant anxieties of the reform movement. During a period in which the consequences either of extending the franchise or of refusing to extend it were equally cause for anxiety,[12] the project of cultural incorporation parallels the equally conflicted dynamics of political incorporation.

The mid-Victorian years have been seen as a crucial stage in the development of ideas about the relationship between culture and class in Britain: one in which the middle-classes exerted and consolidated unprecedented control over the cultural sphere. Eileen Yeo's 1981 essay 'Culture and Constraint in Working-Class Movements', for example, describes the development of a visibly independent working-class culture in the 1830s and '40s, partly in tandem with the political radicalism of that period, and partly in a redirection of political energies to cultural activities as the directly political aims of Chartist radicalism met repeatedly with disappointment. The result, Yeo argues, was an ambitious 'cultural counter-offensive' by the middle classes during the 1840s and '50s.[13] 'Culture and Constraint' documents a remarkable increase, especially after 1850, in the number of voluntary organizations funded largely by middle-class money to cater for working-class leisure and educational 'self'-help: 'These voluntary

[12] While few of those active in the passing of the Second Reform Act believed that the situation in 1866/7 was a potential revolutionary one, there were prominent public figures (including the Queen) who took alarm at such signs of working-class unrest as the London builders' strikes of 1859–62 and the Staffordshire iron-workers' strike of 1865. See Cowling, *1867*, pp. 20–1, 35–40. On the history of working-class radicalism in this period, see E. P. Thompson's classic *The Making of the English Working Class* (London, 1963). For its earlier nineteenth-century context, see Albert Goodwin, 'The Great Debate', in *The Friends of Liberty: The English Democratic Movement in the Age of the French Revolution* (London, 1979), pp. 171–207, and Iain McCalman, *Radical Underworlds: Prophets, Revolutionaries and Pornographers in London, 1795–1840* (Cambridge, 1988), pp. 97–203.

[13] In Eileen Yeo and Stephen Yeo (eds.), *Popular Culture and Class Conflict, 1590–1914: Explorations in the History of Labour and Leisure* (Brighton, 1981), pp. 155–86 (p. 178). Yeo's essay provides a significant development of Raymond Williams's key account of the emergence, after 1830, of a distinct class-consciousness predicated upon the inequality of different classes in culture. See Raymond Williams, *Culture and Society 1780–1950* (London, 1958; Penguin edn, 1961), p. 311; and, for discussion, Julia Swindells and Lisa Jardine, *What's Left?: Women in Culture and the Labour Movement* (London, 1990), p. 102.

organizations often had a tier of vice-presidents who guaranteed financial stability but exerted the direct and indirect pressures inherent in patronage. The accent was on energetic and responsible participation without democratic control.'[14]

Accounts such as Yeo's stress a combative and fixed notion of class which no doubt accurately matches the attitudes of many mid-Victorians. Certainly, it would be easy to depict Dickens's Readings as simply one more blow (and a powerful one) in the middle-class 'cultural counter-offensive'. However, as more recent historical writing has stressed, the languages and material properties of class in the nineteenth century are more fluid than the model of class-war suggests.[15] In accounts of the Dickens Readings, the relationship of different classes to culture is an active question, and the fluidity of class is welcomed. Far from conceding the existence of divergent class interests, under Dickens's active management the idea of the reading public became the means to a liberal celebration of reading as the forum in which all classes could come together, united in the enjoyment of a common sensibility. As I shall be arguing, the consequent seriousness of the issues at stake when Dickens reads to his public – the nature of the hopes involved in his enterprise, and the implications of its possible failure – make for a highly potent fusion of political and cultural concerns, ultimately finding their clearest expression through the rhetoric of contemporary medicine.

Charles Dickens's public Readings originated in his support for a new Industrial and Literary Institute in Birmingham. After learning about plans for the Institute on a visit to the city in 1853, he wrote to the committee offering to give a public Reading of *A Christmas Carol* as a fund-raising event the following Christmas. Working people would be admitted free, and would be unsegregated from paying members of the audience. The Committee accepted. Dickens gave three Readings in December 1853, and their success persuaded him later to take up public reading as a serious professional activity.

Dickens's support for working men's interest in and access to literary culture was well known. A supporter of Gladstone and the

[14] Yeo, 'Culture and Constraint', p. 179.

[15] See particularly Gareth Stedman Jones, *Languages of Class: Studies in English Working-Class History* (Cambridge, 1983); K. C. Phillips, *Language and Class in Victorian England* (Oxford, 1985); and Penelope J. Cornfield (ed.), *Language, History and Class* (Oxford, 1991).

Liberal Party,[16] he spoke regularly at public meetings in support of adult education for working men, visited mutual improvement societies and institutes around the country, and gave most of his later unpaid charity Readings for the benefit of provincial institutes.[17] For four months he also held an appointment on the Central Committee of the Working Classes for the Great Exhibition, established to oversee working-class access to the Crystal Palace (the Committee was dissolved at his suggestion after obstruction from the Commissioners). When granted an audience by Queen Victoria in March 1870, he chose to speak to her about the division of the classes and his hopes for better relations between them (she declared herself impressed by his 'large, and roving mind').[18] Dickens's support for working men's self-improvement was thus public and energetic, and he strongly resisted the press's dilution of his radicalism,[19] but he was also quite explicit about the limits on his support for democracy. Memorably described by Walter Bagehot as a 'sentimental radical', Dickens's own struggle for self-advancement had left him a passionate supporter of working men's self-help, and of financial assistance from the wealthier classes, but he was by no means a revolutionary. He was utterly unsympathetic to mob-vulgarity of the kind he witnessed at the public hanging of François Benjamin Courvoisier in 1840 and even more strongly opposed to mob-violence of the kind depicted in *Nicholas Nickleby*, *The Old Curiosity Shop*, *Barnaby Rudge*, *A Tale of Two Cities* and *Hard Times*.[20] Dickens's Readings reflect a political creed which combines encouragement for the working man's advancement through education into the propertied ranks of society (where he would have earned his right to a say in the country's government) with determined resistance to the working man's enfranchisement by more

16 See Peter Ackroyd, *Dickens* (London, 1990), p. 1036.

17 Ibid., pp. 418, 421, 660, 666–8, 740, 845–6, 958; Collins, *The Public Readings*, p. viii.

18 See Norman and Jeanne MacKenzie, *Charles Dickens: A Life* (Oxford, 1979), p. 387.

19 See, for example, his letter to Macready on 2 March 1870, stating his pleasure that his friend had appreciated his reformist sentiments, and his irritation at their dilution by the press after his speech to the Birmingham and Midland Institute the previous September: 'I was determined that my Radicalism would not be called into question'. Walter Dexter (ed.), *The Letters of Charles Dickens*, 3 vols. (London, 1938), III, 765.

20 See Edgar Johnson, *Charles Dickens: His Tragedy and Triumph*, 2 vols (London, 1953), I, 315, 329–37; II, 813, 826–7, 841–2, 885. Also Ackroyd, *Dickens*, pp. 312–14, 326–7, and 734–41. Some of Dickens's most memorable criticisms of the government's failure sufficiently to respect the moral capacity of the working classes were contained in his speech to the Birmingham and Midland Institute Annual Inaugural Meeting, Birmingham, 27 September 1869; in Kate Fielding (ed.), *The Speeches of Charles Dickens* (Oxford, 1960), pp. 397–408 (p. 407). See also his speech to the Administrative Reform Association, 27 June 1855, pp. 197–208. For an account of class politics in the major novels, see Pam Morris, *Dickens's Class Consciousness: A Marginal View* (Basingstoke, 1991).

violent means. The Readings aimed to assist such an incorporation of meritorious members of the working classes into middle-class culture, and while their success was considerable, they reveal, nonetheless, a discernible alarm on the part of the Reading organizers that this reading public was a precarious entity: one which, in less competent hands than Dickens's, might be liable to violent breakup.

There are two leading eye-witness accounts of Dickens's British Readings. Both are eulogistic, written soon after his death by men closely involved with his reading career. *Charles Dickens as a Reader* was written by his friend Charles Kent and first published in 1872, two years after Dickens's death. *Charles Dickens as I Knew Him* followed in 1885, written by his stage manager, George Dolby.[21] Among the features of Dickens's Readings most frequently and enthusiastically praised by Kent and Dolby is their appeal to men and women irrespective of class background. Kent informs us that

> it was [Dickens's] privilege throughout the whole of his literary career to address not one class, or two or three classes, but all classes of the reading public indiscriminately – the most highly educated and the least educated, young and old, rich and poor.[22]

Dolby notes that the financial success of the tours was

> all the more gratifying as Mr. Dickens had, with that consideration for the masses which ever characterized his actions, stipulated, at the commencement of the engagement, that shilling seat-holders should have as good accommodation as those who were willing to pay higher sums for their evening's enjoyment; 'for', said he, 'I have been the champion and friend of the working man all through my career, and it would be inconsistent, if not unjust, to put any difficulty in the way of his attending my Readings'.[23]

In this, Dickens was going against standard Victorian theatrical practice. As George Rowell, Michael Booth and others have noted, the Victorian theatre was rigidly stratified 'not only in the architectural disposition of its audiences but also in the content of its drama'.[24] Dolby's claim that

[21] These are supplemented by Kate Fields's vivid account of Dickens reading in America, *Pen Photographs of Charles Dickens's Readings: Taken from Life* (Boston, MA, 1868).

[22] Charles Kent, *Charles Dickens as a Reader* (London, 1852), p. 37.

[23] George Dolby, *Charles Dickens as I Knew Him: The Story of the Reading Tours in Great Britain and America (1866–1870)* (London, 1885), p. 3.

[24] Michael R. Booth, *Theatre in the Victorian Age* (Cambridge, 1991), p. 2; see also George Rowell, *The Victorian Theatre 1792–1914. A Survey*, 2nd edn (Cambridge, 1978), pp. 3–4; and Ernest Reynolds, *Early Victorian Drama (1830–1870)* (Cambridge, 1936), pp. 52–4. On the riotous Georgian background to Victorian theatre seating and pricing, see Marc Baer, *Theatre and Disorder in Late Georgian London* (Oxford, 1992).

shilling ticket holders had 'as good' seating as holders of higher price tickets is clearly exaggerated. Boxes, for example, evidently remained privileged seating, but, depending upon the venue, the seating arrangements in the stalls at Dickens's Readings do seem genuinely to have obliged genteel patrons to rub shoulders with members of the audience who would normally have been relegated to the gallery and the pit. The programmes, similarly, were heterodox: usually one long item and one short one, the first being typically more demanding and wider in its emotional and theatrical range than the second, which was generally comic and 'more popular'.[25] The combination was good theatrical practice, but it was also one further indication of the endeavour to appeal to different tastes which, according to the testimony of contemporary theatre managers, directly reflected the class of the audience. The more demanding theatrical pieces would appeal to the gents, the more boisterous comedy would win the lower classes[26] – and Dickens was adept at both kinds of material. He himself testified to the liking for boisterous comedy among the less genteel members of his audience, writing to Georgina Hogarth with amusement on 7 November 1861 that 'The people in the stalls set the example of laughing, in the most curiously unreserved way.'[27]

Dickens was intrigued and delighted at the success of his venture, and particularly at his reception by 'the working people'. After the inaugural Reading in Birmingham, he wrote ecstatically to a friend:

> I never saw, nor do I suppose anybody ever did, such an interesting sight as the working people's night... a more delicately observant audience it is impossible to imagine. They lost nothing, misinterpreted nothing, followed everything closely, laughed and cried with the most delightful earnestness ...[28]

The description conveys hyperbolic pleasure mixed with not a little surprise that these people should have revealed so fine a literary sensibility, such delicate observation. Dickens offers triumphant proof, as he was to do time and again in his letters to friends, of the capacity of the lower orders of society for discrimination, evidenced in their response to him. The sense of an agenda is unmistakable. There is, clearly, a right response to be achieved or missed, so that these people can be said to have 'lost nothing, misinterpreted nothing'.

25 Collins, *The Public Readings*, p. xxvii.
26 See Booth, *Theatre in the Victorian Age*, pp. 2–3.
27 *Letters*, III, 252.
28 Dickens to Hon. Mrs. Richard Watson, *Letters*, II, 533.

Yet just how genuinely or widely 'working class' the Readings were is highly disputable. In university towns many of the 'shillings' (as Dickens labelled the cheap-ticket holders) may well have been students taking advantage of the lower price option, rather than working-class men. For, however concerned Dickens was to make his performances available to all working men, at Readings after 1853 those attending had to be able to afford the basic shilling rate. Real wages are generally held to have increased during the 1850s and '60s for skilled labourers in regular employment, but very many of the working classes did not, of course, come into that category. In 1865 Edward Brotherton and his colleagues on the Manchester and Salford Education Aid Society calculated a minimum subsistence income for an adult at three shillings per head per week exclusive of rent. Brotherton's exhaustive house to house survey concluded that at least twenty-five per cent of the Manchester and Salford workers were in primary poverty.[29] It was, if anything, a conservative estimate. In 1868, Dudley Baxter estimated that forty per cent of the working class in England (exclusive of agricultural labourers, soldiers and pensioners, and female domestic servants) were living below the poverty line.[30] Dickens's one shilling tickets were cheap (given that the regular price for a seat in the stalls was four shillings in 1863, then five until the farewell Readings of 1870 when it rose to seven shillings) but they were still too dear for that large proportion of working men who did not enjoy a regular and sufficient income. They were also considerably more expensive than the one penny entrance fee unskilled labourers would have expected to pay for a concert.[31] For the poorest classes, a ticket to Dickens's Readings would have been an impossible luxury even if it was a desirable one. Moreover, these were events designed for the literate or for those with literate family or friends who could read the Dickens novels aloud. Many labouring men and women still did not fall into either bracket. Though literacy levels were higher and increasing more rapidly in the third quarter of the nineteenth century than ever before, a substantial proportion of the labouring classes had acquired no reading or writing ability. David Vincent's work on marriage registers in England as a

[29] Neville Kirk, *The Growth of Working Class Reformism in Mid-Victorian England* (London, 1985), p. 105.

[30] E. J. Hobsbawm, *Labouring Men: Studies in the History of Labour* (London, 1964), pp. 304–5.

[31] See Hugh Shimmin, 'The Street Boys' Concert Admission, One Penny', *Porcupine*, 8 December 1860; reproduced in John K. Watson and Alastair Wilcox (eds.), *Low Life and Moral Improvement in Mid-Victorian England: Liverpool Through the Journalism of Hugh Shimmin* (Leicester, 1991), pp. 236–8.

guide to literacy in this period has shown that at only 37.8 per cent of skilled labourers' weddings, and 19.8 per cent of unskilled labourers' weddings between 1859 and 1874 were all four signatories to the register (bride, groom and two witnesses) able to write their names.[32]

Dickens's Readings, however extraordinary his popularity, were therefore not as attractive to all levels of the population as he and his promoters claimed. There are, unfortunately, no known accounts of the Readings by the poorest members of the audience, but there is an aside in George Dolby's memoirs which provides an oblique warning against taking the claim to class-inclusiveness at face value – though Dolby himself seems to have remained impervious to the implications of his anecdote. After an unusually poor reception in Aberdeen, Dolby was scandalized to hear the local booking agent's explanation:

> 'Weel, Misther Doalby, I'm no prapared t' state positively what yewr actiel receats 'll be, *for ye see, sir, amangst ma ain freends there are vairy few wha ha' iver haird o' Chairles Dickens*.'[33]

The Aberdeen agent's confession, mangled though it is in Dolby's attempt to render a comically Scottish accent and dismiss the criticism, indicates that while many working-class readers may have been eager to hear Dickens, there existed philistine individuals, perhaps even among the lower-middle-class ranks, who had not read him – who, perhaps, had not even heard of him – and who kept away.

When Charles Kent refers to Dickens's ability to address 'not one class, or two or three classes, but all classes of the reading public indiscriminately', he suggests a further uncertainty behind Dickens's claim to appeal to all sectors of society. The term 'indiscriminately' carries suggestively pejorative as well as positive overtones. More basically, the very meaning of the term class is in question in Kent's formulation. As he uses it, it does not necessarily or exclusively designate a social hierarchy: it refers to divisions according to age and education as much as to wealth and social standing. In so far as it does map on to the modern usage of 'class', it continues to resonate with some uncertainty. The incremental use of the plural attempts to evade a schematism too obvious in the three-class model of society. But how many classes were there? What were the boundaries between classes? When did a man or woman cease to be working-class and

32 Vincent, *Literacy and Popular Culture*, pp. 282–3. On the validity of the marriage registers as a guide to literacy in this period, see pp. 3 and 16–18.

33 Dolby, *Charles Dickens as I Knew Him*, p. 36. His italics.

become middle-class?[34] Most simply, who counts as working-class here? Wally Seccombe, Keith McClelland and Catherine Hall have described the emergence of a new conservatism within the labour movement of the 1840s by which the representative worker increasingly became defined as the male artisan. The politically acceptable face of the lower classes was the respectable, skilled, male labourer in regular employment, able to support a wife and family. The representative artisan gradually came to dominate representations of labour in the 1850s and '60s both from within and from outside the movement, to the exclusion of unskilled labour, female labour and child labour. It was this working man who was most readily encouraged to participate in middle-class culture via working men's clubs and mutual improvement societies.[35] In so far as Dickens *was* welcoming 'the working man' into his audiences, he was addressing this respectable end of the labour constituency.

That Kent, Dolby and Dickens nevertheless believed they were facilitating a true melding of working, middle and upper classes into one reading culture underlines what is at issue. Dickens's Readings represent an attempt to redefine the experience of culture in such a way that it is seen to express the potential irrelevance of class to fundamental sympathies and sensibilities. In Dickens's Readings, reading provides the means to simultaneously recognizing and cancelling class distinctions. By the 1850s Dickens's public was continually represented, as it still is to a considerable extent, as the paradigmatic fiction-reading public of nineteenth-century England and its Empire. He was 'the most popular author of his generation', as Kent tells us. His reading public was celebrated as the most genuinely inclusive readership of the age, in terms of class, gender, age, occupation and nationality.[36] Kent therefore finds it wholly appropriate that 'thanks

[34] On the looseness of the term 'class', particularly 'the working class', see Gareth Stedman Jones, 'Rethinking Chartism', in Jones, *Languages of Class* (Cambridge, 1983), pp. 90–178; Patricia Anderson, *The Printed Image and the Transformation of Popular Culture 1790–1860* (Oxford, 1991), pp. 7–12; David Vincent, *Bread, Knowledge and Freedom: A Study of Nineteenth-Century Working Class Autobiography* (London, 1981), pp. 2, 7–8.

[35] See Wally Seccombe, 'Patriarchy Stabilized: The Construction of the Male Breadwinner Wage Norm in Nineteenth-Century Britain', *Social History* 11 (1986): 53–76; Keith McClelland, 'Some Thoughts on Masculinity and the "Representative Artisan" in Britain, 1850–1880', *Gender and History*, 1 (1989): 164–77; Catherine Hall, 'The Tale of Samuel and Jemima: Gender and Working-Class Culture in Early Nineteenth-Century England', in Harvey J. Kaye and Keith McClelland (eds.), *E. P. Thompson: Critical Perspectives* (Cambridge, 1989), pp. 78–102. See also Robert Q. Gray, *The Aristocracy of Labour in Nineteenth-Century Britain, c. 1850–1914* (London, 1981), pp. 25–9, 33, 38–9, 63–5.

[36] See, for example, G. H. Lewes's review of Charles Dickens's stature as a writer in 1872: 'Dickens in Relation to Criticism', *Fortnightly Review Edinburgh Review* (1872): 141–54. For a good discussion of Dickens and class mobility, see Kate Flint, *Dickens* (Brighton, 1976), pp. 17–20.

entirely to these Readings, he was brought into more intimate relations individually with a considerable portion at least of the vast circle of his own readers' than any other author 'since literature became a profession'.[37] It was a point Dickens himself noted with enthusiasm. He wrote to Forster, seeking to ease his friend's anxiety that Dickens might be using the Readings to escape from personal pressures: 'Will you then try to think of this reading project (as I do) apart from all personal likings and dislikings, and solely with a view to its effect on that particular relation (personally affectionate and like no other man's) which subsists between me and the public?'[38]

Because Dickens's readership was perceived as the widest of his age, when the public heard him read they were in a sense offered their most authoritative experience of *being* a reading public. More than that, they were offered the experience of being a unified public. The 'magic' of the Readings was that they could be seen to demonstrate the incorporation of the reading public in culture. When Dickens read, the crowd responded, according to eye-witnesses, as one body. Kent describes a typical reception:

> Densely packed from floor to ceiling, these audiences were habitually wont to hang in breathless expectation upon every inflection of the author-reader's voice, upon every glance of his eye, – the words he was about to speak being so thoroughly well remembered by the majority before their utterance that, often, the rippling of a smile over a thousand faces simultaneously anticipated the laughter which an instant afterwards greeted the words themselves when they were articulated.[39]

The sense of a unified experience is insistent here, as it so often is in contemporary accounts of how audiences responded to Dickens: one smile for a thousand faces. This is partly the familiar language of the body politic, partly an echo of more recent adaptations of that language in the cause of mid-nineteenth-century liberal reform, emphasizing a holistic model of the body over and above the anatomization of its separate limbs and organs.[40] It is, in other words, a use of the body as metaphor to figure unity rather than class-difference.

Dickens's Readings were, quite literally, authoritative reading: the 'author-reader's' Reading, in Kent's favoured phrase. But Dickens and

37 Kent, *Charles Dickens as a Reader*, p. 38.
38 Dickens to John Forster, [March] 1858, in Dexter (ed.), *Letters*, III, 15.
39 Kent, *Charles Dickens as a Reader*, p. 20.
40 Gladstone, for example, famously welcomed working men as 'our own flesh and blood' during the 1866 debates. See n. 9 above for references to the rhetoric of incorporation.

his co-organizers insisted that the public were doing more than just listening. They were reading with him, through him. At the inaugural Reading in Birmingham, addressing a crowd of two and a half thousand people, it seemed to Dickens as if all two and a half thousand were leaning over his shoulder: 'we were all going on together, in the first page, as easily, to all appearance, as if we had been sitting round the fire'.[41] Dickens's efficacy as a reader makes him the perfect vehicle for the liberal ideal of incorporation. He quite spectacularly banishes all the questions important to recent histories of reading: how people read differently, in what situations? with what competence? alone or with whom? Reading is celebrated here as an experience in common whose mode of practice is held to be self-evident. Centrally, reading can be realized, through Dickens, as public and at the same time familial, intimate, personal: 'as if we had all been sitting round the fire'. Reminiscences of Dickens reading affirm his ability to preserve the illusion of individual address, even as he spoke to crowds as large as that at Birmingham. A little boy, taken to one of the Pickwick Readings in London, remembered having 'roared and shouted with delight and then wept and howled with emotion... I must have been a terrible nuisance to Dickens', he said in later years,

> for I was at his feet, and at least twice I remember very distinctly he looked at me, I am sure with the idea of having me removed.
>
> But my fat friend saved the day for he shouted with glee even louder than I, his bass and my treble chiming in to the great disturbance of our neighbours. My father tried to soothe me for I was getting almost hysterical. But my fat friend could not be removed and we stayed.
>
> At the end Dickens stepped down to speak to my father who presented his guest and me. I remember his rather quizzical look at me but he gave me a most friendly tap or pat of forgiveness on the head.[42]

If Dickens manages the awkward melding of the private into the public, the individual sensibility into the general culture, it is neither an easy achievement nor an unqualified one. While his Readings exemplify the capacity of the public for unification, they also reveal to a striking degree the tensions within the liberal ideal of incorporation. The ideal of a reading public genuinely inclusive of all classes does not mesh as easily as Dickens claimed with an equally powerful valuation of reading as a private, individual experience. The Dickens Readings

41 Dickens to Hon. Mrs Richard Watson, 13 January 1854, *Letters*, II, 533.

42 Eustace Conway, 'My Dickens Episode', in *Anthony Munday and Other Essays* privately printed (New York, 1928), pp. 103–4.

expose a paradox within mid-Victorian notions of fiction-reading. The public's reading of fiction was, in this period, most often represented and experienced as being not in fact public at all, but private, at most familial and friendly (a point that can be made with equal justice of the ostensibly more public friendly societies).[43] Though this configuration of reading is typically associated with the middle classes, Catherine Hall has shown that over the nineteenth century the cult of domesticity had become just as powerful an element in the lives of the labouring classes.[44] Dickens's Readings contribute to a continuing mid-century effort to redefine the perceived working-class experience of culture. They offer a public celebration of what remains, at heart, a private experience, dependent upon a personal capacity for literary sensibility. Culture is, in other words, the public acknowledgement of a shared private experience. It is a definition fundamentally opposed to the possibility that culture might play a role in forging distinct class-consciousnesses.

Moreover, the respectability of the Readings was always in doubt. Beneath the claims that Dickens attracted an audience irrespective of class, there was a continual undercurrent of concern about the appropriateness of his performances for the public. Both Kent and John Forster (Dickens's close friend and his first biographer) felt obliged to counter 'possible objections' on the grounds that the Readings could appear mercenary, or (more evasively) that they were 'derogating, in some inconceivable way, from the dignity of authorship'.[45] Dickens himself voiced concern along these lines when first mooting the possibility of public Readings: 'in these days of lecturings and readings', he mused to John Forster, 'a great deal of money might possibly be made (*if it were not infra dig*) by one's having Readings of one's own books'.[46]

Kent, particularly, was unwilling to afford the Readings the same status as Dickens's writing. The Preface to *Charles Dickens as a Reader* insists that however remarkable they are as performances, they must

43 See Robert Q. Gray, *The Labour Aristocracy in Victorian Edinburgh* (Oxford, 1976), pp. 123–6, for an indication of the private nature of these societies. The nature of the distinction between public and private is, of course, hotly contested.

44 Hall, 'The Tale of Samuel and Jemima' (see n. 27).

45 Kent, *Charles Dickens as a Reader*, pp. 20–1; John Forster, *The Life of Charles Dickens*, 3 vols. (London, 1872–4), III, 4, 165. As Philip Collins has noted, Dickens had considerable support in the fact that Thackeray 'more indisputably a gentleman than himself, had proceeded him in lucrative platform appearances' (*The Public Readings*, p. xlviii).

46 Dickens to John Forster, *Letters*, III, 788 (my italics); and for his earlier exchanges with Forster regarding the propriety of reading for money, *Letters*, III, 12–13.

finally be considered 'supplementary'.[47] This concern to value Dickens's writing more highly than his Readings reflects, of course, a high valuation of the novels; but it further indicates an ongoing disquiet attaching to Dickens's success as a reader even in the eulogistic accounts of his friends and managers – a disquiet which continually returns to the theme of class. A few pages into *Charles Dickens as a Reader*, Kent contradicts himself and admits, after all, that hearing the author give voice to his work brings to the text a fullness of meaning it seems never to have had before. This fullness of meaning is more than simply the immediacy of the voice, or the force of authoritative interpretation, the author-reader's interpretation. It has a specific class-resonance. For Kent, what is returned to Dickens's novels through the author's reading of them is the significance of 'the lesser characters':

> the lesser characters – those which are introduced into the original works quite incidentally, occupying there a wholly subordinate position, filling up a space in the crowded tableaux, always in the background – were then at last brought to the fore in the course of these Readings, and suddenly and for the first time assumed to themselves a distinct importance and individuality.[48]

By 'lesser characters' Kent's examples indicate that he means a class distinction and not just one of consequence within the narrative (the two are, of course, partly related). Lest his description sounds like reading in the service of democracy, reading as a means to sympathy with the poorer classes, the immediate example qualifies the kind of individuality this new distinction permits working men and women.

> Take, for instance, the nameless lodging-housekeeper's slavey, who assists at Bob Sawyer's party, and who is described in the original work as 'a dirty, slipshod girl, in black cotton stockings, who might have passed for the neglected daughter of a superannuated dustman in very reduced circumstances.' No one had ever realised the crass stupidity of that remarkable young person – dense and impenetrable as a London fog – until her first introduction in these Readings . . .[49]

Kent sees Dickens pulling the nameless woman out of the crowd, but only to return her all the more fully to the anonymity of the streets 'dense and impenetrable as a London fog'. Listening to the Reading, Kent recognizes the 'distinct importance' of the humble servant only to gloss that distinctness as, in reality, impenetrably dull. To represent the

47 Kent, *Charles Dickens as a Reader*, p. vii.
48 Ibid., p. 33.
49 Ibid.

nameless 'slavey' means revealing, above all, her palpable and comic lack of an intelligible sensibility.

The degree to which Dickens's Readings are seen to achieve a cultural incorporation of the working classes was more immediately in doubt from the audience. Time and again in Dickens's accounts and in those of his friends, a public success seems to have been snatched from the jaws of public disaster: the unified reading public appears on the point of violent disintegration. In Glasgow, in 1866, there was a recurrence of a problem that had plagued the Reading tour in England. Dolby reports that:

> when the time came for opening the doors, the inevitable 'shilling' rush was apparent. Mr. Wills [Dickens's agent], having had sufficient experience in the shilling market, begged to be excused from assisting in that department on this particular occasion ... he went in for the 'genteel,' as Mr. Dickens described it ... 'Wills is to do the "genteel" to-night in the "stalls," and Dolby is to stem to shilling tide, *if he can.*'[50]

The management's anxiety to maintain some distinction between the 'genteel' and 'the shillings' reflected several earlier experiences of serious overcrowding. At a Reading in Cork in 1858, the crowd was so packed that Dickens had trouble reaching the platform. He described the scene in a letter to his daughter:

> They had broken all the glass in the pay-boxes. Our men were flattened against walls and squeezed against beams. Ladies stood all night with their chins against my platform. Other ladies sat all night upon my steps. You never saw such a sight. And the reading went on tremendously![51]

In Edinburgh, at a first night performance, Dickens

> heard the people (when the doors were opened) come in with a most unusual crash; and was very much struck by the place's obviously filling to the throat within five minutes ... there was a tearing mad crowd in all the passages and in the street, forcing a great turbid stream of people into the already crammed hall.[52]

Again, too many tickets had been sold for the capacity of the building, and, when Dickens appeared, 'fifty frantic men addressed me at once, and 50 other frantic men got upon ledges and cornices',[53] shouting

[50] Dolby, *Charles Dickens as I Knew Him*, p. 23. See also Dickens's letter to Mary Dickens, 7 August 1858, describing the shilling 'torrent' pounding Arthur Helps against the wall and trampling him under foot (*Letters*, III, 35–6).

[51] Dickens to Mary Dickens, 28 August 1858, *Letters*, III, 46.

[52] Dickens to W. H. Wills, 3 December 1861, *Letters*, III, 264.

[53] Ibid.; and see Johnson, *Charles Dickens*, II, 999.

objections and refusing for some time to let the Reading proceed. Quiet was restored and Dickens was about to begin, when a gentleman '(with full dressed lady torn to ribbons on his arm)' suggested that some of the ladies at least might be accommodated on the platform. In a minute the platform was crowded, but then those at the sides of the hall could no longer see. Dickens proposed that the people on the platform (mostly ladies) sit down.

Instantly they all dropped down into recumbent groups, with Respected Chief standing up in the centre. I don't know what it looked like most – a battlefield – an impossible tableau – a gigantic picnic. There was one very pretty girl in full dress lying down on her side all night, and holding on to one leg of my table.[54]

Dickens's uncertainty about whether the scene looked more like a battlefield or a picnic encapsulates a problem in describing the Readings that is ultimately a problem of class decorum. A genteel 'tableau' is made 'impossible' by the sheer pressure of the crowd. 'Ladies', particularly, are obliged to adopt unladylike positions or be 'torn to ribbons'. The extreme violence of the haberdashery metaphor (used repeatedly by Dickens and his commentators)[55] expresses graphically a feared potential of the crowd. Dickens and his co-organizers seem at times uncertain whether they are producing a glorious public event or provoking a public outbreak of hostilities.

At one of the Newcastle readings, the danger of a riot was only just averted. A gas-lantern fell from above the platform

and it looked as if the room was falling. There were three great galleries crammed to the roof, and a high steep flight of stairs, and a panic must have destroyed numbers of people. A lady in the front row of stalls screamed, and ran out wildly towards me, and for one instant there was a terrible wave in the crowd.[56]

So I addressed her, laughing, and half-asked and half-ordered her to sit down again; and in a minute, it was all over... But the men in attendance had such a fearful sense of what might have happened (besides the real danger of Fire) that they positively shook the boards I stood on, with their trembling when they came up to put things right.[57]

54 Dickens to W. H. Wills, 3 December 1861, *Letters*, III, 264.

55 For example, Dickens, letter to Georgina Hogarth, 3 December 1861: 'such indescribable confusion, such a rending and tearing of dresses, ... My people were torn to ribbons. They have not a hat among them, and scarcely a coat' (*Letters*, III, 263–4); and Dolby, *Charles Dickens as I Knew Him*, p. 6, '[in Edinburgh, the door attendants] were all torn to ribbons; they had not a hat and scarcely a coat amongst them'.

56 Dickens to Mary Dickens, 23 November 1861, *Letters*, III, 259.

57 Dickens to Forster, November 1861, *Letters*, III, 261.

The primary danger, then, is not that of Fire, for all its urgent capital letter, but the one 'besides': the other, more terrifying danger of a public riot, whose most powerful symbol is the hysterical woman.

Fear of an outbreak of crowd hysteria appears repeatedly in all accounts of Dickens's performances, most dramatically in relation to the famous murder Reading from *Oliver Twist.* Immediately before Dickens's first rendition of the piece in London in 1868, Sir William Overend Priestley, a prominent women's physician, lecturer on midwifery and obstetrics at King's College, London, and later Professor of Obstetric Medicine there, felt moved to warn him: 'My dear Dickens, you may rely upon it that if only one woman cries out when you murder the girl, there will be a contagion of hysteria all over this place.'[58] The Reverend William Harness (editor of *The Dramatic Works of Shakespeare* (1825)) was also in the audience and evidently felt the same danger. He wrote to Dickens afterward: 'I am bound to tell you that I had an almost irresistible impulse upon me to *scream*, and that, if anyone had cried out, I am certain I should have followed.'[59] 'Sikes and Nancy', more than any of the other Readings, seemed to Dickens and his worried friends likely to disturb the public. Such concern had troubled him as early as 1863 when the idea was first mooted. In the end, public rendition of the piece was only undertaken after a trial Reading before an invited audience, including some members of the press. 'Horror-stricken' but fascinated, they were soothed after the event with oysters and champagne, and with that encouragement, they could hardly contain their enthusiasm. Forster, Dolby and Dickens's son Charley remained opposed, however, though Dickens declared himself more worried by some of his supporters than by his detractors. The actress Mrs Keeley gave him particular pause for thought: ' "The public have been looking out for a sensation these last fifty years or so" ', she told him, "and by Heaven they have got it!" With which words, and a long breath and a long stare, she became speechless. Again, you may suppose I am a little anxious!'[60] The danger of hysteria staring at him through Mrs Keeley's eyes, as it had screamed at him through the other woman earlier, signals what is at stake: the successful integration of the public into one body, or its fragmentation and dispersal into madness. As two respected judges of the physical and spiritual welfare of the public felt obliged to warn Dickens, the cultural incorporation of all classes into one public body

58 Dickens to Mrs James T. Fields, 16 December 1868, *Letters* III, 687.
59 Ibid.
60 Ibid.

involves an extreme risk that the body will be vulnerable to contagion, all too easily slipping hysterically out of control.

The persistent comparison of Dickens's Readings to the performances of a mesmerist needs to be understood in this context. Dickens's interest in mesmerism, or animal magnetism, has been the subject of detailed study,[61] and was widely known and shared at the time. It was a readily available point of comparison for his ability to control the sympathy of a crowd. It is also a particularly revealing metaphor. When Dolby and Kent describe the laughter at his reading of the Trial scene from *Pickwick Papers* as 'of the most magnetic and contagious kind'[62] and claim that 'listening to him we realised what he spoke of by sympathy',[63] or when Kent describes the 'breathless expectation' of audiences hanging upon every inflection of the speaker's voice and every glance of his eye,[64] the overt and implied references to a mesmerist's control over a hypnotized, typically female-body encapsulate the kind of power being exercised here. Through Reading, the public is being made one body, and, more than that, a fully sympathetic body subject to the author-reader's masterly control. The depiction of Dickens as mesmeric master of the crowd picks up a characterization of the mesmerist that was becoming popularized – and vigorously contested – in the 1850s. Alison Winter describes its exploitation not just by pro-mesmerists but by medical anti-mesmerists 'who appropriated much of the culture of mesmerism to portray themselves as doctors of society healing the body politic of a "mesmeric mania"'.[65] William Carpenter, for example, was developing his highly-influential counter-model of mesmerism in the 1850s: an explanation of mesmeric effects as a form of pathology whose proper cure lay with the doctor.[66] The repeated references to Dickens's power as a mesmerist of the crowd therefore convey a complex set of associations: they register both approbation and, potentially, distrust; but, quackery or not, they

61 Most extensively by Fred Kaplan, *Dickens and Mesmerism: The Hidden Springs of Fiction* (Princeton, NJ, 1975).

62 Dolby, *Charles Dickens as I Knew Him*, p. 20.

63 Kent, *Charles Dickens as a Reader*, p. 28.

64 Ibid., p. 20.

65 See Alison Winter, 'The Island of Mesmeria: The Politics of Mesmerism in Early Victorian Britain', unpublished PhD dissertation, University of Cambridge, 1992, pp. 116–17. Also Emma Parry and Alison Winter, '"The Body Which Speaks to the Body": Mesmerism and the Politics of Public Conduct, 1780–1850', paper delivered at a Wellcome Institute Conference, *Medical Radicals*, 19 February 1993, publication forthcoming, for discussion of a similar overlap between debate about the repercussions of franchise reform and the language of contemporary medicine in the 1820s and '30s.

66 Parry and Winter, *The Island of Mesmeria*, pp. 194–230.

identify him over and above the doctor, in this instance, as the man who can quell the threatening hysteria of the crowd by dint of a firm voice and a firm eye.

Philip Collins and Paul Schlicke have both noted the parallels between the Dickens Readings and other popular forms of public entertainment, most obviously the theatre, the one man show and public lecturing.[67] Two further comparisons suggest themselves: Chartist rallies and Methodist preaching. To set the popularity of the Readings among 'working men' in the context of a then recent history of working-class support for radical Methodism and Chartism is to shed light on the perception by Dickens and his friends that a precarious control was being maintained over a potentially hysterical crowd. Methodism's contribution to working-class politics was never purely or uncomplicatedly radical, and by the 1860s the link between the two was more in the anxious imaginations of middle- and upper-class observers than in reality. The working-class domination of Methodist congregations persisted throughout the nineteenth century[68] and the connection of radical dissent with working-class activism in the 1840s and '50s has been well-documented,[69] but for all the Methodist preachers who promoted the People's Charter, there were many others who preached conservatism. Politically radical Methodism was always stronger in Scotland than in England, and was institutionally enshrined there to a greater extent.[70] Dickens's own unflagging hostility to dissent has been thoroughly examined by Valentine Cunningham, but by the time Dickens gave his Readings the radical heyday of Methodism was over and some of the stereotypes he popularized could begin to look dated.[71] The leadership of the church was predominantly middle-class from the 1850s onward, and it seems to have maintained an increasingly respectable and politically moderate, at times even reactionary, character. In the 1860s, radical Methodism and Chartism were more a worrying recent memory

[67] Collins, *The Public Readings*, pp. xlvi-liii; Paul Schlicke, *Dickens and Popular Entertainment* (London, 1985), pp. 234–41 on the influence of Charles Mathews's one-man shows.

[68] See Paul T. Phillips, *The Sectarian Spirit: Sectarianism, Society and Politics in Victorian Cotton Towns* (Toronto, 1982), esp. pp. 4–7, 16–17, 24; and Hugh McLeod, *Religion and the Working Class in Nineteenth-Century Britain* (London, 1984), pp. 14–15.

[69] Thompson, *The Making of the English Working Class*, pp. 350–403; W. R. Ward, *Religion and Society in England 1790–1850* (London, 1972), pp. 92–6, 195–202, 225–30, 270–1; R. Davies, A. R. George and G. Rupp, *A History of the Methodist Church in Great Britain*, 4 vols. (London, 1965–88), esp. II, 233–4; McLeod, *Religion and the Working Class*, pp. 46–7.

[70] McLeod, *Religion and the Working Class*, pp. 48–53.

[71] See Cunningham, *Everywhere Spoken Against: Dissent in the Victorian Novel* (Oxford, 1975), pp. 190–230.

than an immediate threat, and while it is important not to underestimate the force of that memory, it is equally important to recognize a degree of confidence in its being contained by judicious use of political guidance, education and cultural absorption, rather than by force. The aim of class incorporation and the attendant fear of crowd hysteria at the Readings reflect a newly urgent sense that social order is a cultural issue. There *is* anxiety here about how and to what extent working men could safely be allowed representation, in cultural as much as in political life, but it is tempered by considerable optimism.

Only in one area does fear of working-class violence surface explicitly and in a way that is not avoidable or easily recuperable by Dickens and his friends – if, indeed, it was perceptible to them as a class issue. As I have been arguing, the Readings appeared increasingly and obsessively to be in danger of provoking a disturbance which had to be controlled and defused by Dickens's intervention. However, violence was not only a potential of the crowd attending the Readings. It was also something enacted *within* the Readings with growing regularity in the later tours, and it is here that the tensions become most apparent between a safe valuation of reading as private, individual, familial or friendly and the need to promote a collective public recognition and valuation of that reading experience.

The difficulty of melding private and public finally resolves itself into a strange pathologization of Dickens himself, which haunts his representation. That pathology has its adulatory side. Dickens fascinated his audiences with his mimicry. A popular American cartoon of the Readings, much reprinted in biographies, picked up on the theme, depicting him with his body bizarrely multiplied into the several figures of his characters: Dickens as Pickwick, Dickens as Sam Weller, Dickens as David Copperfield, Dickens as Mr Dombey, Dickens as a heavily bearded Little Nell, all jostling for room on the reading platform (see plate 15).[72] Numerous observers testified to his ability to 'be' so many different characters. His face and voice seemed to have an infinite range of expression. 'Spectators noted how monstrous he looked as Squeers, how murderous as Jonas Chuzzlewit, and in their enthusiasm even insisted that in the scene between Fanny Squeers and Nicholas,

[72] This and other contemporary cartoons depicting Dickens's self-transformation into various characters are reproduced in Raymund Fitzsimons, *The Charles Dickens Show: An Account of his Public Readings, 1858–1870* (London, 1970), opposite pp. 112 and 113; Fred Kaplan, *Dickens: A Biography* (London, 1988), between pp. 322 and 323; and J. B. Priestley, *Charles Dickens and His World* (London, 1961), pp. 116, 117.

Plate 15 An American cartoon of Dickens reading, *c.* February 1868. Artist unknown. Cambridge, University Library, S727.c.92.182

one side of his face looked like Fanny and the other like Nicholas.'[73] Recent critical theory has had much to say about the fragility of subjectivity and the ease with which personality disintegrates. Abject bodies, schizophrenic and hysteric bodies, bodies in pieces dominate much current theoretical and literary critical writing. Dickens as Reader offers a quite different spectacle: not a decomposing subject, but a super-composite subject, endlessly multiplying identities. This is not a hysteric performance but, on the contrary, one which answers and quells the threatened hysteria of the crowd.

In the extensive critical and biographical literature on Dickens's reading career, however, the birth of the reading public, to rewrite Roland Barthes, is finally at the cost of the death of the author.[74] The belief that the Readings – and one Reading in particular – caused Dickens's death is one his biographers all agree upon. These were, as the first *Life* saw it, ultimately suicidal performances, and the claim has been repeated by every critic since. Dickens's ill health had been public knowledge from as early as September 1857, when he wrote to *The Times* with some irritation to contradict their report that his American trip was effectively a medically prescribed vacation.[75] General knowledge of his state of health became inevitable when the last provincial tour was curtailed on doctor's orders, but the situation was handled in a way which made it as public as possible, with copies of Frank Carr Beard's medical certificate issued to the disappointed audience along with their refunded money.[76]

There is strong medical evidence that the strain of performing did hasten Dickens's death,[77] but his dying also accrued a particular

73 Johnson, *Charles Dickens*, II, 936.

74 Roland Barthes, 'The Death of the Author', in *Image – Music – Text*, trans. Stephen Heath (London, 1977), p. 148.

75 See Jerome Meckier, 'George Dolby to James T. Fields: Two New Letters Concerning Dickens' American Reading Tour', *The Dickensian* 86 (1990): 171–83 (p. 172).

76 R. D. Butterworth, 'Dickens's Last Provincial Readings', *The Dickensian* 83 (1987): 79–87 (pp. 84–6).

77 See Forster, *The Life of Charles Dickens*, III, 420–2 on Dickens's physical decline in 1869. On Dickens's own perception of the toll the performances were taking on his health, see Forster, III, 274–83, 414–20. The certificate of ill-health signed by Thomas Watson and F. Carr Beard stating that a continuation of the Readings was likely to impair his health permanently is reprinted on p. 422. Less reliably by today's standards, Charles Bray's phrenological reading of Dickens revealed that his most developed organs among the Feelings were Acquisitiveness and Love of Approbation. Bray claimed that, through the Readings, Dickens 'literally killed himself in their gratification' (Charles Bray, *Phases of Opinion and Experience* [1884], p. 28; cited in Collins, *The Public Readings*, p. lxii). A reappraisal of Dickens's ill-health has recently been put forward by a Canadian medical researcher, suggesting that in the last years he was suffering from a tuberculous infection of the kidneys, possibly leading to Addison's disease, see Carol McLeod, 'Dickens's Maladies Re-Evaluated', *The Dickensian* 87 (1991): 77–80.

cultural pathology which has strong resonances for the class politics of the Readings. The murder reading from *Oliver Twist* was widely seen as Dickens's finest achievement as a reader, and the primary cause of his death. That it should be perceived in this light was hardly surprising. Even by today's standards, the 'Sikes and Nancy' reading is shockingly violent. Believing himself betrayed by Nancy, the housebreaker Bill Sikes bashes her to death with a club, smashing the weapon down '*twice* upon the upturned face', then, as she lies moaning, striking at her head 'again and again'.

> Once he threw a rug over [her face]; but it was worse to *fancy* the *eyes*, and imagine them moving towards him, than to see them glaring upward, as if *watching the reflection of the pool of gore that quivered and danced in the sunlight on the ceiling*. He had plucked it off again. And there was the body – mere flesh and blood, no more – but *such* flesh, and *so much blood*!!![78]

Alarmed by the evident toll this particular reading was taking on his health, Dickens's friends and managers urged him in vain to leave it out of the programme. Over the last two years of his life, his doctor had begun to monitor his pulse rate at performances. At the opening night of his last series of Readings, on 11 January 1870, Dr Beard

> found that Dickens's pulse had gone from its normal 72 to 95. From that night on, it rose ominously. Even before the first 'Murder' reading, on the morning of the 21st his fermenting anticipation raised it to 90; at the end it was 112, and even fifteen minutes later had descended only to 100. Dickens was so prostrated that he could not get back his breath for some time and was meanwhile, as he said himself, the 'express image' of a man who had lost a fight... Two days later, when he saw Carlyle for the last time, his arm was once more in a sling.
>
> Nevertheless, he went on, his pulse rising to 114 – to 118 – to 124 ... As he wiped the readings out one by one his feverish excitement and bodily pain grew even greater.
>
> His audiences, however, were almost hysterical with enthusiasm.[79]

Not only his doctor, and his friends, but Dickens too felt that in acting Sikes murdering Nancy, Dickens was murdering himself. Famously, he muttered to Charles Kent, watching from the wings before the final reading of 'Sikes and Nancy', 'I shall tear myself to pieces.'[80] Although, in speaking about this Reading, Dickens often cast himself as Sikes ('I am

78 Charles Dickens, 'Sikes and Nancy', in Collins, *The Public Readings*, pp. 483–4 [Dickens's emphases]. On the history and reception of 'Sikes and Nancy', see pp. 465–71; and Collins, '*Sikes and Nancy*: Dickens's Last Reading', *Times Literary Supplement*, 11 June 1971: 681–2.

79 Johnson, *Charles Dickens*, II, 1144; Kent, *Charles Dickens as a Reader*, p. 87.

80 Ibid., p. 87.

Plate 16 'Charles Dickens Exhausted'. Harry Furniss, pen and ink sketch of Dickens after a reading of 'Sikes and Nancy'. Cambridge, University Library, 454.c.92.42

... murdering Nancy'),[81] he was also an utterly convincing Nancy, electrifying his audiences as he 'shrieked the terrified pleadings of the girl.'[82] The intensity of his identification with her state of mind and her gestures is suggested by a late notebook entry in which he admitted the toll on his health, describing himself as 'extremely giddy ... extremely indisposed to raise my hands to my head'.[83] When Harry Furniss sketched Dickens around this time he depicted him lying exhausted on a couch after reading 'Sikes and Nancy'. Above the author's prostrate body hovers the shadowy figure of Dickens as Sikes, about to bring down his club upon the figure of Nancy which merges, suggestively, into that of Dickens (see plate 16). In the most dramatic of all his

81 *Letters*, III, 681. For further references, see Philip Collins, *Dickens and Crime*, 2nd edn (London, 1964), pp. 267–9.

82 'Mr. Charles Dickens's New Reading', *Tinsley's Magazine* 4 (1869): 62. For more recent insistence on Dickens's effectiveness as Nancy, see Ackroyd, *Dickens*, p. 1032; Fitzsimons, *The Charles Dickens Show*, pp. 161–2; Collins, *The Public Readings*, p. 469.

83 Quoted in Collins, *The Public Readings*, p. 470.

multiplications of identity, Dickens became both murderer and murderee: the drunken, brutal man bashing Nancy to one of the most shocking deaths seen on the Victorian stage, but also Nancy, crying out to her lover for mercy.

Critical appraisals of the Murder Readings have, to an objectionable degree, interpreted them as evidence of a psychological revenge drama on Dickens's part in which he vented his frustration with all the 'horrible' women in his life.[84] The gender significance of the performances has, almost without exception, obstructed any other interpretation. Yet gender is inextricable from a value-laden representation of class in the 'Sikes and Nancy' Reading. This was not 'simply' self-murder. It was the murder of a sympathetic, attractive, feminine representative of the lower classes by one of their most violent and criminal representatives. And it was the murder of the genteel, liberal author-reader by a man of the streets he had, too fully, too dangerously, attempted to incorporate. It is an appropriate, if a disturbing, expression of the degree to which the promotion of cultural incorporation had, in Dickens reading Dickens for the public, one of its most celebrated triumphs and one of its most telling pathologies.

[84] Fitzsimons, *The Charles Dickens Show*, p. 173, argues that 'as the ferocious blows rained down on the imaginary upturned face of Nancy, he was perhaps symbolically enacting his bitterness for his wife and his guilt over Ellen Ternan'. Ackroyd, *Dickens*, pp. 1031–2, claims that Dickens was acting out a complex and finally uninterpretable amalgam of loves, desires and hatreds, starting from his childhood feelings for his mother and sister, and moving through the failure of his marriage and the difficulties of his love for Ellen Ternan. The most striking version of this approach comes from Kaplan, *Dickens*, p. 538: 'In repeatedly murdering her, he expressed himself with displaced violence against the horrible women of his life, his mother and his wife. Perhaps he also expressed some of his occasional ambivalence about what he had done to Georgina [Hogarth] and Ellen [Ternan]'.

Select bibliography

BOOKS

Altick, Richard D. *The English Common Reader: A Social History of the Mass Reading Public 1800–1900*. Chicago, 1957.

Barker, Nicolas (ed.). *A Potencie of Life: Books in Society*. London, 1993.

Baumann, Gerd (ed.). *The Written Word: Literacy in Transition*. Oxford, 1986.

Bennett, H. S. *English Books and Readers 1475 to 1557*. Cambridge 1952; 2nd edn, 1969.

English Books and Readers 1558–1603. Cambridge, 1965.

English Books and Readers 1603–1640. Cambridge, 1970.

Bentolila, Alain (ed.). *Recherches actuelles sur l'enseignement de la lecture*. Paris, 1976.

Booth, Wayne C. *The Rhetoric of Fiction*. Chicago, 1961.

Bourdieu, Pierre, and Randal Johnson (ed.). *The Field of Cultural Production*. Cambridge, 1993.

Burnett, John, David Vincent and David Mayall (eds.). *The Autobiography of the Working Class: An Annotated Critical Bibliography*. 3 vols. Brighton, 1984–9.

Capp, Bernard. *Astrology and the Popular Press: English Almanacks, 1500–1600*. London, 1979.

Carruthers, Mary. *The Book of Memory: A Study of Memory in Medieval Culture*. Cambridge, 1990.

Charles, Michel. *Rhétorique de la lecture*. Paris, 1977.

Chartier, Roger, trans., Lydia G. Cochrane. *Cultural History: Between Practices and Representations*. Cambridge, 1988.

trans., Lydia G. Cochrane. *The Cultural Uses of Print in Early Modern France*. Princeton, 1987.

Chartier, Roger (ed.). *Histoires de la lecture: Un bilan des recherches*. Paris, 1995.

Pratiques de la lecture. Paris, 1985.

trans., Lydia G. Cochrane. *The Culture of Print: Power and the Uses of Print in Early Modern Europe*. Cambridge, 1989.

trans., Lydia G. Cochrane. *The Order of Books: Readers, Authors and Libraries in Europe between the Fourteenth and Eighteenth Centuries*. Cambridge, 1994.

Chrisman, Miriam Usher. *Lay Culture, Learned Culture: Books and Social Change in Strasbourg, 1480–1599*. New Haven and London, 1982.

Clanchy, M. T. *From Memory to Written Record: England 1066–1307*. London, 1979.

Cohen, Patricia Cline. *A Calculating People: The Spread of Numeracy in Early America*. Chicago, 1992.

Collins, A. S. *Profession of Letters: A Study of the Relation of Author to Patron, Publisher and Public, 1780–1832*. New York, 1929.

Cook Morse, Charlotte, *et al.* (eds.). *The Uses of Manuscript in Literary Studies: Essays in Memory of Judson Boyce Allen*. *Studies in Medieval Culture* 31. Kalamazoo, 1992.

Courtenay, William J. *Schools and Scholars in Fourteenth-Century England*. Princeton, 1987.

Crane, Mary Thomas. *Framing Authority: Sayings, Self, and Society in Sixteenth-Century England*. Princeton, 1993.

Cressy, David. *Literacy and the Social Order: Reading and Writing in Tudor and Stuart England*. Cambridge, 1980.

de Certeau, Michel, trans., Steven F. Rendall. *The Practice of Everyday Life*. Berkeley and Los Angeles, 1984.

Davies, W. J. Frank. *Teaching Reading in Early England*. London, 1973.

Davison, Peter (ed.). *The Book Encompassed: Studies in Twentieth-Century Bibliography*. Cambridge, 1992.

Duval, Valentin Jamerey, *Mémoires: enfance et éducation d'un paysan au XVIIIe siècle*, ed. Jean-Marie Goulemot. Paris, 1982.

Engelsing, Rolf. *Der Bürger als Leser: Lesergeschichte in Deutschland 1500–1800*. Stuttgart, 1974.

Fehrenbach, R. J., and E. S. Leedham-Green (eds.). *Private Libraries in Renaissance England: A Collection and Catalogue of Tudor and Early Stuart Book-Lists*. 2 vols. Marlborough and New York, 1993.

Fish, Stanley. *Is There a Text in This Class? The Authority of Interpretive Communities*. Cambridge, MA, 1980.

Flint, Kate. *The Woman Reader, 1837–1914*. Oxford, 1993.

Gilmore, William J. *Reading Becomes a Necessity of Life: Material and Cultural Life in Rural New England, 1780–1835*. Knoxville, 1989.

Goetsch, Paul (ed.). *Lesen und Schreiben im 17. und 18. Jahrhundert*. Tübingen, 1994.

Goody, Jack (ed.). *Literacy in Traditional Societies*. Cambridge, 1968.

Göpfert, Herbert G. (ed.). *Buch und Leser: Vorträge des ersten Jahrestreffens des Wolfenbütteler Arbeitskreises für das Buchwesen*. Hamburg, 1977.

Grafton, Anthony, and Ann Blair (eds.). *The Transmission of Culture in Early Modern Europe*. Philadelphia, 1990.

Hannebutt-Benz, Eva-Maria. *Die Kunst des Lesens: Lesemöbel und Leseverhalten vom Mittelalter bis zur Gegenwart*. Frankfurt am Main, 1985.

Hindman, Sandra L. (ed.). *Printing the Written Word: The Social History of Books, circa 1450–1520*. Ithaca, 1991.

Houston, R. A. *Literacy in Early Modern Europe: Culture and Education, 1500–1800*. London, 1988.

Hull, Suzanne W. *Chaste, Silent and Obedient: English Books for Women, 1475–1640.* San Marino, 1982.
Hunt, Tony. *Teaching and Learning Latin in Thirteenth-Century England.* 3 vols. Cambridge, 1991.
Iser, Wolfgang. *The Act of Reading: A Theory of Aesthetic Response.* Baltimore, 1978.
The Implied Reader: Patterns of Communication in Prose Fiction from Bunyan to Beckett. Baltimore, 1974.
Jardine, Lisa. *Erasmus, Man of Letters: The Construction of Charisma in Print.* Princeton, 1993.
Jauss, Hans Robert, trans., Timothy Bahti. *Towards an Aesthetic of Reception.* Minneapolis, 1982.
Kaster, R. A. *Guardians of Language: The Grammarian and Society in Late Antiquity.* London, 1988.
Klancher, Jon P. *The Making of English Reading Audiences 1790–1832.* Madison, 1987.
Leedham-Green, E. S. *Books in Cambridge Inventories: Book-Lists from Vice-Chancellor's Court Probate Inventories in the Tudor and Stuart Periods.* 2 vols., Cambridge, 1986.
Lennard, John. *But I Digress: The Exploitation of Parentheses in English Printed Verse.* Oxford, 1991.
Love, Harold. *Scribal Publication in Seventeenth-Century England.* Oxford, 1993.
McGann, Jerome G. *The Beauty of Inflections: Literary Investigations in Historical Method and Theory.* Oxford, 1985.
A Critique of Modern Textual Criticism. Chicago, 1983.
The Textual Condition. Chicago, 1991.
McGann, Jerome G. (ed.). *Textual Criticism and Literary Interpretation.* Chicago, 1985.
McKenzie, D. F. *Bibliography and the Sociology of Texts.* London, 1986.
Martin, Henri-Jean, trans., Lydia G. Cochrane. *The History and Power of Writing.* Chicago, 1994.
Mathews, Mitford M. *Teaching to Read: Historically Considered.* Chicago, 1966.
Meale, Carol M. (ed.). *Women and Literature in Britain, 1150–1500.* Cambridge, 1993.
Moore-Smith, G. C. (ed.). *Gabriel Harvey: Marginalia.* Stratford-upon-Avon, 1913.
Moran, Jo Ann Hoeppner. *The Growth of English Schooling 1340–1548: Learning, Literacy and Laicization in Pre-Reformation York Diocese.* Princeton, 1985.
Myers, Robin, and Michael Harris (eds.). *Serials and their Readers.* Winchester, 1993.
Neuburg, Victor. *Chapbooks: A Guide to Reference Material.* 2nd edn. London, 1972.
Popular Literature: A History and a Guide. London, 1977.
O'Day, Rosemary. *Education and Society, 1500–1800: The Social Foundations of Education in Early Modern Britain.* London, 1982.
Orme, Nicholas H. *English Schools in the Middle Ages.* London, 1973.

Parkes, Malcolm. *Pause and Effect: An Introduction to the History of Punctuation in the West.* Aldershot, 1992.

Scribes, Scripts and Readers: Studies in the Communication, Presentation and Dissemination of Texts. London, 1991.

Raven, James. *Judging New Wealth: Popular Publishing and Responses to Commerce in England 1750–1800.* Oxford, 1992.

Rivers, Isabel (ed.). *Books and their Readers in Eighteenth-Century England.* Leicester, 1982.

Roberts, R. J., and A. G. Watson. *John Dee's Library Catalogue.* London, 1990.

Schön, Erich. *Der Verlust der Sinnlichkeit oder die Verwandlungen des Lesers: Mentalitätswandel um 1800.* Stuttgart, 1987.

Sherman, William H. *John Dee: The Politics of Reading and Writing in the English Renaissance.* Amherst, 1995.

Smith, G. C. Moore. *Gabriel Harvey's Marginalia.* Stratford-upon-Avon, 1913.

Spufford, Margaret. *Small Books and Pleasant Histories: Popular Fiction and its Readership in Seventeenth-Century England.* London, 1981.

Stephens, W. B. *Education, Literacy and Society, 1830–70: The Geography of Diversity in Provincial England.* Manchester, 1987.

Stern, Virginia F. *Gabriel Harvey: His Life, Marginalia and Library.* Oxford, 1979.

Street, Brian V. *Literacy in Theory and Practice.* Cambridge, 1984.

Stock, Brian. *Listening for the Text: On the Uses of the Past.* Baltimore, 1990.

Suleiman, Susan R., and Inge Crossman (eds.). *The Reader in the Text: Essays on Audience and Interpretation.* Princeton, 1980.

Tribble, Evelyn B. *Margins and Marginality: The Printed Page in Early Modern England.* Charlottesville, 1993.

Vincent, David. *Literacy and Popular Culture: England 1750–1914.* Cambridge, 1989.

Watt, Ian. *The Rise of the Novel: Studies in Defoe, Richardson, and Fielding.* Berkeley, 1957.

Watt, Tessa. *Cheap Print and Popular Piety, 1550–1640.* Cambridge, 1992.

ARTICLES AND CHAPTERS IN BOOKS

Alexandre-Bidon, Danièle. 'La lettre volée: Apprendre à lire à l'enfant au moyen age'. *Annales: Economies, Sociétés, Civilisations* 44 (1989): 953–92.

Auwers, Linda. 'Reading the Marks of the Past: Exploring Female Literacy in Colonial Windsor, Connecticut'. *Historical Methods* 13 (1980): 204–14.

Bell, Susan Groag. 'Medieval Women Book Owners: Arbiters of Lay Piety and Ambassadors of Culture'. In Mary Erler and Maryanne Kowaleski (eds.). *Women and Power in the Middle Ages.* Athens, GA (1988): 149–87.

Chartier, Roger, trans., Carol Mossman. 'Leisure and Sociability: Reading Aloud in Early Modern Europe'. In Susan Zimmerman and Ronald

F. E. Weissman (eds.). *Urban Life in the Renaissance.* Newark, DE (1989): 103–20.

trans. Arthur Goldhammer. 'The Practical Impact of Writing'. In Phillippe Ariès, Roger Chartier, *et al.* (eds.), *A History of Private Life.* 5 vols. Cambridge, MA (1987–91): III, 111–60.

'Texts, Printing, Readings'. In Lynn Hunt (ed.). *The New Cultural History* (Berkeley, 1989): 154–75.

Clark, Peter. 'The Ownership of Books in England, 1560–1640: The Example of Some Kentish Townfolk'. In Lawrence Stone (ed.). *Schooling and Society: Studies in the History of Education.* Baltimore (1976), 95–111.

Cressy, David. 'Literacy in Context: Meaning and Measurement in Early Modern England'. In John Brewer and Roy Porter (eds.). *Consumption and the World of Goods.* London (1993): 305–19.

Darnton, Robert. 'First Steps Toward a History of Reading'. *Australian Journal of French Studies* 23 (1986): 5–30.

'Readers Respond to Rousseau: The Fabrication of Romantic Sensitivity'. In Robert Darnton. *The Great Cat Massacre and other Episodes in French Cultural History.* London (1984), pp. 215–56.

Engelsing, Rolf. 'Die Perioden der Lesergeschichte in der Neuzeit: Das statische Ausmaß und die soziokulturelle Bedeutung der Lektüre'. *Archiv für Geschichte des Buchwesens* 10 (1970): 945–1002.

Fergus, Jan. 'Women, Class, and the Growth of Magazine Readership in the Provinces, 1746–1780'. *Studies in Eighteenth-Century Culture* 16 (1986): 41–56.

Ferguson, Margaret. 'A Room Not Their Own: Renaissance Women as Readers and Writers'. In Clayton Koelb and Susan Noakes (eds.), *The Comparative Perspective on Literature.* Ithaca, 1988.

Fish, Stanley E. 'Interpreting the *Variorum*'. *Critical Inquiry* 2 (1976): 465–85.

Fox, Adam. 'Ballads, Libels and Popular Ridicule in Jacobean England'. *Past and Present* 145 (1994): 47–83.

Grafton, Anthony. 'Renaissance Readers and Ancient Texts: Comments on Some Commentaries'. *Renaissance Quarterly* 38 (1985): 615–49.

'Teacher, Text and Pupil in the Renaissance Class-Room: A Case Study from a Parisian College'. *History of Universities* 1 (1981): 37–70.

Hall, David D. 'The History of the Book: New Questions? New Answers?' *Journal of Library History* 21 (1986): 27–38.

Houston, Rab. 'The Literacy Myth? Illiteracy in Scotland 1630–1760'. *Past and Present* 96 (1982): 81–102.

Hughes, Helen Sard. 'The Middle-Class Reader and the English Novel'. *Journal of English and Germanic Philology* 25 (1926): 2–78.

Hume, Robert D. 'Texts within Contexts: Notes toward a Historical Method'. *Philological Quarterly* 71 (1992): 69–100.

Hutchinson, Ann. 'Devotional Reading in the Monastery and in the Late Medieval Household'. In Michael Sargent (ed.). *De Cella in Seculum: Religious and Secular Life and Devotion in Late Medieval England* (Cambridge, 1989), pp. 215–28.

Hutson, Lorna. 'Fortunate Travelers: Reading for the Plot in Sixteenth-Century England'. *Representations* 14 (1993): 83–103.

Jardine, Lisa, and Anthony Grafton. '"Studied for Action": How Gabriel Harvey Read his Livy'. *Past and Present* 129 (1990): 30–78.

Jardine, Lisa, and William Sherman. 'Pragmatic Readers: Knowledge Transactions and Scholarly Services in late Elizabethan England'. In Anthony Fletcher and Peter Roberts (eds.). *Religion, Culture and Society in Early Modern Britain: Essays in Honour of Patrick Collinson.* Cambridge (1994): pp. 102–24.

Kintgen, Eugene R. 'Reconstructing Elizabethan Reading'. *Studies in English Literature* 30 (1990): 1–18.

Lamb, Mary Ellen. 'The Agency of the Split Subject: Lady Anne Clifford and the Uses of Reading'. *English Language Review* 22 (1992): 347–68.

Laqueur, Thomas. 'The Cultural Origins of Popular Literature in England, 1500–1850'. *Oxford Review of Education* 2 (1976): 255–75.

McKenzie, D. F. 'Printers of the Mind: Some Notes on Bibliographical Theories and Printing-House Practices'. *Studies in Bibliography* 22 (1969): 1–75.

Ophir, Adi. 'A Place of Knowledge Re-Created: The Library of Michel de Montaigne'. *Science in Context* 4 (1991): 163–89.

Perec, Georges. 'Lire: Esquisse socio-physiologique'. *Esprit* 44/1 (Jan. 1976): 9–20.

Raven, James. 'Selling Books Across Europe, *c*.1450–1800: An Overview'. *Publishing History* 34 (1993): 5–19.

Reay, Barry. 'Popular Literature in Seventeenth-Century England'. *Journal of Peasant Studies* 10 (1976): 255–75.

Rose, Jonathan. 'Rereading the English Common Reader: A Preface to the History of Audiences'. *Journal of the History of Ideas* 53 (1992): 47–70.

Saenger, Paul. 'Physiologie de la lecture et séparation des mots'. *Annales: Economies, Sociétés, Civilisations* 44 (1989): 939–52.

'Silent Reading: Its Impact on Late Medieval Script and Society'. *Viator* 13 (1982): 367–414.

Schibanoff, Susan. 'The Art of Reading as a Woman'. In Elizabeth Flynn and Patrocinio Schweickart (eds.). *Gender and Reading: Essays on Readers, Texts and Contexts.* Baltimore, 1986.

'The New Reader and Female Textuality in Two Early Commentaries on Chaucer'. *Studies in the Age of Chaucer* 10 (1988): 71–108.

Simpson, David. 'Literary Criticism and the Return to "History"'. *Critical Inquiry* 14 (1988): 721–47.

Spufford, Margaret. 'First Steps in Literacy: The Reading and Writing Experience of the Humblest Seventeenth-Century Spiritual Autobiographers'. *Social History* 4 (1979): 407–35.

Taylor, Andrew. 'Fragmentation, Corruption and Minstrel Narration: The Question of the Middle English Romances'. *The Yearbook of English Studies* 22 (1992): 38–62.

Wallace, Ian. '"Examples are Best Precepts": Readers and Meaning in Seventeenth-Century Poetry' *Critical Inquiry* 1 (1974): 273–90.

Wiles, Roy McKeen. 'The Relish for Reading in Provincial England Two Centuries Ago'. In Paul J. Korshin (ed.). *The Widening Circle: Essays on the Circulation of Literature in Eighteenth-Century Europe.* Philadelphia (1976): 87–115.

Index

Printed in the United Kingdom
by Lightning Source UK Ltd.
122907UK00001B/223-255/A

9 780521 023238